Reframing Biblical Theology

Reframing Biblical Theology

The Eternal Design

DANIEL C. FREDERICKS

WIPF & STOCK · Eugene, Oregon

REFRAMING BIBLICAL THEOLOGY
The Eternal Design

Copyright © 2025 Daniel C. Fredericks. All rights reserved. Except for brief quotations in critical publications or reviews, no part of this book may be reproduced in any manner without prior written permission from the publisher. Write: Permissions, Wipf and Stock Publishers, 199 W. 8th Ave., Suite 3, Eugene, OR 97401.

Wipf & Stock
An Imprint of Wipf and Stock Publishers
199 W. 8th Ave., Suite 3
Eugene, OR 97401

www.wipfandstock.com

PAPERBACK ISBN: 979-8-3852-4483-6
HARDCOVER ISBN: 979-8-3852-4484-3
EBOOK ISBN: 979-8-3852-4485-0

VERSION NUMBER 08/22/25

Most Scripture translations are the author's.

Scripture quotes are from The Holy Bible, New International Version®, NIV®. Copyright © 1973, 1978, 1984, 2011 by Biblica, Inc."

Scripture quotes are from New American Standard Bible®, Copyright © 1960, 1971, 1977, 1995, 2020 by The Lockman Foundation.

Scripture quotes are from The Holy Bible, English Standard Version. ESV® Text Edition: 2016. Copyright © 2001 by Crossway Bibles, a publishing ministry of Good News Publishers.

Dedicated to Jeanelle,
Our Justified, Sanctified, and Glorified Granddaughter (2016–2024)

Contents

Abbreviations | ix
Introduction | xi

1 Nature of Creation and Its History | 1
2 Nature of God | 16
3 God's Eternal Design | 29
4 Glory and Holiness | 41
5 Parenthetical Theology | 55
6 God's Kingdom Realms | 67
7 Messiah's Commission | 95
8 Messiah's Universal Kingdom | 131
9 Paul's Kingdom Message | 153
10 Kingdoms' Interactions | 169
11 Israel | 190
12 Dialectical Kingdom | 205
13 Dialectical Consequences | 226
14 Muted Messiah | 251
15 Harmonic Messianic Message | 287
16 New Testament Pronouncements | 303
17 Sanctified Shepherding | 320

Conclusion | 338
Bibliography of Cited Works | 345

CONTENTS

Scripture Index | 357
Author Index | 383

Abbreviations

BDAG	Danker, Bauer, Arndt, and Gingrich, *Greek-English Lexicon of the New Testament*
BDB	Brown, Driver, and Briggs, *A Hebrew and English Lexicon of the Old Testament*
HK	Heavenly kingdom
MK	Messianic kingdom
NE	New Earth
NIDNTTE	*New International Dictionary of New Testament Theology and Exegesis* NK Natural kingdom
SK	Satanic kingdom
TDNT	*Theological Dictionary of the New Testament*
TerK	Terrestrial kingdom
TruK	Trusting kingdom
UBS	United Bible Societies
UK	Universal kingdom

Introduction

WHY IS ANYTHING RELEVANT in life? It is natural to look for relevance primarily within our own personal environment and our immediate experiences. This is how one generally makes sense of life. But what of the world around? How is it relevant? What about ages past and those yet to come? What makes them relevant? Though relevance is perceived in one's life based on their very limited surrounding zone, the way to see the greater extent of relevance is by appreciating the brilliant design within all creation and its history that has always been and always will be. This design explains the pervasive interconnectedness of reality that one is bound to see only scantily in a life focused on the immediate. Fortunately, we need not personally experience all of creation's events to understand their relevance to us or God's comprehensive, eternal design. It is much simpler and more practical than that. The search for such a key to understanding is one of God's greatest blessings to humanity. It drives humanity to inquire about the relevance of all that permeates and surrounds life. The quest might consider the purpose of self, family, and community, yet it only occasionally progresses to the purpose of all creation and its ongoing history. God designed his eternal creation after his own nature; however, creation's design is abused and compromised severely by angelic and human rebellion in this dark "parenthetical age" that fortunately will end at the beginning of a new age.

This study proposes a paradigm that subsumes the narrower focus of any biblical theology paradigm that often centers only on the means of solving this parenthetical issue, not on the eternal practical objective of what the solution will bring. Rather than focusing on the rescue from the parenthetical age itself, the following chapters accentuate the *purpose* for

INTRODUCTION

this rescue and the role of God's eternal design. This proposed paradigm is the foundation and context which forms the most profound theological concepts, e.g., salvation history, Messiah, eschatology, morality, sanctification, history, heaven, and the kingdom of God. This fuller paradigm rests on the following foundational premises:

- God's universal kingdom drives his purposeful eternal design for all creation and its history.
- God's eternal design's historical progression begins in the Trinity's conception and inception of creation and traverses its initial perfect age, this parenthetical evil age, and the everlasting perfect age.
- God's kingdom oversees creation and its history through a kingdom-based substructure, which includes his heavenly, messianic, natural, terrestrial, trusting, and new earth kingdoms.
- The Second Person's divine nature and function was ontologically merged with the original human nature and commission.
- Thus humanity's primary commission from God, to reign, is accomplished in the current universal rule of the Messiah.
- This Messiah, as the perfect image of God, fulfills his multifaceted commission of teaching, judging, interceding, fighting, reigning, and saving from sin and from other adversities.
- The Testaments' message is that God's eternal design blesses believers as they regain their perfect image that God shared with humanity at creation and again with the Messiah.
- In New Earth, God's design will again reach its perfect universal application but not its completion, since the design will continue its productive influence over his universal kingdom eternally.

This study starts by delving into what should be meant by "history" and what its connection is with God and his eternal design for creation.

1

Nature of Creation and Its History

CHRISTIAN THEOLOGY IS NOT fully historical at its core. Of course it refers to history, but Christian theologians, just as professional historians, can dwell narrowly on what they perceive to be *significant* history. For theologians, this limited scope inevitably compromises the precision of their conclusions and misconstrues basic doctrine, so it misleads the world ultimately and fundamentally about the biblical message. This error has not kept the Holy Spirit from convincing persons of the problem with humanity as a whole and with them individually. Mercifully, regeneration occurs without one having a fuller view of history. Nonetheless, this first chapter provides elements of creation and history's nature that will help in viewing them more deeply and broadly.

When considering history, it is clear that it is not the mere written or verbal *recording* of specific events that are retold about what, where, when, how, or to whom it happened, and perhaps what was any god's involvement. Theology and history connect at a much deeper level than just recounting events. So, any cultural explanation of why something happened and to what extent a god or gods had any purpose in what happened forms and expresses an *interpretation* of history's events. An answer to the "why" might begin with the belief that there is no divine reason since a god does not exist, or if it does it no longer cares what happens after reality's inception. Or the answer might be that the god cares deeply about the community and its persons. More likely, the "why" is found at some point along this continuum.

Yet history should be understood at an even deeper level—that is, what is the *nature* of history itself—not what were history's events, nor even their interpretation or implications, but what is history's essence—what makes history what it is regardless of what it chronicles and what its events may mean. Professional historians, encyclopedias, documentaries, pundits, grandparents, friends, social media, religious leaders, and countless other sources will describe history's occurrences and will attempt to interpret their significance; everyone does it. But without a deeper grasp of the nature of history itself, one's interpretations are deficient. Deficiencies of course enter for many reasons, such as incomplete knowledge, errant memory, or intentional revision of the circumstances of an event. What I have just described are the results of how one "does history" or the results of what one does with history—whether one retrieves it, organizes it, analyzes it, interprets it, or transmits it. This process approaches "history" as an object with countless events within. By this approach, one's interest in "history" is defined by the summation of, or parts of, its apprehensible contents. This approach is the discipline of how history's contents are considered and presented by a culture's historians—historiography.[1]

However, historiography does not get to the root of what history is *in itself*. This is the question that is addressed here: what is the *ontology* of history? I have mentioned some levels of historical interest above: recording past events, the interpretation of those events, or revealing the purpose behind those events. But what is critically missing is an understanding of what history *is* in itself versus what its events and subjects have been and whatever they might mean. Failure to understand this will inevitably lead to a narrower focus on a particular event or any length of a series of events in history. The objective here is to acknowledge the importance of history's own nature and to note its impact on understanding the Testaments. So, I suggest that at least the following are ontological properties of history:

---

1. Technical theologies of history are few and far between and without a great amount of interest since sixty years ago and before. Nonetheless, whenever a conscious effort at forming a *theology* of history is attempted, it amounts to historiographic analyses and coincides with the same framework of biblical theologies—the centricity of Jesus Christ's Passion and its role primarily in this parenthetical age. A few examples from that spurt of interest would be Casserly, *Theology of History*; Hult, *Theology of History*; von Balthasar, *Theology of History*.

NATURE OF CREATION AND ITS HISTORY

1. History is codependent and coterminous with creation; therefore,

2. History is as fully comprehensive as the totality of creation's events, and

3. History is as fully integrated as the complete integration of creation's events.

4. A portion of creation exists eternally into the future; thus, history itself is eternal in its future.

5. Creation is contained by space and time; thus, history is always spatial and temporal.

6. Creation is propelled by cause and effect; thus, history is teleological *in time*.

7. God is intentional, so creation and history are teleological *in purpose*, thus productive.

Our pursuit is for a more profound definition of history that is based on what history "is," ontologically, not simply what history is about. Only then might one speak of history's events, which I have defined as any interaction between God and his creation and any interaction among creation itself.[2] So, the approach at this point is not to explore any specific event or any series of events in history. Rather, I begin with identifying the nature of creation and its history, not rushing toward historiography or toward adopting any hermeneutical overlay by which one might interpret any historical event, including the initial creation, flood, Incarnation, Passion, Armageddon, or Christ's final return of the defeated kingdoms to God (1 Cor 15:24–25). These events result from history's nature, but they are not the nature or ontology of history themselves.

---

2. I include as historical whatever was not done which could have been done, since what was not done affects the results of one's actions. To illustrate, "negative space" is where non-existence in space defines and impacts what does exist. By not existing, space and/or time are left out and that absence can affect other existences minimally or substantively. For instance, substantial contributions are made to sculptures by the absence of any nearby shaped media or by what could have been shaped; in music, a whole rest and other rests are real entities, as are the empty spaces in visual art or dramatic pauses within soliloquies. Even if one argued that mere potentiality does not exist, still the *choice* itself between to act or not to act in a particular way does occur in space and time and thus should be considered real. Clearly "missed opportunities," or "negative action," so to speak, has changed historical events, from the least important events to those of the greatest geopolitical, even epochal importance. I assume at least six dimensions within history: space, time, potentiality (what could happen), actuality (what has happened), ideas (mental reality), and subsequent actions (physical reality).

CREATION AND HISTORY ARE CODEPENDENT AND COTERMINOUS

Creation and history are not identical entities, but they are inseparable in time and are codependent in what happens. So to speak, creation's nature is "what" and history's nature is "happens." Of course, whatever happened can then become a "what" as a newly created entity and subsequently create a new event. Using a sentence as a loose analogy, creation is the subject, and history is its verb; neither can function independently. Creation's nature includes the spirit kingdoms: the heavenly kingdom and the satanic kingdom. Creation includes all physical things: both matter and energy, even Christ's incarnate body, each of which determine history. Creation includes the unseen supportive structures and interactions of the natural kingdom; mathematics, physics, chemistry, logic, mind, and spirit have creative abilities and cause history. And all creation is governed by time, space, and cause-effect, which form historical events. In other words, creation creates its history simultaneously with itself each time it produces any event of any magnitude and significance, tiny or epochal.

HISTORY IS COMPREHENSIVE

A historical event may be as routine as a flea pestering a dog or as epochal as if a god appeared on earth for whatever reason. One event is no more historical than another. In this sense one uses the term "historical" for any event in history. On the other hand, when something is considered "historic," someone is ascribing greater meaning, importance, relevance, or implications to a certain historical event or series of events based on one's personal preference of what is significant.

Though constrained by a definition of history within the tunnel of *human* history, Marc Bloch's generalization is one concentric circle short of what is the true "universal history":

> Life is too short, and science too vast, to permit even the greatest genius a total experience of humanity. Some men will always specialize in the present, as others do in the Stone Age or in Egyptology. We simply ask both to bear in mind that historical research will tolerate no autarchy. Isolated, each will understand only by halves, even within his own field of study; for the only

true history, which can only advance through mutual aid, is universal history.[3]

By universal, Bloch means, narrowly, universal *human* history. Bloch realistically concedes that a universal human history is an impossible challenge to synthesize historiographically. *A fortiori*, if "historical research will tolerate no autarchy" is applied consistently, all history should not suffer the tyranny that pays attention to only human history. History is not just "what happened" as recorded in oral or written histories that depend on any human presence. History happens everywhere regardless of human existence, perception, or interpretation. Science tells us a history of the cosmos which is void of any human involvement in its development and routine operations. Black holes were sucking up unseen portions of the universe eons before Eden's Couple, and each cell division and molecular change has been historical, whether perceived or not. Yes, thunder resounds regardless of human presence, and it is indeed historical.

In this sense, "prehistory" is an oxymoron since creation and the history it creates are eternally coterminous and codependent. Nothing is prehistorical apart from God. Of course, by definition, creation is not regressively eternal as only God can be. Intergalactic history, with its peaceful and tumultuous spaces and times, including the history of its atomic interactions, is not prehistoric; instead it creates the physical enclosure of all history within its time-space constraints. Innumerable organisms live and interact within their 240,000 species in the ocean's history. The satanic kingdom's history interacts insidiously within its time-space interactions with the current seven billion souls in the terrestrial kingdom.

As far as academic disciplines go, theology should be the broadest since it starts and ends with the Creator of everything that every other academic discipline chooses to explore. Yet theology has lost any claim as the "queen of the sciences," as it has conceded to the god of naturalism and has starved as reductionist fundamentalism. Beyond any estimation, most history has dealt with anonymous objects, natural creatures, spirits, persons, and cultures, even though God has thoroughly known and has interacted with them all. Yet, since human history is nearly the exclusive interest of most historians, mighty kingdoms are marginalized by compartmentalizing them as specializations of interest to separate historical disciplines. Ever-proliferating information has made this

---

3. Bloch, *Historian's Craft*, 47.

necessary as far as all details, but the trusting kingdom would be so enriched by an awareness of the broad objects of God's awareness, his natural, heavenly, and terrestrial human kingdoms regardless of their size or ethnicity, an inestimable task. Yet the effort of developing a holistic Christian theology of universal history might be distributed among the trusting kingdom's academes, regardless of how overwhelming such an undertaking would be.

HISTORY IS INTEGRATED

God's omniscience includes not only his knowledge of the potentiality and actuality of events but also every intersection and relationship of those potential and actual events—their integration. A comprehensive theology of creation and its history requires at least a conceptual integration as broad as God and creation's integration of all events. Covenants, dispensations, the cross, resurrection, justification, and a millennium are some points of interest, yet as historical realities they are only part of a much broader and theologically integrated consideration. Yes, God's saving reign may be a central concern when considering the nature of history, but he has designed reality and its historical setting to be considerably more than that.

The interaction of all entities within reality is far more complicated than what is commonly considered by most to be history. History is personal; it includes one's own birth, death, thoughts, sleeping dreams, emotions, heritage, and the unique unwritten minute-by-minute, day-by-day biography. Personal histories are hardly ever recorded, much less published, yet they can be indelibly written on memories and can imperceptibly determine future words, actions, and consequences, great and small. History is communal; one's personal history is significantly entwined with the traditions, customs, mores, priorities, and leadership of one's family and community. History is national, formed by communities, cities, provinces, and regions which both share and contest each other's allegiances. History is international; global cooperation and conflict define relationships among ideologies, economies, nations, even whole continents. History is natural; animal migrations, natural disasters, lunar rhythms, and cosmic rays follow God's laws in concert, competition, or indifference with the rest of natural creation.[4] History is spiritual;

---

4. Herbert Butterfield is quick to distance nature's laws from an unengaged deism: "God is in all the motions of the planets—just as he is in all the motions of history."

spirits, both holy and fallen, engage one's historical dimension, impacting one's personal and creation's wider contexts. The combinations and interactions of these personal, communal, national, international, natural, and spiritual arenas in history when conflated are incomprehensible. Creation's indomitably integrated nature and its nearly limitless permutations nearly always occur regardless of human awareness, much less human permission, consent, or desire.

All history is integrated and does not depend on human existence to articulate it since God's awareness encompasses the daily interaction of all creation. His providence is not applied "primarily" to any component; it is just as thorough for Mars as it is for our planet Earth.[5] The same could be said of the components within humanity. God's knowledge, attention, or administration of humanity is not primarily applied to any group; it is just as comprehensive for each, e.g., Israel, the church, Indonesia, Canada, Hindus, Muslims, the poor, the rich, adults, children, disabled, even the deceased. There is no hierarchy where ethnic, gender, age, mortal state, socioeconomic, or religious groups vie and succeed more than the others in garnering God's omniscient attention; there is no detail of creation that occupies God's awareness and interaction at the expense of another detail. Salvation history does not attract God's attention any more than the history of an unknown person in central China, or of the annoying fly buzzing above my head. To form such hierarchies of God's omniscience does not trivialize it; it denigrates it.

The inestimable number of permutations of relationships among seven billion living souls creates an exponentially smaller fraction of the total history that creation creates among its various spirit, natural, and human kingdoms. They represent an incalculably small portion of the total historical interactions just within themselves, not to speak of the number of events among them and their integrated environments. This shows the impossibility of fathoming God's knowledge and wisdom and reveals the power of the Son to uphold all things by his word. Every event in every era and area is an object of which God is aware and to which he reacts actively or passively. He is not oblivious nor unresponsive by

---

He is not interfering with the stars and their rotations—he is carrying them around all the time and in him they live and move and have their being. In his Providence he continues the original work of Creation and keeps the stars alight, maintains his world continually." Butterfield, *Christianity and History*, 7.

5. "The Old Testament is not unaware of the idea of a Cosmos, that is, of a universe organized with wisdom where each thing has its place and is produced in its own time." Jacob, *Theology of the Old Testament*, 136.

action or permissibility to anything. It is within this expanse of creation's history-forming interactions that God exercises his options in his caring management of all details of his universal realm. Or, does one believe he does not care about all of these details? With what degree of deism is one comfortable? He knows all creation's potential actions while he administrates his universal kingdom, and when he does not determine them directly, he chooses to allow them and their implications, or to modify them with different implications, or to disallow them completely, imperceptibly, and unintelligibly. All creation and history is tethered to God's comprehensive omniscience and sovereign will. His infinite awareness either leaves him helplessly lost in the data or it is matched by his ability to govern all creation's products and their history. Unless he masters all the data, he does not master whatever the data represents, so he is finite in power, wisdom, or care.

The interaction exclusively among the atemporal Trinity is not history, by definition. Unless revealed, whenever the Trinity operates within its closed system alone, it defies human perception. This is to say that human perception is not necessary for something to be real. Yet any temporal results to God's atemporal deliberations become "historical." The Trinity's knowledge of potentialities is real (though not historical), and it must know all potentialities; otherwise it would only be guessing at what is wise. The Trinity's knowledge becomes historical only when it is actualized in time and space and by a component of creation which creates history. However, when humans think, those thoughts are always both real and historical events even if only potential, e.g., temptations. When potentialities are not thought by a person, they are only real within the Trinity's omniscience.

The most practical implication for humanity of this comprehensive element of creation and its history is the enormous moral responsibility it demands. To be more like God, that is, to be sanctified, requires one to be aware of the details of the enormous cosmos around them. Making decisions that have the deepest, broadest, and most constructive impact requires one to have the most comprehensive knowledge *feasible*. Otherwise selective ignorance can become neglect and carelessness and thus possibly even become inadvertent mistreatment of others, or it may lead to personal destruction.

CREATION AND HISTORY ARE ETERNAL

There will never be a complete description of creation's history since its timeline is eternal. Of course, by definition, creation is only eternally progressive, not eternally regressive thus coextensive with God. Nor is everything's existence in creation eternally progressive. Vegetation has to die to be eaten, and it is hoped thistles, roaches, asps, and viruses, among many other curses, will become extinct. And the surface of the earth and the believer's body will be destroyed, but they will be restored as indestructible. The Testaments might be stingy on the exact eternal nature of creation, but the promise of the believer's eternal inheritance and reign in New Earth is at least a start.

There will be no end to God's creation nor its descriptive history. Regardless of God's curse of ubiquitous entropy, somehow both creation and its history will extend beyond earth's natural expiration date, even past the life expectancy of our solar system and the entire cosmos. However, we leave that to the Creator of our universe; he has experience in such matters. The universal eternal *direction* of cosmic, global, and personal histories may have moments of "arrival" along their way, but having arrived at any point, they continue on again, departing on new endeavors throughout eternity. Biblical indications of "the end" or "last day(s)" never mean our dimensional universe will shut down, leaving only negative space between the other realities God may have created. These temporal markers were intended only for this parenthesis of dark times between the two perfect ages of history: pre-Fall and new creation.

CREATION AND HISTORY ARE CONTAINED BY SPACE AND TIME

Space and time are codependent and coexistent, somewhat like creation and history. However, creation causes history, whereas time and space operate within creation as well as within each other and so are mutually causal. Furthermore, the rest of creation finds itself contextualized and limited by space and time, though it is not deterministically restrained by them. The freedom of God and humanity manipulates both, but humanity cannot free itself from time and space. God's simultaneous creation of these constraints imposes them as monarchs over the rest of creation with all their powerful and determining authority. Space and time are created "realms" by which God maintains his complete sovereignty. His reign can only be understood in reference to his universal realm of creation, including the "kingdoms" of space and time. Bloch's poetic description is helpful: "Historical time is a concrete and living reality with an irreversible onward rush. It is the very plasma in which events are immersed, and the field within which they become intelligible."[6] Yet, time and space are created realms that are external to God as the "where and when" by which he graciously enters and engages these dimensions and their contents. Though we presume God exists outside of created space and time, he works within them and responds to angelic and human decisions with approval, adjustments, or prohibition. Even the sequences of human thought are space-time historical events since they require time to think and brain space where one ruminates.

I will introduce God's "eternal design" more clearly in chapter 3. However, God's aspatial and atemporal relationship with his spatial and temporal creation is expressed well by Jacques Maritain. He addresses the matter of God's "timing" of his planning and sovereignty and the significance of human agency:

> Now, as regards the divine plan, we must hold that this plan is established, of course, from all eternity. But we must be aware that eternity is not a kind of divine time which precedes time. It is a limitless instant which indivisibly embraces the whole succession of time. All the moments of that succession are physically present in it. . . . In other words, God's eternal plan must not be conceived anthropomorphically as a kind of scenario written in advance . . . The true conception is that divine plan is immutable *once fixed* from all eternity. But it is only fixed from all eternity *with account taken of the free default of man*, which God sees in his eternal present. Man enters thus into the eternal plan.[7]

Time and space pervasively and persistently constrain what, who, how, where, and when something can exist and/or happen, again, most often without compromise. However, animate creation, that is, fauna by its instincts, and spirits and humans by their nature and savvy, can manipulate their time and space restrictions and options for constructive or, unfortunately, destructive purposes. "This age" and the "coming age"

---

6. Bloch, *Historian's Craft*, 27.

7. Maritain, *Philosophy of History*, 120, 121, 122. Cosmologists have a comparable response to the question of what came "before creation," before the Big Bang: like Christianity's God, the Big Bang created "spacetime," so it is nonsensical to ask what happened before it. One cannot have space without time, so it goes, so they must have both been created simultaneously.

are described in the Testaments as space-time epochs: the former epoch's nature as dark and evil, the latter as perfectly glorious. Both are God's realms of time that he rules by his eternal and universal kingdom.

CREATION AND HISTORY ARE TELEOLOGICAL IN TIME

There is an innate, most often unperceived yet necessary operation of one's mind—the insistent process of *cause and effect*. This relentless imposition of thought causes a more perceptible and unavoidable conclusion as an operating principle for all human thought. Creation's time and space *contain* cause and effect, so it is necessary for humanity to apprehend it to understand creation's ontology. This intuition perceives that something, in time or logic, immediately followed "something else" and that it would not have followed for any other reason than that it was inextricably linked to that "something else"; in other words, it was caused by it. This intuition of purpose implies that any cause is meaningful and necessary at least to its effect and to any subsequent effect which in turn becomes a cause in itself to another effect. To continue the analogy of a sentence, inanimate as well as animate creation (subject) causes (verb) an action, and that action as part of creation's history itself becomes a subject for a subsequent verb of action. The sentence, therefore, has a direction. This is a meaning of ontology: whatever the "subject and verbs" might be, specifically, is irrelevant to the natures of creation and history in their own right.

A significant aspect of time is its relationship with change. Some have even argued that change is the definition of time. Perhaps it is better to say that it is the nature of creation to operate within space and time by cause and effect. In other words, cause-effect requires time, which allows for the change it brings. Said differently, change is a means-to-an-end scenario which develops as a progression within time. Change does not create time; it is only a measure of what time allows to progress by its cause-effect nature. Any effect does not exist because it is a co-incidence; rather, it is a post-incidence in time or logic to its cause, which defines a teleological process. What something is, substantially or ontologically, might not appear to change, yet its time-space relationships, its intensity, duration, direction, color, sound, size, clarity, or manifestation will change in any number of ways.

Any one thing in the present has a future of some fleeting or eternal length, meaning anything will change into what it is not yet, however short the "not yet" might be. In other words, everything is "already-not yet." Everything has its own eschatology where something about it ends, its own destination at which point its most significant change is its demise, subordination, different form, or termination. Everything has its season; some things have even an eternal season. Consequently, history is always progressive in time.

CREATION AND HISTORY ARE TELEOLOGICAL IN PURPOSE

God's nature to be purposeful determines the nature of his creation and the direction of history. That is to say, all that has preceded this description of creation and history's nature and properties is the product of his purposive attribute. It is how history progresses: in space and time, by cause-effect, according to his nature, including his purposive nature. The *direction* that time affords is one sense of teleology. Teleology is built into creation by cause-effect in space-time. The *meaning* given to the direction of time is its purposive teleology, beyond the sheer direction of a cause to have an effect. God is decisive when he acts and when he does not act, in his works and in his intentional, selective passivity. He is aware of everything, including all potentiality and connectedness, and he responds in his wisdom to everything either by decisively acting or decisively not acting. So, creation's cause-effect moves this teleological process along within the constraints of time and space but at God's purposive discretion.

Biblical teleology, to an extent, follows the same pattern found in the coterminous and codependent relation between creation and history and between cause-effect and time. That is, biblical teleology is God's coterminous and codependent *purpose* for creation within *time and space*. However, some events may be teleological in mere direction, and apparently not in purpose—they appear purposeless. However, in his omniscience, God works everything for good, including what was only apparently purposeless in itself.

When God's purposes are achieved, creation becomes productive. When the mustard seed produces, its purpose has been accomplished. God's purposes in themselves do not produce anything; instead, he employs creation's nature to implement the purpose by its many properties. Creation is productive only because God's purposes are achieved through it. These purposes are not only "spiritual"; they are very physical and essential for the physical sustenance of creation's various kingdoms. What determines productivity depends on what the purpose is for each part of creation and its means to achieve it.

There is reason to emphasize the coterminous and codependent nature of the two meanings of teleology: quantitative (time) and qualitative (purpose). The former might be applied to history without acknowledging its mutuality with the latter. For instance, while the teleology pertaining to an "eschatological kingdom" acknowledges an eternity, it will often speak in terms of the end of the world or the end of time. This suggests that the temporal end forgoes the purposive end. I will propose, however, that the purposive meaning of teleology necessarily extends creation, history, and time to retain creation's design eternally. One might play with the antanaclasis, "there is no end of time, only the end of time," or "there is no end to the end." In the temporal sense of "end," there is no end; history's eternity has no ending. But in the other sense, there is an "end," the *purposeful* end of contributing to God's eternal design.

I have emphasized God's creative purposefulness and immeasurable omniscience in this chapter as a beginning to the fuller list of God's attributes suggested in the next chapter which pervade his perfect applications in his design of just and merciful blessings, deliverance, and discipline. God built into creation various components that propel it in a purposeful and eternal direction, creating history by its events, by creation's teleology. Creation is designed to be its own agent and thus itself creates its own history while remaining tethered to God's discretion.

Since creation and its history are codependent and coterminous, history is as comprehensive as the totality of creation's events when performed by all creation's various kingdoms, some of which are eternal; thus history is eternal. Personal, social, national, international, natural, and spiritual domains have habitually combined and interacted. These realms' interactions may appear chaotic, mysterious, and uncontrollable throughout history simply because the essence of creation is to be integrated by countless and complex permutations. These kingdoms intersect routinely within themselves and among the other kingdoms, forming the incalculably complex circumstances to which the members of the natural and terrestrial kingdoms react in order to survive or thrive.

Space and time are created "realms" within God's eternal and universal kingdom, and cause-effect brings perpetual and eternal changes. The what, how, where, and when that any entity contributes to creation's history is profoundly and continuously controlled by time and space, causality, and God's discretion. History's events are contained in space and time and are governed by cause and effect, which are not deterministic wherever God allows human discretion to be exercised. The teleology of creation in time, that is, the eternal direction for which it reaches, is the result of this inherent nature of creation and God's purposive nature. His omniscience leaves no cause-effect event unnoticed or without response by his dynamic action or calculated permission. Does he ignore anything? No. Is anything meaningless to him? No. Does it matter whether it appears trivial or inconsequential? No. Must he prioritize his attention, including his amount of attention to any matters? No. God's omniscience is not qualified, proportional, or hierarchical, which is true as well for all his many other attributes when they guide his eternal design collectively.

A specific scenario reminds me to stay on track in this journey to understand God's purposes for his creation. Consider this seemingly mundane event: an unknown pedestrian walks safely through the crosswalk in front of my car. What is the design that includes this specific yet apparent random occurrence? How is this ordinary episode relevant to anything? So what? It would be natural to consider the event as irrelevant, just an event along with innumerable other events that one would never seriously reconsider and describe to anyone else. Nonetheless, this event, like every event, is integrated and moving in a particular direction. Is God more aware of this walking soul than the license plate on my car? Is he more engaged with me because I am a believer than he is with her even if she is not? Does he care what her thoughts and actions were three minutes before crossing the street and what they will be three minutes after? How were those thoughts and actions the results from her birth, from her personality, from her natural environment, or any dark spiritual forces in her life? Is she going home to be lonely, adored, or abused? Has she come from a place of worship or from a funeral? Has God "been in" her life as much as in the life of the apostle Paul or Marco Polo? Yes, she receives no less of God's awareness than King David did.

This is creation's God and the extent of his providence. Reality is not so substantially fragmented, and nothing is inconsequential or meaningless data, especially to God. Does God's infinite and active wisdom incorporate this single pedestrian's act into something beyond simply

God's omniscience? Does he ignore it; is it meaningful to him, or is it so trivial he dismisses it? Does it merit response from him in any way; is it less of a priority than when I cross the road? I propose that there is a design as all creation's "operating principle," thus intrinsic to it and its history. After all, Paul addressed the personal lives of every intellectual elite present on Mars Hill when explaining that one of their own poets acknowledged God's universal kingdom: "He is really not far from each one of us since in him we live and move and have our being," even my fictitious pedestrian (Acts 17:27–28).[8] Paul accentuated every person's (ἑνὸς ἑκάστου ἡμῶν) presence in the milieu of God's sovereignty. This was not a platitude about humanity as a race; rather, it was a pronouncement pertaining to pedestrians as well as philosophers.

What is God's purpose, and what would be his appointed time(s) within an endless history? This study intends to understand God's eternal design and his means of realizing it throughout history. I have contended that Christian theology can be limited in its understanding and expression of God's teleology of his creation and its history. Consequently, certain paradigms need redefinition by better biblical structures. Conventional approaches to biblical and systematic theologies appear to neglect a much broader theological and historical paradigm. Consequently, many unnecessary distinctions and exaggerated discontinuities between God's designs of the past, present, and the eternal future might obscure history's most important and seamless trajectory for God's unending design. The theology of history that this first chapter offers is foundational for understanding God's eternal design and its central role in understanding creation's purpose.

---

8. In Paul: "καί γε οὐ μακρὰν ἀπὸ ἑνὸς ἑκάστου ἡμῶν ὑπάρχοντα. ἐν αὐτῷ γὰρ ζῶμεν καὶ κινούμεθα καὶ ἐσμέν." In Epimenides to Zeus: "For in you we live and move and have our being ('Εν γὰρ σοὶ ζῶμεν καὶ κινύμεθ' ἠδὲ καὶ ἐσμέν)." Jesus had said something similar to the Jewish leadership: "the kingdom of God is in the midst of you" (Luke 17:20–21).

2

Nature of God

MUCH HAS ALREADY BEEN said about God in the first chapter while describing the natures of his creation and its history. Now we describe further his own nature, which is the pattern for all creation. One meets God first as the Creator of the heavens and earth in the Testaments, and the Testaments end with God as the Creator of yet another heavens and earth still with himself as the design. And most basically, this eternal design is formed not simply "by" God but "like" God, after his very nature, which I turn to next. By this brief description of God's nature, what will be explained in the next chapter as the "eternal design" will be shown to derive from these attributes of God.

A few comments first. The following review of God's nature cannot be prioritized since much of the attributes' interconnectedness is mutually dependent and cannot be separated into a hierarchy of logical or otherwise causal antecedents. Furthermore, no attribute is expendable since without it God would not be the greatest conceivable being. Nor can any such listing presume to be exhaustive since he is even greater than the greatest being of whom one's mere finite mentality can only begin to conceive. Further yet, what one knows of God's nature is the summation of only those attributes he has revealed. God has not been required to reveal all of his attributes; he may not have revealed attributes that are not relevant to this creation. In other words, we cannot fully evaluate God's relationship with us even on the basis of general and special revelation since God has selected what he reveals about himself by withholding other information about his infinite self. One cannot assume, obviously, that either general or special revelation exhaust God's nature and its attributes.

Any list of attributes such as the following is bound to be analogous, thus to some extent idolatrous, in that simply a list and its definitions of God's attributes will inevitably contain incomplete formulations perceived and interpreted through the human mind's fallen filters. This is not to say that it is impossible for the finite to understand the infinite. We cannot conceive of infinity, but we can conceive that two plus two equals four. One's view of God's nature is formed by his revelation, which is more than adequate to express truth, not "kind of truth," since his heart and mind communicate in a way that one can perceive the truth by perceptive abilities that he has proactively created and facilitated within us for exactly this and other purposes. In other words, even incomplete and finite lists with definitions of God's attributes can be accurate, though not exhaustive. It is a fool's journey to try to put all the pieces together, believing one can obtain a complete and perfectly systematized knowledge of his nature. Most would challenge or add to the following list and its cryptic comments, which they should, since these explanations focus only on the relevant emphases for this study's purposes. Later in this study, this list and its explanations will structure a discussion of the message of sanctification—one's re-imaging into these same attributes of God's image.

DIVERSITY WITHIN UNITY

Within the ontological unity of the Trinity is their functional unity and diversity. They are always of one accord in the purpose for creation and in their collaboration in designing humanity after themselves. In addition, diversity is exactly what this current list is all about, in that the Trinity's many attributes form a complex nature capable of anything it pleases to do without contradicting itself. Also, their unity in purpose is made effective by their diverse roles, not in any diversity in their attributes. One might be so bold as to suggest that the Persons apply their common essence, their shared attributes, but in different ways according to their functions which are applied to this particular creation. Their roles are not revealed for any other of the Trinity's productions within its eternality; surely God was not dormant before our universe's creation. Moreover, the Trinity's functions are not attributes; they are the products of the common attributes and apply differently to each Person and to the relationships with one another and with their creation. Admittedly, the ontology of the Trinity cannot be known exhaustively; however, it is not contrary to reason, or irrational, though it goes beyond rational.[1]

The different functions among the Trinity's Persons are more than an authoritative polity since they work by love and mutual agreement rather than an insistence on a single Person's own rightful position. Their differences form a functional and cooperative pact with no inferred inferiority because they are equal in their ontology where each Person's nature is God's nature as his attributes below will describe. For example, the First Person is not superior in nature; his leadership role is a service he renders to the other two. So, the nature of the Trinity is not a political hierarchy; it is ontologically egalitarian with differing, servicing roles. Leadership is not a privilege within the Trinity apart from the privilege of service. Then again, the divine Messiah's coregency with the Trinity is considered only a relative coregency given the subordinate ontology of his divine/human incarnation.

COOPERATIVE

The assisting relationship among the Father, Son, and Holy Spirit is seen pervasively in the Testaments where the Father helps the Son, the Son helps the Father, and the Spirit serves the Father and Son. This "helping" is not humiliating, servile employment. To the contrary, it is each divine Person's nature to help since, though the Trinity is diverse in its functions in relation to its creation, its loving coordination of those functions is a consequent attribute given its nature as emotive/loving, active, purposeful, and communicative. It will be clear that this helping relationship is critical for understanding his eternal design, as we will describe in the next chapter.

---

1. Perhaps it is a methodological error to first pursue a metaphysic based on philosophical definitions of ontology rather than to start with special revelation. In other words, one should start with the reality of three Persons as presented by the Testaments. Only then one might go on to define "ontology" in a way where two persons can have identical attributes and not be the same person (God's simplicity). The Trinity's uniquely infinite ontology would not be expected to conform to the limited definitions composed by the finite minds it created.

SPIRITUAL

God is a spirit simply because he is not physical. Depending on one's view of Christ's present ontology in the heavenly kingdom, God is generally considered to be aspatial and atemporal unless he self-restricts by appearing in space and time. Creation reflects this attribute of God in the nature of spirits, either fallen or holy angels, and within the nature of what it means to be human.

ETERNAL

The nature of history starts with God since "In the beginning, God . . . ." God is where an infinite cause-and-effect progression begins. His eternality is the first attribute that one encounters in Gen 1:1, and one can go no further in any theological discipline without it. God's blessing is in his choice to confer eternality to creation's history and design.

CHANGELESS

God is unchangeable in his attributes, though his response to creation, specifically the tethered creative will of humanity, affects his actions within the bounds of his wisdom and righteousness. None of God's attributes conflict among them and cause him to struggle to keep his own nature in balance. Furthermore, none of God's attributes are his aspirations and qualities in which he grows or improves. Passages about God's "repentance" reveal his change in action due to human response to his pronouncements rather than a miscalculation on his part. His actions may change but his nature does not.

ACTIVE

God's nature to act is as necessary as it is for him to exist. His nature is to actively reign over his universal kingdom consistently with all of his other attributes, acting wisely on what he knows, which is everything; he acts creatively, powerfully, righteously, and often emotionally. His actions proceed from his irreducible and uncaused nature with attributes of purposefulness, omniscience, righteousness. However, his actions have no reciprocal impact on his nature in that they are not determinative of his being. God has no deficiency and has no attribute that is ever replenished by his actions, including his act of creation.

OMNIPOTENT

God's nature as a whole is infinite and secured by his impregnable power. Nothing within himself or from any sub-kingdom will successfully challenge his attributes' dominance in all circumstances. Though history is a composite of challenges from the extreme power of the satanic and terrestrial kingdoms, they and the cursed natural kingdom are always controlled. Contrived arguments fail against God's omnipotence when pitting him against his nature, thus making him limited. God cannot do what contradicts his nature, e.g., sin, be unaware, or be anything that compromises any one or more attribute.

OMNISCIENT

Our first chapter affirmed God's awareness of absolutely everything, including the interrelationships of every object, thought, action, and even every potential relationship: "Nothing in creation is hidden from God's sight" (Heb 4:13). His knowledge of how any of creation's interrelationships might be positive or negative is integral to making wise, purposeful, and productive decisions to act. Otherwise, he would be at risk of being wrong. It is important to realize as well that God is no more interested in one detail of creation than he is another. He has an infinite knowledge of each entity and his consideration of its existence and any of its ramifications is just as intense for each mosquito as it is for each quark, person, Norwegian fjord, and Sagittarius A. This fact should impress believers of the purview of God beyond themselves, their family, church, and nation. What he *does* in reference to each detail is rarely made known, and though his actions or inaction are historical, humanity can know only an infinitesimal fraction of them.

LOGICAL

God is infinite and complex in all of his attributes, but he is consistent and non-contradictory among them. His self-awareness coordinates his changeless attributes so as not to be random in action. Reality will at times inevitably defy fallen, finite human perceptions and the presumed logical conclusions drawn from them, but informed human reasoning that is convinced of God's integrity in his attributes will surrender one's presumptions about things unseen in confident faith based on God's predictable, intelligent, though not always perceivable wisdom. He balances emotion with reason and acts in an orderly way based on his omniscient, purposeful, and ethical nature.

INFINITE

God is unlimited in all of his attributes, including any limitation from any of his other attributes. This not a source of dread for those who understand and experience that this includes his righteousness—the source of peace and trust.

PURPOSEFUL

God is fully knowledgeable of every implication of all that he does or does not do, otherwise his actions would be random. His actions might be purposeful but end in uncertain results if all potentialities of his and creation's actions were not known, lest they be destructive, even tragic. Instead, his actions are infallibly purposeful; his omniscience forms and sustains everything according to a perfect eternal design. God thinks teleologically and eternally "ahead," so he has no need for mid-course corrections, including creation's salvation. God determines creation's teleology and he is undistracted and infallible in impelling it eternally and consistently by his design.

EMOTIVE

All of God's emotions have productive implications, including delight, peace, enthusiasm, determination. Even his post-Fall emotions of pity, anger, grief, patience are responses to the moral weakness and rebellion of humanity for fair and disciplinary objectives. Though God's grace is associated with his forgiveness and salvation in justification and sanctification, it is a result of his foundational love to bless his creation not only with eternal existence in the first place but also with its quality of existence.

ETHICAL

Since God is ethical, he acts only ethically; he does not become ethical when he acts; he simply is so. God's righteousness is his standard for shepherding his creation. By it he blesses, delivers, and judges his creation in all love and fairness. If God's nature was not always righteous, his motivations would always be suspect and ominous. The world would look far worse if his Edenic curse was not restricted by his purely righteous nature. However, who would dare to redefine for God what the extent of his Curse should have been? It is within the Curse that his righteousness becomes more fully evident when responding to creation's rebellion since his post-Fall graces are derivative from his righteous nature. His righteous justice, mercy, forgiveness, adoption, and deliverances are examples of his ethical responses to human moral deficiencies, so they will not be needed in the perfected New Earth.

CREATIVE

Creativity is not synonymous with artistry. Art is a particular application of the creative mind whereas the former is an attribute of God and activated whenever innovating anything. That God acts and creates is inevitable, so he did not need an ulterior purpose to create. However, he designed his creation to have a purpose that drives its history in an eternal direction. Since any action is an expression of the actor, God inevitably expressed himself in creation.

COMMUNICATIVE

God's nature is communicative within the Trinity and it is shown to be at creation and throughout the Testaments. So, he reveals himself by his accurate, broad, instructive, and deep revelation that is found in nature, the conscience, and the Testaments. His natural revelation has been, is, and will be perpetual, and his special revelation has been reliably communicated already through physical appearances, his audible voice, visions, dreams, prophecy, and especially during the Incarnation and continued now through the Spirit's guidance of the believer's regenerated spirit. One looks forward to God's additional routine, sensational, and mystifying revelation throughout eternity.

COMPLEX

One cannot comprehend all of the permutations of God's attributes as they combine to determine his thoughts and actions. Through the millennia of his universal kingdom's operation, an entire history of creation and the meaning of all its happenings obviously becomes unintelligible. That is not to say that nothing can be known nor known accurately, only that ultimately the "whys" of personal and global life cannot be known exhaustively, leaving questions and often heartbreaking silence for humanity to grapple with. Yes, God's promises self-limit even his options, but even then, the maximum impact of those promises and the means God takes to keep them evade our perception and appreciation, awe, or even horror.

VOLITIONAL

For any action there needs to be an intentional decision or a subliminal instinct or habit. It is assumed that God's omniscience precludes anything subliminal for him, leaving only his intentionality. However, a decision is itself inadequate for it to be purposeful; action is required. This implies a will to activate the decision. God's will is autonomous of anything but his own nature. An autonomous will and action regardless of his nature would be inconsistent with his changelessness in his attributes. Since he is changeless this is not a possibility. God's will is free to do anything consistent with his nature.

SOVEREIGN

God's attributes are inextricably dependent on his other attributes. One of these attributes that is composed by others is his supreme dominance, his sovereignty. It is not merely an *application* of his attributes shown only in his actions; it is a necessary and intrinsic element of God's nature since he can be nothing other than sovereign given his perfection in all other attributes and the ontological subordination of all he creates. He cannot *become* more or less sovereign since those attributes are never changed or enhanced. In other words, he cannot become any more or any less than the universal Creator, owner, and functioning King of his creation. Otherwise, God's sovereignty would be only a contingent attribute when depending on creation rather than completely on his nature.

GLORIOUS

Like his sovereignty, God's glory is the entire harmonious complexity of his attributes together. Once his nature is understood (but hardly comprehended), no other conclusion could be drawn than that he is glorious. He is "the greatest of all conceivable beings." Yet one should not think that listing his known attributes and summing them up in the term "glory" does him justice as the fullest proof of that; the superlative expression of God's majestic totality is not reflected by this term alone since his glory is *experienced* only when seen, not just heard about. It has to be witnessed, and the Testaments describe his glory as its inexpressible radiance, its brilliant "light." The Testaments' descriptions of God's presence are hardly hyperbolic; rather, they are the best that the authors' finite vernacular could express—only modest understatements. God reveals his nature in his creation, which is designed to mirror and to actualize his attributes while it does not determine or enhance them. Like any mirror, the reflection is limited and incomplete yet still meaningful and productive.

HOLY

The glory of God, that is, the summation and intensity of all of his attributes, is what *sets him apart* as unique from creation. "Holiness" means "separate, set apart" in the Testaments' Hebrew and Greek. The term's fullness certainly does not confine God's holiness to his ethical attribute and actions alone. Rather, holiness is God's necessary position when his exceptional, infinite, conglomerate glory is compared with his creation. His creation is only "common" compared with God's infinite uniqueness. Like all of God's attributes, his holiness is not a goal, something to which he aspires; it is simply his unenhanceable nature.

NOT SELF-GLORIFICATION

It is a common teaching that the world, particularly humanity, was created primarily to glorify God, which in all its ambiguity might be a profound teaching if it were given specific content by testamental support.

Usually, however, one is left with one's own respectful interpretations of it. Did God create everything including humanity *in order to* glorify himself? One might reflect a bit when it is said this bluntly, as if creation is all about him and whether he gets his glory or not.

First, why would he prioritize his own glory since his attribute as glorious is unenhanceable? Even God cannot add a greater volume of an attribute to his already perfect nature or at some point he would have been less than perfect and, therefore, less glorious. Even the millions of praising voices from all those who have benefited from the Passion and the Spirit's sanctification have never added to his glory. There certainly is an increasing acknowledgment and witness to God's glory, but that does not increase it. This witness increases creation's awareness of his glory, both qualitatively and quantitatively, but it does not improve God's attribute of glory. His glory can only be increased in creation's perception and commitment. Otherwise, God's glory would be mutable and finite since his glory would depend on creation rather than completely on his nature as it certainly was during the eternity "before" creation. God *is* glorious; he does not *become glorious*, nor is he made *more glorious* when he acts by combining his perfect attributes or when creation magnifies his glory among itself. God's purpose for creation was not to improve himself.

This presumption about God's purpose for his creation also raises a central ethical question. It would be self-contradicting if he created everything for his self-glorification since it would make morally appropriate exactly what was considered the sin that caused the Fall in the first place. The Couple were tempted to glorify themselves and be like God as his equal. So, were they culpable for raising their self-glorification to the level of an alleged virtue of God—glorifying himself? In other words, would the primary purpose of God's creation contradict what he has revealed and modeled to be a moral virtue? Would God reserve the right to self-glorify but not honor one who carries his image and is motivated by self-glorification? Would what is immoral for humanity be moral for God?

There may be some piety in respecting God, deferring to his "otherness" and allowing him the prerogative to do for himself what he forbids humanity to do. To the contrary, it is quite impious to disrespect the consistency of his moral nature as a pattern for humanity's morality. In an attempt to honor God's glory, one dishonors God's morality. The believer must wish and strive to be like God in his glory, but one's primary objective is not just to *be* like God but to act like him.² Acting to glorify oneself is the sin against humility. Unbelievers are adept at noticing hypocrisy, so it is not winsome or productive to cast God as self-seeking.

On the other hand, no believer would question whether humanity, or the rest of creation for that matter, should glorify God. The question is whether that was creation's purpose. It is an error to say that any result was the *primary* objective of what caused it. For instance, that "the skies reveal God's glory" is not to say that his own glory was the impetus or purpose for creating the skies. Similarly, that "his invisible attributes, eternal power, and divine nature are seen clearly" is not to say that is *why* he created anything (Ps 19:1; Rom 1:20). Given God's omniscience, if his primary intention for creation inevitably *resulted* in it glorifying him, then one could say that he knew that glorification of him would come as well, just as every other result that came from his creation through its cause-effect ramifications. Is the primary purpose of humanity different from that of the whole creation? Again, a result does not make it *the primary* reason for the act. The Testaments command humanity, even all creation, to glorify God, to give him the attention, credit, praise, adoration, worship, just for his nature in itself and for its generous implications. This is incontestable. But the Scriptures do not affirm that his glory was the primary reason for creation's existence—only that his glory is one of creation's significant features. Creation does reveal God's glory, but that was not his motivation, only an inevitable result.

His glorification comes about not in why he created but in *how* he created. Again, God's creation came primarily as another expression of his attribute of infinite love for personal relationships, reflecting the Trinity's love among its Persons. In other words, he created after his own nature. He was not in need of this creation to supplement his perfect communion within the Trinity. Jesus expressed the nature of God clearly when he said he did not come to be served but to serve (Matt 20:28; Mark 10:45). Even more graphically, he said he would be like the master who seats his servants at a table and begins to wait on them, just as he did for his disciples one morning (Luke 12:37; John 20:9, 12–13). One might be confused because Jesus made clear demands of the world as its master.

---

2. God's creative nature is built into creation, and parents exemplify his eternal design. Mutual spousal love reflects the intimacy of the Trinity. And when man and wife "become one" and create another, they lovingly shepherd the child together. Hopefully, a wise child will bring glory to the parents, though that is not why the parents procreated. They wanted to shepherd another who would then shepherd others as they were shepherded.

Yet this is exactly the point Jesus makes: yes, he is the master, and he has demands, but he does not make them to glorify himself but to bless his servants. Serving tables is not demeaning to the Lord; on the contrary, his service to sinners glorifies him, though that is not the reason for his service. The reason is his emotional attribute to love others to death, even death on a cross. After all, again, the Persons have not been serving each other during their eternity to glorify each themselves, but out of loving cooperation with the others.

Various objections raised against this line of reasoning might be based on biblical passages that appear to support God's self-glorification. The Old Testament refers to Israel as his chosen people created and equipped for a unique purpose (Isa 43:6–7; Jer 13:11)—to model for the profane nations what a wholesome, shepherding partnership with God looked like. This was Israel's distinctive purpose for being created and set apart from the other nations. It was by their example to the nations that they glorified him—not as their sole or primary purpose for existence. It was to be a result of her election, and the purpose for her unique creation with the appropriate equipping, including the law and wisdom and the central geographical location between the continents, to glorify God in this particular way, yet not the primary purpose for its people. Furthermore, when Israel failed, he vindicated himself and his glory by disciplining them in various ways, including separating them from their land (Isa 48:9; Ezek 20:14; 36:22–23). His self-vindication defended him from accusations of guilt by association with Israel. It is not wrong to protect one's reputation; however, it is evil to make oneself the first priority of everything and be self-promotional. God himself, in Christ Jesus, showed this by glorifying the Father who had glorified him; yet he prayed also for the glory to be shared with believers (John 17:22).

This unique creation of Israel as an instrument in God's global mission is paralleled in other passages in the New Testament that affirm that creation is "to him" and "for him": "From him, through him, and to him are all things. To him be glory forever" (Rom 11:36); "There is one God, the Father, all things come from him, and for him we exist" (1 Cor 8:6); "for whom and by whom everything exists" (Heb 2:10). Yet these prepositional phrases do not specify in what way creation is "to" or "for" God. Since God's creation is the tight textual context in each of these texts, a preferred translation is that creation is for his use: "to him" and "for him," for his universal kingdom purposes, whatever they might be, like Israel was. In other words, humanity and the rest of creation are for

God's designed purpose, the purpose that is about to be clarified in this next chapter.

The impact from a deeper understanding of creation and its history should cause a deeper appreciation of God's nature displayed in creation's history. It certainly would have impressed humanity regardless of whether there ever was a Fall and will continue to impress the residents of New Earth. Creation's all-encompassing nature that was formed according to God's own nature will continue its design under his dynamic, active, creative, omnipotent, omniscient and wise, sovereign, shepherding oversight. What exactly was that design?

3

God's Eternal Design

THE NATURE OF HISTORY and the nature of God are foundational for understanding how he administrates his universal and eternal kingdom.[1] He built teleology into its properties, including time, space, cause-effect, as well as building his own nature into creation as the pattern for his ultimate and eternal design for it. This "eternal design" has been mentioned at times so far with no accompanying definition, which I now emphasize to be the *summum bonum* of creation and its history, therefore, of the Testaments.[2] This all-encompassing plan gives the deepest meaning to every event of comprehensive history, and this design explains the making of history by God's collaboration with his creation.

God's eternal design is cooperative, intimate, personal, and productive at its core, not a sterile conceptual structure imposed on a passive universe. The Trinity's nature itself is the model of this cooperative design, and by that design God assists each component of his creation. Helping is not a denigrating act for God toward his creation any more

---

1. The eternality of creation is clear because the Testaments tell us that believers have eternal life and that they inherit the planet for eternity. More will be said of this biblical teaching later, but it is a critical underpinning of this study's conclusions.

2. In approaching a theme of "God's order" in history and creation, Charles Scobie understands that the pursuit "expresses the biblical conviction that behind the multiple, complex, and frequently puzzling phenomena of nature and history is a meaning and purpose, a pattern and order that is to be ascribed to the presence and power of the one true God." Scobie, *Ways of Our God*, 94.

than it is among the Persons. "God so loved the *world*"; in other words he loved nature, angels, and humanity, all created components.³ It contributes to his glory even "to help" humanity (Gen 49:25; Exod 18:4; Pss 33:20; 115:9–11; 121:1–2; 124:8). The Messiah is a helping servant to all kings (Isa 49:7). But not only kings. Christ compares his second coming with the actions of a master who himself will serve food to his own *slaves*—something he did before his ascension by serving breakfast on the beach for his exhausted disciples (John 21:13).

> Blessed are the slaves whom the master finds on alert when he comes; truly I say to you, that he will prepare himself to serve, have them recline at the table, and he will come to serve them. (Luke 12:37)

This helping nature could be described variously: to satisfy, please, fulfill, favor, help, give, provide, tend, and care for; be benevolent, considerate, gracious, generous, thoughtful, kind, and compassionate—all conveying the heart of the shepherding God. God's helpful nature forms with his creation's nature the capacity for a wonderful intimacy with him. Yet, his nature also requires massive, sobering responsibilities beyond a calm devotional life and warm Christian fellowship. Mercifully, God has promised to help in these ominous moral responsibilities since the satanic and terrestrial kingdoms prey on the weak, poor, and abandoned.

GOD SHEPHERDS

Paul affirmed in Acts 20:27 that there is one "entire purpose/plan of God [πᾶσαν τὴν βουλὴν τοῦ θεοῦ]." Precisely then, what is God's whole purpose for his creation? What is it that he has built into creation as his teleological operating principle? The means of God's blessing is often described in the Testaments as his shepherding. So, *God shepherds*. This description of his sovereignty is the basis of the eternal design; his shepherding nature

---

3. About *kosmos*, world, Andreas Köstenberger writes: "The term, then, in John as elsewhere in Greek writings, means first and foremost the physical, created universe, as in John 17:5, where Jesus speaks of the glory he had in God's presence 'before the world began.'" Köstenberger, *John's Gospel and Letters*, 281. Edmond Jacob describes the cosmos as habitable and comfortable: "The author of the Priestly creation narrative shows God setting the elements in order like an architect intending to build a house inside which new inhabitants should be entirely at their ease; this house must be substantial, sheltered from dangers, pleasant, with a measure of luxury not forbidden there." Jacob, *Theology of the Old Testament*, 136.

is what determines his relationship with creation, and his caring nature is expected to be imaged by his creation among itself as well.

One might ask what the difference is between God as a *shepherding* monarch and God as a gentle, *loving* monarch. Are they not one and the same? It is true that to shepherd as God shepherds requires his loving attribute. It is also true that to love requires the actions comparable to those of a shepherd. But to be a shepherd emphasizes the various functions that require additional attributes. God's sovereignty is not a more important attribute than his love, but the term "shepherd" denotes a position of influence presumably exercised with affection. God's attributes play different roles, not more significant roles. In this sense, if one were to ask what the difference between God as a shepherding monarch and God as an omniscient monarch was, it would be evident that his omniscience contributes to his shepherding, but it does not adequately describe it. God's love contributes to his shepherding, but it is not adequate alone to describe his shepherding.

Then again, "Sovereign," "King," and "Lord" are examples of accurate and powerful designations of God and his Messiah when considering his eternal design. "Father" is another divine designation yet not one used as frequently in the Old Testament. However, "shepherd" is at times a preferable title and is no more of a metaphor than "king" or "lord," which as descriptive terms restrict one's view of his administration of reality by primarily emphasizing his powerful authority. These terms are of course accurate, but they are not as easily associated with the compassionate, caring role of a shepherd who perfectly and patiently loves, blesses, soothes, protects, delivers, and, yes, disciplines his creation for its own sake. No defense should be necessary for accentuating God's *shepherding* as his relationship with creation. To emphasize its primacy is not a trite, sentimental, or homiletical gimmick. It distinctly communicates God's personal and trusting relationship and should be understood without flannel-graph simplicity. It was a most powerful metaphor used by at least Mesopotamian and Egyptian cultures for their gods and kings as well.

God is mentioned in around fifty literal shepherding contexts in the Old Testament alone because it describes not only God's authority and actions but also his *heart and virtue* in his relationship with his creation. These passages either refer to God as a shepherd or to his appointed shepherds[4] or to anti-shepherds who abuse his sheep.[5] And of course, the New Testament continues the literal shepherding motif,[6] particularly related to Christ, e.g., "May the God of peace, who by the blood of the eternal covenant raised our Lord Jesus from the dead, that Great Shepherd of the sheep" (Heb 13:20). Peter is as comfortable as the rest of Scripture in calling God and his Messiah shepherds:

> You were straying like sheep yet have returned now to the Shepherd and Guardian of your souls. (1 Pet 2:25)

> When the chief Shepherd appears, you will receive the unfading crown of glory. (1 Pet 5:4)

Peter follows the example of Isaiah and Ezekiel, who proclaim a literal "gospel," in Hebrew, *baśar*, namely, that the Lord was Israel's ruling shepherd:

> Bring the gospel . . . Jerusalem, bring the gospel . . . he will care for his flock like a shepherd. He will gather the lambs in his arms and carry them tightly and gently lead them as little lambs. (Isa 40:9, 11)

> I will assign them one shepherd, my servant David, and he will tend them and be their shepherd. (Ezek 23:24)

God was their shepherd, not only the mighty rightful king of the universe but the caring, nurturing shepherd who perfectly blesses, delivers, and disciplines. The Lord had revealed his shepherding nature throughout history already:

> I, the Lord God am compassionate and gracious, slow to anger, full of love, care, and faithfulness for thousands, forgiving sin and rebellion, but not letting the guilty go unpunished. (Exod 34:6–7)

---

4. Gen 48:15–16; 49:24; Num 27:16–18; 1 Kgs 22:17; Pss 28:9; 77:20; 78:52, 71–72; 79:11–13; 80:1–3; 95:7; 100:3; 107:41; 119:176; Isa 40:9–11; 49:9; 53:6; 63:11; Jer 3:15–16; 17:14–16; 23:3–4; 31:10; 50:17–19, 44; Ezek 23:24; 34:5, 11–16, 23, 31; 37:24–26; Mic 2:12; 4:8; 5:2–4; Zech 9:16; 10:2; 11:4–7; 13:7. For more extended explanations of these texts, see my notebook on a biblical theology. Fredericks, *Shepherds*, 24–25.

5. 2 Chr 18:16; Isa 56:11; Jer 2:8; 10:21; 12:10; 23:1; 25:31, 34; 50:6, 17–19; Ezek 34:2–8, 20–21; Zech 11:5, 8–9, 17.

6. Matt 2:6; 9:36 // Mark 6:34; Matt 12:11; 15:24; 25:31–32 // Mark 14:27; Luke 15:4–7 // Matt 18:12–14; John 10:1–29; 21:15–17; Acts 20:28–29; Eph 4:11; 1 Pet 2:25; 5:2–4; Rev 12:5.

One does not denigrate the role of Christ as king or savior while enhancing his role with another testamental designation that more immediately brings impressions of a caring shepherd.

CREATION'S PRIMARY COMMISSION

Because creation reflects the Creator's nature and his deeds, creation is required and equipped by its nature to shepherd as he does. God's image in humanity is one thing, but many might consider it odd to attribute it to spirits and nature as well. Yet, the angels shepherd humanity by their nature and moral obedience in the heavenly realm, something the evil spirits resisted, and so they were banished from that realm. And the natural realm has also been designed to shepherd through its laws of physics and mathematics. Like the angels, humanity's blessing and challenge has been its created moral nature, and moral laws were designed and revealed for humanity by which it is expected to act as shepherds. So, all of creation shepherds. Since God created a shepherding creation, the eternal design which will be the assumption throughout this study is *God shepherds his shepherding creation*. His eternal design for creation is its mutual blessing of all creation; the spirits, the natural world, and humanity were created to bless one another, just as the Trinity does within itself. In other words, God has created everything with the capacity in history to bless all within its space-time reach. That is, God's eternal design for all creation is to experience the blessing to be like him. Again, his purpose for this eternal design is not to be self-serving; rather his purpose for the eternal design is to bless creation. His nature is to serve something other than himself and to bless it with the glory that he has.

So, wording that God "shepherds" his shepherding creation is at least included, if not preferred, in such a foundational definition of God's relationship with his creation. If one rules like God rules, one will be a good shepherd, unlike the seen and unseen rulers and sovereigns of this world whose practice is to rule their surroundings as anti-shepherds by exploitation, oppression, and abuse, rather than by blessing and deliverance. And these counter-productive results accrue by the fallen angels' application of their attributes that in many ways approximate those of their Creator, e.g., active, purposive, volitional, communicative, etc. To live in this fallen world where anti-design behavior is pernicious and far-flung, God and human shepherding should not be visualized as a romantic, docile stereotype of a shepherd who misrepresents God's demanding and intense responsibilities that will take deep concentration, persistent management, and even violent protection of the sheep. Moreover, the eternal design also emphasizes humanity's relationship with him as extremely active, a relationship of dynamic drive rather than mere passive fellowship with God.

God requires the creation he blesses to in turn bless itself. That is a blessing greater than simply "being saved." He has set creation on an eternal journey with him rather than seating us at home with him merely "in relationship."[7] He certainly did not need creation, otherwise it would have been preexistent and coexistent with him. But the eternal design demands that relationship with him to be extremely active, a relationship of dynamic drive rather than a static status, rather than a passive relationship with God. God's expansive and all-encompassing shepherding kingdom is where humanity is blessed to live, thrive, and impact the rest of creation with their Creator now and forever.

Creation's structure was formed after the image of the Trinity and its Persons' functional differences, so creation has differing functional roles among itself as well. The sub-kingdoms within God's universal kingdom will rule their realm differently in important respects. The same relative coregency, where there is a hierarchical structure, applies to the spirits, nature, and humanity, where there are implicit levels of authority, mostly defined by the various levels of power, either innate or granted. Nevertheless, all levels rule their assigned realms because they were so created. They have power required for the interdependent operation of the whole of creation. The soil feeds flora, shorelines select flora, oceans define shorelines, the moon moves oceans, the earth embraces the moon as the sun does the earth. All are necessary functioning parts for the whole to be productively effective, amazing, and beautiful. Each rules but does so relative to its coregent position in God's universal kingdom configuration.

The eternal design parallels the nature of the Trinity and its shepherding nature of all creation. It is not a conceptual overlay, rather it is creation's intrinsic nature to shepherd whether salvation has been

---

7. Popular Christian teaching cherishes the "relationship" between God and believers, which it should. However, this can often imply that "a relationship" with God is the ultimate benefit of regeneration and salvation, leaving it at that. The "inner life" can become an appropriate emphasis, or it can become for all intents and purposes *the* central emphasis. There are many reasons for a believer's enculturation to individualism and its solipsism where one has such a privatized relationship with the Trinity that the dynamism of Christian external responsibilities is marginalized.

necessary or not. Coregency shows its intentions, its teleology, by adding a dynamic structure and method to the shepherding of the eternal design. As one would expect, since the Trinity functions as a coregency, creation's coregency with God and among itself has eternal functions for each of creation's elements.

The eternal design provides the widest context for any history, cultural system, ideology, or worldview. It provides the eternal DNA, the "operating principle" for creation where God's glorious nature is his shepherding model for creation's administration of his universal kingdom's eternal history. The eternal design is not a static framework or arrangement that creation fits into. Rather, it is a dynamic process woven into creation. Nor is it cyclic; its trajectory is linear and productive as it advances through eternity. Cyclicity occurs in only one sense in that, fortunately, there will have been only one cycle: perfect creation, to fallen creation, on to a newly, everlastingly perfected creation again.

The diversity in functions within the Trinity is reflected by the various functions within creation, since creation's functions contribute in unique ways depending on its own nature and abilities. The diversity in function contributes not only to the complexity of creation but to creation's effectiveness in the eternal design.[8] The limitations and options of time-space and causality, however, are used by creation—by the ingenuity of spirits, and humans, and by the innate attributes of the natural kingdom. By these vastly diverse functions, creation's elements bless, deliver, and discipline creation as a whole. More will be said of the spirits' two realms (holy and satanic) and nature's kingdom in chapter 6.

I turn now to humanity's unique shepherding commission and refer to the Trinity's conversations and commands to the Couple in Gen 1:26–28 as the "Primary Commission." It is no less than Jesus' template for his Great Commission.

	Primary Commission Gen 1:26–28	**Great Commission** Matt 28:18–20
Origination	Let us make humanity	Baptize in the name of [the Trinity]
Multiplication	Be fruitful and multiply	Make disciples
Global spread	Fill the earth	of all nations . . .
Human domination	and subdue it	teach them to obey my commands

8. I do not repeat here my extensive description of the ruling and shepherding that God models personally and designed for all creation to follow, including for spirit beings, nature, and humanity. For this, see Fredericks, *Shepherds*.

The designed coregency of the Trinity and humanity is implied in both historic passages: at creation with humanity and again with humanity during the messianic phase of the universal kingdom led by the divine man. Both epochal statements are explicitly presented in the context of the Trinity. Both pertain to humanity's commission from God.

Humanity's primary commission is strong, resolute, and uncompromising in its outcome: "Fill the earth and subdue it" (Gen 1:28). A "softer" statement would have been heard as unexceptional or merely suggestive rather than requiring strenuous effort and force to bring a potentially wild but productive creation into compliance with God's eternal design. This subduing is subsequently described as purposeful and edifying: serving, keeping, improving, and guarding human populations and portions of the natural kingdom (Ps 8:5–6; Jas 3:7). The subjugation commission was necessary even in a "good" creation since the dynamic operations of the natural kingdom were created for human oversight. Unfortunately, it became an overwhelming threat once the Couple set the tone by human non-compliance with God's expectations. Between an extreme and errant understanding of "to subdue" as abuse and a placid understanding of "to shepherd" when frailty is implied, one finds the constructive meaning of balanced management according to God's attributes of omnipotence and love.

The first three chapters and the last three chapters of the Testaments display the eternal design, and between these literary brackets is the parenthetical age. A perfect age was interrupted by this aberrant parenthetical age, which is replaced by the eternally perfect age. The shepherding God blesses, delivers, and judges the Couple in the first three chapters and judges, delivers, and then eternally blesses in the last three chapters. The very first and last chapters of the Testaments include humanity as the coregent with God in the eternal design with a bright thread of revelation showing the means, successes, and failures of humanity's pursuit of the shepherding pattern. The earth had always been given to humanity to rule, but in New Earth, believers will remain as the only beneficiaries. Christ and Paul affirm that believers inherit kingdom citizenship, but they will also own and rule it again since their inheritance is bound with Christ's (Matt 5:5; 25:34; 1 Cor 6:9; 15:50; Gal 5:21; Eph 5:5).

I suggest the broadest theology of history is a convergence of the shepherding sovereignties of God and creation. Especially humanity is equipped with the image of God for each person to pursue one's part in the eternal design: e.g., unity, diversity, spirituality, eternality, communicative, intelligence, purposeful, powerful, creative, active, ethical, emotive, glorious, and holy. We will return to these traits of the human race in chapter 4 and survey their significance for creation's comprehensive primary commission and its implications on its sanctification.[9]

ALL CREATION SHEPHERDS

Again, the agency of angels and the natural kingdom also reflect some of God and humanity's attributes and actions. Since creation is a product of God's glory and holiness, the universal kingdom's various realms synergize many analogous attributes of God. The angels are not said explicitly to be persons by the Testaments, yet as "beings" they reveal attributes of the nature of the divine Persons and of humans. Both holy and evil angels are spiritual, powerful, intelligent beings, which are active and communicative. Their volition is purposeful and appears to be "free" enough to rebel for self-seeking purposes. The fallen angels' willful decision to rebel shows this since they are blameworthy and expelled from the heavenly kingdom. On the other hand, one cannot know whether the holy angels have been granted an ontological impossibility of unethical behavior that foreshadows something comparable to humanity's ontology in New Earth. But the rebellion in the heavenly kingdom speaks to the moral culpability of the satanic kingdom. These attributes of the holy angels alone form their own complexity and glory that set them apart, that is, it makes them "holy" in their perfection. So little is known of the holy angels, but they are a blessing from God to creation as they contribute their designed responsibilities to bless, protect, deliver, and discipline humanity.

---

9. Beale's near existentialist definition of the image of God in Gen 1:28 is inadequate. While affirming the active sovereignty of humanity, he appears to divest it of its ontological causes, yet it is not an either/or proposition, and it was not beyond the earliest readers/listeners to realize this: "Any definition of God's image in humanity at this point would need to explain it as functional rather than ontological; that is, the emphasis in explaining the divine image is that it is something that humans do rather than what they intrinsically are." Beale, *Biblical Theology*, 383, also 30. The *waw* plus imperfect in 1:26 does not require a purposive understanding and can retain its basic meaning of "and," not "so that": see "Let us make humanity in our image and likeness, *and* they will have dominion . . . ." McConville, *Being Human*, 17; also Wenham, *Genesis*, 3–4. McConville later inverts the ontological and functional: "The function of 'ruling,' however, does not constitute or exhaust the meaning of the 'image,' but is better regarded as a consequence of it." McConville, *Being Human*, 20. It is sensible to see the synonymity of "image" and "likeness," contrary to the attempts to significantly differentiate them. For an example of such an equivalence, see Kilner, *Dignity and Destiny*, 125–33.

In respect to the natural kingdom, it is notable that creation starts with its shepherding sovereignty rather than that of humanity. God had already given nature its own primary commission before creating the Couple. Though nature is not free to act outside of its deterministic physics and chemistry, its authority to reign among the realms of creation is no less overwhelming as a coregent in God's universal reign. For example, the lights of Gen 1 alternate their authority yet together define day and night, thus "governing" (*mašal*) the activities of the dark and those needing the light. These lights are an example of the Lord's covenants with day and night (Jer 33:20; Ps 136:9; Hos 2:18). God commissions the various animal kingdoms: "Be fruitful and *multiply*, *fill* the water in the sea and the birds will *multiply* on the earth" (1:22). God shares his generating and shepherding capacities with all life in his natural kingdom.

The cosmos, like God, reveals its attributes of orderliness, creativity, wisdom, and power (Ps 19:1–6). This close and deep relationship between God and nature is described dramatically in Job 37–41. These similarities allow the natural kingdom to shepherd in the same ways as God, his holy angels, and humanity shepherd: by blessing, delivering, and disciplining. Nature blesses creation through its multiplying, swarming, and shepherding laws, providing its food-chain, rain, warmth, seasons, natural shelters, and raw materials. These similarities are not metaphorical in any way; they are structural essentials for all of the natural kingdom's intricate and productive processes that contribute to the eternal design.

The Testaments reveal the natural kingdom's reflection of God's transcendence, but they also make some of his specific attributes intelligible. The heavenly skies are spoken of specifically, and lifeless creations attest to the orderly, logical, complex, powerful, creative, and interactive nature of God. Through the laws of nature, from organisms to higher animals, animated life acts with its own modes of emotion, care, protection, and authority, and these traits may be less anthropomorphic than one thinks. Flora and fauna reveal complexity and interactivity; their realms extend from tiny to vast areas, over a single day or over centuries, from the depths of the seas to the heights of the heavens. Their networks comingle, sustain, and restrain while shepherding their life together. Animals visibly care for their families and communities by nurturing and protecting those within their reach and by disciplining their predators. The scope of sovereignty among life forms is widely divergent, from a single organism's survival and impact on its environment to the pillaging beasts' which dominate various terrains. Admittedly, the rock's depth of wisdom reaches nowhere while the awareness, even intelligence, craft, diligence, and discretion of some species reach that of humans in unique ways. Though one might deprecate this reflection of God's image as merely mechanical or instinctive, nonetheless, nature speaks. One uses such personification in regard to the natural kingdom simply because they, by whatever means, reflect the glory of the Persons, thereby displaying their own glory.

Humanity, of course, has its more far-reaching primary commission to rule the planet as God's coregent by asserting its superior attributes as God's most precise image-bearer in creation. However, humanity and nature coordinate their authority in various circumstances to subdue the earth and skies. Neither the natural nor human kingdoms can act independently; they must negotiate their regencies by mutual submission. People may board up their windows but hurricanes still destroy. Wood will not allow the artist to melt it, nor will stone allow itself to become two-dimensional, yet the artist will cut wood against the grain or cut stone into elegant sculptures with arcs and angles. Still, humanity is ignorant and powerless to govern all of the natural kingdom: "Do you [Job] comprehend the laws of the universe or can you establish their rule over the earth?" (Job 38:33). Nature and humanity's interdependence has both positive and negative consequences: positive when they work together for good and disastrous when either one pursues its own interests without regard for the other. Nature suffers when people consume excessively, and humanity experiences earth's wrath when it renders nature unstable.[10]

SHEPHERDING IMPLICATIONS

Christians can tend to see the rest of the world's individuals primarily as targets of evangelism, but God sees them primarily as targets of his shepherding care, which might include evangelism. One can peer narrowly at humanity through a "winning souls" and "witnessing" lens rather than sheep to be cared for irrespective of their eternal destiny. "If we could *just* get them saved, then . . ." is a mentality that might stand in the way

---

10. "The world, as Yahweh's creation, is not ordered so that some may set themselves over against the whole to their advantage. The world, as Yahweh's creation, requires daily, endless attention to the gifts of creation, for their abuse and exploitation can harm and impede the generosity that makes life possible. Creation, moreover, has within its sanctions to bring death on those who neglect the enhancement of generosity." Brueggemann, *Theology of the Old Testament*, 532.

of caring for needs now. Graciously however, missions and parachurch organizations model shepherding care by providing material, economic, and medical needs for humanity.

Even the nations, regardless of motivations, still shepherd their residents with various measures of care rather than creating a literal and perpetual hell on earth for all. God has always shown his universal kingdom's pervasive grace throughout history while salvation history progresses only incrementally. He has always pursued his eternal design by his "active," not deistic, reign. One should not emphasize the justice in his curse on his creation at the expense of his mercy seen in his pervasive tolerance, blessings, and deliverances of global life from total infernal adversity. Humanity's relentless search for meaning to life finds it already in enjoying relatively peaceful lives in families, neighborhoods, and communities. Admittedly, this equilibrium is interrupted by fallen human oppressors, who more than most others hunger for the greatest portions of power and property. Nonetheless, societies have found ways to connect the dots around them and form a sufferable communal ethos of mutual shepherding support. All religions, even godless philosophies, strain to find complete *shalom* by some hopeful narrative and to assuage their agonies. However, our race finds it all too difficult to wrench itself from the hold of the satanic kingdom and all its enticements to prey on other sheep rather than to adequately shepherd them.

> Kneel before the Lord our creator since he is our God and we are the people of his pasture and the sheep of his hand. (Ps 95:6–7)

4

Glory and Holiness

THE ETERNAL DESIGN IS a collaboration of like agents. As the likeness of God, humanity has been created with his nature, yet as qualitatively finite. In this sense he is not "wholly other," lest revelation has no meaning since it would render all verbiage as equivocal. But he is quantitatively "other" as the infinite model for his finite creation. The significant exception to this is the common eternal nature of God and his creation's future existence. Nevertheless, what is most wonderful about God is his glory. Consequently, what is most wonderful about creation is its glory. The Fall did not void creation's glory since what glory it retains still holds humanity blameworthy for not acknowledging its Creator and his attributes.

GOD'S GLORY

The glory of God is of course a central theme in the Testaments. Though the *purpose* of creation is not God's glorification, nonetheless it is one of many *results* to his creation. The primary Hebrew word for "glory" (*kabôd*) has a wide range of meanings, from the physical weight of an object, to the abstract weight of one's honor or reputation, to the fullest experience of God, including the "weight" of the visual impact of his presence. A generalization of these meanings pertaining to persons including God would be "reputation, honor" and when elevated still, as "majesty." The emphasis is the holistic impact of one's existence in the estimation or experience of others. The predominant Greek word for "glory" (δόξα) also has a wide range in meaning but is mainly within the more abstract fields compared with the wider ceremonial applications in the Old Testament. Both Hebrew and Greek have spectacular meanings in reference to God, e.g., "splendor, beauty, radiance, brightness," which are visually inspiring intensifications of his glory beyond the articulated descriptions of his glory. The Testaments exalt God's glory; they honor him for his greatness, which in every attribute contributes to his infinite, magnificent excellence. God's glory is the reason for his general holiness since it is his comprehensive glory that *separates* him from his creation. Paul extends the meaning of "good news" to include God's glory specifically: "the good news of the glory of the blessed God [εὐαγγέλιον τῆς δόξης τοῦ μακαρίου θεοῦ]" (1 Tim 1:11). Consequently, the glory of Christ as God is also extolled as good news: "the light of the good news of the glory of Christ [τοῦ εὐαγγελίου τῆς δόξης τοῦ Χριστοῦ], who is the image of God" (2 Cor 4:4).

GOD'S HOLINESS

Holiness is a very general term in the Testaments; it is not a synonym for righteousness yet certainly includes it. Holiness "is not really a moral attribute, which can be co-ordinated with the others, such as love, grace, and mercy, but is rather something that is co-extensive with, and applicable to, everything that can be predicated of God."[1] The Hebrew and Greek verbal roots, *qadaš* and ἁγιάζω respectively, mean "to separate [vb], separateness [nn]" and are applied to several objects in the Testaments—from ceremonial bowls, to people, to Christ and God himself (Lev 8:10–11; 19:2; Acts 4:27; Rev 4:8). God is "separate" by his glorious nature; for instance, the Spirit is the "Holy" Spirit due to his glory (Rom 1:4); bowls are deemed "separate" simply by their unique assignment, their "holy" use in the temple. The Sabbath is separate from the other six days (Exod 20:11), and Israel was separate from all other nations as a kingdom of priests (Lev 19:6; cf. Deut 7:6). These examples are literally "holy." So separateness and holiness are comparative terms that emphasize uniqueness compared to something else and often with no moral meaning.[2] In comparison then, God's creation is relatively "common"

---

1. Berkhof, *Systematic Theology*, 73.
2. Acts of definitive separation are a divine and human management skill with legal

by definition, ontologically separate from him, not having his infinite magnitude of glory.

Robin Routledge makes the important point, however, that the separation made explicit in "holiness" is not a deistic concept:

> Holiness, though, is not only about separation; it is also tied to *relationship*. Restrictions and prohibitions exist not to keep God away from humankind but to provide the means and conditions by which One who is *Wholly Other* may have contact with and enter into a relationship with his people.[3]

This study defines this "relationship" to be the eternal design: God shepherds his shepherding creation.

BELIEVERS' GLORY AND HOLINESS

God's holiness in the Testaments includes his moral perfection, but it is his most comprehensive glory that constitutes his "radiance": "Holy, holy, holy is the Lord of hosts; the whole earth is full of his glory" (Isa 6:3). It is God's cumulative glory from all of his attributes, not only his moral attribute, that determines his holiness, his uniqueness, his separateness. Consequently, as one becomes more like God by the sanctification process, one attains one's own holistic glory since the believer becomes more and more separate from the "common" world in many ways in addition to righteousness.[4] A holistic emphasis on holiness will not concentrate exclusively on the moral attribute of the believer any more than it should for God. Consequently, at times in this study holiness will be designated as moral and/or amoral. This means that to exercise one's redeemed attributes is a moral imperative even though the attribute itself is not moral. For example, to have the godly attribute of being logical is not the same

---

tools by which to separate civility from crime, discern wisely between effectiveness and futility or right from wrong, and divide political jurisdiction boundaries, etc. Creation was a series of separations: light from dark, day from night, sea water from sky waters, land from sea, species from species (later named by Adam). Eve is created by a surgical separation. The Curse brought the Couple's separation from Eden. Babel separated humanity into lineages, languages, and cultures. Proverbs primarily divides wisdom from foolishness, aphorism by aphorism. Wars dispute the legitimate separations presumed by national borders. Ironically, separateness can be both a holy goal and an evil bane of this parenthetical age.

3. Routledge, *Old Testament Theology*, 106.

4. This should not be confused with a heretical view throughout church history of an ontological union with the Trinity even if only through Christ (theosis, deification).

attribute of moral; yet, the thinking and thus acting logically is a moral responsibility in personal and social contexts, not in contexts such as mathematics or chemistry.

A very broad but biblical definition of "sanctification" describes the very purpose and the widest scope of humanity's role in God's shepherding of his shepherding creation. Furthermore, sanctification is the purpose of God's revelation in the Testaments as they encourage beyond anything else to be holy as God is holy, both morally and amorally. Sanctification, or holiness, is one's conformity to the glorious nature of God—becoming more "godly" in all of his attributes. In other words, comprehensive sanctification describes the believer's separateness, uniqueness, and holiness in many ways. It is insisted that all creation should reflect God's image and attributes. However, this can be taken too far by not acknowledging David's critical distinction between the Creator and the created in Ps 8:4–6:

> What is humanity that you even remember it, the son of man that you care for him?
> Yet you have made him a little less than God and crown him with glory and honor.
> You have given him sovereignty over your creation; you put everything under his feet.

The natural universe is beyond description. Nonetheless, humanity is responsible for managing a significant part of our planet.

God is not wholly comprehensible, but he is apprehensible, thus not wholly other. Humanity was created to understand who God is, and the Messiah came to verify and expand that understanding. Though it is a commendable attempt at humility, the extreme designation of God as "wholly other" disables a very means of creation's sanctification by rendering God's nature as unintelligible, thus without a standard, so beyond emulation. Infiniteness qualifies God's attributes, but it does not render any reference to them as totally other or equivocal. Continuing in Thomistic terms, even analogical terminology about God does not make God inapprehensible. A mystical "otherness" is theologically misleading and counter to creation's known divine image, especially when applied to both believing and unbelieving humanity and the renewed divine image by the Spirit in all believers. Humanity is to be holy because God is holy, meaning that one first understands what his holiness means and constitutes and, subsequently, how to seek it for oneself; holiness cannot imply an undefined difference whose trajectory is only incoherence. God's separation is quantitative in its volume or infiniteness but not wholly qualitatively separate from creation since creation is in his image, i.e., its qualities are recognizably and relatively analogically the same. Otherwise it would be impossible to be "imitators of God" (Eph 5:1).

Creation, including humanity, did not become totally depraved at the Fall since the image of God which was formed within is still there, though needless to say, it degenerated considerably. For instance, the natural kingdom still operates generally as created in nature even to the extent that it still demonstrates the nature of God (Rom 1:19–20). His nature is still seen in humanity but is miraculously enhanced wherever the Holy Spirit has regenerated and continues to sanctify a trusting soul.

The main implication of God's glory and holiness for humanity is that when imitated by humanity, his attributes lead to effective shepherding according to the operating principle of creation. To accomplish this, God not only has provided instruction for moral behavior, or righteousness, but he has glorified humanity with most of his attributes that have been reviewed already.

AMORAL GLORY

God's concern for creation and throughout eternal history is primarily its sanctification. It was this proper and designed separation and holiness that would be catastrophically interrupted by the parenthetical age but then again regained in a new creation where the attributes of God will be no less needed than they were before the Fall. And they are no less needed during this parenthetical age either. The eternal work that God anticipated to be done is being done, even by unbelievers who inevitably display a significant extent of God's image even though they are not redeemed. Common grace, and an adequate conscience, still contends with Satan's global attempt to frustrate God's likeness within them. It will be done by God's sovereignty and its complex synergy with his other attributes. It will also be done with his coregents whom he instructs throughout the Testaments on how to apply their parallel attributes that equip them in their own sovereignty under his universal kingdom. These attributes are not metaphorical contrivances; they are the actual human attributes which, when renewed by the Spirit, move a believer closer to being truly human as God had designed. And the believer's comprehensive sanctification, moral and amoral, will always be expanding eternally, though of course never reaching God's infinite glory. This expansion of the impact of the eternal trusting kingdom is the already-never-yet of the universal kingdom since the believers kingdom's eternal sanctification will continue to shepherd creation as it had only begun to do in Eden.

Before the Fall, God believed there was an eternal amount of work to be done by the Couple and their descendants. He still does. Before the Fall, his image equipped the Couple and all their descendants for the eternal task of the primary commission. This had nothing to do with redemption and salvation. Before the Fall, human sin was only potential, but when sin entered the world, the Couple were profoundly separate from God, becoming in many ways as common as the rest of creation. Sanctification would bring a simultaneous separation from the common toward the uncommon glory of God.

BELIEVERS' GOD-LIKE NATURE

The following list of human attributes is paired with the list of divine attributes making up God's holy and glorious nature by which creation, especially humanity, was created (chapter 2). To rule in God's shepherding manner requires that one have his attributes. However, the measure of each attribute that the Spirit gives to individual believers will differ now but perhaps be enhanced equally in New Earth; the uneven distribution of the spiritual gifts may be an example of this. The following survey itemizes humanity's attributes and their need for renewal. Many of these attributes can be seen in the spirits and in the natural world as well as in the human race, and at some point it would be enlightening to apply some of them to those realms as well. Another time, perhaps.

Diversity Within Unity

We presume that Genesis refers to an agreement among the Persons within the one God: "Let us make man in our image, after our likeness" (Gen 1:26). The "us" is a unified entity with further differentiations revealed progressively through the Testaments.[5] Consequently, God's unity in his purpose and attributes yet diversity in the Persons' functions are

---

5. The "us" indicates a plurality of some number of Persons within the Godhead.

distributed to his creation. What is true of the Trinity is ingrained in creation in this regard. The eventual unity in purpose by the human race to implement the eternal design will be accomplished effectively by diversity in personhood: personality, ethnicity, gender, location, time, giftings, and function. Creation is further differentiated among the kingdoms of humanity, spirits, and nature, and each will continue to contribute productively to the new creation. An endless and perfect cloning of a single object of creation to a point of utter monism might be conceivable, but it was not the option God took, since unity and functional diversity within the Trinity and creation maintains order, collaboration, and productivity.

Cooperative

The Trinity's internal cooperation is the pattern for creation's nature to be interactive and constructive by coordinating its diverse roles. Again, "helping" or partnering is not a degrading relationship. It is a privilege and pleasure to fulfill this natural inclination of the redeemed and unredeemed alike. Like God's attribute, it proceeds from other attributes such as being loving, active, purposeful, and communicative.

Spiritual

The spiritual attribute of God was given to the spiritual kingdoms where the holy angels are in the lighted heavenly kingdom while fallen angels inhabit the darkened satanic kingdom. The human spirit is frequently an attribute with which God is deeply concerned, including its continuation beyond the body's deadline. Without entering the fray of dichotomy vs. trichotomy, this spiritual attribute contains many of the following human attributes, which need repair by the Holy Spirit's renovating power.

Eternal

God's nature is eternal, as is anything he determines to be eternal. The earth's surface may be scorched, but then it will be renovated to eternal beauty, harmony, and productivity. Eternal life is a capacity activated by God for the sanctified whose patient piety anticipates glory, honor, and immortality (Rom 2:7).

Changeless

That God is changeless in his nature is good news since he permanently created humanity to image his nature. However, the human condition of these attributes needs change, reconstruction. It is the massive change or renewal of one's nature that is the purpose of the salvation which heals those attributes' fallen disorders. The moral implication of God's changelessness should be the same for the renewed person—honesty and other consistencies with moral standards.

Active

Creation is eternally active. From the simplest atom to the incalculable mass and energy of the cosmos, all creation is in motion. All human attributes lead to actions that either contribute to or compromise the eternal design. For instance, one acts wisely or unwisely on what one knows or feels; one is expected to act knowingly, creatively, powerfully, righteously, even emotionally.

(Omni)potent

The human attribute and potential of spiritual, psychological, and physical strength may not be infinite, but it renders little excuse for not exerting oneself intentionally and forcefully to accomplish the eternal design within one's own realm. There are hindrances to one's actions in some instances—a lack of adequate information or overwhelming circumstances. However, when believers cease their strenuous efforts to realize the eternal design and fail to bless, deliver, and discipline others, they weaken the trusting kingdom as a whole—and even one's encompassing secular society. Physical, intellectual, and spiritual strengths should be used lovingly to impact God's order on earth. It is not merely an opportunity; it is a daily responsibility as one works out one's salvation by the power of the Spirit as stewards of the primary commission.

(Omni)scient

The attributes of thinking and awareness are infinite in God, and they are far more present in human nature than one takes advantage of. God's omniscience can be tapped by considering his general and special revelation, from natural law, and humanity's moral conscience. Minds are numbed by entertainment within and outside the home and by the habit of selective ignorance that filters out the inconvenient facts that are vital to living a responsible and sanctified life. Believers should avail themselves of a breadth of information including contentious topics where something might be learned to confirm one's view, adjust it, or jettison it. Believers should think with a different focus than themselves, with a new priority to love God and others by submitting to the Holy Spirit's Testaments that instruct and empower one to reform their framework for goals, actions, and words—to think and pursue knowledge with a renewed mind of Christ.

Logical

The believer rationally accepts the orderliness, rationality, and wisdom of God by recognizing that human perceptions and reasoning are incapable of comprehending his "higher" unheard thoughts. The renewed Christly mind will likewise reason differently ("foolishly," 1 Cor 1:21–27), thus even more logically than the mind of the unbeliever. God's attributes of knowledge, purposefulness, and righteousness will inform the believer to think, plan, and behave differently, even if the carnal mind finds one's decisions to be "irrational." What the world considers strength will often be what believers see as weaknesses and vice versa. This might bring various responses from the world: confusion, frustration, or irritation, or even hatred. This should be expected but endured without compromise, yet with understanding and love. For the believer, humility will lead to a more logical approach for thoughtful action when one knows and consequently submits to God and his instruction. Furthermore, wisdom gives the believer the ingenuity to manipulate what appears to be time and space restrictions and circumvent what only looks to be inevitable.

Purposeful

God's omniscience allows him to determine his own actions in a perfectly wise and moral manner. It also allows him to design and respond to the thoughts and actions of his entire creation. There is no randomness involved in his response, leaving all his purposes perfectly executed.

The believer's transformed mind will be more capable of intentional, focused, and organized thought because of less confusion. A new personal purposefulness that is now focused on the priorities and purposes of God can be coordinated with one's planned routines of daily life. Better stewards of space and time will bring greater effectiveness to one's own life and lead to better shepherding of those for whom one is responsible. Deliverance from sin is for what purpose? Eternal life? Eternal life is for what purpose? Eternal fellowship with God? What is this purpose for eternal fellowship? Better shepherding of creation.

Emotive

Humanity's emotional attribute lays bare a person's deep motivations, whether moral or immoral. Emotion can be a most devastating experience when it expresses an unrenewed heart where only selfish motivations fester and excrete frustration, anxiety, depression, anger, and hatred. The attribute of emotion and its repercussions can appear on the surface to be the same, whether from renewed or an unrenewed spirit. Anger and hatred, for example, might come as venomous retaliation or as righteous responses to circumstances that deserve no less severity. Love for God and others motivates us to do what is right, to shepherd with a heart to bless, deliver, and discipline. Joy is a reward for those who see fruit from their shepherding. On the other hand, remorse can deliver the believer when it motivates repentance for failures.

Ethical

God communicates the details of his own innate righteousness by transcribing them into ethical instructions for humanity. The renovated soul has the capacity to receive and lovingly obey this instruction in God's laws, aphorisms, moral stories, rebukes, and encouragements within the Testaments, which results in his believers fulfilling the eternal design by blessing, delivering, and disciplining his creation in all love and fairness. Moreover, it is within this parenthetical age that righteousness becomes even more realized when responding to the surrounding satanic and worldly rebellion. For example, the fruits of the Spirit of justice, mercy, forgiveness, and deliverances of others are examples of how God and his believers respond ethically to others' moral deficiencies.

Creative

Artistry is only a particular application of the creative mind, but creativity itself is a broader attribute mirroring God's nature; every human has it and uses it daily. It is the responsibility of the sanctified creative spirit to create its own mini-cosmos illumined by one's transformed nature that expresses the glory and holiness of one's renewed, aware, purposeful, emotive, ethical, and complex mind. We are designed to creatively manage all components of our surroundings that are in our personal jurisdiction by spiritual wisdom and discernment. These surroundings, however, are heavily influenced by the spiritual, natural, and terrestrial kingdoms and their intimidating demands. How well one survives or thrives in life requires inventing and crafting responses to small or ominous and complex circumstances. Add to this that while the believer shepherds others, it will inevitably require resourceful improvisations to satisfy their needs.

Communicative

Humanity's nature to communicate is too obvious to dwell on. This divine attribute was designed in humanity to understand, note, remember, enjoy, and obey God's truth as well as to discuss, encourage, educate, plan, love, and otherwise bless one another. The prevalent ethical instructions about human discourse throughout the Testaments are needed since communication by any medium is one of the most dangerous attributes that God transmitted to humanity (Jas 3:5–8); this is shown by Satan and the Couple's conversation.

Complex

The complexity of human nature, though nothing compared to that of God, is beyond the comprehension of the individual and field of psychology. Though an individual's attributes include an ethical/moral awareness in itself, most of one's other attributes have a moral obligation to optimize their impact on one's shepherding of creation. The believer's responsibility is to coordinate one's renewed attributes for the sake of one's own sanctification, as well as for the edification of the trusting community near and far, for the benefit of the world's peoples and for the natural kingdom. One's integration of this complex of attributes while applying the eternal design is why this extensive list of human attributes is important for fulfilling creation's primary commission.

Volitional

God's will is free but not autonomous of his total nature. Since God is infinite, complete, and changeless in all of his attributes, including his will, he is free to do anything his integrated nature allows. On the other hand, finite humanity is not autonomous of God or the natural kingdom, including space and time; it is constrained by forces outside its nature. So, humanity and its individuals are not autonomous, and their will is dependent upon God's will, as all creation is. Nonetheless, persons do have a freedom that is less than autonomous, a freedom defined by what God, human nature (renewed or not), and the natural kingdom allow. The Spirit sanctifies the will, separating it from the "old man" and frees it to decide on conduct that is consistent with the rest of one's renewed attributes.

Sovereign

Like God, humanity's sovereign nature is a compilation of many of its attributes. For example, the complex nature of God and humanity brings together knowledge, morality, emotions, creativity, and communicability in order to exercise their dominion. Sovereignty under God yet over creation is humanity's primary commission. This sovereign nature is restored to believers even more strongly by the Spirit to apply their God-like characteristics in all of their glory to the routines of their life.

Glorious

God's glory is experienced in each attribute itself, and meditating on each individually is a devotional in itself. His glory is overwhelming, humbling, especially when reflected upon in relation to his attributes. This is the first step of the believer's praise and worship—to exalt God's nature. This step marks the renewal at one's regeneration since to accept God's love, his righteous mercy, his sovereign discretion, and the Son's active deliverance contributes to the faith that leads to justification. The re-imaging of the believer by the Spirit into the likeness of God and his attributes can do no other than glorify the believer as well. However, this internal glorification of one's renewed nature is a synergized effort of the Holy Spirit and believer, and the believer is required to externalize this internal renewal of one's God-like image. The believer's transformation is complete when the believer both understands and activates the amoral attributes listed in this section.

Holy

The believer's glory, like God's, is the summation and intensity of all of his renewed attributes that progressively *separate* one as unique from the rest of creation; it makes one "holy." God's aggregated attributes set the renewed person apart from unbelievers as "uncommon"—"unique as God is unique." Apart from the separating perfection declared in justification, the believer's glory and uniqueness, unlike God's, is acquired perfectly only in New Earth, though it is the Spirit's work along the way.

ETERNALLY SANCTIFIED AND PRODUCTIVE

God's purposefulness includes the dynamic development of his creation, and *growth* is a substantive teleological process in God's administration of creation. It is built into nature, from the expansion of the universe to the multiplication of Abraham's seed to the germination of the mustard seed. General revelation shows the beauty of growth. Growth during the parenthetical age is the goal for the trusting kingdom in its numbers, in its geographical expansion, and in its organic growth into the fullness of the body of Christ. The individual is to grow in stature and wisdom as Jesus did. Until humanity has been perfected with the rest of creation so that God is "all in all," everyone will have a hollowness internally since they do not have the fullest image of God within. But for now, the message of sanctification proclaims they will.

Furthermore, growth is an eternal intention of God for his creation as his trusting kingdom impacts the rest of creation throughout this and the coming ages. The believer's maturity will be an ever-fertile foundation for an ever greater depth and breadth in wise activity. So the impact of human maturity will never be complete; rather, it will continue to produce even in its maturity. No longer will nature await the enjoyment and benefits of a renewed, curseless existence. In full cooperation, nature and humanity will pursue the eternal design and shepherd by only blessing creation since their deliverance and disciplinary roles are no longer needed.

Sanctification as a saving process is not eternal since in New Earth all will have been completely saved, forever separated from sin. However, as sanctified persons, creation will continue to emulate God's shepherding nature. The *purposeful* "end" of realizing God's eternal design will have no temporal "end" since there is no end to human history or to the glory of humanity's intrinsic image of God. One will not develop ontologically since one will have attained the pre-Fall state of God's likeness. However, there will be an infinite number of instances of sanctified creative, productive, and successful activity. One can continue speaking of being sanctified eternally, but not eternally *becoming* more sanctified since there is no longer anything to be set apart from, morally speaking. Nevertheless, creation will enjoy the benefits of God's image and succeed in the application of them throughout eternity. Neither does one become infinite in nature, only in one's number of infinite and successful activities. Though believers will live infinitely long and will have the everlasting image and attributes of God within them, humanity's otherwise finite attributes negate any evolution toward divinity. Nonetheless, one will grow in knowledge without noetic impedance, which will result in wisdom, creativity, resourcefulness, and productivity as humanity experiences now, but then without the restrictions of the Curse. Greater knowledge obtained by experiences of any sort would contribute to further creative and productive actions, which would apply a wider, deeper impact on the other components of nature and humanity in New Earth. Imagine where humanity would be now if there had not been this distraction of the parenthetical age!

5

Parenthetical Theology

WE HAVE STARTED BY reviewing the natures of creation and its God and how creation emulates him by his eternal design. This accentuated a deeper and broader structural design that drives and unifies eternal history, developing a productive, eternal trajectory that is constructive, edifying, and successful. Creation has been granted eternity from its inception, though its designed progress has been interrupted by a tragic "parenthetical age." One might focus on this parenthetical age in one's biblical theology, but God has revealed a much more comprehensive and applicable design for history in his special and general revelation. By focusing on the parenthetical, one neglects what is foundational for understanding God's purpose for all creation regardless of which age—its shepherding with him.

What happened to the beauty of the eternal design? Where is the glory of God's nature in the world? When is this cosmic shepherding materializing? A look at the world around might force these questions because the condition of the world is dramatically fallen from its created perfection. In a real sense this is good news since the world has, at least, not vanished; it is not totally depraved, and its history will always be directed by God's purposes. The obscurity of God's eternal design, the limited revelation of God's nature, and the apparent absence of godly shepherding is like an annoying parenthesis in a sentence which is inordinately long. It sidetracks the reader, who then needs to return to the start of the sentence to review what the thought was before the parenthetical distraction and then read the parenthesis in context and move on with the rest of the sentence. The sentence itself has a teleology in time and purpose; it has a syntactical design which gives it coherence; it has a logical order that makes it intelligible; it has punctuation marks that signal how the reader should read the words, e.g., their cadence, their certainty, their significance. But a parenthesis can ruin the experience of continuity in thought. This would be a metaphor for what I would call the current "parenthetical age." As a parenthesis, this age is not the main thought of the historical "sentence." And its length alone (if one were to press the analogy too far, the parenthetical entry turns out to be a run-on sentence, which was an abomination in most English classrooms in the twentieth century and resulted in a poor grade and disappointment to a student and the student's parents, yet . . .) can challenge one's sight of the beginning of the historical sentence. Concentrating on the parenthesis impedes understanding of the historical sentence—that which matters most.

"Parenthetical" does not mean something is unimportant, just less important than what comes before and after it. What makes the parenthetical age important is that though less important, it is the current mire and torturously off-point milieu of creation. It is a tragic digression but only a relatively momentary interruption to the eternal progress intended from the start. The eternal design has been deterred from its endless linear success by this excruciating age that will end only when God's wisdom allows. The detour has not been simply a frustrating distraction—it has been only somewhat less than hell on earth under the prince from hell's administration. This parenthetical age is "this present evil age" (Gal 1:4), "this darkness" (Eph 6:12). This parenthesis in history has temporarily yet substantially blocked creation from pursuing the best of God's eternal intentions for it. The Fall has severely smothered creation, including humanity, from meeting its potential that God had initially built into it. This parenthetical "paralysis," this stunted growth, is Eden's curse.

We live within a tragic parenthesis between two periods when perfection reigns: the age before the Fall and the age of New Earth. The Testaments foresee deliverance as creation-wide, involving nature, nations, cultures, as well as individual believers, for whom comprehensive restorative shepherding must be a priority now. In other words, the pre-Fall and post-restoration New Earth conditions are to be realized as much as possible *during* this restoration period, and believers' attitudes and acts should support the eternal design and its priorities now.

One's gratitude for reconciliation in this age should be accompanied by anticipation of productive endeavors with God during history's everlasting continuum. In this wider paradigm, the pivotal moment in the biblical timeline of history is not the Messiah's Passion, which is meaningful as a means to the conclusion of the parenthetical age. Instead, the pivotal moment is when the Messiah ends this parenthesis by returning the perfectly repaired universal realm of God back to the Trinity so it will be "all in all." God's eternal realm will then continue its journey that began but was so brutally interrupted in Eden. The Testaments reveal that the Passion and parousia are teleological steps in the eternal design; they are not the central or ultimate destination. Neither the Old Testament and its covenants nor even the new covenant point ultimately to the Passion or Christ's parousia. Rather they point toward the Final Testament, the endless destination of creation and its history as both irreversibly continue their adventure of shepherding creation with God.

EXPANDED MEANING OF SHEPHERDING

The eternal design's challenge is not just about sin but about humanity's holistic management of creation. Humanity's capability to effectively manage the skies and earth was compromised by the Couple's sin and God's curse on the ontology of humanness, which would eventually be called the "old man." The completely positive primary commission, which was to bless creation by shepherding it constructively in faithfulness to God, now became a natural, intentional, and pervasive rebellion. Plus, the originally perfect yet finite image of God was crippled beyond the attribute of righteousness. The glory of humanity in all its godly attributes apart from righteousness was glorious no longer. Furthermore, our debilitated race did not have the same environment in which to shepherd, since inglorious humanity, in its weakness, was pitted against the uncooperative, cursed, yet mighty forces of nature. Added to that, humanity has been exhausted by its perpetual clashes with the satanic kingdom and its infestation of the terrestrial kingdom and its infection of its inhabitants.

Two new relationships between the Lord and creation and among creation's realms were introduced by the Couple's mutiny as well as by humanity's additional and perpetual ill-management of creation. The relationship now includes God and creation's shepherding roles of *delivering* creation from adversity and sin and *disciplining* creation. One looks forward to the new creation, where deliverance and discipline will no longer be necessary since evil will have been extinguished. But this age, spanning the Fall to the final judgment, is a brutal but parenthetical age between the two historic eras of perfection.

Creation and humanity are still expected to share with God in the shepherding of creation regardless of their continual culpability. Humanity now shepherds universally in highly destructive ways by neglecting and abusing creation rather than by delivering and disciplining it constructively. Creation needs thorough deliverance, something cultures and ideologies readily admit but strive inadequately to achieve. Since God performs these additional shepherding roles of deliverance and discipline, his eternal design expects his fellow shepherds and image-bearers to perform them as well.

ESCHATOLOGY

Eschatology, the study of the "last things," or "end times," can take on a life of its own as the defining metric of history. The word stresses the importance of the final days leading to the culmination of the conflict between the Messiah and all his enemies. But eschatology can be an inexact measurement of human history; it is only a relative metric. So, when discussing the "last things," one cannot lose sight of the eternal context of God's design for reality. The book of Revelation may describe the last days of the parenthetical age, but it emphatically begins the new and Final Testament. The final judgment and its ominous implications render the last days as a warning for the unjustified and a hope for the sanctified. It does not imply that all reality will cease to exist but that the end of the parenthetical age will become the beginning of the new age; New Earth will be preceded by the last parenthetical days. G. B. Caird remarks on this obvious confusion:

> One characteristic form of Jewish eschatology is the belief in two ages: the present evil age will give place to the coming age of justice and peace, so that the end of the one is the beginning of the other; and in many, if not all, forms of this belief the coming age was conceived as a new and ideal epoch of world history. The danger, then, is that in using the one word eschatology to cover both types of belief we should overlook the fact that we may be using words such as "last," "final" and "end" in different senses.[1]

1. Caird, *Language and Imagery*, 244. There is, of course, acknowledgment of

Eschatology can focus too narrowly on the timing of recovery rather than the purpose for recovery. God's universal kingdom's progression from creation through eternity, including this parenthetical age, cannot be constrained to a finite, temporal calibration concentrating on "the end." Dwelling on the "study of last things" can miss the nature of creation's history. There is no end to the world. "Glory be to the Father, and to the Son, and to the Holy Ghost. As it was in the beginning, is now, and ever shall be, world without end. Amen." "The earth remains forever" (Ps 104:5; Eccl 1:4).[2] Again, the end of the parenthetical age, as dramatic and apocalyptic in nature as it will be, can be a distraction from God's eternal design, which is the very purpose for the means of salvation from this parenthetical age.

This language of finality is pervasive. Christopher J. H. Wright believes the mission of God "will ultimately be accomplished."[3] Thankfully, there is no eternal resolution to the mission of God's universal kingdom and its eternal design. It will never finally "arrive," that is, when creation will have finally accomplished only a finite, in fact infinitesimally small, fraction of what God inaugurated at creation. Instead, there will always be an infinite number of roads to unimaginable destinations for the believer. Beasley-Murray announces the usual premature and final static condition of history: "Thus, the goal of history is reached in the revelation and universal acknowledgement of Yahweh's sovereignty, the triumph of righteousness, and the establishment of peace and salvation in the world."[4] However, God's plan for his creation has never been for it to finally arrive at an intermediate point. To speak of the end of the world's history is not simply a misnomer since its theological implications are

---

existence after "the end." Most prefer not to go any further though. R. E. Clements: "We may, therefore, adopt a broad definition of eschatology which renders it suitable to describe the biblical ideas of God's purpose in history. Eschatology is the study of ideas and beliefs concerning the end of the present world order, and the introduction of the new order." Clements, *Prophecy and Covenant*, 105. And more recently, David G. Peterson: "Eschatology is concerned with the end of human history on this earth and the eternal future of God's people." Peterson, *Hebrews*, 36.

2. Matthew 24:35 // Mark 13:31 // Luke 21:33 are speaking of the passing of the parenthetical natural kingdom: the destruction of this world as we know it before the perfect renovation of it in New Earth.

3. Wright, *Mission of God*, 64.

4. Beasley-Murray, *Jesus and the Kingdom of God*, 20. G. K. Beale sees the eschatological culmination as "the end of history." Later, he refers to "the very end of this age." The latter phrase is valid, but the former is typical eschatological language. Beale, *Biblical Theology*, 887–88.

misleading. It narrows the scope of eternal history to the parenthetical age wherein the Passion is epitomized as the center of that truncated history, whereas eternal history's climax is when Christ returns the world which he perfected to the "all-in-all" Godhead (1 Cor 15:28).

Theology would be better served as a less time-driven eschatology and more deeply as a purpose-laden teleology. Theologies that overemphasize eschatology can obscure the relatively seamless transition from the parenthetical age to New Earth. An analogy would be that just as a believer's personal death seamlessly morphs into a new eternal life with Christ, the "last things" seamlessly morph into a new eternal creation of productive living with God. Yes, during the last days of the parenthetical age the earth's surface may perish, but the unmarred depths, heights, and breadth of the lands, seas, and skies will again flourish and bless the rest of creation, including believers and their continued shepherding efforts by their primary commission. Understanding history's nature will moderate any overstated theological walls one can construct between the creation, the parenthetical age, and the New Earth since the same teleological design traverses all three.

A more detailed discussion of eschatology is deferred to chapter 12.

HISTORY'S NATURE OR HISTORY'S NARRATIVE?

Distinction Between Creation's Nature and Biblical Narrative

The eternal design originates in the nature of God and is built into the nature of his creation. *Since God created the universe after his own nature, that nature became its eternal design.* It is composed by the structure and teleological mechanisms of *creation* that are revealed in general and special revelation. It is fundamentally an all-consuming paradigm that explains God's relationship with his creation. That is, the eternal design is not deduced from a literary narrative; rather, it is sourced in creation's nature as God's design which is imbedded into creation pervasively, so this design is not a narrative in the sense of a story. It is not a literary narrative or center, but a historical design that encompasses any other biblical theology paradigm. There is a much more ambiguous meaning of narrative, however, which would be better deemed a biblical theological framework, maybe a metanarrative. By this less literary definition, the eternal design might be called a metanarrative yet one that encompasses

PARENTHETICAL THEOLOGY

all others. Though semantic arguments might ensue, John Goldingay's distinction of narrative and metanarrative is accepted here as adequate.

> In the use of the word *metanarrative*, the emphasis has thus come to lie on the *meta* rather than *narrative*; the word suggests a master idea or set of ideas, some form of transcendent and universal truth, but not necessarily an overarching story.[5]

The eternal design is derived from the *ontology* of God, his creation, and creation's history, not from a literary structure of special revelation. In either the story or biblical framework definition, one might acknowledge the eternal design, yet it cannot be bypassed or encompassed by them. The eternal design is the only basis on which any narrative or metanarrative can be adequately built. To repeat, any narrative is not the source of the eternal design; it could only be a consequence of it. This distinction of the eternal design is rooted in both creation and God's natures. If one had to use conventional "centric" nomenclature, the eternal design's centricity comes not as a deduction from any narrative or metanarrative in Scripture but is a deduction from the natures of God, his creation, and its history, all of which the Testaments speak of yet can only be understood by both special and general/natural revelation.

More significantly, if any (meta)narrative claimed for itself the same breadth and depth as the eternal design, it would need to substantively include the relevance of the comprehensive, integrative, and teleological nature of *all* historical events. A thorough application and chronicling of each of these attributes of creation and its history for every historical event and its interpretation is not possible or needed. But any proposed narrative structure should do the same as the eternal design is equipped to do in general terms—provide an *eternal* teleology that reflects the natures of God, creation, and history as well as the ultimate practicality of sanctified shepherding. If any (meta)narrative did match the eternal design in all its derivations from God and creation and its history's nature, its definition would be broadened beyond any of its typical meanings. Otherwise, any (meta)narrative approach obscures the pervasiveness and profundity of creation's design for all of everlasting history.[6]

---

5. Goldingay, *Do We Need the New Testament*, 70.

6. Goldingay reflects on his parenthetical focus on a biblical narrative and considers it narrowly as a *total* worldview that presumes an *end* of the narrative. Yet, any biblical narrative can have no end: "In the Bible and Christian thinking, vital importance is attached to the grand narrative that is indeed narrative in form, a total worldview expressed in a story that embraces Beginning and End and the narrative line in between."

For example, one might agree with Christopher J. H. Wright about the Old Testament's story being only a part of a much larger story. Yet he postpones the ultimate *breadth* of the larger story to a future time:

> The Old Testament tells its story as *the* story or, rather, as a part of that ultimate and universal story that will ultimately embrace the whole of creation, time, and humanity within its scope.[7]

But one need not wait for that comprehensive, universal story. That ultimacy is current since the comprehensive, integrative, and eternal teleological nature of creation and its history has always contained "the whole of creation, time, and humanity within its scope." There is no ultimate scope to wait for. That story has been told since creation and contains all creation's stories as histories of every sort, including salvation history. And that universal story is told in terms of God's universal kingdom which has always and will always shepherd his creation dynamically.

Inadequate (meta)narratives of the purpose of God's ultimate direction of history are not deduced from the more fundamental *natures* of creation, history, and God. Instead, theological narratives begin with a biblical narrative. Rolf Knierim is a good example of this.

> Human actions and decisions are not deemed good and justified on the ground that they are historical, but human historical involvement is judged in view of how human actions and decisions serve the meaning and purpose of history. . . . [History's] legitimacy and validity are themselves subject to a criterion which is independent of history, whether in human history in general or in Israel's history specifically. The criterion for either the truth or perversion of history, however, is the salvific intentionality to which history is to be subservient, which determines the purpose and meaning of history, and which is at the same the judge of history.[8]

For Knierim and others, all history is "subservient" to salvation history; history's purpose and meaning is determined by salvation history; salvation history judges all history. I suggest that this inversion where supremacy belongs to salvation history over the nature of history misses the point of God's eternally teleological creation, which has mutual and sanctified shepherding of all creation as its basic and endless objective.

Goldingay, *Do We Need the New Testament*, 71.

7. Wright, *Mission of God*, 55.
8. Knierim, *Old Testament Theology*, 205–6.

PARENTHETICAL THEOLOGY

Limiting one's focus to a culminated age or salvific project cannot suffice as a historical (meta)narrative. Salvation history is no less but no more than the means to getting back to square one of God's eternal design for all creation. We are not expected to be distracted from the pursuit of all that it means to be responsible shepherds in God's universal kingdom until we have first completed the evangelism assignment.

Three more representations exemplify a belief that the center of biblical theology has been found. Christopher J. H. Wright considers his paradigm the "mission of God" as the "overarching, governing perspective" for reading the Testaments:

> The whole Bible delivers to us "the whole council of God"—the plan, purpose and mission of God for the whole creation, that it will be reconciled to God through Christ by the cross.[9]

However, this reconciliation narrative cannot contain the "whole purpose/plan/counsel of God" (Acts 20:27). Has God lost sight that his assignment to humanity to shepherd the earth continues into the endless future? The length, breadth, and depth of history is more thoroughly understood when a redemptive narrative is contextualized within God's much wider and deeper paradigm.

Thomas Schreiner claims succinctly, "The cross and resurrection of Christ are the turning point of history."[10] This may be true of parenthetical history but proves inadequate to address fully the teleology and scope of God's eternal design—it is too limited in its purview.[11] This approach makes reaching back up to zero as the ultimate success both in time and purpose, teleologically speaking. God's corrective measures result in returning creation to pre-Fall perfection and may seem adequate to some, but they do not answer the question when one arrives in New Earth: "Where do we go now as perfect beings in a perfect new age?" Being perfect but without a purpose for perfection is not perfect.

Douglas Moo is another representation of where the focus on the parenthetical age and eschatology throw history off-center:

---

9. Wright, *Mission of God*, 532.
10. Schreiner, *New Testament Theology*, 98.
11. In a survey and supplement to the search for the themes of the Bible, John Walton questions the narrow perspective of redemptive history and personal salvation which center the Incarnation on Jesus' death. To capture a larger picture than salvation, he does not suggest a "center" but rather "an overarching theme, arguably the most dominant and pervasive of themes," i.e., God's presence among his people. Walton, *Old Testament Theology*, 8–9, 24–28.

> The most basic claim Paul makes about Christ, explicit in many texts, implicit in all, is that his coming marks the climax of God's purposes in history. The coming of Christ is "the center of time" (to use Cullmann's language), the climax of all that God is doing in and for creation. It is "the appearing of our Savior, Christ Jesus," that unleashes the eschatological saving events (2 Tim 1:10).[12]

This parenthetical and eschatological center again neglects to see history as eternal by making salvation central as the Savior's accomplishment, though it is only instrumental to an everlasting purpose for God and his Messiah's creation and providence.

But Charles Scobie cautions against a simplistic narrowing of God's gospel about his kingdom to a salvation paradigm, where God's relationship to the broadest creation is constricted to humanity with a particular emphasis on Israel. His outlook is more comprehensive.

> But care must be taken that God's rule/reign/sovereignty/activity not be defined too narrowly. The themes of salvation or redemption[13] ... or of salvation history ... have tended to dominate. Recognition must be given to the dialectic between creation and redemption. God is Creator and Sustainer as well as Redeemer, is active in nature as well as in history, and has a relation to all humankind as well as to Israel.[14]

A different approach than (meta)narratives, though it most often coincides with them by some definition, is a focus on a unifying *theme* in the Testaments. An example of *the* theme that many feel unifies Scripture is God's kingdom. This seems reasonable since it was literally Jesus' theme recorded in at least the synoptic Gospels and Acts 1, and it continues from the Old Testament through the apostles' writings. This theme is mentioned to emphasize that as often as this study will accentuate God's universal kingdom, it is not presented as *the* unifying biblical theme. The point will be made often that God's complex kingdom structure within creation is *one* means of God advancing his priority, the pursuit of his eternal design.

---

12. Moo provides no explicit texts in *Theology of Paul*, 354–55.

13. For this study's purposes, "salvation history" is considered as more precise terminology for the *process* of God's deliverance of humanity, including regenerating sanctification. Terms such as "redemption" and "reconciliation" are derived from Hebrew and Greek terms denoting singular transactions, not processes.

14. Scobie, *Ways of Our God*, 94.

On the other hand, the eternal design does not conflict with whatever one's biblical theological singular point might be as long as that (meta)narrative acknowledges its subordinate place within the more foundational and broader picture and does not purport to take the center stage of biblical theology. The eternal design is not offered *in lieu* of perceived (meta)narratives, stories, or themes. One might find a home for their theology of history in a thematic or story-narrative paradigm, but that is different from looking at God's teleological direction for his creation and how its history was initially and eternally driven by a single design that transcends all ages, whether the age needed saving or not.

The pre-Fall age and the new age are not merely the historical "contexts" wherein parenthetical (meta)narratives flourish. Quite the contrary, the pre-Fall age and New Earth are the substance of the run-on "sentence." The historical parenthetical age, as any syntactical parenthesis, provides secondary, explanatory information. Some have an inside-out theology where the corrective within history has become more central than the main and eternal reason for history.

IN THE MEANTIME . . .

The parenthetical age is one of intense evil, perpetually spawned by the satanic kingdom as far as God's universal kingdom allows. Yet, God's common grace that sustains all things by the powerful word of his Son (Heb 1:3) makes creation's life *relatively* successful. Humanity still has God's image and attributes, even though it continues to exercise them in a contract with Satan rather than in an alliance with the true, benevolent, sovereign King. Sourced in God's nature, the same biblical shepherding standards are required of all cultures. However, most unbelieving societies do not know of them apart from natural revelation, common grace, and communal conscience. Yet they innately seek meaning, some form of rationality, or a unified worldview because the eternal design is imprinted in their godly image. But history shows that left to themselves, unbelieving social units will distort his various revelations and develop pagan perceptions of God and religious traditions that form their own worldview of unseen life, nature, and humanity that is inconsistent with God's direction. Furthermore, Satan exploits their naiveté, weakness, and pride to enlist them unwittingly in his global resistance and attempted destruction of all that God's nature has blessed. "The god of this world has blinded the minds of unbelievers to keep them from seeing the light of the good news of the glory of Christ, who is the image of God" (2 Cor 4:4).

Nonetheless, God is patient and generous and at his discretion trumps Satan's distortions and keeps significant global equilibrium within this callous and cruel world. Indeed, there is horrendous abuse in this age for which glib, aloof, and sanctimonious platitudes sound hollow within God's silent but perfectly wise will. But non-believing humanity is mercifully sustained by God's daily relationship with every individual and by his governance of all societies and nations. Obedience to God's ethical standards, however obtained, will bring a level of practical success for self and community. Healthy societies determine balances of power to manage human activity. Republics, democracies, and tribal councils assure selected leaders have the authority to organize and nurture the community. In the meantime, believers especially are not expected to be distracted by their own admittedly complicated personal history from engaging their surroundings and the majority of humanity and its cultures which operate with their dismal alterations of God's revelations. The trusting kingdom should inform itself biblically about all matters including those generally considered marginal to salvation history. For believers, there is the benefit of learning about creation's offerings of abundance, beauty, and resources with which to better shepherd creation in its damaged condition and to better achieve the primary commission to govern creation with enhanced, godly attributes such as knowledge and wisdom, creativity, productivity, effectiveness, love, and joy.

God's knowledge and wisdom and the providential power of the Son's word are beyond estimation. But Christian theology can marginalize the more theologically integrated construct since its approach is not fully historical when it emphasizes a narrower history at the expense of God's eternal, thus infinite, plans for his creation. If any historiography should show the integration of all history, Christian biblical theology should model the most comprehensive integration of it. God's multiple realms and their productive and collaborative routine intersections would yield far more by such modeling. One published volume, even all published volumes, could never exhaust this contention in detail. With the greatest reluctance, in the most loose sense, and if convention must prevail, the eternal design might be reduced to the designation as the grandest (meta)narrative that alone can contextualize all that creation and its history entail.

6

God's Kingdom Realms

GOD HAS BUILT HIS attribute of sovereignty and all its collaborating attributes into his creation to operate his eternal design. An overall kingdom structure has been and always will be intrinsic to all creation under God's universal kingdom, which oversees creation and its history through its sub-realms where within each are vertically integrated layers of descending authority. The universal realm includes the following sub-realms: heavenly, satanic, messianic, natural, terrestrial, trusting, and New Earth.

UNIVERSAL KINGDOM

God's universal kingdom has been referred to frequently already. It refers to the reign and realm of God over all creation that is cited explicitly and widely in both Testaments. His created realm includes all the original heavenly host, all things seen and unseen, known and unknown, the indefinable smallest elements of energy and matter and the incomprehensible expanse of the cosmos, and the indescribable yet pervasive contexts of time and space. He did not and will not subsequently become the ruler of his creation at any point in history, nor has he ever become anyone's king. He has always been, and always will be, king of all reality despite tumultuous rebellions against him during this parenthetical age. God's sovereignty is the same as his reign, and his realm is everything that he has created and thus owns. Awareness and obedience to God as king may be a global development, but his reign is impossible to develop or enhance; his reign is his universal sovereignty over his created realm.[1]

> Lord, yours is the kingdom and you are exalted as head above all. (1 Chr 29:11)

> Heaven is my throne, and the earth is my footstool . . . because my hand made heaven and earth—that is how they came to exist. (Isa 66:1–2)

> You created all things; they exist because of your will. (Rev 4:11)[2]

The universal kingdom of God has a very material realm to own, to possess. As *the* creating King, he is creation's *sole* owner.

> Everything under the entire heaven is mine. (Job 41:11)

> The skies are yours; the earth also is yours; the world and everything in it. (Ps 89:11)

> From him, and through him, and to him are all things. (Rom 11:36)[3]

God's universal kingdom includes every nation, all of humanity—the terrestrial realm.

> The kingdom is the Lord's and he rules over the nations. (Ps 22:28)

> The decision is commanded by the holy ones so the living will know that the Most High is ruler over the kingdom of humanity. (Dan 4:17)

---

1. Whether both Testaments' languages allow a primary meaning of "kingdom" to be God's reign rather than his universal realm is deferred to chapter 12, where the messianic kingdom is addressed. I will argue there that the Hebrew and Greek do not lead lexically in that direction and neither does logic.

2. Exod 20:11; Job 38:4–12, 19–38; Pss 8:3–4; 19:1; 33:6; 90:2; 93:1; 104:5, 19–20; 115:15; 121:2; 124:8; 134:3; 136:5–9; 145:10–11; 147:4; Prov 3:19–20; 8:22–29; Eccl 11:5; Isa 37:16; 40:26; 45:18; 48:13; Jer 33:2; 51:15–16; Amos 4:13; 5:8; 9:6; Zech 12:1; Acts 4:24; 14:14–15; Rom 4:17; 11:36; 1 Cor 8:6; Eph 3:9; 1 Tim 6:13; Heb 2:10; 3:4; 8:2; 9:11, 24; 11:3; Jas 1:17–18; 1 Pet 4:19; 2 Pet 3:5; Rev 4:11; 10:5–6; 14:7.

3. Exod 9:29; Deut 10:14; Pss 24:1; 50:10–12; 95:3–5; 1 Cor 8:6; 10:26. "If YHWH's saving deeds in Israel's history . . . along with his control of the history of humanity and his banishment of all opposition in the future could all be subsumed under this one image or idea, it has good credentials for being a comprehensive designation of God's relationship with his creatures." Patrick, "Kingdom of God," 73.

> To every nation and tribe and language and people [the angel] said in a loud voice, "Fear God and give him glory, for the hour of his judgment has come; worship him who made heaven, earth, sea, and the springs of water." (Rev 14:7)[4]

Consequently, the Old Testament ascribes the functioning, productive, eternal, and universal creation realm to God; this realm preceded, and will follow, after the parenthetical age. This realm is a never-ending, comprehensive kingdom in no need for a new or parallel eschatological kingdom.

> The Lord Most High is to be revered as a great King over the whole earth...
>
> God is king of the whole earth. (Ps 47:2, 7)
>
> His kingdom rules over everything. (Ps 103:19)

This universal kingdom of God, which includes Israel's more specific national component, was continued from the Old Testament through the Apocrypha and Pseudepigrapha. A few examples:[5]

> Hear therefore, ye kings and understand; learn ye judges of the ends of the earth: Give ear, ye that have dominion over much people, and make your boast in multitudes of nations. Because your dominion was given you from the Lord, and your sovereignty from the most high; who shall search out your works, and shall make inquisitions of your counsels. (Wis 6:1–3)
>
> Lord of lords, God of gods, King of kings... Thou hast made all things, and power over all things hast Thou. (1 En. 9:4, 5)
>
> Blessed be Thou, O Lord, King, great and mighty in Thy greatness, Lord of the whole creation of the heaven, King of kings and God of the whole world.... For Thou hast made and Thou rulest all things, and nothing is too hard for Thee. (1 En. 84:2, 3)
>
> Let us die rather than transgress the commands of the Lord of Lords, the God of our fathers.... And then His kingdom shall appear throughout all His creation, and then Satan will be no more.... For the Most High will arise, the Eternal God alone, and he will appear to punish the Gentiles. (As. Mos. 9:6; 10:1, 7)

---

4. Exod 19:5; Pss 47:8; 97:1; 99:1; 114:2; Isa 24:22–23; 25:6–9; 27:1; Dan 2:44; 5:21; Acts 17:26; Eph 3:9.

5. Translations are from Charles, *Apocrypha and Pseudepigrapha*.

> He is King over the heavens, and judgeth kings and kingdoms. (Pss. Sol. 2:34)
>
> For if I hunger, unto Thee will I cry, O God! And Thou wilt give to me. Birds and fish Thou dost nourish, in that Thou givest rain to the steppe that green grass may spring up, to prepare fodder in the steppe for every living thing.... Kings and rulers and peoples Thou dost nourish, O God. They that fear the Lord rejoice in good (gifts), and Thy goodness is upon Israel in Thy kingdom. (Pss. Sol. 5:10–13, 21)
>
> For the might of our God is forever with mercy, and the kingdom of our God is forever over the nations in judgement. Thou, O Lord, didst choose David king over Israel.... The Lord Himself is our king for ever and ever. (Pss. Sol. 17:3, 4, 51)
>
> O Lord, your mercy is upon the works of your hands forever, your kindness to Israel with a lavish gift.... Your compassionate judgements are over the whole world, and your love is for the descendants of Abraham, and Israelite.... May God cleanse Israel for the blessed day of mercy, the appointed day for the appearance of the Messiah.... (Pss. Sol. 18:1, 3, 5)

Jesus said that God is "the great king" and "Lord of heaven and earth" (Matt 5:34–35; 11:25). Paul proclaims the same: "The God who made the world and everything in it, since He is Lord of heaven and earth" (Acts 17:24).[6] David personalizes the Lord's kingship and includes himself in God's universal realm: "Listen to the sound of my cry, my King and my God" (Ps 5:2). Yet the Lord is also the God of Syria and leprous Naaman, a pagan commander "by whom the Lord gave Syria its victory" (2 Kgs 5:1).

It is clear that there has never been a moment in history when God has not been the ultimate sovereign over creation. The flood, Babel, the patriarchal promises, wisdom literature, the prophetic pronouncements, the Messiah, and his followers confirm God's pervasive rule over the space and time realms since creation, that is, all eras and areas—during all ages and over all places.[7] "To the only God our Savior, through Jesus

---

6. Also Job 34:13; Pss 10:16; 135:6; Dan 4:3.

7. God's providence is more than remote and mechanical; it extends his personal role as Creator into the routine of history: "God created the world long ago but he is also at every time the world's Creator.... But he also does so continually, offering fresh evidence of his creative and innovative activity by preservation and development." Barth, *God with Us*, 29.

Christ our Lord, be glory, majesty, dominion, and authority before all time, now, and forever" (Jude 1:25).[8] Past, present, and future.

We will see later just how common it is to marginalize God's universal kingdom while preferring to speak of his narrower "redemptive kingdom" by way of Israel's national kingdom. However, such a dichotomy is unsustainable from the Old Testament. Two psalms serve as microcosms of the whole Old Testament's kingdom theology in that Israel's covenant kingdom is clearly within the confines of God the King's universal kingdom.

> The Lord Most High is to be revered as a great King over the whole earth. . . . Sing praises to our king. Sing praises, since God is the king of all the earth. (Ps 47:2, 6–7)

> The persistent love of the Lord is forever to those who fear him, his righteousness is to children's children, and to those keeping his covenant and remembering to do his commandments. The Lord has set his throne in the heavens, and his kingdom rules over everything. (Ps 103:17–19)

God has always actively engaged his sub-kingdoms as their supreme sovereign by his shepherding eternal design. And he shares his universal kingdom with the God/man and his messianic kingdom. Both God and Christ tolerate and contain the satanic kingdom and all its attempts to destroy everything within the universal kingdom. God uses the natural kingdom to bless, deliver, and discipline itself and humanity. He shepherds a completely undeserving terrestrial kingdom in its alliance with the satanic kingdom, blessing the nations and their residents, delivering them from Satan's total destruction, but judging their inhumanity, greed, and idolatry of many forms, then saving some from the nations for eternal shepherding along with him in New Earth. God speaks to all nations, thereby presuming his authority over them as his realm. Any prophetic word to non-Israelite entities in the Old Testament implies God's universal kingdom; otherwise he is speaking out of turn and has no authority to be taken seriously. And God shepherds the trusting kingdom in ways only believers realize from his revelation and their own experience.

---

8. Exod 15:18; Ps 10:16; Dan 4:3, 34; 1 Tim 1:17.

HEAVENLY KINGDOM REALM

The heavenly kingdom[9] has three groups of residents: the Trinity, the holy angels, and the deceased believers' souls. Hebrews lists these:

> You have come to Mount Zion, the city of the living God, the heavenly Jerusalem, to myriads of angels, to the assembly and church of the firstborn enrolled in heaven, to God, the judge of everyone, to the spirits of the righteous made perfect, and to Jesus, the mediator of a new covenant. (Heb 12:22–24)

It is a "place" where there is only obedience, and for this reason Satan and his fallen allies were cast out (Ezek 28:11–19). Jesus prays for the Father's will to be done on earth currently as it is in his heavenly kingdom (Matt 6:10), where Jesus would ascend after his Passion (Acts 1:11).

The number of holy angels is uncertain. Though Christ could have mustered twelve legions to defend him from the cross, there is no reason to so limit the total number (Matt 26:52–53). Daniel's vision is variously translated in 7:10 to reflect "thousands upon thousands" or "a thousand times a thousand."[10] The holy angels, who are mighty individually and collectively, worship the Lord, obey him, and are accountable to him for their actions.[11] As far as an angelic hierarchy, Michael is referred to as "one of the chief princes" (Dan 10:13) in addition to at least Gabriel, the only other named holy angel in the Testaments.[12]

Angelic attributes after God's image include their emotions, communicability, purposefulness, activity, and capability of ethical or unethical behavior. They are all aware theologically, so even fallen angels fear and obey Jesus. The holy angels protect and discipline. A few are messengers, encouraging Hagar, the wandering Israelites, Gideon, Samson's parents, and Paul during his shipwreck.[13] They interpreted visions of Daniel,

---

9. Regardless of the reason for Matthew's preferred designation for God's universal kingdom as the "kingdom of heaven" rather than the "kingdom of God," a significant difference lies in his choice to identify the locational source of the kingdom rather than its monarch. Jesus makes the same locational distinction when addressing Pilate: "My kingdom is not of this world . . . my kingdom is not from the world" (John 18:36); and "You would have no authority over me unless it had been given you from above" (19:11).

10. Deut 33:2; Ps 68:17; Dan 7:10; Jude 1:14–15.

11. 2 Thess 1:7; 2 Pet 2:11; Neh 9:6; Job 1:6; 2:1; 38:6–7; Pss 89:5–7; 103:20; 148:1–2; Isa 6:3.

12. Dan 8:16; 9:21; 12:1; Luke 1:19, 26.

13. Gen 16:7–13; 18:1–14; 21:17–18; Exod 23:20–23; 24:40; Judg 6:11–23; 13:2–21.

Zechariah, and the apostle John.[14] They have been involved in human history from Eden to the Incarnation and beyond.[15] It is from the heavenly kingdom where the Trinity and its host of angels enter space and time to shepherd the shepherding believers with blessings, deliverances, and discipline: "Are they not all ministering spirits sent to serve those who will inherit salvation?" (Heb 1:14). On the other hand, a rare insight into the violent spiritual warfare waged on *terra firma* is the revealing episode when Michael fought the "prince" of Persia, a satanic entity, and so was delayed in assisting Daniel (Dan 10:12-13, 20-21).

Angels share in the Lord's shepherding responsibilities and are actively involved in his eternal design. The angels *bless* humanity in their role as messengers. Gabriel blessed Zechariah, Mary, and the shepherds with encouraging news,[16] as did two angels for the women at Jesus' empty tomb.[17] Holy angels deliver and guard humanity in their patrols of the earth, ready to assist in the eternal design.[18] The angels will lead and deliver Israel from harm and their enemies,[19] including individuals: Lot, Abraham and Isaac, Jacob, Daniel and his friends, and all believers whom the holy angels deliver from adversity.[20] After Jesus rebuffed Satan's insults, the angels minister to Jesus in the wilderness.[21] Rather than twelve legions, an angel was sent to encourage Jesus in his agony in the garden. An angel cleared the opening for Christ to walk out of the tomb (Matt 28:2) and broke the chains from Peter. Angels also discipline and judge at God's discretion. An angel kills thousands of Assyrian soldiers (2 Kgs 19:35), seventy thousand Israelites,[22] and Herod Agrippa I (Acts 12:21-23). Gabriel struck Zechariah dumb for his disbelief (Luke 1:13, 19-20). Angels weigh in heavily at Armageddon and the judgment.[23] They serve as witnesses for their assigned persons, as witnesses of persecutions, of

---

14. Dan 7:16; 9:21-23; 10:5-21; Zech 1:9-11, 19; 6:7; and in John's Revelation.
15. Acts 7:35, 38, 53; Gal 3:19; Heb 2:2.
16. Luke 1:11-14, 19, 26-36; 2:9-12.
17. Matt 28:5-7 // Mark 16:5-7 // Luke 24:4-7, 23; John 20:12.
18. Dan 4:13, 17, 23; Zech 1:10-11; 6:7.
19. Exod 14:19; 23:20-23; 32:34; Num 20:14-16; Josh 5:13-15; 2 Kgs 6:15-17; Dan 12:1.
20. Gen 19:1, 15-22; 22:10-18; 24:5-7, 40; 32:1-2; 1 Kgs 19:4-8; Dan 3:28; 6:22; Pss 34:7; 35:6; 91:11.
21. Matt 4:5-6 // Luke 4:9-10; Matt 4:11 // Mark 1:13; Luke 22:43.
22. 2 Sam 24:13-15 // 1 Chr 21:11-14.
23. Matt 13:37-42, 49-50; 2 Thess 1:7-9; Heb 1:7; Rev 14:14-20; 16:1-21.

the justice of local church elders, and all ethical conduct from believers to fallen angels.[24]

Hannah's song articulates a clear conviction of a resurrection of deceased souls, as do some twenty other passages in the Old Testament:[25] "The Lord kills and makes alive again. He brings one down to Sheol but brings one up again" (1 Sam 2:6; 28:11–15). The heavenly kingdom is a place where another believer entered . . . and returned (2 Cor 12:4). Jesus told the crucified thief that he would be his Savior in the heavenly kingdom's paradise (Luke 23:43), and Paul was confident that should he die, he would be with the Lord: "The Lord will rescue me from every evil deed, bringing me safely to his heavenly kingdom" (2 Tim 4:18; also 2 Cor 5:8; Phil 1:23–24).

MESSIANIC KINGDOM REALM

The messianic kingdom will be taken up in detail in chapters 7 and 8.

SATANIC KINGDOM REALM

The satanic sub-realm has its own hierarchy, community, and polity, so it is not included, for our purposes at least, in the heavenly realm.[26] But unfortunately, Satan's kingdom has also always had the most human residents because he is "the ruler of this world" (John 12:31; 14:30; 16:11; Luke 11:18), "the prince" (Eph 2:2): "The whole world lies in the power of the evil one" (1 John 5:19). The influence of Satan is its own narrative in how the parenthetical age starts and ends, Satan's rise to his

---

24. Matt 18:10; 1 Cor 4:9; 11:10; 1 Tim 5:21; Luke 12:8–9; Rev 3:5; 20:2.

25. 2 Kgs 2:11; Job 14:12; 19:25–27; Pss 16:9–11; 22:26; 41:12; 49:15; 61:4–8; 73:24–26; 75:9–10; 115:17–18; 145:1–2; Prov 10:25; 12:19; 14:32; 15:24; 21:28; Isa 25:8; 26:19; Dan 12:2, 13.

26. The administrative center of Satan's kingdom is "in the heavenlies" according to Paul: a perplexing coexistence with God, his holy angels, and the deceased believers supported by the heavenly court in Job. In his thorough analysis of this heavenly setting presented in Ephesians, M. Jeff Brannon considers the arguments for the plural of "heavens, heavenlies" as (1) simply in deference to the Old Testament Hebrew plural term, šamayim, or (2) multiple levels of heavens, i.e., third heaven (2 Cor 12:2–3), or (3) skies/air, the lower heavens. Brannon, *Heavenlies*, 199–218. Perhaps the plural indicates the heavenly kingdom as I described earlier, plus its contiguous outlying heavenly place where Satan and his followers were expelled.

demise.[27] Mercifully, his rule as the "god of this world" lasts only during the parenthetical age,[28] and as immense as his sub-kingdom is, it is only a rebellious zone of God's universal kingdom which is contained by God's ultimate sovereignty and creation's realm. Otherwise, Satan would have already destroyed the terrestrial kingdom he rules, or at least would have brought it to an even worse state of torment.

The operations of the satanic kingdom can be defined simply—they are diametrically opposed to the eternal design. Rather than the shepherding God who protects against predators, Satan himself is the predator: "Your adversary the devil prowls like a roaring lion, seeking someone to devour" (1 Pet 5:8). Anti-shepherding is this kingdom's sole objective, destroying the incentive and abilities of nations and individuals to shepherd as God shepherds. The goal is to neglect God's image in creation, abuse it, and pursue the greatest injustices. It uses the eternal design only as the foil for its own design of not blessing but neglect; not deliverance but abuse; not discipline but temptation. By destroying God's creation, Satan seeks to destroy God's nature that is reflected in his creation: as if shattering the mirror could affect the reality of God, the source of the image. It is as close to assassinating God as Satan could have hoped, apart from his failed attempt to assassinate the Messiah.[29]

Satan's nature is anti-God, anti-glorious, anti-holy, and though the created angelic attributes common with God are retained by the fallen angels, any are used only for destruction, such as sovereignty, creativity, communicability. Yet God tolerates him to manipulate him for his own purposes. Though Satan seeks to deceive and destroy, and though he means it for evil, God includes the intentions and acts in his ultimate

27. Herman Ridderbos describes the battle of God and his Messiah's kingdom against the satanic kingdom: "What he terms in Galatians 1:4 'this present and evil aeon,' elsewhere as 'the power of darkness,' is set over against the royal dominion of Christ (Col. 1:13); and in Ephesians 2:2 he further qualifies walking according to 'his world-aeon' as following the course of 'the prince of the power of the air, the spirit that now works in the sons of disobedience.'" However, he goes too far when generalizing: "The world is therefore in its unity and totality the domain of demonic powers." Ridderbos, *Paul*, 91.

28. 2 Cor 4:4. One should take "as god" as an example of the Testaments' exaggerated designation of divinity applied to entities including the individual, e.g., "You are gods; all of you are sons of the Most High" (Ps 82:6; John 10:35–36).

29. Constantine Campbell attributes the warring realms of God and Satan to the incursion of Christ's future gracious, righteous, and glorious realm into the present realm of sin and death. He bases his two-realm eschatological schema on the presumed inaugural eschatological framework. Yet, the two realms have existed since the Fall. We will pursue this later in chapter 12. Campbell, *Paul*, 59–65.

righteous wisdom and righteousness. Nevertheless, believers defeat the satanic kingdom daily while resisting it and finally delivering the final blow and judgment (Rom 16:20; 1 Cor 6:2–3). More details of these victories will be discussed in chapter 10.

Satan works through his kingdom in the broadest and in the most specific levels. He works through the highest levels of his terrestrial kingdom by various effective governmental deceptions and enticements including carnality, materialism, oppression, and abuse. He further disrupts at the personal level with conniving temptations of the individual's clouded conscience, thereby compromising the natural law within the person who then caters to their fallen selfish ambitions.

This defiant coalition of humanity and Satan that was sealed in Eden defines the fallen world and human nature. But it is worse than a coalition; it is a totalitarianism where his realm's cunning power controls all nations who are spared from total deterioration only by God's shepherding with grace and patience. Satan has so deceived the world that it does not even know who its ruler is; even members of the trusting kingdom may not consider and articulate who directly rules the terrestrial and untrusting kingdom. This deceptive oppression is a key to the parenthetical age within the span of history where God's eternal design is still operating.

Satan's senseless claim that he himself could give away Jesus' jurisdiction over all the nations was only made because he thought he could deceive and take advantage of the human nature of Jesus as he had with Eve and Adam. However, Jesus answered one temptation of Satan in the most authoritative way possible, telling him not to test him because he was God: "You are not to test the Lord your God" (Matt 4:7). Jesus was then tempted to allegedly acquire all the nations by worshiping Satan. This was also answered by Jesus by inferring that he was God: "You are to worship and serve only the Lord your God," which of course was Jesus (4:10). In other words, "Go away. Do not tempt me, but worship me, for I am God." This vain testing was more than jousting with Scripture; it was the infinite Creator putting his finite diabolical creature in his place. Essentially, Satan was offering Jesus what already belonged to him as the divine, the terrestrial kingdom. Within days Satan and his demons would obey the Lord, only more publicly: "God disarmed the rulers and authorities. He made a public display of them, triumphing over them through Christ" (Col 2:15).

The demons know God and tremble (Jas 2:19; Luke 8:28), and Satan can do nothing unless the Lord allows it. God allowed Satan to curse Job and curse Paul with his "thorn of the flesh" (2 Cor 12:7). Paul even exploited the core evil of Satan to deliver at least three sinners to humble, discipline, and deliver their souls (1 Cor 5:5; 1 Tim 1:20). So, even Satan and his destructive intents serve the king of creation. Satan has never been the autonomous ruler of the nations. He may have had a long leash, but that is the serious nature of God's curse due to the Couple's choice for such an alliance. God employed Satan's anti-eternal design nature to attain his eternal design discipline of the world even more indirectly.

Satan's ongoing battle with the Messiah is predicted in Zech 3:1–8, where God rebukes Satan for accusing Joshua, the high priest, who was a symbol of the coming priestly Messiah. Satan even desired to "devour" Christ at his birth (Rev 12:4). This assault on the Messiah continued from the wilderness temptation and is countered by the Messiah's restrictive boundaries set for Satan, including the dramatic exorcisms. John's designation "anti-Christ" accentuates this kingdom battle involving the Messiah, and not only as a sin-Savior (1 John 2:18, 22; 4:3; 2 John 1:7). God enlists his believers in an incursion on Satan's kingdom and his anti-eternal design strategies to neglect, abuse, accuse, and destroy (Eph 6:12).

Jesus demonstrated his kingdom superiority by binding Satan (Matt 12:29); to what extent he has been bound will be debated until he is finally doomed. Jesus had seen in his pre-existence how Satan and his minions were permanently ejected from the heavenly kingdom (Ezek 28:11–19; Luke 10:1); he was at the scene in the Second Person. At least two other stages in Satan's subjugation are clear: "God's kingdom within Jesus' teaching has a two-fold manifestation: at the end of the age to destroy Satan, and in Jesus' mission to bind Satan."[30] This binding of the demons (2 Pet 2:4; Jude 1:6) is considered adequate for now, but the expulsion of the satanic kingdom from the heavenly kingdom will eventually be expanded to its permanent expulsion from the world as well (John 12:31), leaving a peaceful eternity in New Earth's universal kingdom.[31] Yet, the satanic kingdom will not be eradicated even then, simply contained in a torturous abyss. This was a primary objective for the Incarnation: "The Son of God appeared for the purpose to destroy the devil's work" (1 John 3:8; cf. Heb 2:14). Paul reminds us that Satan and his kingdom would be dealt a

---

30. Ladd, *Theology of the New Testament*, 64.
31. 1 Cor 15:23–24; Heb 2:14; Rev 12:9; 17:12–14; 20:2.

head-crushing blow, alluding to Gen 3:15: "The God of peace will soon crush Satan under your feet" (Rom 16:20). God's verdict against Satan had already been announced; he was condemned (John 16:11; 1 Tim 3:6).

NATURAL KINGDOM REALM

The natural kingdom is unique among the eight kingdoms in its apparent passivity and lack of intelligent self-direction, whereas the other seven kingdoms have conscious spirit or human leaders. Peter describes the animals unflatteringly, "unreasoning animals, born as creatures of instinct to be captured and killed" (2 Pet 2:12). Admittedly, this forces one to speak anthropomorphically about all of the natural kingdom. For instance, nature "obeys" God perfectly through its physical laws until God suspends them for exceptional miracles: "even the wind and sea obey him!" (Mark 4:41). However, nature is not just another and less significant sphere in the Lord's universal kingdom; it is the largest and most powerful of the sub-realms in known and yet-to-be-known ways. Our planet is a speck drifting in the cosmos (Job 26:7; 38:33; Ps 8). Though subject to space-time, cause-effect, and God's purposes, the natural kingdom's commanding reign has daily impact on itself and the life of humans, making for wonderful days of enjoyment to horrendous days of tragedy and death.

Still, the natural kingdom groans under the overpowering force of God's intense curse that it suffers because of the Fall and will continue to feel until Christ returns (Rom 8:25–28). Nature was unwittingly but nevertheless guilty by association with the serpent and the Couple's conscious and willful disobedience. So, natural disasters, thorns, plagues, and diseases are God's natural tools used against nature itself and the rest of creation to discipline and judge. Nonetheless, God still shepherds what he has cursed because he so loves the world: "The Lord is good to everything and merciful to all his creation" (Ps 145:9); "The world is full of the Lord's love and kindness" (Ps 33:5). God has eternally "covenanted" with the natural kingdom to bless it (Gen 9:9–17; Job 38:41; Ps 104; Hos 2:18; Matt 6:26–30).

One speaks of a creation/cultural mandate or primary commission for humanity (Gen 1:26–28), but nature was also given its own creation commission. God commissioned nature to "be fruitful and *multiply, fill* the water in the sea and the birds will *multiply* on the earth" (1:21–22).

So, God gave nature its realms to rule once it had filled its kingdom. He covenanted (Jer 33:20) with the cosmos to rule over temporal reality, including the sun, moon, and stars: "God set them in the sky to give light on earth and to *rule* the day and the night" (Gen 1:17–18; Ps 136:7–9).

In over forty verses the Lord recounts his unique relationship with his natural kingdom, which is incomprehensible and uncontrollable by humanity (Job 38). The natural kingdom has its own laws and enforces them strictly. Nature determines the contours of shores, rivers, weather, species, etc. The rhythm of celestial bodies enables nocturnal predators, flora growth, cosmic gravitational cohesion, and seasonal precipitation. Nature's formidable power and its extreme variety reveal the danger of human tampering with its tiniest atomic particles. Nature has its own cosmic "temptations" if celestial bodies were to stray too closely to black holes or animals were lured to their prey. In other words, nature governs itself and humanity with great might and tireless consistency. Consequently, without trusting and worshiping the Creator of nature, the terrestrial kingdom resorts to worshiping "mother nature" and her formidable authority in the attempt to find a less meddling personal power than a truly nurturing God who is the true source of their sustenance (Deut 4:19; Rom 1:22–23; Acts 14:17).

However, nature serves others as well as itself, in its compliance to the eternal design, by shepherding itself and humanity. For example, the soil blesses and sustains all life when nurtured by humanity, the clouds, the sun, the seasons, and even by the decay of the same flora and fauna that it had fed. Nature can negate the ravages of sickness and death by its immune systems, herbs, and sunlight. Nature delivers itself and humanity as well in its shepherding role in the eternal design and is the Lord's tool many times: wilderness subsistence, Elijah's ravens, and Jonah's saving fish. As a disciplining, judging, even cursing agent, nature works counter to human efforts and defends itself against abuse, whether by the maternal protectors of offspring or the soil becoming even more stubborn in its production when overused. Since the Fall, the kingdoms of nature and humanity have been adversaries in many ways. Nature might react to its abusers with severe consequences. Nature may retaliate against annoying its wildlife or polluting its water, land, and air. The components of creation have battled each other since Eden, so the natural kingdom has been perpetually groaning because of humanity's sin since Eden:

> Creation was subjected to futility, not willingly, but because of Him who subjected it, so that creation itself also will be set free from its slavery to corruption into the freedom of the glory of the children of God. For we know that the whole creation groans and suffers the pains of childbirth until now. (Rom 8:20–22)

Nonetheless, whether interpreted as hyperbole, metaphor, or a changed nature of fauna, the new creation will relieve the natural kingdom from its suffering during the parenthetical age:

> The wolf will dwell with the lamb, the leopard with the young goat.... And a little boy will lead them.... The nursing child will play by the cobra's hole, and the weaned child will put his hand on the viper's den. (Isa 11:6, 8)

But the parenthetical age does not end for the natural kingdom until fire leaves the fallen earth scorched[32] so God can begin a re-created perfect New Earth that he has always planned planet Earth to be.[33] Comparable to the believer's physical body at death, nature will be destroyed only to be raised a new creation, and it will help sustain the exciting life ahead for the trusting kingdom within New Earth. Psalm 104 is an image of New Earth as it portrays a perfectly balanced natural kingdom in its contribution to the eternal design. Permanent destruction is not what the natural kingdom awaits at the end of the parenthetical age since its history is not ended. But a temporary purging comes that does not compromise the New Earth's new wine by applying the old wineskins of the parenthetical age. Nature may groan and even be destroyed, but in New Earth it will be renewed and shepherded by the Lord and humanity, and the natural kingdom will continue shepherding itself and the remaining humanity.

TERRESTRIAL KINGDOM REALM

The terrestrial kingdom is composed of all nations, peoples, tribes, and tongues, and it is the universal kingdom's focus. And it is this kingdom's sanctified shepherding by the authority of the primary commission that is the Testaments' focus. The first and last books of the Bible are about the nations. Genesis 1–14 begins and Revelation ends with God's relationship

---

32. 2 Pet 3:7, 10, 12; 1 John 2:17. For a good survey of the earth's demolition before its renovation, see Middleton, *New Heaven, New Earth*, 179–95.

33. Hos 2:18, 21–22; also Pss 96:10–13; 98:7–9; Isa 11:1–3, 6–9; 35:1–2; 51:3; 65:17–25; 66:22; Ezek 36:30; 2 Pet 3:10–13; 1 John 2:17; Rev 21:1.

with all nations at front and center. Dynastic empires of Egypt, Mesopotamia, Israel, and Persia are prominent nations in the Old Testament. Jeremiah and Paul were a "prophet to the nations" and an "apostle to the nations" (Jer 1:5; Rom 11:13). Obadiah, Jonah, and Nahum are mainly about non-Israelite nations, and Melchizedek, Joseph, David, Solomon, Nehemiah, Mordecai, Esther, and Daniel ruled in nations other than Israel. Specifically, the Messiah was commissioned to significantly impact the nations in Pss 2, 72, 110; Isa 42, 49, 52; Dan 7; Mic 5; and Zech 9. Both Testaments proclaim God as the only king of the terrestrial kingdom: "The Most High rules the kingdom of humanity and gives it to whom he will and sets the lowliest of men over it" (Dan 4:17).[34] Jesus said exactly this to Pilate's face while under interrogation: "You would have no authority over me unless it had been given to you from above" (John 19:11), something Herod was soon to find out with his wormy demise (Acts 12:20–23). All sovereigns are appointed by God,[35] and it is by his authority that the nations' realms and their durations are assigned[36] whether it is Pilate representing the gentiles or the religious leaders when representing Israel in Christ's crucifixion. John accentuates Jesus' theme of the "world" heavily in his writings, particularly in his Gospel where he quotes Jesus referencing the world nearly eighty times.[37]

The primary commission singled out humanity as the highest sovereign component in creation: "Subdue the earth and rule" (Gen 1:28). This is neither a command nor permission to exploit the earth; rather, it is a privilege to reign as God does, that is, with God and with his shepherding heart in all its strength, resolve, and love. Yes, the earth and all that is in it is the Lord's (Ps 24:1), but he made humanity to rule over all things he created (Ps 8:6), so it could be said, "The Lord has given the earth to humanity" (Ps 115:16)—to rule wisely, fairly, and with compassion. The Couple developed into numerous families and eventually all

---

34. 2 Kgs 19:15; 2 Chr 20:6; Pss 22:28; 66:7; Jer 10:7, 10; Dan 2:44; 5:21; Matt 28:18–19; Col 1:16; 2:10; Acts 10:34–36, 43; Rev 1:5; 14:6–7; 17:14.

35. Isa 44:28; 45:1–3; Dan 2:20–21, 37–45; 5:18, 21; 7:12–22; Hag 2:21–23; Rom 13:1–2.

36. Gen 11:8–9; 12:1–2, 6–7; Exod 3:7–8; Deut 2:5, 9, 12, 19–21; 32:8; Josh 1:2–4; 3:10; 2 Sam 7:10; Pss 60:6–8; 86:9; 135:10–13; 136:17–22; Acts 17:26.

37. The references are not always about the world's population alone, but they include the natural kingdom as well. John's repetitive use of *kosmos* "underscores impressively the controlling nature of the Johannine worldview that has stamped its imprint indelibly onto its presentation of Jesus in the gospel." Köstenberger, *John's Gospel and Letters*, 281.

the peoples. Cities and agrarian communities emerged. Art and artisanship, mining and manufacturing, and social order formed and expanded (Gen 4:17–22).

Unfortunately, human history shows how the terrestrial kingdom's privilege of sharing rule with the Almighty instead became the proud and pervasive opposition to him, century after century, millennium after millennium. The struggle against, rather than cooperation with, the Trinity is the tragedy of the terrestrial kingdom. History rarely reflects a partnership between God and humanity but instead reflects a duped kingdom that only continues to pursue what it believes to be its own ways, when they ultimately contribute to Satan's diversionary ways. Blessing, deliverance, and discipline are to be the shepherding fruit of the eternal design; instead, the terrestrial kingdom acts as its invisible anti-shepherds, supporting Satan's mission to contradict the eternal design by neglect, abuse, and injustice. The monolith of humanity as a whole under the overwhelming influence of the satanic kingdom is the reason for the terrestrial kingdom to be written in the singular when "terrestrial kingdoms" might sound more natural. Though the terrestrial kingdom has had innumerable nations, people, ethnic, and dialectical groups, it is a unit in its submission and subjection under the satanic sub-realm.

Satan's subordinating reign over all nations, yet under the universal kingdom, is what he won temporarily by Eden's insurrection. That victory for him was a loss for humanity that resulted in all nations suffering tyranny under his regime. His reign cuts a cruel and destructive wound on every society's cultural conscience, which inevitably becomes morally infected. He assists in developing and pimping alternate worldviews, ideologies, and religions, including those that physically bow before him or simply wink at him through their artistic or popular culture. Yet, consider the even more horrifying scenario if there were an absence of any of God's common grace and natural law intervention within a society's governing ethics and laws.

Unbelievers live relatively ethical lives (Matt 5:46–47; Luke 6:32–33), often outperforming believers in this regard while motivated only by common grace and their moral conscience:

> When Gentiles without the written Law instinctively keep the Law . . . they reveal the work of the Law written in their hearts; their conscience and thoughts accuse or defend them. (Rom 2:14–15)

Admittedly, all hearts are compromised by a fallen, debilitated human nature, even believers' hearts while being renewed by the Spirit. Yet, the terrestrial kingdoms do shepherd in compliance and in dissent to God's universal kingdom ethics, and there is enough goodness to ward off total social anarchy. Paul's instruction to comply with Roman laws was based on whatever goodness and justice those laws and their enforcement contained. Were they perfect like the Old Testament laws, wisdom instructions, and the moral commandments of Christ and his apostles? Hardly. Were they still helpful? Immensely (Eccl 8:2–5, 11; Rom 13:3–7; Titus 3:1; 1 Pet 2:13–14). Mercifully, the satanic kingdom lacks complete obedience to its commands, and God's discretion relies on the remaining goodness within all cultures to maintain a relatively balanced society where the leaders he has determined or approved should be obeyed. Paul confirms Jesus words on taxes: "Give back to Caesar what is Caesar's and to God what is God's";[38] "Authorities are the servants of God. . . . Pay taxes to whom taxes are due" (Rom 13:6–7); "Everyone must submit to the governing authorities since all authority comes from God" (Rom 13:1).

Enough positivity about the terrestrial kingdom's leaders! All leaders of the earth are graced to be called "shepherds" and God has created a global system where he holds them accountable for their treatment of their sheep: "The Lord has a judgment against the nations. . . . Weep and moan, evil shepherds! Roll in ashes, leaders of the *flock*! Your time for slaughter is here" (Jer 25:31, 34). Humanity still has God's image within itself that empowers it for aggressive, effective work and achievements. However, it continues to invest those God-like characteristics in its contract with Satan rather than in alliance with the shepherding King. That contract eventually stipulated that the terrestrial kingdom execute God's Son. Again, ironically, this pernicious injustice accomplished the perfectly righteous will of God who required a human sacrifice for the world's sin. There are brief periods in the history of the trusting kingdom when its faith has been a state religion or has had regional or national moral influence, thus somewhat protected from Satan's animosity. However, this is not the status generally: "I chose you out of the world so you are not of the world and the world hates you" (John 5:19; Jas 4:4). Multiple nations afflict the trusting kingdom by diabolical laws and ferocious village raids, which show their hatred by the terrestrial kingdom for the Lord's lambs. Persecution of believers is at its highest level in history. Christians and

---

38. Matt 22:21 // Mark 12:17 // Luke 20:25; also Matt 17:25–27.

the rest of the world wrestle not with terrestrial forces alone but with heavenly principalities in battles that take place on earth, often inflicting horrific bodily harm, even death.

After all that might be said of the terrestrial kingdom's rebellion, it is still blessed by God's shepherding common grace and by his natural kingdom's provisions regardless of its Satan-instigated rebellion:

> He let all the nations go their own way, but he has not left them without witnessing about his character by revealing his kindness in giving you rain from the skies and predictable crops in their seasons; he provides you with plenty of food and fills your hearts with joy. (Acts 14:16–17; also Rom 17:24–25; Matt 5:44–45)

God's love for the nations persists: "the good news of the kingdom will be proclaimed to all nations, then the end will come" (Matt 24:14). Then, all remaining humanity will follow Christ, and all nations will be represented in New Earth (John 12:31–32).[39] New Earth will see all nations bowing to the Lord.[40] At the final fall of the total satanic kingdom, God will gather believing representatives from all the nations to him in peace, ready for productive work, not for constant war (Mic 4:3).

TRUSTING KINGDOM REALM

Holy Nation

The trusting kingdom is a separate kingdom surrounded by the satanic, natural, and terrestrial kingdoms. It is not to be identified with the church at any level since the trusting kingdom's composition is solely made of individual believers. Organizations do not constitute a trusting component since all "Christian" organizations of any size either are systemically weeds or goats themselves or are a mix of believers and unbelievers, e.g., state churches, denominations, local churches, parachurch ministries. History proves that the church has had chapters of heinous abuse of humanity, has acted arrogantly from a presumption of cultural

---

39. Isa 1:25–26; 4:3–4; 32:15–16; 52:13—53:12; Jer 31:31–32; Ezek 36:25–26; 37:23–24.

40. Pss 22:7; 46:10; 66:3–4; 68:30–32; 72:17; 86:9; 102:21–22; 126:2–3; 145:21; 148:11–14; Isa 2:4; 12:4–5; 19:20–25; 25:6; 42:1–4, 10–12; 45:22–25; 55:3–5; 56:6–7; 60:7; 61:5–7; 66:18–19; Jer 3:17; Dan 7:27; Mic 4:1–5; Zeph 2:11; 3:9; Hab 2:14; Zech 8:20–22; 14:16; Mal 1:11.

superiority, has confused the sheep doctrinally, and has been led by those who serve personal wealth rather than God, and those who have wasted the Lord's resources on pretentious edifices that are empty both in bodies and saving faith.

A person is a citizen of heaven or not and belongs to an intimidating counterculture to the world. Individuals in the trusting kingdom may be part of simple or complicated administrative structures where these churches or organizations only assist the trusting kingdom; they do not define it, just as secular social, legal, and political structures may even assist the trusting kingdom without these structures being included within the trusting kingdom. The church has any number of polities, but it is not a distinct kingdom. Even when a subscription to a faith statement is required for some form of membership in a church there is still the important distinction between those who simply believe in God (like the demons) and those who trust him with their lives and commitments. To refer to the trusting kingdom as the "believing kingdom" would be a term too generous for a kingdom that included those who believe but do not trust.

Believers make up the kingdom of the redeemed that reside in all of the terrestrial kingdom's levels of social order: families, churches, denominations, communities, regions, peoples, the globe. There are no physical borders for this kingdom which populates rather than dominates. The trusting kingdom in the Testaments is God's assembly of his chosen, repentant, and trusting souls. God had already designated Israel as "a kingdom of priests and a holy nation" (Exod 19:6), and Peter applies this to New Testament believers as well, whether Jews or gentiles (1 Pet 2:9–10).[41] Christ has "made us a kingdom, priests to his God and Father" (Rev 1:6), and that kingdom priesthood is a royal, ruling priesthood that parallels the messianic roles of king and priest (Ps 110:2, 4). The trusting kingdom is dispersed throughout the globe in ever-increasing areas and in ever-increasing numbers. Like the tribe of Levi, including its priests who resided within forty-eight designated cities throughout Israel, the trusting kingdom is made up of believers who are priests, mediators, instructors, prophets, and servants of God throughout the terrestrial kingdom where they live. Gentiles are merged with Jews in this "holy nation": "holy, set apart" from the terrestrial kingdom, among whom the

---

41. Peter is addressing a mixed group of Jews and gentiles who were residents of five provinces of Asia Minor. Regardless of whether the congregational makeup of these five regions was predominantly Jewish or gentile, this salutation sees a single audience.

trusting kingdom is scattered yet where tribalism will be no longer, only pan-tribal affinity in New Earth (Eph 2:14–16).

Paul tells the multi-ethnic believers at Ephesus, "You are fellow citizens with the saints and are members of the household of God" (Eph 2:19; also Phil 3:20; Heb 3:6; 1 Tim 3:15); "[God] raised us up with him and seated us with him in the heavenlies in Christ Jesus" (Eph 2:6). They are rescued from the domain of darkness and transferred to "the kingdom of His beloved Son" (Col 1:13). Other designations for the trusting kingdom are God's friends (John 15:14–15; Jas 2:23), his family (Eph 5:1; 6:23; Col 1:2; Titus 1:4; 1 Pet 5:9; 1 John 3:2; 2 John 13), his body (Eph 1:22–23; 5:29–33), his army (Phil 2:25), and his fellow-laborers (Col 4:11).

Real Realm

It would be simplistic to consider the trusting kingdom as only a "spiritual" realm. There is a power, profundity, stability, and functionality to the trusting kingdom's culture that challenges persons around it and their cultures. It is a political entity whether activist or passive. It acts and is acted upon. The trusting kingdom thinks deeply about the breadth of the human experience. It congregates in numbers that can be small within its social context, and yet its influence can be destabilizing or seen to be so by a culture. It shows its generosity to all and humbly convicts cultures of their shepherding deficiencies. It is often seen as a competing, potent challenge to those around them, especially when its kingdom citizenship and allegiances grow. The trusting culture's shepherding within itself and to the surrounding society ironically can bring oppressive kingdoms jealously against it. It is also simplistic to believe that believers are not impacted when caught in the grip of repression and tragedies common to all humanity because of the Curse. The point is that there are very physical realities for the trusting kingdom as it impacts its surroundings through its believers.

The individual believer's realm is where one reigns over a jurisdiction containing space-time dimensions. The believer's citizenship in the heavenly kingdom has significant terrestrial implications for the other kingdoms, the satanic, terrestrial, and natural kingdoms, and it affects the family, marketplace, church, community, nation, and world. The trusting kingdom may not have a unique landmass, but the nations contain believers who, by not belonging to the dark satanic kingdom, can thrive from their kingdom of light. In fact, as citizens of the trusting kingdom and containing the Spirit, they are told to resist and overcome Satan (Eph 6:11–12; Jas 4:7; 1 John 2:14), not obliged to the dark realm's unbelievers (2 Cor 6:14–15) nor submitting to their false worldviews (Col 2:8). Belonging to the trusting kingdom equips for conquering (Rom 8:37–39).[42] Just as Israel was to be the community who impressed the nations with her relationship with the only God, Paul stresses that the New Testament trusting community should also impress the world: "Your light must shine in such a way that people will see your good works and glorify your Father in heaven" (Matt 5:16).

Believers possess and manage their own space and time where they conduct themselves as both citizens of heaven and a kingdom on earth. They have real estate, material things, physical and spiritual influence over the world, and they govern small-to-expansive areas. Living believers are not bodiless souls; they are active, instrumental, and influential members of a powerful distributed province within God's universal kingdom.

Global Reign

The trusting kingdom's inheritance of global reign with God in New Earth is a great promise. Believers reign currently but only over portions of the universal kingdom, where it is surrounded by the other sub-realms. But New Earth will belong solely to believers and God as he now calls and develops those who will do as he has intended since Eden; the trusting kingdom re-inherits what the Couple surrendered.

> The sovereignty, authority, and greatness of all the kingdoms under heaven will be handed over to the saints of the Most High. His kingdom will be an everlasting kingdom, and all rulers will worship and obey him. (Dan 7:27)

The Messiah came to continue redeeming future shepherding residents of New Earth and populate it with all the Old Testament, New Testament, and subsequent believers: "Do not be afraid, little flock, because your Father has decided to give you the kingdom" (Luke 12:32). The primary

---

42. Fleming Rutledge: "We have tried to show . . . that the Christian *participates* in the cosmic struggle, that she stands with her Lord under the world's sentence of death, that she is equipped for the fray with the armor of light, that she is clothed with the righteousness of God, that she bears the sword of the Word into battle, that she must bear her cross." Rutledge, *Crucifixion*, 390.

commission of Gen 1:28, "Subdue the earth and rule," continues through the trusting kingdom's influence from Genesis through eternal New Earth. Genesis first promised it, and Psalms, Isaiah, Daniel, Matthew, Paul, John, and Hebrews reaffirm it. Believers are named in the estate of New Earth and in many ways already draw from it, yet eventually they will inherit and rule it all: "To whoever is victorious and obeys me to the end I will give authority over the nations" (Rev 2:26). The Testaments' first and last chapters stress a trusting kingdom's reign in the universal kingdom (Gen 1:28; Rev 22:3–5).

Humanity will not metaphorically "inherit" the earth as mere residents with benefits; they will own and rule it[43] as God commissioned humanity. It can be lost that the momentous occasion of the Messiah's reception of the universal kingdom in Dan 7:13–14 continues the believers' reception of the commission to reign. The kingdom given to the Son of Man is given to the trusting kingdom following its verdicts over the world and angels (Dan 7:13–14; 1 Cor 5:2–3).

> The saints of the Highest One will receive the kingdom and take possession of the kingdom forever . . . . That horn was waging war with the saints and prevailing against them until the Ancient of Days came and judgment was passed in favor of the saints of the Highest One, and the time arrived when the saints took possession of the kingdom . . . . Then the sovereignty, authority, and greatness of all the kingdoms under heaven will be handed over to the saints of the Most High. His kingdom will be an everlasting kingdom, and all rulers will worship and obey him. (Dan 7:18, 21–22, 27)

This eventuality does not negate the trusting kingdom's duty to shepherd now. The difference is that in New Earth it will not have a scattered rule but a united and planet-wide rule. Paul applies this truth of the future sarcastically to those who acted as if they already ruled to this degree: "You have everything you want already. You are already rich and have started reigning without us. How I wish that you really had started to reign so we might reign with you" (1 Cor 4:8).

Like the primary commission of Gen 1:28, the Great Commission paraphrases Dan 7:14 with five important components in nearly identical sequence.

---

43. Dan 7:22; Matt 25:34; Luke 12:42–44; Acts 20:32; Rom 8:16–17; 1 Cor 3:22–23; 6:9–10; 15:50; Gal 4:7; 5:21; Eph 1:11; 5:5; Col 1:12; 3:24; 2 Tim 2:10–12; Heb 12:28; Jas 2:5; Rev 3:21; 5:10; 22:5.

Matt 28:18	Dan 7:14
All authority in heaven and on earth	Dominion, honor, and a kingdom
has been given to Me . . .	was given to Him so that
make disciples of all the nations . . .	all the peoples and nations
teach them to follow all that I commanded you.	will serve Him.
I am with you always, to the end of the age.	His dominion is an eternal dominion.

The trusting realm is expanded by recruiting obedient and serving disciples from all nations under the Messiah's authority. "If we died with him, we will also live with him. If we endure, we will also reign with him" (2 Tim 2:11–12). "Those receiving the abundance of grace and the gift of righteousness will reign in life through the One, Jesus Christ" (Rom 5:17).

Meanwhile, God's believers will be hated by the world, tortured, raped, imprisoned, and executed by the terrestrial realm led by the satanic kingdom (John 15:19). The trusting kingdom understands that its constant clash with the world is not merely two-dimensional; it is a multidimensional conflict among itself and the terrestrial and satanic kingdoms, in addition to the natural kingdom. In less ominous circumstances, believers have a defense against the satanic kingdom which demands the precaution of not giving the enemy an occasion to distract them (Eph 4:27) and also resisting until the enemy flees (Jas 4:7): "Resist him, firm in faith, knowing that the same suffering is felt by your brothers and sisters who are in the world" (1 Pet 5:9). The promise is encouraging and final: "The God of peace will soon crush Satan under your feet" (Rom 16:20).

Eternal Design

Ethical conduct is a way believers proclaim God's excellencies: "A people for his own possession and zealous for good works" (Titus 2:14). Jesus' commission continues to assemble a global trusting kingdom and instructs it in its vehement opposition to the dark kingdom, in its call for urgent deliverance, in its service to persons in the terrestrial kingdom, and in its care for the natural kingdom. New Earth will bring unimpeded obedience from the trusting kingdom, and the challenge for the believer is to live that New Earth life now. This includes the trusting kingdom's obligation to "do good to all men," just as God sends rain to all of humanity (Luke 6:27; Gal 6:10). The trusting kingdom has multiplied and is filling the earth and shepherds the earth and its nations. It has been successful in convincing many communities, even nations, that it is a great yet humble kingdom, "wise and understanding" (Deut 4:6–7). Health care, water management, nutrition, literacy, shelter, microeconomics are only examples of the application of Christians' shepherding worldview to millions. The trusting kingdom is working to serve Christ and his universal messianic kingdom. Every hour, ministries of the trusting kingdom deliver the nations' abused, trafficked, homeless, physically ill, emotionally scarred, illiterate, starving, addicted, displaced, orphaned, and disabled. No single nation has responded with sustained appreciation for God's grace, and this global ingratitude will remain until New Earth. Until then, there will always have been a trusting kingdom, God's faithful nation of priests. It has grown to be a massive influence around the globe. The trusting kingdom, however dense or rarified its population may be, must continue and intensify its collaboration to impact all its spheres of influence.

NEW EARTH'S KINGDOM REALM

God's holistic plan of salvation was to send Christ to save "the world," which includes the terrestrial, trusting, and natural kingdoms (John 3:16; 1 John 4:14). All creation awaits the salvation of humanity, including the holy angels, who will undoubtedly be relieved when the intense spiritual battles are finally over. Every biblical reference to eternal life refers to that life's venue, namely, the promised new creation and its glory—not merely to live forever, but "they will reign *on the earth*" together with God (Rev 5:10).

The New Earth kingdom is clearly presented as a terrestrial kingdom on this planet, not another dimension called "heaven."[44] Though New Earth is described somewhat, too little is offered to presume what it will look like in any detail. One can reasonably extrapolate what the nature of New Earth might be by observing what God originally intended, how his universal and messianic kingdom has operated during this parenthetical age, and the Testaments' specific prophecies. The cursed creation will no longer fight and groan among its inhabitants: animals, vegetation, and

---

44. "Saints will enjoy their freedom from sin and its effects in this regenerated earth that is liberated from its present state of imperfection and decay . . . not in a spiritual, disembodied heaven 'up there.'" Waltke, *Old Testament Theology*, 562. Even a "new Jerusalem" is described in its descent to the earth (Rev 21:1).

human managers. The call to shepherd the world will still be in effect, but there will only be reciprocal respect and assistance between the trusting and natural kingdoms. Both nature and humanity will be relieved of their cursed existence once God's highest vice regents are finally perfectly free from the sin that oppresses all creation (Rom 8:18–22). "He will wipe away every tear from their eyes; and there will no longer be death; there will no longer be mourning, crying, or pain; the first things have passed away" (Rev 21:4). The Final Testament will have arrived.

Second Peter 3:7–10 reminds one of the prophecy in Isaiah of a re-creation of earth and skies after their destruction by fire. Surfaces will be burnt away, leaving an even more fertile earth and cleansed sky to produce a beautiful global "Eden." After all, the rainbow is an "everlasting covenant" (Gen 9:16). The tranquility of New Earth is portrayed by peace among its fauna, beauty, and fruitfulness of its flora and the protection of humanity from natural predators (Isa 11:6–9; 35:9; 51:3–4; 55:12–13; 65:17, 25; 66:22; Ezek 34:28).[45]

It is an amazing statement that the future glory in New Earth will be far greater than its inverse, the sufferings in this present world: "I consider the sufferings of this present time are not worthy to be compared with the glory that will be revealed to us" (Rom 8:18). This is a profound way to put suffering in perspective, a strong premise for any theodicy! New Earth will not simply be better than the current human and natural situation; it will be far more exciting than current suffering is distressing, more exhilarating than oppressions are now agonizing. The temporary intensity of creation's curses calibrates the even more inestimable, eternal glories of New Earth.

All citizens of the trusting and terrestrial kingdoms will finally be the identical population; the terrestrial kingdom will then be the trusting kingdom. All those who "entered" the kingdom during the parenthetical age were simultaneously recorded as future New Earth citizens. And all terrestrial kingdoms will have come to realize that they were always simply provinces within the universal and messianic kingdom, though they followed the most insidious of kingdom princes in this age. And though the population will be the remaining trusting and terrestrial kingdom,

---

45. Exaggerations are expected in apocalyptic literature as found in Isa 60:20; Zech 14:7; Matt 13:43; Rev 21:1; 22:5. New Earth will be so radically different, even strange, one can only humbly project and separate exaggeration from actuality.

hopefully their cultures in all their delightful variety will be retained as a beautiful tapestry of diverse and colorful threads.[46]

Revelation 22:3 describes New Earth in a most efficient and encouraging way: "nothing will be cursed anymore." Whatever was cursed since Eden will have been delivered. Creation will again be "good."[47] The absence of evil deception, jealousy, tears, disappointment, infidelity, naïveté, projection, guilt, death, dissatisfaction, intense labor, pests, pain will be replaced by perfect and eternal contentment, joy, honesty, loyalty, brilliance, efficient work, success, and comforting environments (Ps 96:11–13; Isa 65:17–18; Zech 14:11; Rev 21:4, 27). The fruits of the Spirit will be unfettered by the previously fallen dispositions and priorities; they will be dispensed routinely by believers and enjoyed in peace and love.

God's creation and its inherent eternal design should be taken seriously rather than assuming he relented on Plan A and will move to a new paradigm in New Earth. Yet, there is no reason to expect another extreme either, where New Earth defaults to the utter primitive condition of Eden. Given a punishing physical scorched earth, still, the trusting kingdom might build on the wisdom and knowledge that humanity had acquired during the parenthetical age. Creation's "return to Eden" implies a continuation of the eternal design, not a reversion to a primordial earth. The primary commission still applies; nature will need to be controlled and cultivated since it was created originally to grow. The interdependence of creation for assistance and productive results will remain, but the absence of sin and its curses will no longer impede the eternal design's perfect shepherding impact. The trusting kingdom will finally shepherd its inherited kingdom perfectly as he intended before he created anything: "Then the King will say to those on his right, 'You who

---

46. Gordon H. Johnston conveys the spirit of the difference in God's approach to polity in the Old Testament and New Earth's Final Testament; however, the application of his portrayal of the egalitarian nature of Zion would be equally true for the global population: "Although the house of David would play a role in the future eschatological deliverance of Zion, it would not function as the primary focus of Yahweh's blessing as it had in the past. Rather, it would share this honor with the ordinary citizens of Jerusalem as well as the common farmers of Judah. In essence, the traditional preexilic honor of the house of David as the agent of Yahweh would be democratized in the coming age." Johnston, "Zechariah," 206.

47. "The new creation will be a place where the effects of Adam's transgression against God's command are reversed.... In summary, the new creation will return to a condition qualitatively like its condition prior to Adam's sin." Thielman, *Theology of the New Testament*, 716, 717.

are blessed of My Father, come inherit the kingdom prepared for you since the foundation of the world" (Matt 25:34).

If there had been no Fall, the trusting kingdom by now would have had millennia of uninhibited minds and hearts acting with far greater depth and variety in producing far more extraordinary, beautiful, and edifying effects. If one were to extract everything good that has been developed, subdued, shepherded, and accomplished by humanity in the parenthetical age, immeasurably more could have been done by now if not for the constraints of the Curse and humanity's sinful nature. So, one might extrapolate from these enormous and innumerable achievements during this present age what human successes in New Earth might bring endlessly. It is doubtful that the Messiah will be satisfied as the almighty king of a global retirement home. Believers have been justified for practical terrestrial purposes, not a vague platonic "relationship with God in heaven." As true and gracious as it is to be at peace with God, there is practical teleological progress that amounts to more than an uninterrupted tea with the Trinity.

Unfortunately, history has seen a parenthetical suspension of humanity's immeasurable potential, but believers will see their own personalities, gifts, talents, and interests combined with others' complementary assets to populate communities across the globe who worship God by their faithful, productive, everyday shepherding and management. Every attribute given to reflect God's image will be expressed by the trusting kingdom, and these expressions will synergize perfectly through eternal history. The condition of God's universal kingdom as "good" was not just its assessment at its inauguration; its goodness is the teleological aspiration and eternal goal for God and his trusting kingdom, which will be experienced throughout the Final Testament. Though the earth's surface may be torched, humanity's divine image will not. The learning curve of human culture will not be thousands of years; it will pick up where it left off, with powerful intellectual, imaginative, and inventive productivity. Though his finite creation can never show God's infinite glory, creation's eternality will allow it to develop an infinite number of successes as it adds and shares only its blessings to God's universal kingdom.

The divisions of Babel and the rich variety of ethnic and cultural strengths and emphases that have transpired will then stimulate the united trusting kingdom in the new creation, not with competing and clannish prejudices but with celebrated diversity. A glory of the current terrestrial kingdom is its variety in customs and its innovative collaborations with creation to produce diverse foods, art, clothing, shelter, music, etc., and their diverse colors, smiles, beauty, voices, and ceremonies will delight everyone in New Earth. In other words, when one analyzes the full variety of what it means to be human, perhaps one could project those blessings even if enhanced further into the new creation as well. Maybe individuals will continue doing in New Earth what their callings and enjoyments have been during this compromising parenthesis but without being fallen, easily distracted, and biased in self-centered minds and hearts.[48] As prevalent as formal worship is displayed in Revelation, it will have the same qualified function as in the Testaments. God has always desired acts of blessing, humility, and kindness over ceremonial minutiae. One does not read in Genesis that Adam and Eve were to spend their lives on their knees in worship; they were to be on their knees praying while cultivating, tending, subduing earth's potential excesses, and producing with and for creation far more than what they were to sacrifice to God.

---

48. Shaw and Gitau capture an appreciation of this current Christian cultural diversity while describing the World Christianity movement: "It is interdisciplinary, utilizing history, theology, linguistics, missiology, and the social sciences to uncover the movement of the Spirit in the church around the world as it raises up new expressions of the faith and revitalizes older expressions. World Christianity focuses on both non-Western expressions of Christian faith and non-Western perspectives on the movement on this Christianity around the world. Applied to Christian historiography, such an approach is ecumenical in its breadth and inclusiveness, evangelical in its roots and core commitments, and contextual in its mission and sensitivities." Shaw and Gitau, *Kingdom of God in Africa*, 9.

7

Messiah's Commission

THE KINGDOM STRUCTURE THROUGHOUT creation and its eternal history creates a dynamic intersection of powers and authority centers within God's universal kingdom. During this cursed parenthetical age, the intersections can be anything from pleasant and productive to contentious and destructive. Conflict is most noticeable since it challenges humanity in an extremely intimidating world. However, God's universal realm is in this condition until he decides the time has come for the parenthetical age to end and the new creation to begin. We deferred the messianic kingdom's description to this point because of its resounding prevalence in God's kingdom structure by which he administers his universal kingdom. Since all of the sub-realms of the previous chapter are under the jurisdiction of God and his Messiah's universal realm, this eighth kingdom plays the unifying role among the other seven kingdoms.

Along the way in this age, in his mysterious timing, God personally modeled what the eternal design should look like and would look like—what humanity should have done before this age, what it should do now in this parenthetical age, and what it will do after this age. He came as the Messiah, as the Second Person melded with human chromosomes in a woman's womb to become the divine man. The Messiah's humanity was a necessity if God's plan for human sovereignty was going to be modeled; the Messiah's divinity was a necessity for the modeling to be perfect. And since the Old Testament's unblemished sacrifices foreshadowed the requirement for an unblemished human sacrifice, the Messiah's unblemished humanity was a necessity as much as his divinity was. This Messiah came as the Shepherd for humanity to better reign over the entire realm of creation. And he came as the high priest, king, prophet, judge, teacher, intercessor, warrior, and the savior of individuals and nations from their various adversities.

JEWISH UNDERSTANDING OF A MESSIAH

The Testaments' message is seen more fully once the Messiah's commission is understood.[1] Understanding the complete scope of the Messiah's roles prepares one to define the kingdom of God and its impact on the ubiquitous kingdom structure within the eternal design and throughout the New Testament and since. However, frustratingly so, too little from those who spoke about Jesus' messiahship in the Gospels indicates what exactly they were looking for in a Messiah. Mainly, the assumption was that a Messiah would bring a visible victorious kingdom. Yet, Jesus responds to John the Baptist's inquiry with evidence that he was a prophet (Matt 11:4–5 // Luke 7:22; Isa 61:1–2). Certainly a killed Messiah was not expected by Peter, his fellow disciples, or anybody else for that matter, even while considering Jesus to be the Messiah (Matt 16:16 // Mark 8:29 // Luke 9:20; Matt 16:22–23). What criteria made Andrew certain that they had found the Messiah (John 1:41)? The Samaritan woman was certain the Messiah would explain everything, but what role did she believe the Messiah would play as the "explainer" (John 4:25–26)? A clearer understanding was proclaimed about the Messiah after his ascension, when regardless of Jewish expectations the apostles evangelized the messianic realities. However, before this, they only admitted that they had heard and seen much greater things in Jesus' ministry than they had from all other previous prophets' teachings and miracles, including John the Baptist.

---

1. Texts considered "messianic" for this study are passages found in the following chapters: Pss 2; 72; 110; Isa 9; 11; 42; 49; 50; 52–53; Jer 23; 30; 33; Ezek 21; 34; 37; Dan 7; 9; Hos 3; Mic 5; Zech 3; 6; 9; 12; Mal 3. This list does not deny that other messianic texts could be found, but as a limited scope, it is intended to keep the subject focused without rejecting other pertinent material relevant to the whole matter of Old Testament messianic expectations. Also, texts that simply point to a messianic age are not included here unless the text is explicitly about the Messiah himself. Admittedly, these are moves of expediency, yet they should not compromise my primary conclusions.

MESSIAH'S COMMISSION

We are missing a thick straight line between the Testaments that tracks a continuum labeled "the intertestamental kingdom of God." Yet, a Messiah had come who met some expectations. Jesus was close enough to whatever expectations for some to wonder whether he was the one (Matt 11:3; Luke 3:15; John 11:27). What exactly had been the Jews' expectation when the apostles pronounced that "Jesus is the Christ" (Acts 2:31; 3:20; 5:42; 9:22; 17:3; 18:5, 28)? We know in hindsight what it meant, but exactly what they were expecting in a Messiah before then is vague, apart from Judaism's presumption of a realized political kingdom in general.

This undefined expectation by those voicing their curiosity or certainty is understandable. N. T. Wright notes that there was no "fully formed outline picture of 'the Jewish expectation of the Messiah.' . . . Jesus' Jewish world offers instead a flurry of confused elements, some of which may be present in some messianic movements."[2] In other words, there was no lengthy public checklist of anticipated functions of the Messiah. Nonetheless, there was an excitement about any indication that he may have arrived: "The people were waiting expectantly, all wondering if John might possibly be the Messiah" (Luke 3:15). A politically delivering king was the expectation most widely held, though most misunderstood it; so for most, Jesus proved a disappointing candidate. For this reason, Jesus did not publicly and literally pronounce himself to be the Messiah but did so only privately to the Samaritan woman, who took it upon herself to tell her town. He knew to do so would incite a knee-jerk, imprecise, and tragic nationalistic hysteria, and his premature execution.

Jesus' literal claim to be the Messiah was either by a response during a conversation or by baiting the disciples. He did not make it an explicit proposition that he set about to argue. The Samaritan woman deferred theological controversies until the Messiah came, to which Jesus responded only, "You are talking with him" (John 4:25-26). He also affirmed or absorbed the title of Messiah when he was with his disciples (Matt 16:15-16, 20; Mark 8:29; Luke 9:20) and when answering Caiaphas (Mark 14:61-62). The demons identified Jesus as the Messiah, which he did not deny verbally—he only affirmed it by his actions (Luke 4:41).[3]

---

2. Wright, *Victory of God*, 483. Fitzmyer: "Though the messianic expectation or hope was widespread among Jews in Palestine, it was not uniform in its conception or formulation and not universally held, even in the Diaspora." Fitzmyer, *One Who Is to Come*, 132.

3. Howard Marshall correctly describes Jesus' nuanced approach to any repetitive, thematic pronouncements of his own about his messiahship. Jesus pursues the active proof of this fact rather than merely the announcement of it: "What Jesus does is

The Baptist comes the closest in understanding Jesus to play the priestly messianic role as the Lamb of Isa 53:7–12. But even this was evidently wasted on all who heard John since there is no recorded acknowledgment of it until after the Passion. John deflected attention from himself to "the one" following him (John 1:29, 36). Others asserted or wondered about his Messiahship, including Andrew and Philip (John 1:41, 45, 49). The public was at least perplexed (John 7:25–27, 31, 41–42; 10:24; 12:34). Jesus did not feel it necessary to explicitly and publicly self-identify nor self-implicate as the Messiah; others did it for him.

THE CHRIST

Since "Messiah" was a designation commonly used by Jews and Samaritans as a title for the expected one, it was the title that became a designation for Jesus, an epithet of title.

> Simon Peter answered, "You are the Christ, the Son of the living God." (Matt 16:16)

> The woman said to Him, "I know that Messiah is coming (he is called Christ); when that one comes, he will declare all things to us." Jesus said to her, "I am Messiah, the one speaking to you." (John 4:25–26)

Subsequently, the apostles continued to use and even preferred the designation "Christ/Messiah" and its many compound constructs because of its breadth and richness. One encounters "the Messiah" in seventeen texts concerning Jesus in the Gospels.[4] As the Messiah, Jesus taught and exemplified what the Old Testament was unclear and "mysterious" about and what the intertestamental period did little to clarify. He is still proclaimed as "Jesus" in early Acts, but the preferred designation of "Messiah" becomes more prevalent as the book goes along. The apostles announced "the Christ" early in Acts, and "Christ" and its compounds eventually became the predominant designations for the post-ascension

---

announce the coming of the kingdom rather than his own coming as Messiah, but he speaks and acts with authority in such a way as to raise the question of who he is and what his role is in relation to the kingdom." Marshall, *Theology*, 79.

4. Leon Morris counts Luke's use of "Christ" in his two books: "[Luke] uses twelve times in his Gospel, and twenty-five times in Acts. Almost invariably he has the article with it: he refers to 'the Christ'—i.e., 'the Messiah'—and does not use 'Christ' as a proper name as does Paul." Morris, *New Testament Theology*, 162–63.

Jesus.[5] The apostolic designation in various permutations of Lord/Jesus/ Christ indicates a commitment to the fully orbed function of the Christ/ Messiah, and "the Lord" designation provides the divine context for the multifaceted messianic roles that Jesus filled.

The title "Christ" is often discounted to be only a common reference, as a name rather than a title in Acts and the letters. However, the apostles set out to prove that Jesus was more than his given name's etymology, savior. Their pronouncement that "Jesus was the Messiah" deliberately accentuated his title, not his name. Allegedly, at some point this became no longer a priority and "Christ" was used only as a name rather than an intentionally emphasized title. For example, Darrell Bock prioritizes the role of "Christ" as a name over any view of its weight as a title: "The term 'Christ' functions as a constant designation for Jesus, almost like a family name, whether it still retains its titular force or not."[6] Leonhard Goppelt is more grudging in accepting a significant titular force, concluding that Christ became a proper name "for the entire Hellenistic church" but that it "had become an epithet with the capacity to speak. The name Jesus was common, the epithet 'Christos' was unique. The latter retained a type of titular emphasis."[7] Donald Guthrie goes a little further in retaining an importance of the role of the title in designating Jesus in his ambivalent assertion: "We note first that 'Messiah' (Christ) in the epistles of Paul has now become a proper name. . . . But the forms 'Jesus Christ' or 'Christ Jesus' or 'Lord Jesus Christ' . . . show how basic the Christ concept was in the apostle's thought."[8] Craig Blomberg contends for the other pole of the discussion: "There is no unambiguous evidence to demonstrate that 'Christ' in any of its 531 New Testament uses ever 'degenerated' into a mere second name for Jesus."[9]

---

5. In the Epistles and Revelation, "Christ" is used alone nine times more than the use of "Jesus" alone. The compounds using "Christ" and/or "Jesus" occur ten times more than the use of "Jesus" alone. The pertinent permutations are Jesus Christ, Christ Jesus, Lord Jesus, Lord Jesus Christ, Jesus Christ . . . Lord, Christ Jesus . . . Lord, Jesus, and Christ. Gordon Fee provides a chart of these with their number of occurrences. *Pauline Christology*, 26–27.

6. Bock, "Messiah Confessed," 331. "Titular" might not be the best word here since in English vernacular it has a diminished, even denigrating meaning as only a token title.

7. Goppelt, *Theology of the New Testament*, 2:67. Comparably, Matera, *New Testament Theology*, 16. See Fee, *Pauline Christology*, 26.

8. Guthrie, *New Testament Theology*, 248.

9. Blomberg, "Messiah in the New Testament," 141. N. T. Wright's resistance to "Messiah" being reduced to a name as opposed to a deeper resonance as a title is

That Jesus was the Messiah was not only a profound thought that might have inspired some to consider Jesus to have the title "Messiah." Rather, it became a repetitive apostolic proclamation whenever "Messiah" was spoken or written. Luke's shorthand in Acts for the message of Peter and the apostles was that "Jesus was the Messiah" (5:42). This pronouncement also was a customary message for Paul in his journeys, for example in Damascus, Thessalonica, and Corinth (Acts 9:22; 17:1–3; 18:5; cf. 18:28 [Apollos]). It is unreasonable that such a central Old Testament messianic expectation and persistent New Testament talking point in the public ministry of the apostles would become in their letters just a second name with minimal if any significance as Jesus' title as the Messiah. Douglas Moo inadvertently voices the inconsistency of holding to the significance of the messianic commission while he marginalizes the force of the titled designation, Messiah:

> While "Christ" has lost any clear theological significance in Paul, calling Jesus "Christ" serves to remind early Christians, whether Jewish or gentile, that he is the fulfillment of the Old Testament expectation about an eschatological redeemer.[10]

Surely, something as important as "the fulfillment of the Old Testament expectation about an eschatological redeemer" would not have lost "any clear theological significance in Paul."

Furthermore, there is no perceivable transition from Paul's insistent, public oral contention that Jesus was "the Christos" to his alleged use of "Christos" primarily as a name in his letters. Paul's investment in the Corinthians was large, sending at least two lengthy letters and spending an extended time living with them (Acts 18:2–5). So, during Paul's journeys and simultaneous writings there is no evidence while using "Christos" (much less "*the* Christ") that he toggled between title and a mere name depending on whether it was his spoken or written assertion.

"Christ" is no more simply a name in the designation "Christ Jesus" than that of many Caesars. Though "Caesar" was initially a family name, it became a title of political supremacy, even divinity. "Christos," like the title "Caesar," was a designation too loaded to be reduced to the function

---

welcomed. However, if the reason is found only in the Messiah's kingship and its union with the people of God, then the reason may be just a start. The title denotes a much wider messianic commission than a royal role. Wright, *Climax*, 41–55.

10. Moo, *Theology of Paul and His Letters*, 366.

of merely a name in utterance and hearing.[11] Paul's appeal to Caesar was not a diminutive appeal to simply the ruler's last name—it was an appeal to the most supreme position.

Moreover, "Christ" is no more simply a name in Paul's letters in the designation "Christ Jesus" (around eighty times) than does the title "Lord" become only another name for Jesus in the designation "Lord Jesus" (nearly twenty times) or "Lord" in "Lord Jesus Christ" (nearly fifty times). Obviously, "Lord" as a title was much more than a generic term for "master." So, as in its compound terminology with "Lord" and used as an obvious title, "Christ" should be understood to retain the same title role as that of "Lord." Plainly, "Christ" as a title in these compound designations is replete in the Epistles, reaffirming the apostles' public pronouncements that "Jesus is the Messiah." The anticipated divinity of the "coming one" does more to qualify the identity of Jesus than his birth name, and "Messiah" covers more ground as the full meaning of the Incarnation in the way the common name "Jesus" does not. The apostles recognized this and were careful and persistent to couch "Jesus" in this fuller messianic picture by their many compound phrases involving "Christ." The preeminence of the Incarnate's messiahship is accentuated by the apostles' preference for referring to him with the uncompounded name "Jesus," which totals only ten times in their letters combined[12] compared with over two hundred uses of the uncompounded "Christ."

Given the heft that the term "Messiah" had amassed by the time of and during the Incarnation, it is difficult to imagine that the verve of the apostles about Jesus' main identity would marginalize the title to a byword that carried only an equivalent value as his common name, "Jesus."[13] One cannot say that an anarthrous "Christos" should be translated as "*the* Messiah," but it should be said that it does not only connote but denotes the promised divine who would fulfill many messianic functions. Rather than assuming a discontinuity with the early apostolic emphatic pronouncement that Jesus was the Christ, a continuity in that emphasis should be acknowledged, especially since the most common

---

11. Though Caesar was originally a family name that became a title for some Roman emperors, the inverse does not apply to Christ. Incidentally, even "name" in the New Testament milieu can carry with it the connotation of authority: "in the name of..."

12. Not including Hebrews.

13. "For Paul a cognomen that can have titular overtones." Schnelle, *Theology of the New Testament*, 153.

element within the apostolic designations for Jesus is "Christos," reaffirming the centrality of Jesus' identity as the "Messiah." One should not be tempted to see "Christ" as a last name that nears becoming only a habit. There is no reason that New Testament believers would not have been comfortable meaning literally "Jesus Messiah" when voicing the Greek translation "Jesus Christ" just because of it feeling clumsy for today's English-speaking believers to refer to him as "Jesus Messiah" rather than Jesus Christ.

JESUS' FOUR EXPLICIT MESSIANIC GOALS

Jesus mentioned three of his commissioned purposes. A couple of these are found within his interrogation by Pilate: "You are correct that I am a king. It is why I was born and have entered the world—to testify of the truth" (John 18:37). The Second Person came in the flesh (1) to reign as king and (2) to speak prophetically to that truth. Jesus had said the same thing earlier in Luke 4:43: "I must proclaim the kingdom of God . . . since I was sent for this purpose" (cf. Mark 1:38). It was the public accusation and very charge for Christ's execution that he claimed that he was a king (Luke 23:2; John 19:12). (3) Also, Jesus said the purpose for his life was his Passion: "What shall I say, 'Father, save me from this hour'? No, it was for this exact reason I came to this hour" (John 12:27).

A fourth purpose for the Incarnation is found again in John, his first letter: "The Son of God appeared for this purpose, to destroy the devil's work" (3:8; Heb 2:14, 17)—something seen dramatically as his ministry progressed from Satan's wilderness defeat to the numerous exorcisms along the way until his final defeat at Armageddon. But this destruction was demonstrated with a more far-reaching purpose: "God's purpose in all this was to use the church to display his wisdom in its rich variety to all the unseen rulers and authorities in the heavenly places. This was his eternal purpose, which he carried out through Christ Jesus our Lord" (Eph 3:10–11). God's eternal purpose eclipses his redemptive purpose since the latter is only the means to the former. His rich wisdom includes but is not limited to his salvation history.

Certainly, other goals for the Incarnation are inferred in the New Testament. For instance, and most generally, the Incarnation revealed in real time and space what God's nature is and what should be the renewed sanctified nature of the believer. Jesus was the physical manifestation of

God's attributes, as far as Jesus' human nature allowed. Furthermore, he lived the sanctified life of wisdom, righteousness, love, and all the fruits of the Spirit as the model of a sanctified life: "Imitate God!" (Eph 5:1).

CONFLUENCE OF MESSIANIC FUNCTIONS

This Messiah, "the anointed," was prophesied to be a king and a high priest, the two offices that required anointing in the Old Testament (Ps 110:1–4; Zech 6:12–13). So, it is incorrect that "the Messiah" means "the anointed king." The messianic commission is richer than reigning and dying/rising, and this breadth of the Messiah's responsibilities is the subject of this chapter. The New Testament emphasis on "the Christ" sets a precedent for the New Testament to accentuate Jesus' holistic incarnational purposes in addition to coming as king.

By messianic "expectations," God's expectations and commission are meant, not those of intertestamental or New Testament Judaism. No one would have envisioned the Messiah to have the exact collection of the following messianic functions. Nonetheless, an Old Testament profile of God's expectations of the Messiah could be said to have three ontological expectations (divine, human, righteous) and at least six functional expectations (king, priest, prophet, judge, and national and personal deliverer). The functional roles are familiar from Israel's civic history, as they were performed by official and unofficial leaders. These were not all uniquely defined functions; some overlapped in significant ways, which was common for kings of the surrounding nations as well, like Melchizedek.

It is tempting to include another Old Testament social "position" in this amalgam of messianic precursors—the sage. There were those in Israel who were engaged in the acquisition and collection of national and international wisdom, yet there is inadequate proof and descriptions of any formal court or otherwise commissioned sage position. Collectors of wisdom and their collections are mentioned in Prov 25:1, 31:1, and Eccl 12:9–12, but a substantial wisdom establishment is at best a shadow compared to the explicit definitions of positions such as kings, priests, prophets, elders, and generals. Nonetheless, attributing Jesus' supremacy to previous holders of these societal roles was a way of claiming he also held at least the essence of those roles. So, Jesus was greater than the prophets

Jonah (Matt 12:41), the Baptist (John 1:30), and a high priest (Matt 12:6), and to our point, greater than the sage Solomon (Matt 12:42).[14]

This overlap among the various civil responsibilities of the king, priest, prophet, elder/judge, and geopolitical deliverer defines responsibilities of the Messiah—he assumes the role of all five administrative functions which could also intersect with one another. For instance, as king, David took responsibility for certain *cultic* functions (2 Sam 6:13–18 // 1 Chr 15:27; 2 Sam 24:25 // 1 Chr 21:28), and his descendants were even referred to as "priests" (2 Sam 8:18). David also served as a *judge* at a higher level than the local/regional judges/elders (2 Sam 15:2–6). David and Solomon were *prophets*, at least by their revelatory composition of psalms. Israel's desire for a military king as an adversity *deliverer* was a main reason for their demand for a monarchy.

This functional confluence involved other leadership roles as well. Priests had cultic responsibilities in addition to instructional and hortatorical duties pertaining to the law's ethical and legal teaching (Lev 10:8–11; Deut 24:8; 27:14–26; 31:9–12; 33:8–10; Ezek 44:15, 23; Hos 4:1–6; Mal 2:4–8). Priests were God's *spokesmen* on various occasions with blessings and encouragements (Num 6:22–26; Deut 20:1–4).[15] They also served as *judges* alongside the judging elders (Num 5:29–31; Deut 17:8–12; 19:15–19; 21:1–5; 2 Chr 19:8–10; Ezek 44:15, 24).

Prophets often were not "official" but were chosen by the Lord directly from various backgrounds. They interpreted, applied, defended, and proclaimed the law's ethical teaching, as did the priests. Prophets supported the law as it was supposed to have been taught. As God's spokesmen, however, they not only excoriated sinners (particularly the religious leaders) and warned of impending doom, but they, like the priests, spoke the Lord's blessings and encouragements to the people.

Before the monarchy, elders/judges were the secular administrative leaders within Israel's society, responsible for every non-cultic operation. At that time, by default, they were responsible for Israel: her legal, political, economic, as well as foreign relations, including when war was

---

14. For a position presenting a more formal description of sages, see Brueggemann, *Theology of the Old Testament*, 680–85.

15. Goldingay mentions the overlapping of the priests and prophets in some roles, e.g., declaring and teaching God's instructions, common sanctuary participations, and Levites who prophesied: "The roles of priest and prophet could therefore be hard to distinguish." Goldingay, *Old Testament Theology*, 3:752. More specifically, Walther Zimmerli points to the priests' occasional reception of oracular revelation similar to that of the prophets. Zimmerli, *Old Testament Theology*, 96, 102, 104.

required. During the monarchy they continued more of their legal functions but under the hegemony of the throne.

These societal functions were magnified in the Incarnation beyond their routine purposes in Israel since they would continue as global messianic roles for millennia, with far greater reach, power, righteousness, justice, and effectiveness. Furthermore, the messianic roles are not mutually exclusive, so a composite of roles might not have been a startling concept for those awaiting a messiah or for those who witnessed his words and works. The Messiah, therefore, personifies the totality of Israelite leadership in these cumulative, harmonious, overlapping, and integrated roles. Neither king, nor any one role, or summation of two or three roles are comprehensive enough to contain all that God considered necessary for a coming messiah's optimum shepherding of humanity. Similar to the Persons' different functions, communities have multiple leadership positions to operate them. In this sense, they are parallel to Christ's one body, the church, which is empowered by the various functions of the spiritual gifts.

In fact, cultures across the globe are inclined toward a similar construction to attempt a functioning society: king, priest, prophet, sages, judges, and various deliverers. These more or less official structures reflect a common grace from the Creator to the terrestrial kingdom's various civilizations. Over the millennia, all cultures have developed with these common features of social management. So the Messiah came to replace the failed Couple in their management of creation, and he did so by personifying and balancing all leadership roles that are necessary for godly shepherding of a worldwide community. In this sense, none of the leadership roles in Israel are types of Christ. Rather, Christ is himself a "type" of most cultures worldwide. Their societal structures share very similar roles to those of priest, prophet, king, general, elder, judge, and sage.

Lastly, these messianic functions are not to be reduced in number nor prioritized as if one role is more important than the others. Given their overlapping and mostly integrated relationships, to emphasize one of these messianic roles is at the expense of the others. Each of them contributes equally to the Messiah's commission. A biblical theology might be simplified if it accentuates one over the others and misses the comprehensive integrated glory of the Incarnation. It is marginally better to limit the Messiah's commission to a traditional *musus triplex* (prophet, priest, king) since these are not the only offices he filled, and prophets were not anointed anyway. Christ fulfilled these three and more official functions.

A frequent deficiency in Messiah theology is the popular reductionist principle that central to messianism are the roles of sin salvation and/or the eschatological king. However, the New Testament pronouncement that "Jesus is the Messiah" is more complex than this, as the following survey demonstrates. Again, the first three expectations are ontological; the remaining roles are functional.

DIVINE

The Old Testament's ontological expectations of the Messiah were that he be divine, yet human, yet a perfectly righteous human. These attributes conflate mysteriously, evading human imagination and comprehension. An incarnation in the first place and then a human void of original sin defy logic, yet it is the clear teaching of the Testaments.

There are numerous passages that affirm Jesus' deity. For instance, that the Messiah would be divine is revealed by Isa 9:6, where one of his designations is "Mighty God." Paul writes in Col 2:9 that within Christ's humanity, the fullness of divinity is contained: "The complete fullness of God lives in bodily form." Thomas was turned from a doubter of Jesus to a worshiper of Jesus as God (John 20:28). John the Baptist repeats Mic 5 about the Messiah's preexistence: "He existed before me" (John 1:15), and Christ himself said, "Before Abraham, I am" (John 8:58). Christ's preexistence implies his involvement in the creation of the world, a fact that John the apostle felt significant enough to serve as the introduction to his Gospel and that Paul paraphrases: "Everything has been created through him and for him" (Col 1:16), and even more directly, "the Messiah, who is God over all, praised forever" (Rom 9:5). Hebrews 1:8 converts a generic "God" passage (Ps 45:6–7) to be about the Son: "Of the Son it is said, 'Oh God, your throne is forever and ever.'"

Jesus' bold and unambiguous self-acclamation not only pronounced God as his Father[16] but accepted the name "Son of God" several times, e.g., from demons (Mark 3:11), the disciples (Matt 14:33), Martha (Luke 11:27), and a centurion (Matt 27:54). By accepting this divine

---

16. John's Gospel reflects Jesus' balance in his comments about divinity. He preferred to identify and equate himself as God in terms of his personal relationship with the Father rather than politically and prematurely declaring that he was God or even a king. He was one with the Father (John 10:30). More than patriarchal position, it was a relationship of love (John 17:24). This is a significant theme of John's and perhaps why he limits most of his "kingdom" content to the later Passion context.

designation, Jesus incites Caiaphas to charge him with blasphemy (Matt 26:63-65). Jesus himself argues deftly from Ps 110:1 that he was David's Lord, thus God (Mark 12:35-37; Matt 22:41-45).

"Lord" is also a title for Jesus—a title that could designate any master, including God himself. The transition from an honoring salutation for the man Jesus as *a* lord to a submissive deference to his divinity as *the* Lord God lies on a continuum that would be hard to chart. Nonetheless, its frequent equation with Yahweh is eventually proven in many cases.[17]

HUMAN

Christ came as fully human; he ate, slept, felt, suffered, and was tempted, but he was born sinless and lived sinlessly. As the Good Shepherd he perfectly obeyed the Father and gave up his life yet began a new *human* reign that would succeed in the primary commission that God had given to Adam and Eve: to bless, to tame, even to subdue his good but wild earth. He was commissioned then to come and exemplify flawless blessing, deliverance, and discipline of humanity and the natural kingdom.[18] Priest, king, prophet, judge, and deliverer were official human roles, not angelic or beastly roles. These roles are found pervasively in religions and are general revelation's testimony to the necessity of human agency. It was necessary for him to arrive as a human so he could accomplish what no human had done successfully before.

Micah predicted the divine Messiah would be born to be a *human* shepherd (5:2). The "Father/Son" terminology is anthropomorphic, reflecting the Middle Eastern political, cultural, and theological

---

17. Fitzmyer recognizes the coregency revealed in the use of "Lord." The messianic implications of this Lord's world dominion parallel that of the title "Son of God." "The frequency of Paul's use of *Kyrios* for Christ is remarkable, in comparison with his use of the title 'son of God,' and reveals that *Kyrios* is the title par excellence for Jesus in the Pauline writings. . . . The titles Father and Son, being relational words, suggest distinction and even subordination. But *Kyrios* ascribes to both Yahweh and Jesus a dominion over creation and a right to the adoration of all creation." Fitzmyer, *Pauline Theology*, 34, 37. Christopher J. H. Wright concludes that for any Greek-speaking Jew of the first century, "it was second nature to read *ho kyrios* and think 'the Name,' YHWH." Wright, *Mission of God*, 108.

18. Wayne Grudem lists seven reasons why God's Incarnation was the preferred intervention: representative obedience, substitutionary sacrifice, mediation between God and humanity, human rule over creation, exemplary living, a pattern for our redeemed bodies, and providing a sympathizing high priest. Grudem, *Systematic Theology*, 540-42.

vocabulary. But the unique obstetrical genesis of the God/man cannot be ignored either. The Messiah would be formed in the womb (Isa 49:5–6) as a man-child (Isa 9:6; Mic 5:3). Born by the Holy Spirit and Mary, the Messiah was literally God's only "begotten Son."[19] The Messiah was twice over the "image of God": as a human descendent of Mary thus carrying the image of God, and as God, the Second Person.

Daniel identified the Messiah to be "like a man's son" (7:13–14), and Jesus adopts "Son of Man" as a self-designation, identifying himself with the commissioned divine Messiah. Complementing the humanity of the Messiah as a son of David is the more generic and universal line of descent from the human race, accentuated by his genealogies (Matt 1:2–16; Luke 3:23–38). By referring to himself as the Son of Man, the entire council of elders condemned him because of the inference of divinity. He knew what he was saying. In fact, Luke 22:66–71 measured the designations "the Messiah, Son of God, and Son of Man" as equally blasphemous.[20] Even the common Jew equated the Son of Man to the eternal Messiah: "We have heard from the Law that the Christ remains into the αἰών. Why do you say that the Son of Man must be lifted up?" (John 12:34). For this reason, we take the nearly ninety New Testament references to Jesus as the Son of Man to designate the role of the Messiah's regal reign and realm. Otherwise, the Messiah chose repeatedly to use what would be a misleading allusion to himself from an obvious messianic text. On the other hand, this rich and multifaceted self-designation also fits in with Jesus' intentionally obscure and evasive statements that would baldly self-identify as deity. It was a not-so-secret code.

But he would also be the required *human* sacrifice for the rebellion of the human race. Hebrews summarizes the role Jesus had to play as a man on behalf of humanity's failure in shepherding Eden and the rest of the world.

---

19. The profound explanations of the "begotten" as a designation of privilege should be balanced with the plain fact of the human and divine contributions to Jesus' embryonic state.

20. "The mysterious heavenly figure of Dan 7:13–14 is the closest Hebrew Scripture came to a revelation of the heavenly origin and divine nature of the eschatological Messiah.... He is of heavenly origin, yet he looks human." Bock, "Messianic Trajectories," 188. Many find it difficult to connect the dots of the son of (a) man in Dan 7:13–14 and Jesus' frequent self-designation as the "Son of Man." See Guthrie, *New Testament Theology*, 270–29, for an outline of the optional interpretations. John seems to connect the dots in Rev 1:13; 14:14.

> We see him who was made for a little while lower than the angels, Jesus, because of his suffering death he is crowned with glory and honor; so by God's grace he tasted death for everyone. (Heb 2:9)

The Son has always owned the cosmos with the Father and the Spirit. But in a new arrangement in history, Jesus owned the earth as the *human* shepherding king. The titles Son of Man and Son of God explain Christ's Incarnation perfectly, ensuring success this time for each of his words and acts since they are human and divine. Significantly, a man did not become God; rather, God became man (Phil 2:7–8).

RIGHTEOUS

God's Nature

A third ontological expectation of the Messiah, that is, an attribute of his nature, was his moral perfection, honored by his epithets the Righteous One and the Holy One. Being righteous is an attribute among many others in the more holistic designation of the divine as "holy." This moral expectation was certain to be true of the Messiah, since even with a human nature he was the incarnate God. Jesus was necessarily righteous in spite of his human composition, so his moral perfection was commendable and exemplary but obviously inevitable. So, one need not prove his sinlessness only inductively; it can be assumed deductively. Yes, he was tempted, but he was unable to sin. He felt the tension but could not bend (Heb 4:14). God had ensured there would not be a second Adamic failure.

Isaiah first speaks of the Lord's glory as the Righteous One (Isa 24:16; 40:25), then applies the same honor to the justifying, suffering, serving Messiah (Isa 53:11). Peter, Stephen, and Paul each refer to Jesus as the Righteous One (Acts 3:14; 7:52; 22:14). Peter had confessed earlier that he and other disciples knew that Jesus was the Holy One of God, which was confirmed even by the satanic realm (John 6:69; Luke 4:34). Again, Peter referred to Jesus as the Holy One and in prayer with the apostles referenced him as God's anointed holy servant (Acts 4:27, 30). Paul's commentary echoes Isa 53:11: "On our behalf he made him to be sin who knew no sin, so that in him we might become the righteousness of God" (2 Cor 5:21). The anointed Holy One in turn anoints the believer (1 John 2:20).

Righteousness Predicted

Isaiah predicts that the Messiah's reign and the peace that it would bring would only expand globally and eternally into the era of New Earth (9:7). He would be empowered with the gifts and fruit of the Spirit. He would be given the gifts of wisdom, understanding, knowledge, fairness, honesty, and kindness.[21] Given these gifts, he would shepherd righteously, revering and obeying his Lord and Father.[22] He would persevere in this righteous obedience, even to the point of humiliation and death.[23] The righteousness and humility of Zechariah's servant Messiah would accomplish the peace brought into the world through his salvation from sin and from the horrendous results of the Eden rebellion (9:9-10). Jesus is the completely sanctified one, the lone human to be utterly separate and pure, and his ethical behavior matched his ethical teaching. He perfectly observed and modeled all his words and works since he was incapable of hypocrisy.

Jeremiah assumed that the Messiah would love righteousness and justice to the extent that "his name would be 'The Lord is Our Righteousness'" (33:15-16; also 23:5). By this name alone, Jeremiah affirmed Isaiah's good news of the righteous, serving Messiah's substitutionary righteousness and death (Isa 53:11; Heb 2:14-15). Furthermore, the Son of God and Son of Man, the righteous and holy Messiah, would shepherd his people through endless blessings, deliverances, and judgments. Jeremiah blasts the leaders of Israel as "shepherds who destroy and scatter the sheep of my pasture . . . and who have not cared for them" (Jer 23:1-2). But the Lord promised to remove their abuse so his people could again "be fruitful and multiply," the very words of the primary commission. The solution will come through his righteous Messiah king who would bring peace and quiet to his sheep as the Good Shepherd (Jer 23:3, 5-6; John 10:11), bringing deliverance for the poor and oppressed.[24]

> O Bethlehem . . . a ruler will come from you who will shepherd my people, Israel. (Matt 2:6)

---

21. Isa 11:2; 11:4; 53:9; Jer 23:6; 33:15-16; 1 Cor 12:8.
22. Isa 11:2-3, 5; 50:5.
23. Isa 42:3-4; 50:5-7; 53:7-9.
24. Ps 72:2-4, 12-14; Isa 11:4; 61:1, 2.

> When he saw the crowds, he had compassion for them, because they were harassed and helpless, like sheep without a shepherd. (Matt 9:36)

God shepherds his shepherding people.

Submission to God

The Messiah's experiences are frequently phrased by passive syntax, indicating his humble acquiescence to God's formidable commission for him. Yet his submission was deliberate, profound, unremitting, and born of the infinite love and humble collaboration within the Trinity. It is the servicing synergy of the First Person with the Second and Third Persons, the synergy of God and his human servant. In many capacities he was the passive recipient of his Father's and others' actions. For example, he would be made king;[25] he would be made victorious (Ps 110:1-2) and be given attentive ears and an enlightened tongue (Isa 50:4-5). He would be appointed (Mic 5:4), supported,[26] prospered (Isa 53:10), honored (Isa 49:5, 7; 53:12), announced (Isa 42:1), presented (Dan 7:13), anointed with the Spirit (Isa 11:1), made wise (42:1), and told to sit at God's right hand (Ps 110:1, 5).[27] Though he could have called a myriad of angels to defend him, he deferred and was struck, spat upon, crushed, afflicted, forsaken, grieved, humiliated, falsely accused, and assigned a grave and buried. In no Old Testament passage does the Messiah refuse, object, or offer any alternative to the assignments God gave him; rather, he humbly submitted to his Father's anointing and commissioning.

> I love the Father so I do exactly what my Father has commanded me. (John 14:31)

> Jesus, the apostle and High Priest was faithful to the one who appointed him, just as Moses was faithful in all God's house. (Heb 3:1-2)

The most pervasive and frequent Old Testament projection about the Messiah is his role as God's willing servant. Micah makes it clear that

---

25. Pss 2:6; 110:2; Isa 9:7; Jer 23:5; 30:8-9; 33:15; Ezek 21:25-27; 34:23-24; 37:24-25; Dan 7:14; Mic 5:2; Zech 6:11, 13.

26. Isa 42:1, 6; 49:5, 7; 50:7-8a, 9; Mic 5:4.

27. Also Ps 110:1; Luke 22:69; Acts 7:55-56; Eph 1:20; Col 3:1; Heb 1:3, 13; 8:1; 10:12-13; 12:2; 1 Pet 3:21-22.

the Messiah would come on behalf of God, "for God" (5:2), by whose initiative, strength, and authority the Messiah would accomplish his commission *for* "the Lord his God" (5:4). Jesus reaffirms this structure in John 17:4 when reviewing his success in his messianic commission: "I have glorified you on the earth by completing the work you gave me to do." Jesus' human nature had to acknowledge God as "my God" (Matt 27:46; John 20:17; Rev 3:12), so it is appropriate that he would say "the Father is greater than I am" (John 6:38; 14:28; 17:4).[28] The Messiah's faithfulness to God is clear in Isaiah: "The Lord God has opened my ear, and I was not rebellious" (Isa 50:5), and his commitment to God was consistent from a teenager to the eve of his execution just as Isaiah's "Servant Songs" predicted (42:1–4; 49:1–6; 50:4–9; 52–53; Luke 2:49; 22:42). Peter and others referred to Jesus as God's "anointed" servant (Acts 3:13, 26; 4:27, 30). Matthew highlights the humble servant heart of the Messiah by quoting Isaiah's predictions (Matt 12:15–21; Isa 42:1–4). Jesus reaffirms repeatedly that he does nothing on his own, only what his Father required. For Jesus, *God* is "the great king" and "Lord of heaven and earth" (Matt 5:35; 11:25). The reason for Jesus' exaltation was his humble nature to comply with God's every command, to suffer thirty years within the fallen world, to tolerate the perpetual disrespect during his three-year ministry "until" (μέχρι) his death, even on a cross (Phil 2:8–11).

PRIEST

Besides the Messiah's anointed royalty, he was commissioned with another anointed position, the high priest, making the Messiah anointed twice over. This Judahite high priest would be like Melchizedek, a king and a non-Levitic priest (Ps 110:4; Gen 14:18–20; Heb 7:11). The doubly anointed Messiah is also anticipated by Zechariah, who realigns the tribal lineage of this prophesied high priest from the Levitic line to the Messiah's Judahite lineage as the Branch of David and Judah.[29]

> A man named Branch will "branch out" from where he is; and he will build the temple of the Lord. Yes, he will build the temple of the Lord, and he will receive majesty and sit and rule on his

---

28. John 6:38; 14:28; 17:4.

29. Hasmoneans' royal priesthoods were intended to be temporary, not a permanent attempt to correspond with any messianic prophecy. Bock, "Messiah Confessed," 353.

throne. So, he will be a priest on his throne, and there will be peace between the two offices. (Zech 6:12–13)

The Jews may have been looking primarily for an immediate national political king, but instead they were provided an immediate teaching and self-sacrificing priest.

Teaching Priest

Old Testament priests were the official teachers of the law, so teaching would be expected from the royal and priestly Messiah as well: "The lips of a priest must guard knowledge, and the people should look forward to his mouth's instruction, for he is the messenger of the Lord of hosts" (Mal 2:7; also, Lev 10:8–11; Deut 33:10).[30] The Old Testament priesthood facilitated reconciliatory sacrifices for a sincere nation and its individual sincere citizen, yet the same priesthood taught and interpreted the law. The priest's role was not simply a reconciler of the believer *via* the sacerdotal system; he was the believer's discipler for sanctification. Ezra was an exemplary priest: "Ezra had set his heart on studying the Law of the Lord, to do it and to teach his statutes and rules to Israel" (Ezra 7:10; also, Neh 8:1–3). Yet, just as all types of social leaders of Israel were guilty of dereliction of duty far too often in her history, the priests also failed in their teaching (Jer 2:26–28; 8:1–2; Zeph 1:4; Ezek 22:26; Zeph 3:4; Mal 2:8).[31]

An unfortunate omission from biblical theological approaches to Christ's priestly role is this teaching role of the priest.[32] A fixation with the last portion of each Gospel leads one to believe that the first portion, which highlights Jesus' teachings, is only secondary. This can become a foundation for justification-centered theologies as opposed to a fuller theology that emphasizes sanctification. As the high priest, he taught the

---

30. Also Deut 24:8; 27:14–26; 31:9–12; 33:8–10; 2 Chr 17:7–9; Ezek 44:23; Hos 4:1–6; Hag 2:11–13.

31. "Israel's very spiritual leaders tripped them up spiritually. Instead of having true teaching in their mouths and thus turning many people from waywardness, they have made many people fall through their teaching (Mal 3:8)." Goldingay, *Old Testament Theology*, 3:753.

32. T. Desmond Alexander's theological approach to the priesthood of Christ is helpful in its soteriological focus, yet it lacks the critical teaching and interpretive role that was archetypal for the Old Testament priesthood. Alexander, *Face to Face*. For details on the theological impact from Jesus' parables and designations on his priestly profile, see Perrin, *Jesus as Priest*. However, one might find several lines drawn between texts to be quite faint.

laws of his kingdom, the ethical standards for following creation's intended design. Ironically, he himself was the necessary sacrifice for those who trust him and repent of their non-compliance to his standards.

Jesus fulfilled this teaching requirement as a priest but not as a Levite, instead as "rabbi" and "teacher." He reaffirmed the teaching of the law[33] and gave his own additional instructions by his exhorting, convicting, blessing, and encouragements.[34] A thorough description of his teaching in this priestly role would end in simply reciting a large portion of the Gospels' content. However, a few examples of Old Testament law that are continued under the Messiah's teaching include the following.

- Adultery   Exod 20:14; Matt 5:27–28
- Prostitution   Lev 19:29; Luke 15:29–30
- Gluttony   Deut 21:20; Matt 11:19
- Drunkenness   Deut 21:20; Luke 12:45–46
- Impartial courts Exod 23:6; Matt 23:23
- False testimony   Exod 20:16; Matt 15:19
- Care for widows   Exod 22:22–24; Mark 12:38–40
- Care for disabled Lev 19:14; Matt 4:24
- Care for the poor Deut 15:7, 11; Luke 14:13
- Withholding wages Lev 19:13; Matt 20:8–9
- Lending   Exod 22:25–26; Matt 5:42
- Respect parents   Lev 19:3; Matt 15:4–6
- Love neighbors   Lev 19:18; Mark 12:31
- Divorce   Exod 21:10–11; Matt 5:31–32
- Coveting   Exod 20:17; Mark 7:21–22

33. John Bright understands the ethical unity of the Testaments: "For if anything is clear, it is that Christ did not come to contribute a new ethic. There has never been a higher ethic than his, yet it was essentially the ethic of Judaism. . . . Nevertheless, if compared point by point, the ethical teaching of Jesus find their parallels in Judaism and in the faith of ancient Israel . . . he simply did not come to teach Judaism a higher ethic and to understand the New Testament in that light is fundamentally to misunderstand it." Bright, *Kingdom of God*, 194, 195.

34. Possibly due to the hegemony of Pauline theology over that of Jesus' theology, Jesus' obligation to be a law teacher as an anointed priest is surprisingly a relatively underdeveloped subject.

- Murder   Lev 24:17; Mark 7:21
- Stealing   Exod 20:15; Luke 3:14
- Royal privilege   Deut 17:14–20; Matt 23:25–35

Pharisees, scribes, the crowds, common individuals, his disciples, and Jesus himself called Jesus a "teacher" in over forty Gospel accounts. It is clear that Jesus struck the people as an amazing authoritative teacher, one who intimidated the religious leaders as a skilled and dangerous rhetorician, one who modeled un-hypocritically whatever he taught, and the one who demanded obedience to his own divine commandments. The apostles highlighted the teaching of Jesus in various texts, at times quoting him, other times referring to his teaching; for example:

> Fathers, do not irritate your children to anger; bring them up by the Lord's discipline and instruction. (Eph 6:4)

> Anyone who drifts too far and does not remain in Christ's teaching does not have God. (2 John 9)

Jesus avoided extensive reaffirmations of the current ceremonial law, specifically. He was also aware of the obsession that the ceremonial law could become at the expense of the moral law, a concern of Old Testament prophets and the Jerusalem council (Acts 15:10, 19–21). Old Testament teaching prioritized "moral" over "ceremonial," e.g., Ps 51:16–17; Mic 6:7–8, and Jesus, the High Priest, repeated the sentiment: "If you had known the meaning of, 'I desire mercy, and not sacrifice,' you would not have condemned the innocent" (Matt 12:7; also 5:23–25; 12:11–12; Mark 2:25–28).[35]

Christ corrected the "scribes and Pharisees" and their abuses of the old order before his Passion redefined the new sacerdotal order. For example, heartless interpretations of Sabbath laws that were traditions rather than revealed law supposedly disallowed his several Sabbath healings, e.g., Mark 3:1–6. Just picking one's snack was considered "work" (Luke 6:1–2). These teachers of the law were incapable of discerning the relative weight of some laws over others (Matt 23:23). The dedication of funds to a generous God was presumed by religious leaders to be non-retractable, even to save one's parents from serious adversity (Mark

---

35. Bright writes about Jesus' sparse teaching on the ceremonial law: "[His] moral demands are stated quite without that mass of ceremonial regulations upon which Judaism laid such stress." Bright, *Kingdom of God*, 194. Jesus commanded that his messiahship was to be kept quiet (Mark 8:29–31).

7:10–12). These were not exceptional practices: "You negate the word of God by your tradition that you have handed down. And you do many things like this" (Mark 7:13). A mode of Jesus teaching in his Sermon on the Mount was interpretation of the law, explaining its application in ways some would not have understood it, particularly in Matt 5:17–48, where his rhetorical structure goes, "You have heard it said . . . but I say to you . . . ." This interpretive approach touches on the subjects of murder, adultery, divorce, vows, and retribution.

The Great Commission is introduced by Jesus' claim to have received the universal kingdom as his royal realm (Matt 28:18). He then followed this with his high priestly commission to his priestly disciples to teach all of his royal decrees, his sanctifying law, his commandments to the world. As a passage, it reflects his dual anointing as a commanding king and as a priest who gives and interprets his own law.

Judging Priest

At least occasionally in the Old Testament adjudication overlapped between priests and judges when applying the law to everyday life.[36] Other texts seem to cloud the matter on which priests were the judges (Deut 17:8–10; 19:17; 21:5; Ezek 44:24).[37] It would be expected that the role of the priest in teaching and interpreting the law might require their presence in the court to guide the elders in their decisions, if not participate in the judicial proceedings even more directly. Jesus obviously was not an official Jewish judge, and he sat on no judgment seat within any city gate, so he explicitly deferred his own role in formal judiciary proceedings to the final judgment (John 3:17),[38] where his final judgments will be soothing for some, severe for others.

---

36. A tribunal evidently consisted of judges and priests apparently when a case was adjudicated at a sanctuary, when priests were of course hosts and participants. These passages reflect "difficult cases," not necessarily every case. Furthermore, the priests maintain the consistency of legal *interpretation* as the teachers of the Old Testament law. These three passages do not clarify the precise role of the priests with the judges but do show their significant role in the judicial process.

37. Also Num 5:29–30; Deut 19:15–19; 21:1–5; 2 Chr 19:8.

38. Regardless of whether John 8:1–8 is considered authoritative tradition, the scenario is not relevant since Jesus was not engaging a judicial setting; it was a test of Jesus, not a quest for justice.

Ceremonial Priest

The Incarnation was already a major change from the Old Testament law since Christ, the new, eternal high priest was a descendent of Judah and David, not Aaron. The Messiah starts a new legal and ceremonial arrangement that replaced the ceremonial arrangements in the Old Testament.[39] His new cultic order replaced the sacrifices, feasts, and holidays, role of the temple, and the many positions reserved for the Levites: "When these things are forgiven, an offering for sin is not required" (Heb 4:18). Now, since his coming, Christ was greater than the temple and the Sabbath because his position as the high priest replaced those older formalities.[40] Where the high priest stood in God's presence in an earthly temple building, now Christ sits as high priest at the right hand of the Father (Heb 9:24; Rom 8:34; Eph 1:20; Col 3:1). This is a better arrangement than the older one, though the older one was God's perfect plan for those times. The ease with which he could and did raise up a new "temple" discounted the physical structure in lieu of himself (John 2:19–22). Zechariah confirms the identification of the Messiah as one who will "rule as *king* from his throne and will serve as *priest* from his throne with harmony between the two roles" (Zech 6:12–13).

Jesus' words about his anointed, priestly function are infrequent; perhaps it would have been too inflammatory to be a constant theme. Jesus' command to keep his messiahship quiet (Mark 8:29–31) was not only because he was the anointed king but because he was also the anointed priest; a High Priest that descended from Judah would be an irritating threat to Judaism's Aaronic dynasty. Touching on sacerdotal law any more than Jesus did may have accelerated his coming Passion; it would raise the topic of his own substitutionary atonement, something he kept to himself except for only vague allusions. Prophetic and instructional pronouncements about non-cultic laws were less intimidating.

A new priesthood under Christ was a blessing for all the nations because now the flood of gentiles entering the kingdom of God could come without the burden of the complicated ceremonial expectations, which Peter thought to be burdensome even for him and all Jews (Acts 15:10). Since the new high priest was not a descendant of Aaron, a foundational stone of the ceremonial laws was removed, and the Old Testament religious structure toppled: "When the priesthood changes, the law must be

---

39. Heb 12:24; also 7:22–24; 8:4–6.
40. Matt 12:6–8 // Mark 2:28 // Luke 6:5.

changed . . . since obviously our Lord descended from Judah" (Heb 7:12, 14). This radical change in the ecclesio-political structure of God's royal priesthood led Paul to a sarcastic moment while under his abusive court inquisition, which included a rebuke for disrespecting Ananias, "the high priest and ruler of Israel." Paul's cheeky reply to the accusation implied in the most profound way that because of the Messiah's royal priesthood Ananias could no longer claim to be the high priest nor ruler of Israel: "Brothers, I did not know that *he* was the high priest" (Acts 23:4–5).

Jeremiah reaffirmed the priesthood of this future king from the tribe of Judah by speaking in sacrificial terms that Old Testament Israelites would have associated with a priest. The prophet portrays David's descendant king and priest as one who would, in Old Testament terms, offer burnt and grain sacrifices (Jer 33:17–18). A final sacrifice by way of a New Testament execution by crucifixion would not have made sense to Old Testament ears. The Messiah would come as the high priest to *his* temple (Zech 3:7–8) and purify his down-line priests and religious workers, the Levites (Mal 3:1–4). When the Christ came, he maximized the meaning of the promise of the purification of the faithful and formation of a new kingdom of priests from believers from tribes and peoples around the world, a new priesthood of all believers. Hebrews spends much of its time explaining the implications of the Messiah's role as the new high priest. However, the New Testament as a whole mitigates the cultic aspects, reducing them from standards to metaphors.

Populist Priest

When Jesus arrived, he redefined the holy, the sanctified, the "other." God's condescension to become a human priest to a significant degree brought anti-"ceremonial holiness," an anti-"separateness." Jesus the God/man entered the world as a commoner. The Old Testament's contrived imputation of holiness/separateness by ceremonial fiat is crushed by the truly holy Christ and his priestly but populist sub-culture of non-Levites who wore blue, not clerical, collars. As soon as Christ says the kingdom of God is at hand, he starts recruiting sovereign shepherds from a cross-section of society, not from the ecclesiastical elite but from the masses.

The dramatic and spectacular venue created by the ceremonial code has now become the ordinary in the way that Luther's common vernacular translation of the Bible threatened and replaced the ceremonial Latin cultus. The Jewish ceremonial legal system that was clumsy and burdensome was now obsolete. Nonetheless, the trusting community immediately and over the centuries re-ceremonialized what Christ had made common and for centuries has flaunted its opulent edifices and bloated bureaucracies in cities and suburbs around the world. It has done so with the mite of the widow, the very one who deserves the material means for a more dignified life.

Disrespected Priest

Disrespect for the Trinity has been the practice of humanity throughout the parenthetical age. But this whole span of rebellion has been surpassed by God's faithfulness to humanity nonetheless. Humanity's constant neglect and distortion of God's nature and grace, and its persistent disloyalty by aligning with the enemy, eventually brought the Messiah to his deathly demonstration of loyalty to humanity. Three of the Servant Psalms reveal this disrespect for the Messiah. The Christ would be abhorred and despised by Israel (49:7). Eventually he would suffer physical torture and humiliation, including scourging and being spat on (50:6) to the extent that his body would hardly appear human (52:14). Isaiah 53:3–9 then mounts the indignity upon indignity that the Messiah would suffer in his generous act of deliverance from sin. He would be despised, rejected, grieved, punished, pierced, crushed, wounded, slaughtered, killed. The Shepherd! The King! The Creator! God! Christ suffered this disrespect from the intimidated and jealous religious and political leaders throughout his ministry.

Ironic Priest

John the Baptist deflects the notion that he was the Messiah and announces that Jesus was the "Lamb" of Isa 53 who would take away not only Israel's sin but the sins "of the world" (John 1:29, 36; Acts 8:32). Jesus prepared his followers for his death while walking voluntarily toward it, while patiently hinting, then becoming emphatically clear about it, in his last months. He does enlighten them about the events, yet not clearly, if at all interpreting the events as salvific (Matt 20:28; 26:28; Mark 10:45; Luke 22:19–20).[41] So, the change in the sacrificial system included not

---

41. Matt 12:38–40; 16:21–23 // Mark 8:31–32 // Luke 9:21–22; Matt 17:22–23 //

only a new and permanent high priest but a high priest who was *himself* the sacrifice. The Old Testament high priest oversaw the whole sacrificial process, stewarding forgiveness for Israel and her citizens. However, the Messiah turns around and lays his own back on the altar to become the final sacrifice. Jesus is the "ironic priest"—the one who sacrifices himself for the sheep rather than sacrificing them. By offering himself, he was both mediator and medium, thereby releasing believers from their deserved and permanent verdict of death.

KING

The expectation of a messianic king was the most dear for Israel as a nation and for its frequently oppressed individuals. Israel had always seen a king as the solution to their woes from the time of the judges on, and David gave them their best model. God continued indulging their preference for a human king, but especially within the final king who was a failsafe divine/human "David," whose dynasty was anxiously awaited.[42]

The Old Testament clearly presents Israel's God as the king of all, whose kingdom spans from the time of creation through eternity and encompasses all reality as his realm. Furthermore, the universal kingdom's reign and realm was promised to, and accepted by, the Messiah. As the king of kings he holds his fallen and fractured universal kingdom together by blessing it perpetually, controlling its nemeses, and sending the Third Person who was empowered to recreate humanity again after the image of God. A more thorough commentary on the Messiah's reign and realm will be presented in the next chapter.

Mark 9:30–32 // Luke 9:43–45; Matt 20:17–19 // Mark 10:32–35 // Luke 18:31–34; Matt 17:9–12; 20:28; 21:36–39; 26:1–4, 12, 24, 26–32, 61; 26:31–32 // Mark 14:27; Matt 26:61 // Mark 14:58; Mark 8:31, 34; 12:1–12; Luke 13:32–33; 24:25–26; John 2:19, 22; 3:14; 12:6–8, 32–34; 13:33; 14:25, 29.

42. Matthew records what was a prevalent criterion for the Messiah: he must be a descendant of David: Matt 1:1, 6, 16–17, 20; 9:27; 12:22–23; 15:22; 20:30–31; 21:9, 15; 22:41–42. Luke does the same: Luke 1:27, 32, 69; 2:4, 11; 18:38–39; 20:41–44; Acts 13:22–23; 15:16. The Epistles' global perspective show less interest in David since Christ is the incomparable King of kings.

PROPHET

The Messiah was the quintessential prophet since, as God, he spoke his Father's mind about the past, present, and future while performing prophetic signs of adversity salvation. He spoke whatever God instructed, including interpretations of past events, current moral evaluations, and predictions into the future. Moses conveyed the Lord's promise that he would send prophets to speak for him: "The Lord your God will raise up for you a prophet like me from among you . . . I will put my words in his mouth, and he will speak all that I will command him" (Deut 18:15, 18).[43] Though this does not refer to Christ specifically, he was the ultimate example, speaking only what God wanted said through the Spirit (Acts 3:22). Jesus combined his prophetic and royal roles when responding to Pilate: "You are right, I am a king. That is why I was born and have entered the world, to testify to the truth" (John 18:37). The Samaritan woman expected the Messiah to explain "all things" when he came (John 4:25–26). This is a teaching/prophetic/priestly role that was apparently expected of the Messiah by some.

The greatest prophetic concern in the Old Testament was the moral condition of the Israelites. It focused powerfully and sharply on poor moral behavior requiring repentance. Though the prophets at times verbally convicted, even condemned the people, they also blessed and encouraged them. Their prophetic ministry fully engaged the shepherding eternal design in its messages of judgment yet very often conveyed blessings and deliverance as well. The priests' commission to teach the law was complemented by the prophets' assessment of the moral compliance that was taught by the law; thereby, the law was retaught by the

---

43. The hermeneutical controversy is acknowledged here, but a parallel is proposed between this promise from the Lord and the Davidic covenant (2 Sam 7:12–16). Both are phrased and contextualized as promissory within the Old Testament political milieu. They were administrative promises with immediate, successive, and official human fulfillments, not explicit nor implicit predictions of a "Messiah." They might be considered messianic either as a hidden, indiscernible intention among the Trinity, or because *any* Old Testament official position was messianic since Jesus fulfilled them all. That this particular promise was seized as a messianic credential mistakes the singular form of "a prophet" to refer to "the Prophet" rather than simply one from the succession of prophets like Moses who initiated that succession. The same error is made when the Davidic covenant is seen as messianic, where David's "seed," singular, a *sinful* seed at that (7:14), is the subject.

prophets. A few examples of prophetic assessments on the basis of the law would include the following.[44]

- Adultery — Exod 20:14; Jer 23:10
- Prostitution — Lev 19:29; Isa 57:3–4
- Incest — Lev 18:10; Ezek 22:10–11
- Drunkenness — Deut 21:20; Isa 5:22
- Impartial courts — Exod 23:6; Isa 1:23
- False testimony — Exod 20:16; Ezek 22:9
- Bribery — Exod 23:8; Isa 5:23
- Care for widows — Exod 22:22–24; Isa 1:17
- Care for orphans — Deut 16:11; Jer 22:3
- Care for the alien — Exod 23:9; Jer 22:3
- Care for the poor — Deut 15:7; Isa 3:15
- Care for servants — Lev 25:39–40; Jer 34:8–10
- Collateral — Exod 22:26–27; Ezek 18:7
- Divorce — Exod 21:10–11; Jer 3:1
- Idolatry — Lev 26:1; Hos 8:4–6
- Withholding wages — Lev 19:13; Jer 22:13
- Sorcery — Deut 18:10; Jer 27:9
- Lying — Lev 19:11; Isa 59:12–13
- Coveting — Exod 20:17; Mic 2:2
- Murder — Lev 24:17; Jer 22:17
- False measures — Lev 19:35–36; Hos 12:7
- Stealing — Exod 20:15, Deut 5:19; Mic 2:2
- Royal privilege — Deut 17:14–20; Jer 22:14–15

44. When the examples of common elements of prophetic ethical pronouncements in the Old Testament that were listed under the messianic role as teaching priest are matched with these common elements of the Law and the Prophets, the continuity of ethical commandments from Law to Prophets to Jesus is shown. The continuity could be shown to extend through the apostolic writings as well.

Isaiah anticipates the Messiah's own words about God's initiative in instructing him: "The Lord has instructed my tongue . . . He awakens me and my ears each morning to listen and be taught" (50:4). So the Messiah prophesies his Lord's decree to the nations in Ps 2:7–9: "I will tell of the decree of the Lord. He said to me . . ." And the Messiah's recitation of the Father's words is exactly how Jesus publicly explained the source of his own words as God's prophet.

> The things that I heard from him, these I say to the world. (John 8:26)

> The words that I say to you I do not speak on my own, but the Father who lives in me does his works. (John 14:10)

Jesus described himself literally as a prophet; his entire daily ministry was that of a prophet: "A prophet is not without honor except in his hometown and household" (Matt 13:57; John 4:44).[45] On his way to his Passion he insisted, "I must journey today and tomorrow and the day after; for a prophet cannot perish outside Jerusalem" (Luke 13:33).[46]

The Jews were looking for such a prophet to come, so Levites and priests were sent by their leadership to question the prophet John about his own identity. After using their multiple-choice test, they had reservations about his authority (John 1:20–25): "Why are you baptizing if you are neither the Christ, nor Elijah, nor the Prophet?"[47] Some concluded from Jesus' prophetic gift that he was simply "a prophet,"[48] while others concluded that Jesus was not just "the Prophet" but also the messianic

---

45. Though Jesus' self-declaration as the "Son of Man" has an undeniable connection with Dan 7:13–14 at least at some level, the same is true in connection with Jesus' and Ezekiel's prophetic role. The nearly one hundred instances of the designation of Ezekiel as "son of man" would hardly have been of no interest to those familiar with the prophetic book, especially given the frequently articulated anticipation of a coming prophet in the Gospels.

46. Bock links the Old Testament benchmark for the Messiah from Isa 61:1–2 and Jesus' shrewd self-designation as the prophecy's fulfillment (Luke 4:16–30): "Jesus is also more than a prophet, for he brings the salvation he proclaims. This extraordinary prophetic role led to Jesus' typical rejection of a prophet by national authorities due to an anti-establishment mission, e.g., prophet John versus executioner Herod." Bock, *Luke-Acts*, 189.

47. "Popular opinion compared Jesus in three ways with a prophet. (1) He was the prophet Elijah . . . who was to return before the end of the world. (2) He was the reincarnation of John the Baptist, who was executed by Herod . . . (3) He was in general 'a prophet, like one of the prophets.'" Goppelt, *Theology of the New Testament*, 1:165.

48. Matt 16:13–14 // Mark 8:27–28 // Luke 9:18–19; Matt 21:46; Mark 6:15; Luke 7:16; 9:8; 24:19; John 4:19; 9:17.

King (John 6:14; 7:40-41). "The whole work of Jesus in revealing the truth about God and the kingdom may be seen as the climax to the prophetic office of the Old Testament."[49]

A further and significant connection between the prophetic ministries of Jesus and the Old Testament prophets is the similar miracles associated with the prophets Moses, Elijah, and Elisha: leprosy healings of Miriam by Moses, and Naaman by Elisha (Num 12:13-16; 2 Kgs 5:10-14). Jesus' authority over the violent waters of Galilee reminds one of the prophetic parting of waters by Moses, Elijah, and Elisha (Exod 14:21-22; 2 Kgs 2:8, 14; Matt 8:26; 14:25, 28, 32). Jesus raised the dead, as did Elijah and Elisha (Luke 7:14-15; 8:54-55; John 11:43-44; 1 Kgs 17:17-24; 2 Kgs 4:34). In Elijah's case it is noteworthy that the miracle of raising the widow's son was confirmation to her that he was *certainly* a prophet. In the same vein, Jesus' exponential multiplication of food was also precedented by Elijah and Elisha (1 Kgs 17:14; 2 Kgs 4:4, 43). In fact, it was the crowd's primary conclusion that Jesus was a miracle-working prophet when he fed thousands from nearly nothing, affirming intentionally that he was the Messiah: "When the people saw him do this miraculous sign, they exclaimed, 'Surely, he is the Prophet we have been expecting!'" (John 6:14).

JUDGE

Israelite tribal judges/elders were assigned the routine task of hearing local/regional disputes. They assessed the arguments and witnesses, determined innocence or guilt, and decided and applied the appropriate means and extent of any punishment. As we saw under the Messiah's role as priest, the judges and priests shared judging responsibilities, and kings were involved in legal disputes as well. Jesus' messianic role merged his royal, priestly, and prophetic teaching, proving further that the various social responsibilities of the king, priest, prophet, judge, and adversity savior define the responsibilities of the Messiah—Jesus personifies the role of at least five administrative functions. So, the Messiah would be expected to judge as a foundational function of his comprehensive portfolio.

Psalm 2 warns the kings and judges of the earth to worship the Lord and his Son with reverence and joy or to perish (9, 12). The positive aspect of God's judgment is to bless, deliver, and protect those who worship him and his Son (12). Psalm 110:5-6 is more graphic in the depiction of

---

49. Goldsworthy, *According to Plan*, 205.

the Messiah's judgment: crushing nations and their leaders and filling those nations with corpses. For Solomon, deliverance of the innocent, the vulnerable, and the oppressed entails the Messiah's judgment on the callous perpetrators of anti-shepherding evils (Ps 72:2–4).

The Messiah will judge wisely and righteously throughout the world to punish wicked and abusive authorities: "May he vindicate the afflicted of the people, save the children of the needy, and crush the oppressor" (Ps 72:4). Isaiah says the Messiah will judge those who oppress the poor and are his enemies; they will be tormented, die, and be left for scavengers to devour (Isa 11:4; also 42:1; 50:9, 11; Mal 3:3, 5). And Malachi prophesies that the Messiah will discipline the Levites. God originates judgment (Matt 18:34–35; Heb 12:23), but the appointed Christ and his coregency will include being the lead judge in the process (Acts 17:31; Rom 2:16). "All the nations will be gathered to him to separate them as a shepherd separates sheep from goats" (Matt 25:32). He claimed this role and everyone will stand before him (τοῦ Χριστοῦ) as their judge: "We all will be required to appear before the Messiah's judgment seat so each person will receive what they deserve for their works" (2 Cor 5:10). Paul is repeating here what Christ already had said about coming again to judge (Mark 8:38). And John the Baptist had already paved the way for Jesus' words about his judging role (Matt 3:12).

Several texts speak to the Messiah's judgment, both his retributive judgment and its inverse, celebrated vindication.[50] Christ publicly accepted this responsibility before the Jewish leaders and people: "All the nations will be gathered to him to separate them as a shepherd separates sheep from goats" (Matt 25:32).

Though God did not send Jesus the first time to judge the whole world (John 3:17), that claim is contextualized within his frequent criticism of many in Israel: religious leaders, his followers, demons, temple trespassers, the localities of Jerusalem, Chorazin, Bethsaida, and Capernaum, even an unproductive fig tree. Jesus refers in John 3:16–17 to his judicial, formal, and final judgment, which he explains later in John 5:22–27. Yet even during his ministry, he speaks of his discerning judgment's implications for those immediately around him, not his eschatological, final judicial decisions with the Father: "I came into this world for judgment" (John 9:39).

---

50. Also Matt 27:11; Acts 10:42; 17:6–7, 31; Rom 14:9; 1 Cor 15:24–28; Eph 1:10, 20–22; Phil 2:6–11; Col 1:13, 16–20; 1 Tim 6:15; 2 Tim 4:1; 1 Pet 4:11; Rev 1:5–6; 17:14; 19:16.

Judgment is commonly thought of as negative when in fact it is fundamentally positive. It employs a necessary part of God's eternal design since it blesses the moral person, delivering them from evil, while it sets an ominous and dangerous standard against injustice. The judgment of Christ is not only against the sinner but also for the sinned-against. Judgment is against the oppressor, but it delivers, frees, and relieves the oppressed. Furthermore, Christ's judgments of believers are disciplinary, intended to guide toward further spiritual maturity and practical success in life. In other words, the disciple should look forward to the Messiah's sanctifying judgment. It is a blessing; it delivers from sin as well as ironically exonerates one before the world and one's adversaries: "The Lord disciplines who he loves" (Heb 12:6).

In the same way, the skies and earth will be judged and destroyed by fire; this too is a blessing to the New Earth and its inhabitants. After all, even now, forest fires benefit the soil by replacing the accumulated and choking debris with new, healthier growth. Better and uncompromised production will come from a world no longer made toxic by God's curses and by humanity's continuous moral and physical pollution.

ADVERSITY DELIVERER

There are at least four instances in the life of an individual who is delivered: by justification, sanctification, and glorification, yet also from adversity, both physical and mental: "Be gracious to me, O Lord, for I am languishing; heal me, for my bones are troubled. My soul also is greatly troubled" (Ps 6:2–3). God's deliverance in his eternal design becomes a central piece in biblical revelation activated by the believer's "saving faith" in all four applications. Though the first three apply only to the regenerate who have experienced the sin salvation through the Messiah's priestly role, adversity salvation applies to all humanity. It is experienced regularly by both believers and unbelievers, and to misunderstand this is to overlook God's universal kingdom and his routine salvation as the shepherd of individuals (and nations) from the satanic, terrestrial, and natural kingdoms.

A theology of human history must address the prevalent volume of *personal* histories with all their traumas and ecstasies. They combine to form the most important historical events for the individual, and they contribute to the most important historical events to one's close family and friends. One's intimate personal experiences and histories are of great interest to the heavenly and satanic kingdoms: the former to bless, the latter to destroy. Terrestrial authorities monitor compliance with civil laws and frequently make individuals the target of oppression. Even one's peers take an interest by restricting one's freedom and demanding unnecessary conformity.

Powerful kingdoms surround the individual; the heavenly, satanic, natural, terrestrial, and trusting kingdoms do not ignore anyone—they chase the individual instead. A person's history is the result of these kingdoms converging in various combinations to mold one's circumstances and create scenarios requiring petty to extraordinary decisions or realistic resignation to the inevitable. The individual too often attracts unwanted attention from some kingdoms. Nevertheless, the believer's personal history will reveal one's intimate relationship with God as the Shepherd as it reveals one's trust and wise relationships and responses to their surrounding threatening mega-kingdoms.

It would be grace enough for believers to live only temporary lives in God's family, to experience his design and then die eternally. Apart from his promises, God would not be required to extend eternal life even to believers. His love would have been just as sincere without granting everlasting life. Thankfully, however, that was not his design for creation. Rather, he has conferred immortality to his followers for endless, productive activity with him in New Earth. Life now is already an infinitesimally small segment of that exciting journey with God, giving a satisfying taste of the glories ahead. Every promise of eternal life is a reference to the coming age when ceaseless pursuits will bring unceasing joy and success.

Deliverance from adversity recorded in the Testaments was a blessing from which a nation or individual is saved so that they could get on with what God called them to do. These deliverances were not for the sake of deliverance alone but so that the delivered could continue accomplishing their responsibilities. Any salvation, restoration, and deliverance is not God's ultimate design in themselves; rather they are critical prerequisites for continued shepherding success during the parenthetical age. Adversity salvations in the Old Testament include the mundane reclaiming of a lost tool or more dramatic deliverances from destitution, disease, the dead, despots, and defeat from one's military foes.[51]

---

51. Unfortunately, hermeneutical devices can distract and dull the original intent of revelation by imaginative poetic parallels formed by well-meaning exegetes. For instance, in referring to Israel's military deliverance in Judges: "Israel's temporary

On the other hand, the Testaments often make it difficult to detach sin from adversity deliverances since they are so closely related. Jesus forgave and saved individuals from sin as well as from physical and spiritual adversity, as in the case of the paralytic in Mark 2. Jesus' messianic kingdom proved his concern for the individual by saving many from simple dilemmas to grave disasters. As the powerful king over God's universal kingdom, Christ exercised his authority over the spirits and nature by exorcisms, healings, resurrections, and frequently bending nature's laws. He even healed those who did not know him or did not appreciate him for who he really was as their adversity savior (John 5:13; 9:30–38).

Deliverance for the afflicted was an obvious messianic expectation. Psalm 72:12–14 describes the care the righteous would receive from the Messiah:

> He will save the needy when one cries for help, the afflicted, and the one with no helper.
> He will have compassion on the poor and needy, and he will save the lives of the needy.
> He will rescue their lives from oppression and violence.

He opened his ministry by announcing the adversity deliverance prophesied in Isaiah:

> The Spirit of the Lord God is on me, because the Lord anointed me to bring good news to the humble, he has sent me to heal the brokenhearted, to announce the release of captives and freedom for prisoners ... to comfort all mourners. (Isa 61:1–2; 42:6–7; Luke 4:18–19)

Jesus answers the Baptist about whether he was the Messiah by emphasizing his adversity deliverances. This is "good news" from Jesus that he brought before his pronouncements about or his submission to the Passion.

> The blind receive their sight, the lame walk, lepers are cleansed, the deaf hear, the dead are raised, and the poor have good news proclaimed to them. (Matt 11:5)

---

deliverance at the hand of these 'judges' or 'leaders' finds its typological fulfillment in the permanent deliverance that Christ wins for his people." Moo, *Theology of Paul*, 468. Not everything in Scripture is designed with a hidden, eschatological purpose. At least some texts mean only what they say.

The salvations by Christ from death, disease, demons, and disasters were not just the teasers before the Passion; they are commensurate with the Passion; they confirm that the sacrifice was divinely qualified. They are not only a show of compassion and power; they are the public display of Jesus' messiahship.

More general promises are given to believers—promises that assure Christ's adversity salvation for the believer who is in the midst of affliction from powerful kingdoms. Jesus asked the Father to continue protecting believers (John 17:11–15). If John could not catalogue all of the Messiah's salvation acts in the first century, one should consider that his acts of deliverance have increased exponentially over the last two millennia (John 20:30; 21:25). He has continued to guide the lost, console the confused, calm with his voice, and resurrect, heal, and shield from Satan.

God's nature is emotionally balanced; his love, anger, joy, and grief are never obsessive. Isaiah adds this to the Messiah's deliverances. His words will strengthen the burdened believer: "The Lord God has given me the tongue of disciples, so that I may know how to sustain the weary one with a word" (Isa 50:4). When the Messiah arrived, "he felt compassion for them, because they were distressed and downcast, like sheep without a shepherd" (Matt 9:36; also 11:28–30). His concern was not only for one's physical wellbeing but also for emotional strength and stability (Matt 6:34; 10:28–31; Luke 12:22–31; John 14:1–4). He also sent the Holy Spirit to comfort and console (John 14:16–19, 26).

NATIONS' DELIVERER

Much has already been said about God's vision for the global inclusion of the terrestrial kingdoms into his universal kingdom's New Earth. It has been emphasized that the terrestrial kingdoms and their primary commission are the focus of God's universal kingdom and revelation. However, the nations are currently part of the satanic kingdom and most often the enemy of the trusting kingdom. The fundamental adversity that any nation faces is its immediate and long-term affliction of sin, yet the believers from the nations will represent all nations in New Earth's diverse population.

The nations are the objective in both Testaments—they are the beneficiaries and the benefactors of New Earth. This is an element of creation's teleological eternal design that is evident in its various outworkings through history. God blessed the nations by promising the patriarchs that their impact would be international: "In your offspring shall all the nations of the earth be blessed" (22:18; also Gen 18:18). God's promise to Abraham was God's covenant with the nations—a great blessing for Abraham and an equally great blessing for the nations. Eternal and intimate fellowship with the nations was the Lord's objective, not only to die for them, but to live and rule with them.

> I will bless those who bless you, and whoever curses you I will curse; and all peoples on earth will be blessed through of you. (Gen 12:3; also 18:18; 22:18)

The descendant of the patriarchs would bless the nations:

> May people be blessed in him—all nations call him blessed. (Ps 72:17)

Isaiah introduced the Messiah to be God's means of salvation.

> I will give you to be a covenant to the people, a light to the nations . . . so my salvation may reach to the ends of the earth. (Isa 42:6; also Isa 49:6; Luke 2:32; Acts 13:47; 26:23)

So, Jesus claimed to be that Light:

> I am the light of the world. (John 8:12; also, 12:46)

> They will come from east and west, and from north and south, and recline at table in the kingdom of God. (Luke 13:29)

The contention between the Messiah and the nations ends in peace and blessings (Ps 2:10–12), and of course, Israel is included in this merciful change from national antagonism to eternal peace (Isa 53:8, 11; Jer 23:5–6; 30:8–9; Zech 3:9–10). Nonetheless, the Samaritans were expecting the Messiah to be the "world's savior" (John 4:42). Christ promised he would draw all humanity to himself, but it was necessary for the Spirit to continue to convict the nations of sin, righteousness, and judgment (John 12:32; 16:8–10).

Finally, the trusting kingdom, by faith and practice, contributes to the Messiah's deliverance of the nations as it shepherds the world in its love and wisdom through its churches and missions. The trusting kingdom's history describes the practical assistance that its clergy and laity, at their own risk, even death, have given the nations.

8

Messiah's Universal Kingdom

THE SEVENTH KINGDOM UNDER God's universal kingdom is the messianic kingdom, and it completes the cohort of kingdoms that were introduced in the last chapter: the heavenly, satanic, natural, terrestrial, trusting, and New Earth kingdoms. The matter of Messiah's kingdom will now guide the rest of this study because it subsumes the other kingdoms, since it is by his word that all creation and its kingdoms are upheld (Heb 1:3). However, one cannot address the messianic kingdom separate from a foundational subject of the Testaments: the kingdom of God. This is not a new subject introduced by Christ in the New Testament; rather, he continues its teaching just as it was pronounced throughout the Old Testament.

EQUIVALENT KINGDOM PHRASING

Many have been concerned that equivalent Hebrew wording for the New Testament phrase "kingdom of God" (βασιλεία τοῦ θεοῦ) does not occur in the Old Testament. First, one should realize that it is only a hermeneutical presumption that an Old Testament concept and its Hebrew expression should conform to a New Testament Greek linguistic pattern.[1] Nevertheless, idiomatic or semantic equivalents do exist in the Testaments. Hebrew possessive phrasings pertaining to God and his kingdom

---

1. "The idiom 'kingdom of God' itself was not used in the Old Testament, though the concept is found in the prophets." Bock, *Luke–Acts*, 206.

are syntactically synonymous to the Greek. Bruce Chilton affirms this concerning Daniel in particular:

> It is true that the exact phrase "kingdom of God" does not appear word for word in Daniel. But to insist on that point seems pedantic, since the word "kingdom" does appear with "his" in contexts which the unequivocal antecedent is God.[2]

Likewise, Dale Patrick:

> The Old Testament does contain ample antecedents of the Greek expression. If one assumes YHWH to be a semantic equivalent to Elohim, we have a number of exact equivalents in Hebrew and Aramaic to the Greek βασιλεία τοῦ θεοῦ . . . . Obviously at a purely statistical level, the expression "the kingdom of God" has sufficient antecedents in the Old Testament to justify Jesus' use of it.[3]

The following are examples of these equivalent phrasings from the Old Testament and intertestamental literature.

"Kingdom of the Lord" (1 Chr 29:11)

"The kingdom is the Lord's" (Ps 22:28–29)

"Yours is the kingdom, O Lord" (1 Chr 29:11; Ps 145:11–13)

"His kingdom rules over all" (Pss 103:19; 114:2; Dan 4:3)

"Kingdom of the Lord over Israel" (1 Chr 28:5)

Examples from apocryphal and pseudepigraphal passages:[4]

> When a righteous man was a fugitive from a brother's wrath, wisdom guided him in straight paths; she showed him God's kingdom [βασιλείαν θεοῦ] and gave him knowledge of holy things. (Wis 10:10)

> They that fear the Lord rejoice in good (gifts), and Thy goodness is upon Israel in Thy kingdom[5] [τῇ βασιλείᾳ σου]. (Pss. Sol. 5:18)

---

2. Chilton, *Pure Kingdom*, 25. Similarly Waltke, *Old Testament Theology*, 146.

3. Patrick, "Kingdom of God," 72–73. He quotes John Bright as well. Bright, *Kingdom of God*, 18.

4. Charles, *Apocrypha and Pseudepigrapha*, 2:638.

5. Kenneth Atkinson sustains Buchanan G. Gray's translation (Charles, *Apocrypha and Pseudepigrapha*, 2:638) by translating "your kingdom." Atkinson, *Psalms of Solomon*, 118. R. B. Wright translates less literally as "as you rule." *Psalms of Solomon*, 103.

There is more than enough Old Testament precedent for contextualizing Israel's kingdom within the wider governing universal kingdom of God. And it plays the foundational role for Jesus' kingdom matrix of words and works which demonstrate his meaning of the "kingdom of God." It was shown earlier that it was the universal kingdom that the Messiah was granted in the Old Testament and that he accepted, proclaimed, and demonstrated prevalently in his ministry. Nowhere does either Testament see the scope of the Messiah's kingdom to be constricted as anything less than the universal kingdom apart from its synecdochical meanings of the trusting kingdom and/or New Earth.

Furthermore, it has already been noted in chapter 6 that the universal kingdom of God included a more specific national component continued from the Old Testament into the intertestamental literature, e.g., 1 En. 9:4, 5; 84:2, 3; As. Mos. 9:6; 10:1, 7; Pss. Sol. 17:4, 5, 51. Particularly in Pss. Sol. 17:4, the identical phrase, βασιλεία τοῦ θεοῦ, is found to express the same pervasive "kingdom of God" pronouncements as those of Jesus and his followers in their letters. Not only did Jesus mean the universal kingdom, but it had been voiced as such literally and identically as "βασιλεία τοῦ θεοῦ" a century before as an equivalent translation from the Hebrew.[6]

> For the might of our God is forever with mercy, and the kingdom of our God [ἡ βασιλεία τοῦ θεοῦ ἡμῶν] is forever over the nations in judgement.

The Apocrypha and Pseudepigrapha, then, not only acknowledge the universal kingdom in general terms, but at least in this passage in all its translations, the kingdom is expressed here exactly as Jesus expressed it in his proclamation of God's gospel, βασιλεία τοῦ θεοῦ—the reign of God which encompasses all nations as part of his comprehensive realm. Psalms of Solomon 17 as a whole pleads that God by his eternal universal reign would bring a new and righteous "messianic" Davidic king. This prayer is in the context that all nations from the ends of the earth were subjects within God and his Messiah's universal kingdom.

The Psalms of Solomon is the most comprehensive intertestament source about a coming Messiah, and so it plays a significant intermediate

---

6. The Hebrew vorlage of these psalms has been lost, but they are estimated to have been written in the first century BCE based on several factors, including its historical allusions. The eleven Greek manuscripts from 900–1500s have no variants in this kingdom phrasing apart from two omitted words, "in judgment" (ἐν κρίσει), in only three manuscripts. Wright, *Psalms of Solomon*, 176–77.

point on the Testaments' continuum in the meaning of the "kingdom of God": "There is more substance to the ideas concerning the Messiah in the Psalms of Solomon than in any other extant Jewish writing."[7] Though the intertestamental literature is generally diverse and imprecise on the subjects of a messiah and the kingdom of God, when the Psalms of Solomon uses the phrase "kingdom of God," one is forced to look at the phrase's context to determine its probable meaning. In particular, on chapter 17 alone: "Ps. Sol. 17 remains the longest, continuous description of the messiah that we possess from pre-Christian Judaism."[8] This should be a serious consideration when determining whether Jesus, by this phrase, meant his possession of God's universal kingdom.

MESSIAH'S COREGENCY

God's eternal design required a human who was incapable of sin in order to perfectly follow Genesis's primary commission for humanity to shepherd his creation. So, the Messiah came to bless as the benevolent king, the self-sacrificing priest, the encouraging and edifying teacher/prophet, the insightful sage, the liberating judge, and the powerful deliverer of nations and individuals.

The Messiah's ontological nature as the divine sovereign of creation as the Second Person, melded with his assigned role as the sovereign of the earth with a human nature, finally created an entity that would rule the world perfectly with complementary natures which were both anchored in the image of God to fulfill the eternal design together. Jesus the man, having the divine nature, was not divested of divine sovereignty over all creation; he was God, the Lord, the universal King, by definition of his Second Person attribute of sovereignty. In the Incarnation, he did not become a king or try to become king, nor was he nor will he be made a king; he was and is King. And Jesus, the human sovereign, the second Adam, who by his divine nature had shepherded the universal kingdom since creation as a Trinity member, and now as a human, was the designated shepherd in a more direct way (Mic 5:2–4). The Old Testament's commissioning of the Son, therefore, was a confirmation of what was already true—the coming divine Messiah was already king of the universe.

---

7. Wright, "Psalms of Solomon," 2:643.
8. Trafton, "What Would David Do," 157–58.

What was new, however, was revealing the mystery that the divine nature of the Messiah was inexplicably united with the perfect human nature.

The Messiah came to focus on what the Old Testament focused on—God's kingdom and his generous sharing of his attributes including sovereignty with creation's kingdoms, especially with humanity. He continued his prerogatives when, as the Second Person, he accepted the more direct, personal, in-the-flesh responsibilities as the Messiah. Unlike David, who only had a heart like God's, Jesus ministered by a heart that was God's:[9] "If you have seen me, you have seen the Father." So, the universal kingdom is not a new kingdom for the Second Person. Newness came in his ontological melding with a descendant of Adam so that humanity's sovereignty over creation would again be secured. Upon the transfer of the messianic universal kingdom back to God (1 Cor 15), sanctified humanity will look back at this parenthetical phase of the universal kingdom as a catastrophic episode in eternal history that temporarily postponed humanity's primary commission's fullest effect to shepherd as God shepherds.

The consensus is that the gospel from Jesus Christ was that of the kingdom of God, and it is this kingdom that will be given some attention for the remainder of this study. Luke represents the gospelers and gives the fullest New Testament description of Jesus' gospel of the kingdom of God within Luke's "Gospel," which comes in two parts: Luke and Acts. These two parts reveal God's central interest within a continuous historical narrative, which, telling from Jesus' own pronouncements, was God's universal kingdom, including all creation, but more particularly all the nations. The trajectory of Luke's Gospel and Acts is about the universal kingdom of God and humanity's conduct within it. The framework of Luke–Acts melds the two books' united message by clearly accentuating the kingdom of God in Jesus and his apostles' pronouncements. Luke Timothy Johnson reviews the references by which Luke constructs the kingdom of God thematic framework that fuses his Luke–Acts:

> From the beginning of Luke–Acts (Luke 4:43) to the very end (Acts 28:31), the "kingdom/rule of God" has been the constant

---

9. While discussing Jesus' divine and human nature, I have done so in terms of Grudem's systematic theology where "whatever can be *said of* one nature or the other *can be said* of the *person* of Christ. . . . Anything that is *done* by one nature or the other is *done* by the *person* of Christ." Jesus "is free to talk about anything done by his divine nature alone or his human nature alone as something he did." Grudem, *Systematic Theology*, 561.

content of preaching both with Jesus (Luke 6:20; 7:28; 8:1; 9:11; 11:20; 12:31–32; 16:16; 17:20–21; 18:29; 19:11; 21:31; 22:30; 23:42; Acts 1:3) and with his prophetic representatives (Luke 9:2; 10:9–11; Acts 8:12; 14:22; 19:8; 20:25).[10]

New Testament history, then, continues the Old Testament's trajectory of God's revelation of his eternal design for his universal kingdom. His revelation continues to encourage personal, national, and global shepherding conduct by humanity. The trajectory does not lead to humanity's completion of its recovery from the effects of the Fall on its own, but it expects humanity's perpetual attempts to mitigate those effects until the Messiah, himself human, completes that recovery at his parousia. The Old Testament canon is fundamentally about his relationship with the nations and their constructive or destructive contribution to his creation's design. A historic link is made immediately in the New Testament when Jesus begins with his ministry theme of God's universal kingdom (Mark 1:14–15) and continues throughout his three years to advance the divine agenda of sanctified living.

Again, as reviewed in chapter 6, the Old Testament view of God's universal realm has always extended over the entire world, to the ends of the earth, forever with no end, and this theology was continued in the Second Temple literature. The Messiah's kingdom is predicted to be nothing less than God's universal realm, as the following passages pertaining to the Messiah attest:[11]

> Ask me, and I will certainly give the nations as your inheritance, and the ends of the earth as your possession. (Ps 2:8)

> May he rule from sea to sea, and from the Euphrates River to the ends of the earth. (Ps 72:8; Zech 9:10)

> The God of heaven will set up a kingdom that shall never be destroyed . . . it will stand forever. (Dan 2:44)[12]

---

10. Johnson, *Acts*, 470.

11. Scobie supports this generalization in reference to Psalms' ascription of God's kingship: "Some of these psalms envisage God enthroned in Zion and refer to his rule over Israel (Pss 97:8; 99:6–9), but much more frequent is the declaration that God is king over all the earth and all the nations." Scobie, *Ways of Our God*, 107.

12. The fifth realm of Dan 2:44 is the messianic kingdom, though the Messiah is not mentioned. The prior four realms are sequential and *contiguous*, implying the fifth is contiguous yet endless.

MESSIAH'S UNIVERSAL KINGDOM

> This is what the Lord says ... to the Servant of rulers: "Kings will see and rise; princes will also bow." (Isa 49:7)

> He will rise and shepherd his flock by the strength of the Lord ... then he will be great to the ends of the earth. (Mic 5:4)

Since God has always ruled his kingdom by his eternal design, he commissioned the Messiah to shepherd the Trinity's universal kingdom by that same design beyond the last days of the parenthetical age: "He will reign over the house of Jacob forever, and his kingdom will have no end" (Luke 1:33).

This equivalence of God and his Messiah's kingdom could not be shown more clearly than Daniel's parallel descriptions of their kingdom(s). Both receive the same glory, honor, and praise, and both have authority over the same realm which cannot be destroyed but is eternal. Speaking of God prophetically, Nebuchadnezzar and Darius declare God's eternal and comprehensive reign and realm, by which he is glorified.

> His realm is everlasting, and his authority is from generation to generation. (Dan 4:3)

> I praised the Most High and I honored and glorified him who lives forever, for his authority is everlasting and his kingdom endures from generation to generation. (Dan 4:34)

> His realm will not be destroyed, and his authority will be forever. (Dan 6:26)

Then, Daniel's depiction of the Messiah's reign and realm is identical to God's, and their kingdoms' scope deserves the same glory and praise.

> To him was given authority, glory, and a realm ... His authority is an everlasting authority which will not pass away, and his realm will not be destroyed. (Dan 7:14)

These predictions of the Messiah's comprehensive ownership and reign over God's universal realm were confirmed by Jesus and his followers; his kingdom's realm is as comprehensive as his reign over his Father's kingdom—it *is* his Father's kingdom. The following texts attest to God's sharing his universal realm with the Messiah.

> The Father loves the Son and has given everything into his hand. (John 3:35)

> He is Lord of all. (Acts 10:36)[13]
>
> God has put everything in subjection under his feet. (1 Cor 15:27)
>
> And he put everything under his feet. (Eph 1:22)
>
> By him everything holds together. (Col 1:17)
>
> Everything was created through him and for him. (Col 3:16)
>
> At the name of Jesus every knee of those in heaven, and on and under the earth will bow. (Phil 2:10)
>
> He upholds everything by his word's power. (Heb 1:3)
>
> Angels, authorities, and powers having been subjected to him ... (1 Pet 3:21–22)[14]
>
> He is ... the ruler of all kings of the world. (Rev 1:5)

There is no indication in these passages that God shared only part of his universal kingdom with his Messiah and/or that he deferred a complete sharing of it until a future stage.[15] In fact, Eph 1:20–21 explicitly specifies that the Messiah now reigns completely over all authorities as his realm in this parenthetical age as well as after the eschaton in New Earth.

> He seated him at his right hand in the heavenly places far above all rule and authority ... not only in this age but also in the one to come. (Eph 1:20–21)

The Messiah himself attests to his own reception of the universal realm and reign that had already been shared among the Trinity and was now in his possession during his Incarnation, not eventually sometime

---

13. "He sent the message to the Israelites, proclaiming the good news of peace through Jesus Christ—he is Lord of all." The phrase "he is Lord of all" is often reduced to a mere parenthetical comment "(he is Lord of all)," e.g., ASV, ESV, KJV, NASB, NET, RSV. Yet, since Peter's Jonah-like ethnocentrism had just been shattered by his vision of forbidden food, he now conveys to Cornelius that Christ's lordship is over all nations. This *is* "the good news of peace through Jesus Christ"—a statement to be underlined, not parenthesized.

14. Matthew 13:41 speaks of the Son of Man sending "his angels."

15. Ridderbos responds to an interpretation of Phil 2:8–11 where Christ is elevated to his highest level of sovereignty only post-ascension: "This pre-existence of Christ with the Father so emphatically declared by Paul underlies his whole Christology and makes it impossible to conceive of all the divine attributes and power that he ascribes to Christ exclusively as the consequence of his exaltation." Ridderbos, *Paul*, 68.

in a future eschaton. Most verbs in this case are present tense; though the perfect tense is in Col 1:17, Heb 1:8 is a nominal sentence.

> Everything [realm] has been handed over to me by my Father. (Matt 11:27)

> All authority [reign] in heaven and on earth has been given to me. (Matt 28:18)

> Jesus [knew] that the Father had given everything [realm] into his hands. (John 13:3)

> Everything [realm] that the Father has is mine. (John 16:15)

> You gave [me] authority [reign] over all humanity. (John 17:2)

> Everything [realm] I have is yours, and everything you have is mine. (John 17:10)

Paul and Hebrews' identification of the Messiah as divine accentuates his trinitarian role as the Second Person in conjunction with his reign and realm as the second Adam.

> After all, "The Messiah is God over everything [realm]." (Rom 9:5)

> Of the Son it is said, "Oh God, your throne [reign] is forever and ever." (Heb 1:8)[16]

The Messiah's rule over the universal kingdom is christologically necessary and is exegetically proven. Again, there is no indication from Jesus that he accepted anything less than the universal kingdom in his Incarnation. And there is nothing written that indicates that there was more of God's universal kingdom for Jesus to receive at some point in his future. It is improbable that when Jesus spoke of the kingdom of God that he meant anything less than both his Father's and his universal kingdom. He deflected any assumption that he came to reestablish Israel's national kingdom. Yet he did say that he owned, thus shared, God's universal kingdom.

Paul attributes divinity and the universal kingdom to both God and the Messiah in Rom 9:5 (Messiah as God is over all), and the implication of the equation is frequently affirmed elsewhere in the New Testament.[17]

---

16. Here, the Old Testament's generic "God" is converted to mean the Son.

17. Christ is the King of the kingdom for Paul (1 Cor 15:24–28; Col 1:13) though God is considered the King in Paul's other kingdom texts; both Christ and God are kings in 1 Corinthians and Colossians (1 Thess 2:12; 2 Thess 1:5; 1 Cor 4:20; 6:9–10; 15:50; Gal 5:21; Col 4:11). Fee, *Pauline Christology*, 110.

For example: "Anyone who is sexually immoral or impure, or who is covetous (that is, an idolater), has no inheritance in the kingdom of Christ and God" (Eph 5:5).

The following paraphrased passages also express interchangeable attributions of the universal kingdom to both.[18]

- God is the "only Sovereign," yet both God and Christ are "King of kings, and Lord of lords" (1 Tim 6:15–16; Rev 17:14; 19:16).
- It is the Father's kingdom and the Messiah's kingdom (Matt 13:40–43).[19]
- Both God [Lord] and Christ have the same kingdom (Rev 11:15).
- Believers are possessed as God's people (Acts 15:14)[20] and the Messiah's people (Titus 2:14).[21]
- "I will write on them the name of my God . . . I will write on them my new name" (Rev 3:12).

John's Revelation also affirms the singularity of the kingdom and the "throne" as one place belonging to the two Divines. The authority of the terrestrial kingdoms of the world are subsumed directly under "the kingdom of our Lord *and* of his Christ" (Rev 12:10). Furthermore, the landscape of New Earth surrounds the single throne where both the Lord and Christ the lamb sit.

> The angel showed me the river of the water of life, bright as crystal, flowing from the throne of God and of the Lamb . . . . No

---

18. In defense of Christ's divinity, Morris lists passages where the divine subjects are interchangeable: "[Paul] assigns a number of functions indifferently to God and to Christ," e.g., kingdom of God/Christ; grace of God/Christ; gospel of God/Christ; church of God/Christ; Spirit of God/Christ; peace of God/Christ; day of God/Christ; judgment seat of God/Christ. "The Septuagint word for Yahweh, 'Lord,' he uses freely of Christ." Morris, *New Testament Theology*, 47.

19. God's kingdom: Matt 13:43; 26:29. Christ's kingdom: Matt 16:28; Luke 22:29–30; John 18:36.

20. Luke 1:68; Acts 15:17; 1 Pet 2:9–10; Rev 21:3.

21. Matt 1:21; Luke 1:77. Other examples of joint ascriptions to God and Christ: The Father's and Jesus' "hands" are strong, and the believer is secure in them (John 10:27–29). God and the Lord Jesus direct and comfort simultaneously (1 Thess 3:11; 2 Thess 2:16–17). God and his Messiah will defeat the latter's enemies (Ps 110:1–2). God judges (Matt 18:34–35; Heb 12:23), but he does so through Christ (Acts 17:31; Rom 2:16). God is the Savior (1 Tim 1:1; 2:3; 4:10; Titus 1:3; 2:10; 3:4), and Christ is the Savior (Matt 1:21; Eph 5:23; Phil 3:20; 2 Tim 1:10; Titus 1:4; 2:13).

longer will there be anything accursed, but God and the Lamb's throne will be in it. (Rev 22:1–3)[22]

The incomprehensible relationships within the Trinity will persist within frustrating finite minds, yet revelation is meaningful, so one is left with what cannot be defined in any other way than a *relative* coregency of God and his Messiah. Where Revelation's visionary license speaks of one throne, there are few phrases that are repeated as often in the Testaments than about Christ "sitting at the right hand of God/Father," presumably indicating two foci of authority, not literal separated thrones. The Messiah's deity is never in question, but his relative status is clear: he is God, yet he is God's prince as well (Isa 9:6; also Ezek 34:24; Dan 9:25). Humbly, only at God's side, was his preferred identity over equality with God just as he confirmed his subordination to the Father constantly and publicly in word and deed (Phil 2:6).

The unity and diversity within the Trinity's nature is a model built deeply into its creatures. Unity in its ontology and purpose yet diversity in the Persons' functions make their coregency over the universal kingdom perfectly synchronized and inevitably and wonderfully successful. The Trinity's eternal design is assured by the Second Person's four relationships of unity, coregency, purpose, and function,[23] where one relationship leads to the next. (1) His *ontological* coregency within the Trinity leads to (2) the *functional* coregency of the Father and his Messiah of the universal kingdom. This functional coregency required (3) the *ontological* merger of the divine Messiah with a human, leading to (4) the *functional* coregency with humanity as the coregent with the rest of his creation.

The unity/diversity model among the Trinity led to the Second Person's commission to a new locus of coregency between God and his Messiah who would be of the same nature as God and holding to his same purposes but with a new human nature that was assigned specific functions to substitute for the defiant human race and to exonerate it in preparation for its eternal pursuit again of the eternal design in New Earth. This Messiah rules the universal kingdom with God and, as God,

---

22. John's pervasive creation theology, his overwhelming global apocalypse, and his vantage point as the last New Testament writer who had seen the successful expansion of the faith refers to the "world" most often as God's universal realm: nearly half of the New Testament instances and three-quarters of the Gospels' uses.

23. "As God, the Son's rule is inseparably one with that of the Father . . . and of the Holy Spirit. As Man, the Son is inseparably one with us." Hughes, *Revelation*, 131.

and he is a teaching, judging, and ceremonial priest, a miracle performing prophet, and a king with a realm that reaches to all creation's sub-kingdoms.

The Incarnation finally ensures humanity's success in its primary commission (Gen 1:28) by forming another ontologically unified coregency after the image of the Trinity—a divine coregency of God and humanity in the flesh. There is no difference in God's nature and the divine nature within Jesus to shepherd by blessing, deliverance, and discipline. The Messiah came to continue his rule of the universal kingdom of God as he had always ruled as the Second Person.[24] In Jesus the Messiah, the universal kingdom comes that much closer to humanity: not just visiting the Couple in Eden or eating a meal with Abram and Sarai but living daily in human flesh.

This coregency of the Father, Son, and Holy Spirit over their universal kingdom is what Jesus meant by the "Kingdom of God has arrived." It is the overriding, most general kingdom concept in the Old Testament, and it was the explicit understanding between God and his Messiah as they communicated with each other and as Jesus revealed in his last years of daily life.

KINGDOM OF GOD

There are two polar views of the phrase "kingdom of God." One extreme has a definition that is too wide; the other is so specific that it is inadequate to incorporate God and his creation's natures as defined in our first two chapters. The first is represented by the suggestion that the New Testament "kingdom of God" is a "tensive symbol." Norman Perrin suggests that a mythic nature of Scripture implies that a phrase like "the kingdom of God" is a tensive symbol that can "evoke a whole range or series of conceptions." For example, "the kingdom of God is in the midst of you" where "the symbol of the kingly activity of God on behalf of his people confronts the hearers of Jesus as a true tensive symbol with its

---

24. It is a difficult balance what is hidden in the nature of the Trinity to retain the Son's subordination without diluting the equal extent of universal authority and realm that he was given. The main reason for this subordination is probably due to the human nature of the Son. For a good explanation of a vice-regency of the Incarnation see McCartney, "Ecco Homo." For this reason, describing Jesus' role as a "vice-regent" rather than "coregent" might be a bit too modest and subordinating.

evocation of a whole set of meanings."²⁵ Dale Patrick agrees with Perrin: "Jesus employs the expression βασιλεία τοῦ θεοῦ ('kingdom of God') to arouse in his listeners a complex of ideas, associations, and metaphors."²⁶ However, Robert O'Toole objects aptly to the ultimate subjectivity of any tensive symbol approach since there would be no objective restraints to one's imaginative interpretations: "Perrin has not attended sufficiently to the objective content or limited nature of a symbol. A symbol cannot say everything, nor can it be deprived of some definite content."²⁷ The other extreme is to truncate God's universal kingdom to the extent that it refers to primarily Israel's national kingdom. This extreme will be engaged later in chapters 11–13, where the meaning of the "kingdom of God" has been limited in many ways.

Two considerations are important for a definition of the kingdom of God: (1) when the Old Testament uses kingdom terminology as God's universal kingdom, which has already been discussed, and (2) whether there is a figure of speech involved in the uses of the phrase "kingdom of God." The phrase is often used as a figure of speech when used as a synecdoche, i.e., when the whole, the "universal kingdom" is used to represent only one of its parts: the trusting kingdom or New Earth. Believers enter two kingdoms in the New Testament: the present trusting kingdom at one's justification and the future kingdom at one's resurrection into New Earth. The same population, the trusting kingdom, is the part-for-the-whole that lives in both this age and the one to come, so both are designated as parts that are separate-yet-the-same kingdom within God's universal kingdom. One does not enter the universal kingdom; one is conceived into it. But one can enter the present trusting realm, thereby having a guaranteed admission to the realm of the new creation; one enters the kingdom of God at conversion and continues by entering it at glorification. This is not a unique use of the phrase "kingdom of God"

---

25. Perrin, *Language of the Kingdom*, 33, 45. He adopts Phillip Wheelwright's description of these symbols. Wheelwright, *Metaphor*, 93–96.

26. Patrick, "Kingdom of God," 70. R. T. France opts for this explanation as well. *Mark*, 93. Guthrie also follows this model in *New Testament Theology*, 431. Boring adds yet another visual obstruction, a "translucent" window between the reader and what is an obscure tensive meaning. Boring, "Kingdom of God," 131–32, 134. Similarly, Rudolf Schnackenburg suggests that the kingdom in Mark 1:15 is "intentionally ambiguous" to allow for an already-not yet interpretation. Schnackenburg, *God's Rule*, 141–42.

27. O'Toole, "Kingdom of God," 147. I would suggest that a better example of a tensive symbol, minus the presupposition of myth, is the church's use of the terminology "the gospel."

as a synecdoche since commentators recognize the part-for-the-whole when they read certain texts as either the "already" part or the "not-yet" part within their understanding of an eschatological kingdom. This synecdochical approach to the phrase is easily understood without opening interpretation to the unconstrained parameters of tensive symbols.

Past and Present Universal Kingdom

Jesus announces God's gospel as "the time is fulfilled, the kingdom of God is here [Πεπλήρωται ὁ καιρὸς; καὶ ἤγγικεν ἡ βασιλεία τοῦ θεοῦ]." The Old Testament universal kingdom had always been "here," including the present, but when Jesus accentuated that it had arrived (or would arrive soon) at a proper time, πεπλήρωται ὁ καιρὸς, he indicates that there is some development in the universal kingdom.[28] Something new was happening. The new development was that the Old Testament promise about God's universal kingdom now would be developed in many ways by a merciful human; now creation is graced with the incarnate, empathetic ministry of the Messiah. The time of the coregent universal *messianic* kingdom had arrived in a divine human who would be king, priest, prophet, judge, and a deliverer from adversity.[29]

Determining what ἐγγίζω means in a New Testament passage depends on the contexts at the sentential, paragraph, or book levels. It can mean "here, near, now, soon," etc. All options have their proponents in the case of Mark 1:14–15 and in other cases involving the kingdom of God. However, the strongest argument that it means "here" or "has arrived," apart from the universal meaning of "the kingdom of God," is the finality of the preceding phrase, "the time is complete [πεπλήρωται ὁ καιρὸς]," indicating the present reality of the universal kingdom since they are both perfect indicatives.[30] Paul affirms Jesus' meaning here when

---

28. A spatial meaning rather than a temporal one; "nearby" is a minority position. However, it is feasible, e.g., Cranfield, *St. Mark*, 66.

29. "It is important to see that Jesus did not come because the time was fulfilled, but rather he fulfilled the time by coming. Fulfillment is not a reference to history in general, but the way Jesus fulfills all the expectations of the Old Testament at the time appointed by God." Goldsworthy, *According to Plan*, 72.

30. For a successful argument for "here" over "near," see Bock, *Dispensationalism*, 40–47. Also see his treatment of ἔφθασεν ἐφ᾽ ὑμᾶς ἡ βασιλεία τοῦ θεοῦ in Luke 11:20. Bock, *Luke-Acts*, 206. Others preferring "here": Caird, *New Testament Theology*, 33; Stein, *Mark*, 73; Beasley-Murray, *Kingdom of God*, 73; Gundry, *Mark*, 65; Voelz, *Mark 1:1—8:26*, 146; Wenham, *Paul*, 48; Marshall, *Theology*, 78; Chilton, *Kingdom of God*,

in Eph 1:9–10 he writes about this new phase in the universal kingdom: "[God] planned in him, in the fullness [πληρώματος] of times, the uniting of all things in the Christ [the Messiah], things in the heavens and on the earth." Both Jesus and Paul speak of the Christ's current reign over the universal kingdom.

The reason the time was now complete was because the Messiah had arrived to rule over all creation as the Father had appointed him during the Old Testament. Since then, he has been the sovereign shepherding human above every authority and in his every realm.[31] This God/man shepherds his kingdom[32] with a heart like God because he is God.[33] In other words, when Jesus spoke of God's universal kingdom as God's good news, he was referring to his own messianic kingdom, which he had always ruled as the Second Person; nothing could be taken from his rightful realm and reign while he was incarnated. Though some limitations apparently ensued because of his finite human nature, the Trinity's coregency extended to and through him. The universal kingdom of God had always been the Old Testament's reference point in place and time for everything, and the anticipated Messiah had finally come, solving mysteries that were hid in times past about the future of God's universal kingdom in history.[34] So Jesus announced in Mark 1:14–15 that this coregent messianic phase of the universal kingdom had arrived.

Whether ἤγγικε in Mark 1:14–15 is temporal, spatial, here, or near becomes inconsequential very soon since these questions were settled by the time of Jesus' first exorcism only eight verses later in 1:23–28. Furthermore, he said the kingdom of God was already in the Pharisees' midst, either because he personified the kingdom as he stood before them or because the universal kingdom had always been the context of reality and could be seen, hidden in plain sight (Luke 17:20–21). So, Jesus himself said the reign and realm of God were "here."[35]

14–15; France, *Mark*, 92–93.

31. Matt 28:18; John 3:35; 17:2; Acts 10:36; Eph 1:20–22; Phil 2:9–10; 3:21; Col 1:16; 2:10; Rom 9:5; 14:9–11; 1 Pet 3:21–22.

32. Luke 22:69; Acts 2:33; 5:31; 7:56; Rom 8:34; Eph 1:20; Col 3:1; Heb 1:3, 13; 8:1; 10:12–13; 12:2; 1 Pet 3:21–22.

33. Matt 1:6; 2:4–6; Luke 1:32–33; John 7:41–42

34. Eph 1:10–11; 3:2, 9–11; also Matt 13:35; 25:34; 1 Pet 1:20; Rev 13:8.

35. Dale C. Allison surveys the interpretations of these two passages in particular and their bearing on a present/future debate of Jesus' kingdom. Allison, *Constructing Jesus*, 98–102.

> If I cast out demons by the Spirit of God, then the kingdom of God has come upon you. (Matt 12:28)[36]

> The kingdom of God is not coming in ways that can be observed, nor will anyone say, "Look, here it is!" or "There!" Look, the kingdom of God is already in your midst [ἐντὸς]. (Luke 17:20–21)

Jewish leaders could only explain Jesus' exorcisms as the work of the satanic kingdom. But Jesus explains that no kingdom can stand if divided, and since the satanic kingdom could not stand against the Messiah then the universal messianic kingdom was here. And the kingdom of God could not be observed if those observing were looking only for what they assumed all kingdoms had: armies, robed kings and princes, coinage, and palaces. One might as well be blind if awaiting a physical David-like kingdom—it could not be "seen." On the other hand, if one was looking for the more profound evidences of a kingdom powerful enough to defeat Satan, to bend nature, and to rule the entire creation, then one's sight might be perfect. The universal kingdom of God was already in their midst; it was not on its way.[37] This is why there is such frequent pairing in the Synoptics when Jesus' and his disciples' announcements on the arrival of the kingdom of God were accompanied by wonders of healings, resurrections, and exorcisms. The message, authority, and power of the universal kingdom was both proclaimed and demonstrated over the natural, satanic, Jewish, and gentile nations within the terrestrial kingdom (Matt 4:17; 9:35; 10:7; Luke 9:2, 11).[38]

Admittedly, in Luke 17:21, ἐντὸς is somewhat ambiguous (within, among, in the midst). Yet, it is unlikely that Jesus would have directed the Pharisees, of all people, to personally look "within themselves" to see the kingdom of God. However, if the meaning was that the kingdom of God was "among" or "in the midst of" them, it would have been significant since they were familiar with this frequent and theologically

---

36. In Luke's parallel words, "If it is *by the finger of God* that I cast out demons," one is reminded of the pagan Egyptian witness to God's miracle performing universal kingdom (Exod 8:19).

37. If it means temporally "near," it is a matter of days when the kingdom of God appears, not years or millennia. Gundry asks how "near" might be preferred: "What does this combination of fulfilment and nearness indicate, the nearness of imminent arrival or the nearness of an arrival that has taken place?" Gundry, *Mark*, 64. "Near" works if it really means near.

38. See Ben Witherington's discussion of the suggested options for the meaning of ἐντὸς: "within you," "among you," and "within your grasp." *Jesus, Paul*, 71–72.

loaded phrasing in the equivalent Hebrew term, *qereb*.[39] That the Lord was *among* and *reigned* the realms of Israel, Egypt, Moab, indeed the whole earth, would not have been wasted on the Pharisees standing before Jesus, eye to eye. For example, *qereb* is used spatially in the following:

- It is a form of good news that the Lord, the righteous Holy One, is in Israel's midst (Ps 46:5; Isa 12:6; Jer 14:9; Hos 11:9; Joel 2:27; Zeph 3:5, 15, 17; Zech 2:5; 8:8).
- The Lord is in the midst of the whole earth (Exod 8:22; Ps 135:8–12; Isa 19:19; 25:10–11).
- The Messiah will reign in the midst of his enemies (Ps 110:2).
- The Lord brings salvation to the midst of the earth (Ps 74:12).

Jesus, the incarnate Lord, was claiming to be the Old Testament messianic Expected One. Whether the universal kingdom itself was in their midst or Jesus meant the kingdom of God was personified in himself does not matter since in either interpretation, God and Jesus were the coregents of the universal kingdom that was in the world's midst.

The universal kingdom of God is behind numerous Gospel passages. Jesus' parables convey that the universal kingdom should be sought and invested in at any cost as Jesus had said similarly in Matt 6:33, "Seek first the kingdom of God" (Matt 13:44–46). It is the universal King who forgives indebtedness and expects the same (Matt 18:23–35). The universal King's blessings are always fair, even if not equal (Matt 20:1–16). Jesus' encouragement and modeling of prayer speaks to the current shepherding power of his Father's universal kingdom.[40] The Testaments' invitations to pray for daily provision, rulers, protection, forgiveness, health, assumes that God's universal kingdom, his reign, delivers his grace to his realm. Jesus refers to the present kingdom where there is a "least" person, which would not be found in New Earth (Matt 11:11 // Luke 7:28). His kingdom parables may also show the synecdochical nature of

---

39. The Hebrew meaning of *qereb* in this context can be the "midst" within the human body, or the "midst" surrounding it, whether the immediate social, national, or the remote global surroundings. *BDB*, 899.

40. "Nothing is more important for the cause of religion at the present day than we should recover the sense and consciousness of the Providence of God—a Providence that acts not merely by a species of remote control but as a living thing, operating in all the events of life—working at every moment, visible in every event. Without this you cannot have any serious religion, any real walking with God, any genuine prayer, any authentic fervour and faith." Butterfield, *Christianity and History*, 4.

the kingdom of God. The parables phrased as similes, "the kingdom of God is like . . .," might invite too literal and forced interpretations. It is perhaps better understood when the connection idea "is connected with" or "relates to," which gives more elasticity. So, the world's trusting kingdom is the point of several of these parables: the kingdom's growth is like the mustard seed (Matt 13:31–32 // Mark 4:30–32 // Luke 13:18; also Mark 4:26), and like the growth from leaven (Matt 13:33; Luke 13:20). One might accept an invitation to enter the trusting kingdom, but eventually any insincerity and disrespect will not be tolerated (Matt 22:2–13). Or one's commitment to the kingdom can be too flaccid and unwise, thus ineffective (Matt 25:1–13). Jesus rebukes the religious leaders not only for refusing to enter the kingdom themselves but discouraging others from entering as well (Luke 11:52 // Matt 23:13; 21:31).

Future Universal Kingdom

Paul's use of kingdom phrasing also shows how it is used in terms of a synecdoche. Jesus and Paul speak of the believers' "inheritance" in the kingdom of God, which appears to be the future New Earth itself. The earth had always intended for humanity to rule (Gen 1:26–28; Pss 8:6–8; 115:16), and in the restructured, eternal New Earth the only remaining humans will be believers as the beneficiaries of that function. Believers do not simply inherit citizenship but are owners and rulers as stewards over New Earth since their inheritance is bound with Christ's (Dan 7:18, 22, 27; Rev 2:26; 22:3, 5; Rom 8:17; 1 Cor 3:21–23). Jesus had promised, "Blessed are the gentle, for they will inherit the earth" (Matt 5:5; 25:34), and Paul phrases a future inheritance as well, often in the negative, e.g., "Do you not know that the unrighteous will not inherit the kingdom of God?" (1 Cor 6:9; also 1 Cor 15:50; Gal 5:21; Eph 5:5). Other examples of future meanings of the "kingdom of God" in New Earth refer to those who will find it difficult to enter it (Mark 10:23–25) and those who will have honorary seating there with Christ and feast with him and the patriarchs (Matt 20:21; Mark 14:25; Luke 13:28–29).

John pronounces a current fact followed by the future New Earth's continuation of what was intended from the start in the Edenic commission: "You have made them as a kingdom and priests to our God; and they will reign on the earth" (Gen 1:28; Rev 5:10; also Rev 1:6; 20:6). Again, the total population of the trusting kingdom from this parenthetical age will be the same population of New Earth. However, the venue changes radically, from a fallen world infested by the satanic kingdom and its poisoning impact on the natural, terrestrial, and trusting kingdom to the glorious perfection of a renovated and advanced rendition of Eden in its coordinated successes of the other kingdoms.

NEWNESS OF THE NEW TESTAMENT

God has perpetually grown and enhanced his universal kingdom even during this parenthetical age, continuing the Old Testament's trajectory with the same common eternal purpose. But God becomes in his Incarnation even more intimate in Jesus, the compassionate human shepherd who grieves over the shepherdless (Matt 9:36). Jesus continued the Trinity's teaching and example of the shepherding good news of the kingdom established in the Old Testament in his blessing and disciplining, and in his innumerable deliverances of healings, exorcisms, resurrections, and bendings of nature (Isa 61:1; John 20:30–31). The same Old Testament focus on God's kingdom and his generous sharing of sovereignty with humanity was behind Christ's proclamation of God's kingdom gospel and behind the miracles that proved the arrival of the messianic stage of the pre-existing universal kingdom—not a new kingdom, but the same universal kingdom that was shared with the Couple but now also shared with the Messiah.

It is reasonable to ask then what exactly is new in the New Testament if there is such a continuity in God's universal kingdom. There are at least five significant aspects of newness. The newness of the kingdom of God was not in its universality but in its divine/human coregency, its cultic order, its ecclesiastical order, the trusting kingdom's exponential growth, and the Spirit's more transparent role.

Coregency of God and His Human Messiah

The mystery of the divine Messiah is solved now in Christ Jesus. Regardless of the dominant continuity between the Testaments in the fabric of the teleological progression of the eternal design, it cannot be denied that when God's universal kingdom was shared with the Messiah, a definitive, eternal, and royal episode erupted into creation.[41] There is a quiet re-

---

41. God's eruptions are his way throughout history. Waltke, after reviewing major

definition of some things by Christ, but his ministry was no less than an invasion of creation by a human king that overcame the satanic kingdom, penetrated the terrestrial kingdom, subdued the natural kingdom, will finally destroy all rebellious zones, and then reconstruct the New Earth and skies.

Again, for the Second Person, this was not an inaugural event, but for Jesus, it was. Wherever and whenever the Second Person is, the universal kingdom is present. What *is* an inaugural development is the coregency of God and the divine human who had arrived to perform God's primary commission of shepherding creation perfectly. The Messiah was the solution to the mysteries veiled in the Old Testament:

> Through him we have redemption by his blood, the forgiveness of our sins according to the riches of his grace which he rained upon us by all wisdom and insight. He revealed to us the mystery of his will, consistent with his good intention which he planned in Christ in the fullness of times, the uniting of all things in the him, things in the heavens and on the earth. (Eph 1:7–10; also Col 2:2; 1 Cor 2:6–10; 1 Pet 1:10–11, 20–21)

New Cultic Order

We find in Lev 19:23–25 a precedent for God establishing a Mosaic law that would expire after three years, showing the divine prerogative to build change and development into his legal administration. Granted, the new cultic order where the royal priesthood which Jesus brought was a more radical development than timing Israel's agricultural rhythm, yet in both cases there was a fulfillment of time that brought forward those changes in divine law.

Jesus, the self-sacrificing priest, ended the pre-Passion sacerdotal system: "When the priesthood is changed, the law must also be changed" (Heb 7:12; 10:14). This change was a relief from what was publicly described by Peter as a yoke "that neither our fathers nor we have been able to bear" (Acts 15:10). The old cultic system was now void, replaced by a decentralized, populist culture, since the central practice of sacrifice was obsolete due to the new divine high priest from Judah. He was the final

---

historical blocks of the Old Testament, writes: "The holy and merciful God continually irrupts into history in order to establish his kingdom." I would presume to substitute "shepherd" for "establish" here. Waltke, *Old Testament Theology*, 167.

priest and Lamb. Plus, there were new supplemental teaching and commandments from this high priest and from his Spirit-inspired servants.

Exponential Growth

Within the New Testament's details of the success of the Spirit's continued micro-generative mission in the believers' life of saving faith is his macro-generative power for the expansion of the whole trusting kingdom and his role in convicting and converting the world. A significant global expansion of God's trusting kingdom is powered by the Spirit and the Incarnation's messianic implications. A broader call of all peoples, including the widely dispersed Jews, is relentless to the extent of the current trusting kingdom's extensive reach and influence in many of the world's cultures.

New Ecclesiastical Order

Related closely to the new cultic order was the new structure of a New Testament church which necessarily morphed from the Israelite national, political, social, and legal structure to a more organic community that still lived under the despotic Rome. A decentralized community as God intended Israel to be after Babel, and under the judges, returned under the monarchy of God's Son. The millennia since the Incarnation have continued with the terrestrial and satanic kingdoms' collusion against God's universal kingdom, while his trusting kingdom has survived as a nimble, diversified, and self-supporting alliance of cells. Consequently, given the forthcoming globalization of the church, a populist structure was necessary.

Holy Spirit's More Transparent Role

Now, greater clarity was revealed in the New Testament about the Holy Spirit and his role in regeneration and sanctification of believers. What was vague or hidden in the Old Testament about the believer's dependence on the power of the Spirit to become a new creature is revealed in the New Testament. It is only reasonable that the fallen nature of humanity was equally ingrained in the people of both Testaments, and the renewal of their souls equally required the Spirit's creative force to bring them to the loving, trusting, saving condition for their salvation. Contrary to presumptions, God was not required to explicitly and frequently emphasize this role of the Spirit in the Old Testament.

SUMMARY

The Messiah was granted the same extent of God's universal realm as his own "kingdom of God" (Pss 2:8; 72:8; Zech 9:10; Dan 2:44; 7:14; Isa 49:7; Mic 5:4). He was commissioned to shepherd his universal kingdom by the eternal design during the remaining days of the parenthetical age. Jesus accepted this reigning role over the universal kingdom in its entirety and proved his authority of the heavenly, satanic, natural, terrestrial, trusting, and New Earth kingdoms, and his followers' commission made this clear as well (Matt 11:27; 28:18; John 3:35; 13:3; 16:15; 17:2, 10; 1 Cor 15:27; Eph 1:22; Col 1:16; Heb 1:1–4, 8–13; 2:1–10; 8:1; 10:12, 13; 12:2). Ontologically speaking, there is no Old Testament or exegetical reason for Jesus not to have meant in Mark 1:15 that the universal kingdom of God was present now under his divine human jurisdiction. The "kingdom of God" may appear to be an ambiguous statement in Mark 1:15, but soon any ambiguity would be clearly removed by Jesus' works and words as he claimed and proved even during his pre-Passion life to have universal authority over everything. The Old Testament foundational principle of the universal kingdom of God substantiates Christ using the same foundation for his authority and ministry. The "fulfilled time" continued the Trinity's universal kingdom indefinitely in Jesus the Messiah until he would raise it to God as a perfect realm again.

9

Paul's Kingdom Message

EVERYTHING FALLS WITHIN GOD'S created kingdom structure: the spirits, nature, and humanity. This kingdom structure has contained all of the efforts and events of the seven kingdoms which have and will either follow or distract from God's universal kingdom's shepherding eternal design. However, I do not suggest that the kingdom of God plays *the* central and prominent position in revelation, though it is an extremely prominent element. Jesus' gospel from God was the arrival of God's universal kingdom under Jesus' human sovereignty as the divine Messiah. The two writings of Luke are best suited to present the New Testament's kingdom theme since it forms 25 percent of the Testament and spans the ministries and kingdom pronouncements of Jesus and his followers, including Paul. From beginning to end, Luke-Acts presents God's universal kingdom gospel as a central piece in the Testaments.

Jesus acknowledged his commissioned role and visually verified his authority as coregent over the universal and its heavenly, satanic, natural, terrestrial, and trusting sub-realms. And his followers reaffirmed his commission in their own commissions as well. After three years of ministry, Jesus was still proclaiming the kingdom of God. His fuller explanation of his messianic commission and his Passion including resurrection did not displace God's gospel while "appearing to them for forty days and speaking in regards to the kingdom of God" (Acts 1:3). And its importance remained throughout the apostles' ministry as Paul and others emphasized it explicitly in their proclamations to Jews and gentiles.

RHETORICAL CONNECTIONS OF LUKE-ACTS

The dominance of the kingdom of God for Luke is evident rhetorically in Luke-Acts in at least six ways. The following Luke-Acts syncopation guides the trajectory of this Lukan theme.

Luke 4:43—Luke 24:46–47—Acts 1:3—Acts 1:8——Acts 28:30–31

> I must also proclaim the kingdom of God to the other cities since I was sent for this purpose. (Luke 4:43)

> It is written that the Christ would suffer and rise from the dead on the third day and that repentance for forgiveness of sins would be proclaimed in his name to all nations, beginning in Jerusalem. (Luke 24:46–47)

> He also showed himself alive by many convincing proofs after his suffering, by appearing to them for over forty days and speaking of matters regarding the kingdom of God. (Acts 1:3)

> You will be my witnesses both in Jerusalem and in all Judea, Samaria, and as far as the furthest part of the earth. (Acts 1:8)

> Paul stayed on for two full years . . . proclaiming the kingdom of God and teaching things about the Lord Jesus Christ. (Acts 28:30–31)

1. Two enclosing brackets were referenced earlier[1] that place Jesus' kingdom of God gospel at the beginning of his teaching (Luke 4:43) and at the end of Paul's teaching (Acts 28:31) as the *termini a quo* and *ad quem*.

   Luke 4:43————————————————————Acts 28:30–31

2. Within these brackets, a rhetorical hinge between the two books links Luke's Gospel ending and his Acts beginning. Luke's Great Commission from Jesus in his last Gospel chapter instructs his disciples to spread the proclamation of forgiveness beyond Jerusalem to all nations under his authority over all nations, his universal

---

1. See L. T. Johnson's framing of Luke–Acts by Jesus and the apostles' accent on the kingdom of God referenced in the previous chapter: Johnson, *Acts*, 470.

kingdom (24:46-47). Then, immediately, Acts opens with the same commission to spread the proclamation beyond Jerusalem to all the nations (1:8). Luke's way of joining his two volumes is by the ever-expanding reach of Jesus' authoritative teaching.

Luke 24:46-47————————Acts 1:8

3. Again, Luke's Gospel begins by recording Jesus' demonstration and teaching on God's gospel of the kingdom (Luke 4:12-43), and Luke's opening verses of Acts also begin with Jesus' teaching on God's gospel of the kingdom. Luke introduces Jesus' teaching in each book to be about his kingdom of God.

Luke 4:43————————Acts 1:3

4. Jesus' teaching about the kingdom of God at the beginning of Luke's Gospel ends with Jesus' geographical *implications* of that universal kingdom of God found at the close of Luke's Gospel, marking its *termini a quo* and *ad quem* as a single book (4:43 => 24:46-47). Parallel to this development, and within a much smaller window in his second book, Luke condenses and thus summarizes his Gospel's *termini* when Jesus' gospel of the kingdom of God (1:3) ends with the geographical *implication* of the universal kingdom, namely spreading the message to the nations (1:8).

Luke 4:43—Luke 24:46-47 // Acts 1:3—Acts 1:8

5. Jesus spoke primarily of his kingdom of God in Acts 1:3, and Luke has Paul ending Acts with Jesus' kingdom of God message still in 28:31, forming an additional *termini a quo* and *ad quem*.

Acts 1:3————————Acts 28:30-31

6. In the midst of these rhetorical considerations are the literal, verbatim, sustaining, adhesive texts that confirm a central concern of Jesus and his apostles for the universal kingdom of God: Luke 6:20; 7:28; 8:1; 9:2, 11; 10:9-11; 11:20; 12:31-32; 16:16; 17:20-21; 18:29; 19:11; 21:31; 22:30; 23:42; Acts 8:12; 14:22; 19:8; 20:25; 28:23.

Furthermore, the apostles announced the kingdom of God by affirming and arguing explicitly that Jesus was the Messiah (Acts 2:31; 3:20; 5:42; 9:22; 17:3; 18:5, 28). The universal kingdom reign of the Messiah was implicit in this and included his full commission in addition to being the universal King, e.g., self-sacrificing and law-teaching priest, prophet, adversity savior, exhorter, and as judge of believers and non-believers. Since the apostles' intention was to identify Jesus as the Messiah, it is not surprising that Luke closes Acts by describing Paul's success in persuading some of his visiting Jewish leaders that Jesus was the Messiah of the Old Testament prophecies (28:23).

PAUL'S PRINCIPAL MESSAGE IN ACTS

The emphasis in this chapter is on Luke's four summaries of Paul's message during his journeys and imprisonments and their consistency throughout his public pronouncements and writings. These four summaries reveal that Paul proclaimed the universal kingdom of God until the very end of his life.[2]

> He entered the synagogue and for three months spoke boldly [παρρησιάζομαι], discussing [διαλέγομαι] and persuading [πείθω] them about the kingdom of God. (19:8)
>
> I know that none of you among whom I have gone about proclaiming [κηρύσσω] the kingdom will see my face again. (20:25)
>
> From morning till evening, he explained [ἐκτίθημι] to them by testifying solemnly [διαμαρτύρομαι] to the kingdom of God and trying to persuade [πείθω] them about Jesus both from the Law of Moses and from the Prophets. (28:23)
>
> He lived there two whole years at his own expense, and welcomed all who came to him, proclaiming [κηρύσσω] the kingdom of God and teaching [διδάσκω] about the Lord Jesus Christ with all boldness and without hindrance. (28:30–31)

In Luke's two books and by these specific idiomatic summaries, he accentuates the continuity of Jesus' main pronouncements in the Synoptic Gospels and the apostolic message of Paul. Luke's summaries of Paul's ministry-long pronouncement of the kingdom of God are pivotal in understanding the New Testament message—pivotal not only theologically but rhetorically, since they form the axis between the Gospels and Paul's letters.

2. A fifth instance of "the kingdom of God" by Paul in Acts 14:21–22 is not an overall summary of his teaching as are these other four: "We must enter the kingdom of God through many tribulations." In this case, Paul chose to use "kingdom of God" to indicate the synecdoches of either the believing or New Earth kingdom as a part of the Messiah's universal kingdom, which he refers to in 19:8, 20:25, and 28:23, 31.

It is consequential that Luke stresses the numerous rhetorical scenarios *in* which Paul pronounced and *by* which he pronounced his kingdom of God message. As one reads the above texts, one should not miss that it was not by his public speeches alone that he emphasized the kingdom of God; it was his theme regardless of setting or form of verbal intercourse. Luke intentionally heaps forms of communication by which Paul conveyed his seminal message. Certainly, the following would have overlapped within a single venue, but the cumulative effect of this variety of scenarios heightens Luke's emphasis on just how pervasive Paul's theme was and when and how he communicated it: παρρησιάζομαι, διαλέγομαι, πείθω, κηρύσσω, ἐκτίθημι, διαμαρτύρομαι, διδάσκω.

One would expect Paul's emphases of Jesus' gospel of God's kingdom that are recorded by Luke would be consistent during his journeys, imprisonments, public pronouncements, and in his letters; nothing in Paul's writings contradicts Jesus' understanding of the universal kingdom of God. For instance, Paul refers to the universal kingdom: "The kingdom of God is not about talk, but power" (1 Cor 4:20). The relation of kingdom and power is seen as definitional by most: the reign of God is powerful. Later in 1 Corinthians he refers to Christ's presentation of the perfected universal realm to the all-in-all God: "Then the end comes when he delivers the kingdom to God the Father after destroying every rule, authority, and power" (1 Cor 15:24). In Col 4:11, Paul commends his Jewish co-workers "in" or "for" (εἰς) the kingdom of God, by their work for God's global realm: "These are the only men of the circumcision among my fellow workers in [εἰς] the kingdom of God."

Christ's coregent universal reign as God's judge of all past and present residents of the nations' realm is an impetus for proclaiming good news: "I charge you before God and Christ Jesus who will judge the living and the dead, and by his appearing and his kingdom—proclaim the word!" (2 Tim 4:1–2; cf. where Christ's appearing is eschatological in 4:8; 1 Tim 6:14; Titus 2:13).

The trusting and New Earth kingdoms are the parts that are expressed in terms of the whole, as synecdoches. Distinguishing these two synecdoches can be an uncertain task at times since the members of both parts of the universal kingdom are the same population, separated by time and the believers' eventual ontology—separated in time, because the trusting kingdom is current and New Earth is the believers' future inheritance (1 Cor 6:9–10; also Gal 5:21; Eph 5:5 [cf. Paul's comment in Acts 14:21–22]). The believers' ontology is somehow different as well:

"We have borne the image from the earth, so we will also bear the image of the heavenly.... Flesh and blood cannot inherit God's kingdom; nor does the perishable inherit the imperishable" (1 Cor 15:49–50). One aspect of walking in the glory of God's nature is to prioritize community harmony over dietary scruples: "God's kingdom is not about eating and drinking but of righteousness, peace, and joy in the Holy Spirit" (Rom 14:17). This is because they have been delivered from "the domain of darkness" to a different domain within the universal kingdom, "the kingdom of God's beloved Son" (Col 1:13–14). This transfer to the Son's kingdom brought with it the transformation of the old man into the glorious image of God: "We were exhorting... each one of you as a father would his own children so that you would walk in a way worthy of the God who calls you into His own kingdom and glory" (1 Thess 2:11–12). Paul alludes to one's current kingdom citizenry: "You are fellow citizens with the saints and members of the household of God" (Eph 2:19).

OCCASIONAL NODS

A few will affirm innocuously that Luke's four summaries of Paul's public pronouncements are a continuation of Jesus' foundational message. For instance, James Dunn notes Luke's determination to reveal the preservation of Jesus' kingdom teaching within the New Testament church:

> The twin emphases of Paul's testimony were the kingdom of God and Jesus (28:23). The fact that this twofold emphasis recurs in the very last verse (28:31) indicates that the choice of themes was neither accidental nor frivolous. As with the repeated emphasis in 1.3 and 6, Luke evidently wanted the continuity with Jesus' own proclamation of the kingdom in the Gospel to be clear beyond doubt.[3]

Others have noticed Luke's summaries stressing Paul as an example of the dependence of the early church on Jesus' primary theme of the kingdom of God. Eckhard J. Schnabel on Acts 20:25:

---

3. Dunn, *Beginning from Jerusalem*, 1005. Elsewhere from Dunn: "Luke goes out of his way to indicate that 'the kingdom of God' continued to be a feature of earliest Christian preaching and teaching. Particularly noticeable is the fact that 1.3 forms an *inclusio* with 28.31: the final note of Paul's preaching ('proclaiming the kingdom of God') matches the chief and last topic of Jesus' instruction." Dunn, *Beginning from Jerusalem*, 143; also 1008.

Paul describes his ministry in Ephesus in terms of proclamation (κηρύσσων), whose content he summarizes with the term "kingdom" (βασιλεία) . . . a term that underlines the continuity between the preaching of Jesus (Luke 4:43; 8:1; 9:11; Acts 1:3), of the Twelve (Luke 8:10); and of the Jerusalem church (Acts 8:12).[4]

Leon Morris:

> It is noteworthy that Luke continues to refer to "the kingdom of God" when he writes the Acts. . . . From all this we see that Luke took the sovereignty of God very seriously. Clearly he deeply appreciated what Jesus had said about the kingdom, and he makes it clear both that Jesus taught about it often and significantly, and that this preaching continued in the early church.[5]

George Eldon Ladd in reference to all four summaries by Luke:

> We may assume that such passages mean that the apostles proclaimed in summary form what had been the burden of Jesus' message.[6]

David Wenham:

> Luke goes on to portray Paul as someone who taught about the "kingdom of God" (19:8; 20:25; 28:23, 31), thus also as someone who taught the sort of traditions that he, Luke, has presented in his Gospel.[7]

However, acknowledgments like these about Luke's summaries of Paul's kingdom of God message are only simple observations for commentators followed by no substantive interpretation or description of what the pervasive impact on Paul and New Testament theology would be from this most profound source of theology—the words of the Messiah about his kingdom of God. This is concerning since one must assume Luke provides these summaries not as narrative padding but as loaded repositories with at least the same weight as his Gospel's summaries of Jesus' message about the kingdom. Worse, it will be addressed in chapter 14 how Jesus' full kingdom message has been pervasively disallowed to impact the epistles' content. The ramifications of the continuity of the kingdom of God in Luke's

---

4. Schnabel, *Acts*, 586.
5. Morris, *New Testament Theology*, 148.
6. Ladd, *Theology of the New Testament*, 369.
7. Wenham, *Paul*, 405.

Gospel and Acts should be absorbed much more deeply as foundational for the overall theology of Paul and the Testaments.

DISTRACTIONS FROM PAUL'S MESSAGE

Even more distracting from the significance of Paul's continuity with Jesus' kingdom teaching is the unsurprising yet frequent redefinition of "kingdom of God" rendering it more consistent with what most feel to be Paul's central theology. In Acts 20:24, Paul speaks of "the gospel of God's grace" that he proclaimed to the Ephesian elders:

> I consider my life as nothing to me; I aim only to finish the race and complete the task the Lord Jesus has given me: testifying to the good news of God's grace.

The next verse states,

> I know that all of you among whom I went about proclaiming the kingdom, will not see my face again. (Acts 20:25)

According to some, due to the proximity of the terms "gospel" (24) and "kingdom" (25), one might conclude that the meaning of the "kingdom (of God)" became synonymous with "the gospel of God's grace" in the early church, which is equated to some message of salvation, usually centered on the Passion. For instance, Richard I. Pervo implies that Luke has left his own Gospel's meaning of kingdom of God for another paradigm when he writes his Acts and now refers to it as "the gospel." He posits this on the basis of the objective genitive in Acts 20:25:

> This combination (κηρύσσω + βασιλεία, "proclaim" + "kingdom") is used in Acts only here and in the last verse of the book (28:31). The noun indicates that, for Luke, "kingdom" as object of proclamation was essentially the same as "gospel," which is one of the variants.[8]

Craig Keener and Simon Kistemaker are two further examples of those who synonymize "gospel" and "kingdom" based on this supposed parallel of pronouncement terminology. But the parallel is broken when essentially a new paragraph has begun between these phrases. Paul begins

---

8. Pervo, *Acts*, 522. Yet, no Bible translation uses this variant. Later Pervo writes of Acts 28:23, "'Dominion of God' means, in effect, the message of the gospel." *Acts*, 684. Others equate the "kingdom of God" and the "gospel": Schnabel, *Acts*, 1071; Kellum, *Acts*, 100, 317.

verse 25 with a change of perspective: "And now, listen carefully [Καὶ νῦν ἰδοὺ]."[9] Others specify the "kingdom of God" to mean, narrowly, the message of salvation, probably assuming God's "grace" could only refer to his saving grace and not to the grace of the messianic commission in its fullness.[10] Surprisingly, David Wenham broadly attributes this equation of the gospel and kingdom to refer to salvation even to a complicit teaching of Jesus, ironically inverting even the Messiah's teaching to be the Pauline gospel: "It is clear that Paul is familiar with 'kingdom of God' language: He uses it as a sort of catchall phrase to describe Christian salvation—in a way not dissimilar to that of Jesus."[11]

This parallel equation that some suggest between these two verses as an evolution in kingdom meaning in the early church works both ways, however. A symmetrical retroversion rather than an evolution is an equally viable application of this suggested equation: if the "kingdom of God" means "the gospel" then "the gospel" means "the kingdom of God." However, most would not care for this arithmetic. Jesus combined the terms "gospel" and "kingdom of God" from the beginning and throughout his ministry (Mark 1:14-15). This is not a place where many would like to return in respect to Paul's theology, where Jesus proclaimed God's gospel as the arrival of Jesus' coregency over the universal kingdom. However, it is one thing to cast Paul's message in the same terms and understanding of Jesus' message of the kingdom of God. It is quite another to substitute another gospel, whoever that might be, for that of Jesus' message of the "kingdom of God" in Luke's Gospel and Pauline summaries in Acts. Frequent examples of this substitution will be shown in chapter 14.

Marshall offers another alternative to the plain equivalence of Luke's kingdom of God phrasing in Jesus and Paul, yet the alternative is still in the salvific sense. He argues that the kingdom of God in Acts became

---

9. Keener, *Acts*, 3:3022. Kistemaker: "In Acts, to preach the kingdom of God means to proclaim the Word of the Lord, that is, the gospel . . . in 20:24-25. [Luke] uses the terms *the gospel of grace* and *the kingdom* as synonym." Kistemaker, *Acts*, 683; also 967. Moreover, it is gratuitous to assume that God's grace should be limited to the Passion and its justification implications since that is not the connection Paul makes later in the same address to the Ephesian elders in verse 32, where God's grace refers not to the Passion but to sanctification: "Now I entrust you to God and to the word of His grace, which is able to build you up and to give you the inheritance among all those who are sanctified."

10. See also Williams, *Acts*, 21; Polhill, *Acts*, 216-17; Strauss, *Mark*, 80; Larkin, *Acts*, 297; Schnabel, *Acts*, 844.

11. Wenham, *Paul*, 73.

associated more with repentance for the forgiveness of sins and the kingship of Jesus than it had earlier:

> In the former period, the Law and the Prophets were the controlling factors. From then on, the good news of the kingdom is being proclaimed. This proclamation continues after the death and resurrection of Jesus as the followers of Jesus also made the kingdom the object of their preaching (Acts 8:12; 19:8; 20:25; 28:23, 31), although there is a shift in the accent as the theme is expounded more in terms of the king (Acts 17:7) and the call to repentance with the offer of forgiveness of sins (Lk 24:47).[12]

However, repentance for the forgiveness of sins and kingship was not a new context for the kingdom in Luke's Gospel or Acts since it is reflected from the start of Jesus' ministry, even before, in John the Baptist's ministry. In fact, the call to repentance for forgiveness in reference to the king is a perpetual message of both Testaments.

> The kingdom of God is here/near. Repent and believe. (Mark 1:14–15)

> Jesus came into all the region around the Jordan, proclaiming a baptism of repentance for the forgiveness of sins. (Luke 3:3)

> John the Baptist appeared in the wilderness, proclaiming a baptism of repentance for the forgiveness of sins. (Mark 1:4)

Furthermore, the idea of Jesus as a king is an explicitly significant emphasis in Jesus' Passion week according to Luke (Luke 19:38; 23:2–3, 37–38). So, "a shift in the accent" is untenable since there is only continuity between Jesus and his apostles in the Gospels and Acts on the subjects of the kingdom of God, repentance, and Jesus' kingship. Marshall is correct, however, in seeing the continuity extending back to the Law and Prophets, e.g., Isa 30:15.

Luke's summaries are obligatory to address in the commentaries; still, New Testament theologies or even specific theologies of Paul rarely, if ever, consider how these passages cumulatively have a substantive role in Pauline theology.[13] Perhaps, to contend for such proximity between

---

12. Marshall, *Theology*, 145.

13. Pervo attempts a theological explanation of the use of "kingdom of God" in Acts in a footnote that references Karl Barth's dictum concerning apostles leaving the words *from* Jesus behind to advocate for their own words *about* him: "By using the same words to characterize the message of both Jesus and Paul, Luke helps overcome the gap between 'proclaimer' and 'proclaimed.'" Pervo, *Acts*, 522. This hermeneutical

the central message of Jesus and Paul would be disruptive to the narrative of discontinuity between Jesus and Paul that pervades Pauline theology to various degrees. Yet, this simple acknowledgment that the meaning of the kingdom of God is the same whether used by Jesus, Luke, Paul, or the early church is a stronger position than morphing the phrase to mean something else in Acts that results in an unnecessary discontinuity. A paradigm shift where Paul's message was the kingdom of God, as summarized by Luke, would be nearly scandalous. Yet one should take Luke's kingdom of God summaries in Acts as consistent with what he does in his Gospel.[14] Luke's understanding of the "kingdom of God" is consistent in both of his books since there is nothing to indicate otherwise. No conversion of its meaning is found exegetically, nor should it be imposed on the text by a preferred theological paradigm.

What might be standing against my position is the pervasive and debilitating hermeneutical presupposition that the New Testament message should be divided between the Gospels' message *from* Jesus and the apostles' message *about* him. We will look at this theorem again in chapter 14.

GOD'S INTENTIONAL, ETERNAL, AND ENTIRE PURPOSE

Ephesians 1:8–10: God's Good Intention

Especially in Paul's written communication to the Ephesians one hears of God's designing attribute that is seen in the teleology of his creation and its history. I suggest that each of three passages contain key words identifying God's design as intentional, eternal, and comprehensive.

---

principle which Pauline theology considers axiomatic will be returned to in chapter 14.

14. C. K. Barrett's understanding of Luke's summary in 20:25 and the kingdom of God sounds reasonable enough in one sense: "It means in effect the recognized content of Christian preaching, and is so expressed in order to bring out the continuity between the preaching of Jesus and the preaching of the post-resurrection church." Barrett, *Acts*, 2:973. But comments elsewhere on 8:12 obscure his exact position on the issue by dismissing Jesus' meaning of God's kingdom as irrelevant to the use of the meaning in Acts: "It seems clear for Luke in Acts *kingdom of God* can serve as a general summary of Christian belief and preaching (e.g., 28:23); it is not necessary to go back to the gospel tradition and inquire exactly what the expression meant in the teaching of Jesus." Barrett, *Acts*, 1:408.

God's good intention	Eph 1:8–10	Messiah's universal kingdom
God's eternal purpose	Eph 3:8–11	God's eternal design achieved through Christ
God's entire purpose	Acts 20:27	Kingdom (of God) and Ephesians' sanctification

In Eph 1:9–10, by three words of clear intentionality, Paul asserts that it was God's "will (θελήματος)" and his "good intention (εὐδοκία)" to "plan (προτίθημι)" for all creation to be united (ἀνακεφαλαιώσασθαι) in the Messiah (τῷ Χριστῷ).

> God made known to us the mystery of his will according to his good intention which he planned in him in the fullness of times, the uniting of all things in the Christ, things in the heavens and on the earth. (Eph 1:9–10)

Christ's universal kingdom was planned and has already been accomplished: "All that the Father has is mine" (John 16:15). He says this tautologically as the Second Person but incarnationally as the God/man.

In Col 3:11, Paul claims "Christ—all, and among [ἐν] all" as shorthand for what he had already written earlier in 1:16–17: "Everything has been created through him and for him. . . . He is before all things, and in him all things hold together." "Christ—all" abbreviates the Messiah's universal kingdom and providence. That Christ is "among all" indicates that all demographics and classes are united with him since they all have believers among them. Based on Eph 1:10, everything falls under his lordship, everything is summed "in Christ" and everything is affected by his agency, including all benefits of salvation.

Ephesians 3:8–11: God's Eternal Purpose

Paul repeats later in Eph 3:8–11 that it was God's complex, wise plan (οἰκονομία) that achieved his *eternal purpose* (πρόθεσιν τῶν αἰώνων) through Christ. What 1:8–10 asserts about God's will and good intention is now said in 3:8–11 to have been a mysterious plan, which in God's wisdom has already been achieved and revealed to the heavenly kingdom by the trusting kingdom.

> This grace was given [to me]: to proclaim to the Gentiles Christ's immeasurable riches, and to enlighten all people about the mystery's plan that for ages has been hidden in God, who created all things; so that the rich variety of God's wisdom might now be made known through the church to the rulers and authorities in the heavenly places. This was according to the eternal purpose which he carried out in Christ Jesus our Lord.[15]

What was this eternal purpose that God carried out through Christ? It was to unite everything in the universal kingdom from 1:8–10, under the Messiah's lordship.

Acts 20:20–35: God's Entire Purpose

Returning now to Luke's summation of Paul's teaching in Acts, it is not unreasonable that this good and eternal purpose, this universal kingdom of the Messiah that is referenced in Paul's letter to the Ephesians in chapters 1 and 3 is what Paul has in mind in Acts 20 when bidding goodbye to the elders of Ephesian when leaving Miletus. Paul was convinced God's good and eternal intention could be taught "wholly." So in Acts 20:20–35 we finally hear about the good, eternal, and *entire* plan of God (πᾶσαν τὴν βουλὴν τοῦ θεοῦ).

I would offer a different defining parallel in the more immediate context of Acts 20:25–28, which most editions separate as starting a new paragraph:

> I know that all of you, among whom I went about proclaiming the kingdom, will not see my face again. So, I testify to you this day that I am innocent of the blood of all men. For I did not shrink from declaring to you the entire purpose of God [πᾶσαν τὴν βουλὴν τοῦ θεοῦ]. Be on guard for yourselves and for all the flock, among which the Holy Spirit has made you overseers, to shepherd the church of God which he purchased with His own blood.

Paul parallels his proclamation of the *kingdom* with his declaring of God's *entire purpose*, not with a narrower message of salvation. So, in keeping with Luke's summaries of Paul's kingdom pronouncements, rather than limiting Paul's perspective, and if parallels are important,

---

15. Of course Markus Barth's translation for "the eternal purpose" as "the design concerning the ages" is welcomed by this study: "This is the design concerning the ages which God has carried out in the Messiah . . ." Barth, *Ephesians 1–3*, 326, 345.

then "proclaiming the kingdom" provides a much wider berth since the closest parallel is "the entire purpose of God." It may be an adequate restriction of God's entire purpose to see history only parenthetically and through the lens of salvation history primarily, or alone. However, that window is inadequate to grasp God's "entire purpose" for his creation. His reign over his universal realm according to his shepherding eternal design is the explicit implication of his pronouncements in verse 28, and the episode of the Passion is the conduit for living the sanctified life eternally. I believe the following excerpts are a fair rendition of Paul's thinking here: "I went about proclaiming the kingdom . . . declaring to you the whole purpose [βουλὴ] of God. . . . So shepherd the church of God which he [God/man] purchased with his own blood."

There is a definite continuity in emphasizing God's purposefulness in his creation's history within these three passages that are addressed to the Ephesian laity and elders.

History is eternal and entirely contains all of creation's time, space, events, and all divine and human purposes. So it should be obvious that salvation history and its salvation increments do not compare with the comprehensiveness of God's eternal design. The salvation history which is only found within the parenthetical age does not apprehend the richness of God and his Messiah's universal kingdom and its eternal sub-realms.

OBJECTIVE OF PAUL'S TEACHING

Luke summarizes Paul's overall message four times, and in turn, Paul himself summarizes his overall message as the kingdom of God in his farewells to the Ephesian church's leaders: "I have gone about proclaiming the kingdom" (Acts 20:25). Consistent with the Testaments throughout, religious leaders bear responsibility for their trusting community. They have been gifted as shepherds to tend their flock, as Jesus repetitively stressed to Peter over breakfast one morning (John 21:15–17). So, the Ephesian elders, who were "among the sanctified" (20:32) were to model the renewed life from within the community. In addressing the elders, Paul combines specific shepherding instructions with the most general theological construct, something he does often in his letters. In this presumably edited length of Paul's comments and his last opportunity to "say it all," Luke crystallizes the most profound features of both Jesus and Paul's theology including the kingdom of God. Paul reminds the elders that he had commented publicly and privately "anything" that was of benefit (20). This would have included the lofty "entire purpose of God" as well as one's routine "working hard" and from the widest soteriological process of grace and sanctification, to the most immediate requirement, the episode of one's justification. Paul begins this speech where Jesus began, referring to instructions about repentance and faith (20:21; Mark 1:15), the two requirements for sanctification's post-justification progress for those yet to believe and for those already believing. He speaks in the most general terms of God's blessings, his grace (24, 32; cf. 14:3; 1 Pet 5:12), which is Paul's first and greatest wish for all of his parishioners when he begins each letter by requesting God's continual "grace and peace" for them.

Paul, in this departing speech to the elders, then begins to apply the implications of God's grace to those responding in repentance and trust thus redeemed by the blood of Christ (28). In so doing, he traverses the basics of the eternal design: blessing, deliverance, and discipline. Deliverance from sin, deliverance from the assault of infiltrating wolves, deliverance of the vulnerable from their pressing needs. Paul speaks to them in literal shepherding terms: vigilance and sober alertness are required for the Ephesian "shepherds" (28–31). It is God's word of grace (32) and the words of the Lord Jesus (35) that build the believer up to the point of the sanctified's eternal inheritance. Paul himself does not presume on others to support him (33), but in self-reliance he shepherded his entourage (34). He challenges the elders toward diligence as well in their shepherding the weak within their flock by quoting the agraphon of Jesus: "It is more of a blessing to give than to receive" (35).

Like the administrative closings to Paul's letters, one might be tempted to dismiss these practical examples of sanctification as if Paul trails into everyday things. However, Paul's closings are the routine of holy living as Paul works out his theology and works out what God had transformed within him and what he wishes to see believers work out in their own repentance and trust. Though Acts 20:18–35 is addressed to the Ephesian elders who were among the sanctified, the letter sent to all Ephesians is replete with ethical expectations from the renewed believers. These practical ethical matters are the motivation and essence of this letter.

- Harmony   1:15; 2:12–18; 4:1–16, 25–29; 4:31—5:2, 21; 6:18
- Sexual ethics   4:22; 5:3
- Justice for the weak   4:28
- Stealing   4:28
- Greed   4:19; 5:3, 5
- Violence   4:26, 31–32
- True worship   5:5; 5:18–20
- Deception   4:22
- Foul speech   4:29; 5:4
- Drunkenness   5:18
- Marriage   5:22–33
- Children's obedience   6:1–3
- Fathers' kindness   6:4
- Slaves' obedience   6:5–8
- Respect for slaves   6:9

God's *intentional, entire, and eternal* plan for the Messiah was not only to come and close out the parenthetical age. The Messiah rules forever,[16] even when the eternal design's shepherding functions of deliverance and discipline will no longer be needed. God's eternal design does not simply raise creation out of its parenthetical hole, back to ground zero, but the eternal design picks up where it left off in Eden to continue creation's management of itself under God's shepherding direction. In other words, eternal teleology still matters, and its objectives will not change.

---

16. 2 Sam 7:13; Dan 7:13–14; Luke 1:32–33; Eph 1:20–21; 2 Pet 1:11; Rev 11:15. An arguable solution to this eternal reign of Christ and the expectation of handing the reign and realm to the Father is that Christ's reign is a necessity "until" he has vanquished all his enemies and their realm. This only accentuates that his reign must last *at least* until then. The syntax does not demand that he then ceases to reign. Presenting a perfected universal kingdom to the Father recognizes that the Father's reign from and throughout eternity was shared temporarily with the God/man who will continue at this central eschatological point of history only as the divine Son, not necessarily as a God/man.

10

Kingdoms' Interactions

KINGDOM THEOLOGY IS FAR more than defining Jesus' gospel of the kingdom of God. A kingdom structure throughout creation and its history has been shown in this study to permeate the Testaments' understanding of God's relationship with his creation. So, the kingdom interactions surveyed in this chapter will show the significant role they play in the historical drama of the eternal design within this parenthetical age. The Testaments' narrative could not have been written without chronicling the encouraging as well as terrifying intersections of any two or more of the eight kingdoms. These kingdom crossings are inevitable, given that history is as fully integrated as the complete integration of creation's events. To this incalculable volume of kingdom interactions, add their massive domains and power. Only then does one begin to comprehend the enormity of God's kingdom structure and his administration of them as they determine all of history's contents. Nevertheless, this structure operates within the context of the eternal design, whether constructively or destructively. Regardless of being constructive or destructive, all events operate by the same constrictions, from the nature of creation and its history as presented in our first chapter, including God's fully integrated and wise teleological thrust.

Fortunately, the Messiah's success in holding all things together by his powerful word requires the positive cooperation of most of the kingdoms a sufficient amount of the time. But this cooperation is frequently allowed to dissolve into conflicts, small or global, as ramifications of God's Eden curse among any rebellious alliance of the spirits and humanity. Family, neighborhood, societal, regional, national, global, and spiritual conflicts are not always due to moral equivalence; rather, they can be one-sided aggressive assaults at each of these levels at the expense of the "innocents." Nevertheless, all battles between the heavenly, trusting, terrestrial, satanic, and natural kingdoms are still subject to the discretion shown by God as he dynamically exercises his universal reign over his universal realm. Creation's history in its incalculably complex, eternal, comprehensive, relational, integrated, and teleological nature testifies to how God keeps order in his universal kingdom by his shepherding sovereignty, making God's universal kingdom manifest now.

The kingdom interactions in this epoch are integral to the Testaments, not mere landscaped backgrounds and props for whatever theological narrative one might see as a biblical story. Rather, it is the nature of history, including the parenthetical age, to intersect all sub-realms under God's active universal reign, thus composing the history of all creation. These kingdoms cooperate and clash everywhere on the planet in different arrangements as they conform to or resist the eternal design. They bless, deliver, and discipline each other, or they ignore, neglect, afflict, or act unjustly to the other kingdoms, depending on the diverse and countless situations in which the kingdoms are engaged, in which era and area, and by whom; thus, all of history is kingdom-based. Again, the eternal design is the pattern for the kingdoms to follow. How well humanity's sanctified shepherding goes, so goes history. Put more generally, how well the kingdoms shepherd is exactly how positive a span of history is.

This forms a far broader and more complex matrix within which to place all of creation's historical and conceptual components than within a limited biblical theological narrative such as salvation history. A (meta)narrative may itemize some of history's content, but it cannot begin to fathom the effect of the operating principle by which the eight kingdoms engage outside that narrative. It is a matrix for which a focus on any segment or genre of history does not suffice. Tragically, the parenthetical age is not only about the progress of salvation, but the progress of humanity's self-incrimination and intensification of the Curse and the ramifications of this perpetual intensification. Yet this fallen condition of creation is by far the more prevalent milieu of the sub-kingdoms and their interaction with each other's realms while advancing or tragically impeding the eternal design's realization. It requires the believer to be aware of more than redemption history and to be interested in much more than evangelism. The kingdoms' serious complications require navigation by wise and resourceful responses as the believer becomes more apt to do so by progressive sanctification.

The Testaments consistently use the term "kingdom," yet its pervasive significance is not shown only when the word itself is found. Where the term may not be explicit, the kingdom structure of creation and its history no less saturates the Testaments, which relentlessly reveal the various interactions of the eight kingdoms. Since the kingdom of God is a foundational theme in the Testaments regardless of one's theological framework or how the concept is defined, one might miss its pervasive presence and significance if only searching concordances for the word "kingdom" and its lexical field of related terms—one must look more conceptually.[1] The following analyses of the sub-kingdoms' interactions are based on the concept of their ubiquitous presence and role that each plays within the universal realm. Each of the following New Testament examples are concluded by the initials of the kingdoms that are explicitly woven together in that passage.

UK	Universal kingdom:	Integrated realm by the eternal design: all creation, kingdoms, and ages.
HK	Heavenly kingdom:	Where the Trinity, holy angels, and deceased believers dwell and function.
MK	Messianic kingdom:	The universal kingdom granted to Christ to rule as the Father directs.
SK	Satanic kingdom:	Satan's exiled realm from where fallen angels impact other kingdoms.
NK	Natural kingdom:	All creation except spirits and humans souls. But the body is included.
TerK	Terrestrial kingdom:	The peoples, including their national and civil divisions.
TruK	Trusting kingdom:	All those trusting the one God, thus are justified.
NE	New Earth	Where all kingdoms except the satanic kingdom continue to interact eternally.

1. So Schreiner, as an advocate for the relevance of the kingdom of God in the Testaments concludes, at least literally, "The kingdom of God cannot be a central theme if we count up how many times the words 'king,' 'kingdom,' or 'rule' and 'reign' appear, for in many books of the Bible they do not appear at all." Schreiner, *Beauty*, xiii.

Over sixty texts are considered among the categories of Gospels: Acts, Paul, John, and other writers. Of course, disagreement is expected on the details of the analyses and the number of kingdoms referenced in each passage, but a fuller commentary on each with interactions with secondary sources would be far beyond what is necessary, since the cumulative point here is that all creation's kingdom history is comprehensively integrated in the way they advance or impede creation's pursuit of the eternal design.

INTERACTIONS IN THE GOSPELS

Within the Gospels, the supremacy of the Messiah's universal kingdom over the satanic is shown in various ways. Jesus' explanations of his messianic kingdom's dominance were punctuated by his exorcisms that were characteristic of his and his followers' ministries (Mark 1:32–39; Luke 10:17–20). John records Jesus to say that his purpose for coming was to destroy Satan's works (1 John 3:8), something the demons knew before being exorcized (Mark 1:24 // Luke 4:34). In the New Testament, this began with Satan's ludicrous presumption that he could grant Jesus something that the Second Person already possessed—ownership of all the nations (Matt 4:8–9; Luke 4:5–7). Jesus subsequently bound Satan repeatedly as he plundered and divided his kingdom (Matt 12:29; Luke 11:21–22). Satan and his subordinates were cast out and judged, but the satanic kingdom's demise will be completed only at the end of the parenthetical age (John 12:31; 16:11; Luke 10:18; Rev 20:1–3).

Jesus' kingship over the cursed natural kingdom was also shown routinely by his healings, resurrections, and by bending the laws of nature: its waters, the fish within them, a fig tree, and by multiplying one meal into thousands.

The judicial proceedings of Jesus were not merely introductory material before the Passion. They were venues within the terrestrial kingdom for his direct confrontations with Jews and gentiles when he succinctly affirmed his possession of the terrestrial kingdom within his messianic universal kingdom. He claims the messiahship and kingdom before Caiaphas (Mark 14:61–62) and Pilate (John 18:37). Jesus' contemporary enemies were both Jews and gentiles, but his own simple binomial division of people is a universal principle: "Whoever is not with me is against me" (Matt 12:30). The residents of the terrestrial kingdom then belong either to his kingdom or Satan's (Luke 12:51–52).

Matthew 4:8–10 // Luke 4:6–8: In this epochal event, Satan attempts to replicate the Fall in Eden by subduing the second Adam. He pretends to have an ultimate authority that he does not have, i.e., supremacy over the nations. It worked catastrophically with the Couple but not with the Messiah. Implicit in the Second Person's response is that this is an ominous conversation between Satan and God himself. Satan should have knelt before the very one he was standing before, the one who already ultimately owned all the terrestrial realms. Satan was correct in saying he had authority over the realm of the nations, but it was a sorry attempt to sell sleeves from his vest by confusing authority with ownership. God had handed this ruling "prince" a subordinate role in managing the world, but Satan had no authority to give it to another. The preeminence of the divine human over the satanic and terrestrial kingdoms was already in motion here in the wilderness. *MK, SK, TerK*

Matthew 12:28–30 // Mark 3:23–26 // Luke 11:18–20: When Jesus exorcized by the power of the coregent Spirit from the heavenly kingdom, the Messiah's authority over the satanic kingdom proved that the universal kingdom of God had arrived in him. The leaders could not deny that exorcisms were taking place but could only explain it by Satan's own kingdom. *HK, MK, SK*

Matthew 13:37–43, 49–50: This scene portrays the intersection of the six kingdoms during and at the end of the parenthetical age. The messianic Son of Man and his angels from the heavenly kingdom will enforce justice on all, depending on which kingdom they belong to. Those from the terrestrial kingdom who do not live according to God and Jesus' commandments and instead follow the leader over the satanic kingdom will be separated from those in the trusting kingdom at the end of this age and punished. However, the trusting kingdom will live on in God's new creation. *HK, MK, SK, TerK, TruK, NE*

Matthew 20:25–28 // Mark 10:42–45: The trusting kingdom should do the opposite of the terrestrial kingdom in their mode of leadership. They are not to dominate but to serve like the Son of Man serves as the ruler of the messianic kingdom. This exemplifies the eternal design of blessing and delivering others—in this case, sacrificing his life to ransom the trusting kingdom from the satanic kingdom. *MK, SK, TerK, TruK*

Matthew 22:21 // Mark 12:17 // Luke 20:25: Jesus acknowledges a citizen's responsibilities within both the terrestrial and trusting realms.

Though one might reason that by funding the government one is complicit in combating God's universal kingdom, Jesus obviously rejects that "logic." Later, the Jews were desperate to lie to Pilate about Jesus' stated position on paying taxes (Luke 23:2). *UK, TerK, TruK*

Matthew 24:3–36 // Mark 13:3–37 // Luke 21:7–36: All created kingdoms, physical and spiritual, are involved in the excruciating process of closing out the parenthetical age. This harrowing end is creation's last effort under Satan's final flare of devastation to destroy all that is good. This end of the age involves messiah imposters, false prophets, ultimate sacrilege, wars between terrestrial realms, natural disasters, and the trusting kingdom's martyrdom by the nations. Earth and sky as we know them will disappear, but all peoples will have heard the good news before the Messiah returns from the heavenly kingdom with his angels. The angels will gather the globally scattered trusting kingdom to enjoy eternal New Earth. *HK, MK, SK, NK, TerK, TruK, NE*

Matthew 25:31–40: Jesus, the "King," will come from his heavenly kingdom with his angels and judge the nations. Individuals from the satanic terrestrial kingdom will be separated from those of the shepherding trusting kingdom whose citizens complied with the eternal design and blessed and delivered others from the physical adversities of hunger, thirst, loneliness, nakedness, imprisonment, and sickness. These blessed shepherds will inherit the kingdom of the new creation. *UK, HK, MK, SK, TerK, TruK, NE*

Matthew 26:51–53 // Mark 14:47 // Luke 22:49–51 // John 18:10–11: A multi-kingdom confluence at Jesus' arrest occurs when Peter, representing the disciples' readiness to defend Jesus against the terrestrial kingdom leaders, attacks and wounds Malchus. The Messiah rebukes Peter and reveals his own authority to call on his own angels as an even more effective defensive force. Jesus restores Malchus's severed ear, showing his authority over the natural kingdom. *HK, MK, NK, TerK, TruK*

Matthew 27:11, 29, 37, 42 // Mark 15:2, 12, 18, 26, 32 // Luke 23:3, 37–38 // John 18:36–37; 19:10–15, 19: The discussion between Pilate and Jesus was at the highest level that either of them had confronted since they spoke from the position as authorities under the authority of a superior divine being, Caesar and the Father, respectively. Jesus said he was a king, just not one sourced from this world, implying it was sourced in the heavenly kingdom. This was more seditious than claiming one's own authority since Jesus bypasses Caesar's authority, saying Pilate would have no power except from the Lord. Pilate's wife receives an ominous vision from the heavenly kingdom. The Jews pit Rome against Rome by calling Pilate a traitor for tolerating another king, Jesus. Rome taunts Israel by Pilate's sarcastic exchange with the Jews and their religious leaders, ending in his unwitting, ironic insistence on the truthful declaration posted above the assassinated Jesus: "King of the Jews." *UK, HK, MK, SK, NK, TerK*

Matthew 28:2–8 // Mark 16:2–6 // Luke 24:1–6: An angel appears to agents of the terrestrial kingdom and paralyzes them with fear. The natural kingdom responds to the heavenly kingdom by shaking the tombstone loose. *HK, NK, TerK*

Matthew 28:18–20: The Messiah, who now has all authority over the universal kingdom, demands that the disciples expand the baptized, trusting kingdom by discipling believers from all terrestrial kingdoms by the universal authority of the Trinity. The discipling meant teaching obedience to all of the Messiah's wisdom and commandments. *HK, MK, TerK, TruK*

Luke 10:17–19: This passage has three allusions to the vanquished satanic kingdom. (1) The commissioned disciples return from their Luke 9 mission excited about their exorcisms and the demon's submission to them because of Jesus' universal authority, something the Couple failed in because the satanic serpent inverted the commission and subdued them instead (Gen 1:28; 3:4–6). (2) Jesus quotes the Old Testament allusion to Satan's expulsion from the heavenly kingdom (Isa 14:12–14) as well as (3) the trampling of the serpent (Gen 3:15) that Paul reaffirms (Rom 16:20). The same delivering and disciplining functions of the eternal design that the Messiah modeled was extended to his disciples. The shepherding Messiah shepherds his shepherding disciples. *HK, MK, SK, TruK*

John 11:47–48: Jerusalem's leaders were concerned about the ceremonial and political implications of Jesus' success in attracting believers. They did not deny his signs but feared losing their influence over their terrestrial kingdom of Israel and attracting too much attention from Rome. It was a political matter for them as they vied for both their terrestrial kingdoms. *TerK, TruK*

John 12:31–34: Jesus announces the kingdom meaning of the Passion week, a week of judgment in two senses. (1) Satan will be judged and "driven out" from his princely role over all the nations, including Israel, and (2) the judgment against the Messiah and his sacrificial death will accelerate his draw of the whole world to himself and his kingdom. That Jesus would be "lifted up" was a poetic foreshadow and the only pre-Passion hint in the Gospels about the means of his death. *MK, SK, TerK*

John 16:33: Jesus tells his believers what he had said in so many words earlier (12:31–34; 14:30–31): that he had already overcome the world and its terrestrial kingdom. This is not a complete overcoming, only proof of what will be complete. That is, he has accelerated the demise of the enemy and the growth of the trusting kingdom. The trusting kingdom will find peace in its King even while distressed by the fallen world. *MK, TerK, TruK*

These Gospel texts integrate the kingdoms and demonstrate the preeminence of the messianic universal kingdom as it accelerates God's global objective that he has pursued since Genesis. The passages reveal the reasons for the acrimony between the messianic kingdom and the satanic kingdom, which includes what was ultimately and already Jesus' terrestrial realm. But the texts also reveal the Messiah's authority to direct the course of history by governing the sub-realms of his universal kingdom. One observes in these Gospel texts that the kingdom substructure and its interrelationships conflict and at times collaborate.

INTERACTIONS IN ACTS

Luke's Acts of the Apostles includes the same signs and wonders as the acts of Jesus in the Gospels, showing the supremacy of the universal kingdom over the satanic, terrestrial, and natural kingdoms. These kingdom interactions in Acts are still under the authority (in the name) of the ascended Jesus Christ the Lord (3:6–7; 4:7, 29–30) since Peter says more directly to Aeneas, "Jesus Christ heals you" (9:34). The Lord is the one who blinds Elymas directly as he healed Paul on the way to Damascus, without human mediation (13:10–11). The apostles brought healing for many, exorcisms for others, even at least one resurrection (9:40–41). Christ's followers continued the purpose of the Incarnation by defeating Satan's house through exorcisms (5:12–16; 6:8; 8:6–7; 10:38; 13:10; 16:18). Satan overpowers Ananias and Sapphira, but divine justice prevails and executes them (5:3–10). Simon the cultic magician is outdone by Philip's works, so by his message of "the kingdom of God," Simon converts (8:12–13), exemplifying what it means "to open their eyes, so that they may turn from darkness to light and from the power of Satan to God" (26:18).

Furthermore, in the same way as Jesus clashed with the terrestrial kingdom, the apostles debated Jewish and gentile leaders by his authority.

Sadly, this conflict continued with Israel's leaders and escalated to Rome in the most direct ways (13:46-48). Acts is composed substantially of the apostles' interactions with terrestrial leaders and their courts. Their judicial proceedings with Jewish and gentile administrators drew just as clear jurisdictional lines at this point in history as the frequent and final conflicts of Revelation. Acts begins with apostolic charges against the terrestrial kingdom leaders of Israel and Rome for executing the universal King, and Peter continues these charges in his court appearances. The book concludes with extended passages about Paul's legal confrontations. Paul teaches to submit to the authorities, and he will even use their laws to protect himself and the success of his mission. Paul not only highlights the interactions of the kingdoms, but he also presents them as staged examples to be seen publicly by the inhabitants of the terrestrial, heavenly, and satanic kingdoms (Rom 9:17; 1 Cor 4:9; Eph 3:10; 1 Tim 3:16; 5:21; 6:13).

However, it is not purely a political clash of authority, but as subsequent history proves, it is an ideological clash determined by the relatively shallow wisdom of the terrestrial kingdom's rulers as they are strapped with an empirical philosophy of history rather than the revealed theology of history's teleology (1 Cor 2:6-8, 12-13). Again, the terrestrial kingdom's oppression of the brave and ever-sustained trusting kingdom illustrates the simple truth that within the universal kingdom, one is a citizen either of the trusting kingdom or the satanic kingdom, a reality in Acts and throughout history until the new creation.

According to Luke, as explained in our last chapter, Paul's pronouncements about God's universal kingdom were common in his mission to the gentiles. The success of his call to the gentiles was due to the message and demonstration of God's superiority to pagan gods, not only in their alleged power but in their abhorrent care for the world. The universal kingdom was a necessary matter to address to the nations since it was the widest context within which salvation could be proven necessary. The gentiles would have had very little interest in yet another terrestrial kingdom. Whereas Jesus' Jewish audience had an awareness and interest in Yahweh's universal reign, Paul and other apostles in their global commission had to begin with the gentiles' ignorance of the Old Testament and with Israel's apparent insignificance in world politics. So, while in Lystra (Acts 14), in Athens (Acts 17), and on a voyage with international passengers (Acts 27), Paul identifies God not as mythical but as the Creator of all. He is a God whose discretion allows humanity to stray from his truth while at the same time blessing them with rain, food, and other pleasures. God is significantly engaged with all humanity, determining its time and space parameters, and blessing, delivering, and disciplining all humanity. God's constant provision of sustenance is punctuated with episodes like the Maltese shipwreck, when deliverance from adversity and the wrath of nature is answered by the encouragement of angels that God's purposes could not be restrained.

Acts 1:6–8: Jesus did not answer the disciples' question about the restoration of the terrestrial kingdom of Israel. Rather, he reminded them of the Father's reign over the universal kingdom that sets the definite and suitable times for the epochs of *all* nations—God's primary objective from Genesis. The disciples' question about their kingdom was off point; Christ was concerned only about the next phase, which was the Spirit's guidance on their global mission. Rather than Israel, the more relevant, immanent, and beneficial future pertained to the Spirit's global, terrestrial pursuit of the Great Commission (John 16:7–11). Angels encouraged the disciples that Christ would return from the heavenly realm. This recalls his predicted descent from the clouds in his first Incarnation when he was promised the universal kingdom (Dan 7:13–14) and his future return (Matt 24:30; Acts 3:21). *UK, HK, MK, TerK, TruK*

Acts 2:1–12: The natural kingdom's wind and fire are employed to stress the Spirit's inspiration of messages through the "Galileans" spoken in many languages of the terrestrial kingdom from three continents. The rapid expansion of the trusting kingdom had now begun, starting with these carriers of Christ's message, who upon returning home to their terrestrial kingdom would ignite an evangelistic explosion. *UK, HK, NK, TerK, TruK*

Acts 4:26–28: In this prayer, the extent of God's powerful rule over the times and events within his universal realm is blatantly professed. Consistent with Ps 2, Herod, Pilate, gentiles, and Jews—in other words, all peoples—conspired against God's servant, the "Anointed." The teleology of history under God's complete sovereignty predetermined that humanity's resistance led to their means of salvation in the Messiah's self-sacrifice. This confirmed what Jesus had told Pilate that the terrestrial kingdom's authorities have political power only from God whether they acknowledge it or not (John 19:11). *UK, MK, TerK*

Acts 5:29–31: Peter and his fellow apostles affirm the priority of obedience to God over terrestrial authority. Clashes are inevitable between a perfect universal kingdom and the fallen terrestrial kingdom.

Though it is God's universal kingdom, it is also the kingdom of the coregent Messiah, "the one whom God exalted to His right hand as a Prince and a Savior," the one terrestrial leaders had executed. *UK, MK, TerK*

Acts 12:21-23: The most dire end is in store for one who does not acknowledge that one's terrestrial kingdom is only assigned to him by God and must not to be taken for granted. All authority is subject to God's universal kingdom, including the heavenly kingdom from where the angel came to kill Herod and including the natural kingdom's worms that added a grotesque touch. *UK, HK, NK, TerK*

Acts 14:11-17: Paul tells the people of Lystra that they have misplaced their worship, giving it to worthless Zeus and other pagan gods when instead it must be directed to the kind Creator-God "who made the heavens and the earth and the sea and everything in them." Paul explains that God had let the nations go their own way (Rom 1:21-32) by their own rebellious, confused interpretation of the world order. Yet God still shepherds and blesses them through the natural kingdom with rain, crops, food, and joy (Eccl 2:24-25). The contrast of all cultures' worldviews with God's natural and general revelation is the bane of any society while it struggles within the domain of darkness. Nonetheless, he still shepherds them as they, in their best moments, shepherd others. *UK, NK, TerK*

Acts 17:18, 22-31: Paul defines a broad scope for a correct theology and teleology of history for the Athenian philosophers. As in Lystra, he explains God's universal kingdom and how he serves the world as the great benefactor. He creates the nations, ensuring their distribution, their national boundaries, and historical epochs. He tolerates humanity's fumbling around while searching for the God who is in plain sight (Rom 1:19-20). This God shepherds by blessing everyone with life, breath, and whatever sustains life. He pursues his eternal design: he blesses, he delivers by resurrections, and he disciplines in the final judgment by the appointed "man." *UK, MK, NK, TerK*

Acts 27:22-24: During Paul's shipwreck experience near Malta, he revealed to the travelers the convergence of the heavenly, natural, terrestrial, and trusting kingdoms. God's revelation came through an angel to him, a trusting believer who "belonged to the God he worshiped." God would control the natural elements because God's plan would not deter his evangelistic and political plan for Paul to contend with the Roman terrestrial kingdom authority, Caesar. *UK, NK, TerK, TruK*

INTERACTIONS IN PAUL

We saw earlier that in Eph 3:8–11 and elsewhere that God's singular design has a comprehensive and eternal purpose for all creation. Paul's theology is immersed in the context of the interacting kingdoms under the universal kingdoms of God and his Messiah. In Romans, for instance, God's attributes are seen clearly enough in his general revelation that humanity is culpable for its unappreciative, disrespectful, and unrighteous responses. So God's judgment was to allow personal and cultural naturalism to dissolve into self-denigration until his and Christ's final judgment (1:18–32; 2:15–16). His realm includes the cursed natural kingdom, which he will then emancipate along with the trusting kingdom so both will survive into his eternal new creation (8:18–20). Paul's robust creation theology, when itemized, adds to his conviction of God's universal kingdom.

Nothing in God's universal realm can threaten his protective, shepherding care for his believers: neither the heavenly and satanic kingdoms, the natural kingdom, nor the terrestrial kingdom (Rom 8:37–39). The persistent rebellion of the satanic and terrestrial kingdoms does not postpone God's successful operations over the universal kingdom. It does not compromise his comprehensive reign over his universal realm of creation. This is Paul's argument in favor of submission to the terrestrial kingdom leaders since all authorities and their realms, including their borders, have been set by God. Paul affirms their divine ordination to serve God's purposes regardless of their oppressive grip (Acts 14:15–17; 17:26; Rom 13:1–7). Paul's conviction is that the universal kingdom restrains the terrestrial kingdom's leaders and their erratic tyrannical and vicious reign, and he expects believers to pray that God within his wisdom will provide sufficient balance for their peace and safety in which to live orderly, predictable, and sanctified lives (1 Tim 2:1–2).

Behind the terrestrial kingdom's intimidation of the trusting kingdom is of course the contending-yet-controlled satanic kingdom, whose leader the God of peace will soon crush under the human believers' feet, as he had promised the human Messiah in Ps 110:1 (Rom 16:20). The depraved and perverted "spirit" of this parenthetical age originates in the satanic kingdom, so the "wisdom" of the terrestrial kingdom is woefully superficial, willfully neglectful, thus too foolish to understand much less follow the purposes of God. On the other hand, the Spirit's revelation and transformation prevail for the trusting kingdom (1 Cor 2:6–8, 12–13) whose believers are to take every thought captive and reveal the terrestrial kingdom's foolishness. God's wisdom will humiliate humanity and its supposed knowledge whether it capitulates or not (1 Cor 1:20–24; 2 Cor 10:4–6). Shallow cultural traditions, in stories, ethics, myths, philosophy, and religions will eventually be disgraced (Col 2:18–23; 2:8–10; 1 Tim 1:3–4; 4:7).

Paul's letters primarily address the trusting kingdom as it grows spiritually, while frequently engaging the other kingdoms. If Paul is obsessed with anything for the believer and the believing community it is with their progress in re-imaging the likeness of God and his Messiah. For Paul, the shepherding eternal design in its most intimate depth and breadth was the sanctification of each edifying community and each of its believers—God's everlasting primary objective. So, whereas Paul's communications in Acts are mainly prophetic, evangelistic, cross-cultural, and apologetic, his letters are more priestly—instructional, ethically demanding but encouraging.

Basic to Paul's messages in Acts about the interactions of the kingdoms, Luke references and summarizes Paul's messaging to be about the universal kingdom of God (Acts 14:22; 19:8; 20:25; 28:23; 28:30–31). Paul also speaks literally of the "kingdom of God" in eight of his letters. Yet, beyond these passages, one need not read literal kingdom terminology to see his awareness of the coregency of the Trinity over the universal kingdom and the interactions of its sub-realms.

Romans 1:18–32: The terrestrial kingdom has no excuse for suppressing the truth about God and his universal kingdom: his invisible attributes, eternal power, and the nature of his divinity. Though in themselves they do not bring justification, these are reasonable inductions from his created order and appreciation should lead to honoring him appropriately, even if not salvifically. All peoples are affected directly by God's nature, having been created in his image and carrying his moral nature and his expectations in their hearts (Rom 2:14–16). Yet, God allows naturalism to reign, which will progressively overwhelm the intrinsic imprint of God's divine nature and character, causing individual and social decline. The conscience-driven, partial compliance with God's moral laws proves that any culture can do better. But in trying to be wise and developing alternate worldviews, their foolishness is obvious since they worship themselves, each other, or the lower lifeforms and strata of creation that they were supposed to subdue (23; 1 Cor 8:4–6; 10:19). God gave them over to the satanic kingdom and allowed them to pursue their aberrant thinking and conduct, including deviant sexuality, as they encouraged others to join them in their rebellion. *UK, NK, TerK*

Romans 8:18–20: This is a relieving statement; the future glory in the new creation will be far greater than the inverse, the sufferings in this present world—an overwhelming way to put present suffering in perspective. How horrendous are the sufferings of humanity and nature now? New Earth will not be simply better than the current human and natural situation; it will be far more exciting than evil is currently distressing. Herein lies a theodicy, an explanation of the duration of the agonizing parenthetical age. Nonetheless, God did subject nature to relative futility compared to its future abundant productivity after its own and humanity's emancipation from the Edenic curse. *NK, TruK, NE*

Romans 8:37–39: All of the sub-realms are at war, each with varying success and failures. Yet the universal kingdom of God and his Messiah subsumes all of creation's sub-realms that might threaten to negate God's love for his believers but to no avail. Fallen angels and their passion for destruction, the natural kingdom and its dangers, the terrestrial authorities' oppression, the present and the future, the spaces above and below; all creation fails to separate the believer from God's love. *UK, HK, MK, SK, NK, TerK, TruK*

Romans 13:1–7: Every authority or kingdom has been approved or set by God. Here, Paul is focusing on higher levels of terrestrial authority; however, the principles apply to every level, including ecclesiastical and parental. Since God is sovereign on every level, his placement of authority is purposeful. There are oppressive, even sadistic authorities in every culture. But as brutal as Caligula and Nero were in his lifetime, and villainous despots are in any age, Paul still believes in their divine ordination to serve God's overall universal administration, even preferring them over the anarchy that would only lead to worse conditions. *UK, TerK, TruK*

Romans 16:20: The God of peace will soon crush Satan under the believers' feet. *UK, SK, TruK*

1 Corinthians 1:20–24: Though Paul argues in Rom 1 that the terrestrial kingdom should know much about the transcendent God, here he says that in composing alternate interpretations of reality it was not able to know and depict God fully enough. Humanity could determine the obvious, that they were subordinate to "a god," and from conscience alone that they were morally impoverished. However, the terrestrial kingdom's religions and philosophies do not lead to knowing God's means of

sin salvation or precise sanctification standards. So believers receive the "foolish" message about a crucified Messiah who was necessary to correct the inadequate "wisdom" of all terrestrial cultures. *UK, MK, TerK, TruK*

1 Corinthians 2:6-8, 12-13: The most profound thinking by the terrestrial kingdom during the parenthetical age is wholly inadequate for understanding the reasoning, wisdom, providence, and purposes of God (3:18-20). An epistemology that ignores the Spirit's impact on true knowledge will define its own "spirit" of this parenthetical age. That spirit is promoted, even enforced, by the satanic kingdom's ruler, the anti-shepherd who reigns over the rulers and their subordinates in the terrestrial kingdom. Satan has intentionally disabled his terrestrial kingdom so it cannot make sense of the good news (2 Cor 4:3-4), but the supremacy of the Trinity's revelation of wisdom in multi-dimensional ways leads his followers to victories along the way. *UK, HK, SK, TerK*

1 Corinthians 4:9: The massacre of the martyrs is witnessed by the heavenly, satanic, and terrestrial kingdoms within the arena of creation; it is even perpetrated by the latter two. *HK, SK, TerK, TruK*

1 Corinthians 15:24-28: All creation is currently subject to Christ, yet when he ends the powerful satanic kingdom and when the rebellious terrestrial kingdom is finally obedient, he will present to God as perfect again what his human nature could claim to be his universal kingdom. *UK, HK, MK, SK, NK, TerK*

2 Corinthians 10:4-6: Kingdom warfare is spiritual warfare propelled by divine power and the trusting kingdom against the satanic and terrestrial kingdoms' "fortresses." Believers and their trusting kingdom are to take every thought captive and destroy speculations and arrogant objections against the knowledge of God (Acts 17) that should have led humanity to submission in the first place (Rom 1). *UK, TerK, TruK*

Ephesians 1:8-12, 22-23: The coming of a messianic kingdom was not a mystery; that was clear enough from the Old Testament prophets. The mysteries were God's timing of that purpose and with whom exactly God would share the universal kingdom. God's revealed mystery is that Christ's messianic kingdom now subsumes all reality; he reigns over all realms, their rulers, authorities, and kingdoms. The trusting kingdom consists of all God's adopted children so they have the inheritance in New Earth that Christ alluded to in the Beatitudes and elsewhere, e.g., Matt 25:34. *UK, HK, MK, SK, NK, TerK, TruK, NE*

Ephesians 2:1-10: The terrestrial kingdom walks in the "spirit" of the parenthetical age under the wicked influence of Satan, whereas the trusting kingdom's believers are citizens in the heavenly kingdom with their gracious and loving God (Phil 3:20). Eventually God will show Christ's even richer grace of the New Earth. Until the new creation and eternally thereafter, one will continue working as sanctified partners with God. Believers have been created for good works that the Spirit has prepared within them (Phil 2:12–13). *UK, HK, SK, TerK, TruK, NE*

Ephesians 3:8–16: God hid his multifaceted plan for his creation until the worldwide trusting kingdom could reveal it to the rulers and authorities in the heavenly kingdom. This wise, eternal purpose that God revealed to the heavenly kingdom leaders is not a single-faceted plan of salvation but a plan that includes all that the Incarnation brought through the Messiah (Eph 1:9–10; Acts 20:27). *UK, HK, MK, SK*

Ephesians 6:11–12: Believers are to equip themselves appropriately, that is, spiritually, to withstand and defeat the spiritual rulers and forces sourced in the satanic kingdom located outside this world. As is true for the messianic kingdom, though the satanic kingdom is not *of* this world, its domain is certainly *in* this world. *SK, TruK*

Philippians 2:8–11: Every "knee" of the believing, satanic, and terrestrial kingdoms will succumb and bow to the coregent Messiah as the divine Lord because of his obedience to God, which included his temporary submission to death: "Not my will, but your will be done" (Luke 22:42). *UK, HK, MK, SK, TerK, TruK*

Philippians 3:20–21: The believer's citizenship is in the heavenly kingdom (Eph 2:1). But, yet to be completed is the physical transformation of the believer's physical body in New Earth by the power of Christ to whom everything is subject. *HK, MK, NK, TruK, NE*

Colossians 1:13–20: The Second Person's role in the universal kingdom was expanded by God in the Incarnation of Jesus to be creation's reconciler and inheritor. Beyond that, he is the sustainer of everything in the cosmic order: the heavenly, satanic, natural, terrestrial, and trusting kingdoms. Within the universal kingdom, one is transferred from the satanic kingdom into the trusting kingdom because of the Messiah's sin deliverance. This good news goes to all creation and publicly humiliates the satanic kingdom (2:15). *UK, HK, MK, SK, NK, TerK, TruK*

Colossians 2:18–23: Combating the erroneous theological and philosophical ideas that infiltrate the church was a significant concern of the apostles. Cultural traditions, "wisdom," ethics, lore, particularly dealing with angels in Colossae's case, were not tolerated to compromise the pristine truth from Jesus and his apostles (2:8–10; 1 Tim 1:3–4; 4:7).

Errant responses to God's natural law, general revelation, and the conscience are the fabric of all cultures and generate self-made religions, teachings, and philosophies with shallow but destructive restrictions and taboos. Those in the trusting kingdom are exempt from such foolishness and are to think differently, having taken every thought captive. *HK, NK, TerK, TruK*

1 Timothy 2:1–2: The interactions of the kingdoms are generally negative according to the New Testament, where harassment, contention, imprisonment, oppression, even martyrdom are experienced by the trusting kingdom. Nonetheless, believers are expected to pray for their leaders including tyrannical Caesars so that the terrestrial kingdom's intimidation and suppression adds less to the already prevalent pressure from the satanic kingdom. The ultimate objective? A godly and dignified life, i.e., sanctification. *UK, TerK, TruK*

INTERACTIONS IN JOHN AND OTHER WRITERS

John's Gospel passages were covered earlier along with the Synoptics, but his letters touch on the purpose for the Messiah's Incarnation, "to destroy the devil's works" (1 John 3:8), i.e., the works of the anti-messiah who has enslaved the terrestrial kingdom (1 John 4:3; 2 John 7). Satan's works will be finally destroyed when the world's non-believers perish and the earth's surface and skies pass away, leaving room for the new creation (1 John 2:16–17).

The kingdoms' intersections are too obvious and thorough in Revelation to itemize and comment on here. Revelation depicts the end to the parenthetical age and the resumption of creation's Genesis perfection in the new creation; the universal kingdom of God and his Messiah continues to prevail into eternity (1:5; 17:14; 19:15–16). The chapters describe the battles of the satanic, terrestrial, heavenly, and trusting kingdoms until the trusting kingdom of priests finally inherits New Earth in its intended excellence in the final two chapters (1:6; 5:9–10). The angels of the heavenly kingdom subdue the satanic kingdom (12:7–9; 19:20; 20:1–3, 9), the world war rebellion of the terrestrial powers fails, the divine final judgment concludes the parenthetical age (20:4–15), the new creation is regained from Genesis (21–22) where the trusting kingdom will reign and shepherd with God (2:26–27; 3:11, 21; 22:5), and the natural kingdom will finally find its repose.

Throughout the New Testament the coregency of God and his Messiah rules over the sub-realms of their universal realm. He allows the implications of his curse, compounded by the sin of cursed humanity, to characterize the kingdoms' interactions. A gracious amount of blessings and deliverance balance the treachery of the satanic and terrestrial kingdoms, and what the natural kingdom generously provides is interrupted in this age by its own disciplinary episodes that humanity deserves.

Hebrews 1:1–4: An interest of Hebrews in the angels of the heavenly kingdom, like Colossae, puts their power in perspective compared with the authority of Christ at the right hand of God (1:13; 8:1; 10:12; 12:2). His role in the creation, his inheritance of all kingdoms, his reception of authority over all kingdoms, and his maintenance of cosmic order are his claim to preeminence (2:5, 8–10). *MK, HK*

1 Peter 2:13–14: The trusting kingdom is to submit to terrestrial governing authorities regardless of their injustice in many ways and in varying degrees; even only some civil order is better than none. *TerK, TruK*

1 Peter 3:21–22: All angels, fallen and holy, had already been subjected to Christ even before his ascension, as the exorcisms and angelic messages of good news demonstrated. *UK, HK, MK*

2 Peter 2:4–13: Mockers are reminded of the flood and told that the Creator will by fire destroy creation including the ungodly at the judgment. The present sky and earth's elements will be burnt off and holy, godly people will live to see a new creation where righteousness will be the environment of all life. *UK, NK, TerK, TruK, NE*

2 Peter 2:4–5, 9–13: The judgment of the Lord has already come upon the satanic kingdom and its followers who disrespect the Lord who has bound them until they are finally and permanently judged. The wicked are not only lower than the angels; rather, they are on the same level and will be destroyed as unreasoning animals at the earth's destruction, reminiscent of God's judgment by the flood. *UK, HK, MK, SK, NK*

Jude 6–10: Again, as in 2 Pet 2:4–5, 9–13, the Lord is already keeping fallen angels in eternal bonds for the judgment, but it is not for even the archangels to judge. The fallen angels' human disciples, however, reject authority and contend with the holy angels. An eternal fire will destroy these antichrist disciples along with unthinking animals. Five realms interact: the universal, heavenly, satanic, natural, and terrestrial kingdoms. *UK, HK, SK, NK, TerK*

POLITICAL NATURE OF THE MESSIANIC KINGDOM

Though the Jews' political expectation of the Messiah was an immediate and visually realized kingdom in a conventional terrestrial sense, what Jesus established instead was a kingdom with a global reach where his burgeoning trusting kingdom impacted the politics of many nations. In the typical sense, Judaism was wrong again about the Messiah since in Jesus' commissional sense, the very definition of political—the impact of ideas on a society's civic discourse and structure—was the most pervasively political movement in history.

Israel's ultimate, international, and political purpose was to be a world witness in word and deed to the truth that there was only one God who alone ruled all realms as their Creator.[2] So, one should not read "Render to Caesar . . . and render to God" as a dismissive assessment of politics since it marks what has always been the terrestrial kingdom's battle against the universal kingdom. It does not dismiss either side; to the contrary, it highlights their coexistence and demands avoiding unnecessary conflict. Jesus' birth and Herod's attempted assassination, his contentious ministry and secular execution, and his continued battles between his terrestrial and trusting kingdoms prove that Jesus' Incarnation was certainly political.[3]

Isaiah summarizes how international politics work on an everyday basis. Isaiah looks above immediate history to the global politics under God's rule, as did Hannah in her prayer of praise (1 Sam 2:9–10).

> The nations are like a drop from a bucket, accounted as dust on the scales. . . . All nations are as nothing before him, accounted by him as less than nothing and emptiness. . . . He stretches out the skies like a curtain, and spreads them like a tent to live in. He brings princes to nothing, and makes the rulers of the earth as emptiness. (Isa 40:15, 17, 22–24; also Prov 8:15; 21:1)

---

2. Deut 4:35, 39; 2 Sam 7:22; 1 Chr 16:25–26; Isa 37:20.

3. In reference to Jesus' expression "the kingdom of God," Patrick confirms the inevitable impact of Jesus' central pronouncement: "It is in his proclamation that we meet this term as a comprehensive, synthetic scheme for interpreting Scripture and tradition. His choice of this expression to designate the coming intervention of God gave the event a particular coloring, namely, a political and legal coloring." Patrick, "Kingdom of God," 78. Schnelle: "Jesus's claim to authority and his message of the present and coming kingdom could not long remain apolitical, even though it was not fundamentally conceived in political terms." *Theology of the New Testament*, 91.

The Jews' messianic expectations were primarily nationally and internationally political, and Revelation is a thoroughly political account.

Jesus' point made to Pilate was about the source of his kingdom's authority, that it was not *of* this world and that even Pilate's own political position was sourced from God above. Jesus had accepted coregency *over* this whole world. Actually, his kingdom *is* this world, so it is foundationally political. If not, why does Paul encourage prayer for political authorities?

Christians are persecuted, mutilated, tortured, and killed not because their leader is a Savior but because he is a political and social threat! His kingdom was the excuse to martyr Christ and his followers. A Jewish king would be in conflict with Caesar, so the Jewish leaders portray themselves disingenuously as aligned with Rome in making their political argument for Jesus' execution (John 19:12). As much as one might be tempted to distinguish a "political" kingdom from another qualification such as "spiritual," such a distinction did not get the Messiah and the apostles killed. Caesar's kingdom objected to the Christians' core political views. Christians objected to the Caesars' core political views. Again, neither Christ nor his apostles nor countless thousands of martyrs since then have been executed merely because of their beliefs. They were politically executed because of their persistent faithfulness to a higher authority than the state. That's called politics.

The implications of the lordship of Christ and how it has been interpreted and reacted to with both love and hate have been globally momentous. The political nature of the clashing kingdoms throughout history, particularly the trusting and terrestrial kingdoms, is far from primarily "spiritual" whether the context involves ancient Rome, Israel, Christians, Islam, missions, North Korea, the history of the church, continental exploration, despotism, democracy, or social justice. Only a narrow, theologically technical definition of "political" would say that Jesus did not see himself as a political figure. To maintain that political matters pertain only to terrestrial political positions, to typical government edifices, protocols, and ceremonies, is far below the profundity of Jesus' impact on the political spheres of the world. The universal kingdom of God and his Christ is in the midst of us, not only by the Spirit, but by its daily engagement, even clashing with visible terrestrial and natural realms or with the invisible heavenly kingdom.

The trusting kingdom experiences the same implications of the kingdoms' interactions as other kingdoms: believers experience disease, natural disasters, wars, pollution, etc. The difference is that the believers' release from sin and sanctification equips them for valuable service and ministry not just among themselves but to the terrestrial and natural kingdoms as well. Living among the kingdoms constitutes the trusting kingdom's daily struggles, but the believer's progression in becoming more like God and his nature brings victories in those battles. The vigilant believer intentionally and thus wisely and hourly both blesses and fights the other kingdoms as renewed souls by the Holy Spirit.

11

Israel

Israel has an eternal covenant with God, as does the natural kingdom, as does the terrestrial kingdom and all its nations. But it is all nations that continue as the Testaments' most general focus, yet it is even more widely realized and rebalanced in the New Testament's history and in its message. The difference is in a different strategy of each Testament. The Old Testament had a greater emphasis on a single nation's sanctification as a very small plot in the middle of three continents. The New Testament's kingdom is a rarified trusting kingdom within a multi-continental global community. The New Testament's trusting kingdom, in its global expanse, no longer operates within a single covenantal nation as a witness to a few surrounding nations. Instead it has become a powerful scattering of community-based witnesses *within* nations.

Israel has never been a trusting kingdom because it is has not been inhabited by believers exclusively. Inevitably, as any other nation, it is one nation among all the others within the terrestrial kingdom. Obviously, however, she will always have a unique relationship with God as his chosen nation and in this way is separated from the others. This election, then, raises Israel's eternal kingdom to a prominent role within his universal kingdom, but she is contextualized therein:

> If you truly obey my voice and keep my covenant, then you will be my own possession among all the peoples, nonetheless, all the earth is mine. (Exod 19:5)

> The Lord is God in heaven above and on earth below; there is no other. So you must keep his statutes and his commandments which I am giving you today. (Deut 4:39-40)
>
> Are you not God in the heavens? Are you not ruler over every kingdom of the nations? (2 Chr 20:6)

A MEANS TO THE NATIONS

Israel's significance was to be a microcosm of God's intentions for all nations, a means to humanity's eternal *shalom* and shepherding. The patriarchal promise portrays Israel's role as an instrument to bless all nations: "In you all the families of the earth shall be blessed" (Gen 12:3; 18:18; 22:18; 26:4; 28:14).[1] It was God's designed objective for Israel to not only have a unique relationship in its intimacy but to have a purpose for that intimacy to publicly display God's future relationship with all the peoples.

> Announce his glory among the nations, his marvelous works among all the peoples. . . . For all the gods of the peoples are worthless idols, but the Lord made the heavens. (1 Chr 16:24, 26)
>
> [Lord], do according to all the foreigner asks of you, so that all the peoples of the earth will know your name and fear you, as your people Israel do. (2 Chr 6:33)
>
> Give thanks to the Lord; call on his name and reveal his deeds among the peoples. . . . May God be gracious to us, bless us, and make his face to shine on us . . . . That your way may be known on earth and your saving power among all nations. (Ps 67:1-3)
>
> O Lord our God, save us from Sennacherib's hand, so all kingdoms of the earth will know that you alone are the Lord. (Isa 37:20)

---

1. When putting Israel's meaning in the context of creation, Knierim posits two possibilities: "In the former, creation would have its meaning by standing in the service of Israel. In the latter, the meaning of the history and existence of history would be to stand in the service of God's creation of the world. This alternative cannot be dissolved in a 'both-and.' In fact, many interpreters will readily admit that Israel's election is to serve God's creation." His further analogy shows how pervasive this relationship is on a cosmic scale: "It is a basic fact that our history depends on the existence of this globe in our solar system, while the solar system, let alone what lies beyond it, does not depend on our global history." Knierim, *Old Testament Theology*, 181, 185.

In other words, the nations were the ultimate objective of God's revelation, and this was to be exemplified by Israel's own relationship with him. Jeremiah was God's "prophet to the nations" as were the New Testament's apostles/prophets (Jer 1:5; also Acts 26:17; Matt 28:19; Rom 11:13; Gal 1:16). He even called pagan rulers with questionable devotion to God to acknowledge his wisdom and power, e.g., Nebuchadnezzar and Cyrus. The nations are represented by the worshiping eastern wise men who journeyed to Jesus' manger. All nations are the audience for John's "eternal gospel," the good news about the justice that will come to them from their Creator (Rev 14:6–7).

The Psalms frequently called Israel to tell of, and the nations to hear of and respond to, the glory, faithfulness, salvation, and judgment of God. The purview for the Old Testament psalmists' world and its nations was of course not global, but it included at least Africa, Asia, and Mediterranea, not just the Fertile Crescent:

> When the LORD restored the fortunes of Zion, we were like those who dream. Then our mouth was filled with laughter, and our tongue with shouts of joy. Then they said among the nations, "The Lord has done great things for them. The Lord has done great things for us; we are glad." (126:1–3)

> Kings of the earth and all peoples, princes and all rulers of the earth! Young men and maidens together, old men and children! Let them praise the name of the Lord, for his name alone is exalted; his majesty is above earth and heaven. (148:11–13)

> Why should the nations say, "Where is their God?" Let the avenging of the outpoured blood of your servants be known among the nations before our eyes! (79:10)

Israel's wisdom and successes in all areas of life were to demonstrate God's eternal design to all his nations, where wisdom and care for all creation reflects the nature of God himself, not only as Israel's God but the only God. His covenant and its instructions, when kept, would lead to an impressively vigorous nation in every regard, at each social level (marriage, family, tribe) and in every way: morally, economically, spiritually, politically, health-related, and in all military confrontations. Israel's covenant with Yahweh was to be respected by the nations and to lead to their holistic national prosperity, as it will be in New Earth. Israel's covenantal relationship was to be so successful that no nation could reasonably hold to an inferior worldview, so it would eventually admit and submit to Yahweh's supremacy. On the other hand, God would not tolerate Israel's persistent misrepresentations of him and his nature if they were to continue as his international instrument as a living apologetic. That would only convey to the peoples that Yahweh was not the only God but instead that he was an inferior god to their own deities and idols.

Israel was also instrumental in initiating the eternal Davidic dynasty. The promise was . . .

> My servant David will be king over them, and they will all have one shepherd; and they will walk in my ordinances and keep my statutes. (Ezek 37:24)

The identity of the Messiah was the mystery unveiled in the Incarnation, but it is not recorded that the New Testament Jews sought a literal reincarnated David when anticipating the Messiah. However, a reincarnated prophet, Elijah, was considered (Mark 6:15; 8:28). But, without a prophesied name for the Messiah, the Old Testament used a generic, superlative name, which could only be "David." Beyond the Messiah's kingship, his more comprehensive commission was to bring the nations to their intended eternal purpose, to shepherd the natural kingdom and themselves. Israel was a means to the purposeful end of redemption and sanctification of all nations. In this sense, the Old Testament and Gospels are no more about Israel than Acts and the letters are about Mediterranea. The objective of both is about the world and the intermediate steps to evangelize and sanctify it.

Israel's significance became more that of a venue for Jesus' proclamation of the kingdom of God. Israel is not at center-stage in the New Testament; it *is* the stage—the stage that frames and provides the background and props for the process of God's interaction with all humanity through his Messiah. The sad irony was that his own people received him not, yet Israel was blessed to continue as the ethno-geopolitical venue for the Incarnation. God's unique terrestrial kingdom was the first to benefit from the pronouncements of Jesus, and the synagogues were the first to be blessed by him, which became the routine for the apostles' itineraries. In both Jesus' and his apostles' case, the gentiles were second in sequence. It was God's strategy which limited the reach of the Messiah's commission during the Incarnation: "I was sent only to the lost sheep of the house of Israel" (Matt 15:24; Luke 4:43–44). Jesus was sent to the Jews, and he sent his disciples first to the Jews and their synagogues as an administrative expediency since they could not effectively establish a believing base if bypassing the synagogues and marginalizing "God's people" because of a premature global zeal in their great commission.

COVENANT

The Old Testament covenant was God's written tool to express and enforce his eternal design for sanctified shepherding within the covenant community. It expressed his desire to work *with* the Israelites as individuals and a nation. It was the instrument that itself modeled the eternal design's objective—to do something together, as the Trinity acts together. The covenant was a means by which God would enlist Israel in sanctified shepherding by service to one another and the wider world around them. It was not a "center," though it was a reference point along the way to the primary and central objective. And it was still a reference point in the New Testament, most apparently by its reaffirmation of the covenant's moral law. However, the societal infrastructure provided by the covenant's legal and ceremonial nature was about to become inapplicable in the Gospels, and they were finally inapplicable in Acts. Covenant is not recorded as a talking point for Jesus, nor is it a fundamental doctrine in the letters. The populist polity of the early church and the relativity of the ceremonial laws left the accoutrements of covenant far behind. What was left was the ethical instruction of community laws and wisdom literature and the narratives of biblical characters who exemplified that instruction positively or negatively. The fundamental unity of the Testaments is found in this ethical guidance on living and loving within a mutually nurturing community and world; it is a covenant arrangement to shepherd as God shepherds.

Covenant theology describes the arrangements needed during this fallen parenthetical age to achieve what would have happened naturally before the Fall and will happen naturally in New Earth: love, trust, and obeying one's loving and faithful God in order to succeed in productive and edifying shepherding with him. Covenant theology provides a legal structure like the marriage ceremony in that the covenant formed only a seal of what is the most important—the loving, mutual commitment to the Couple's productive efforts in their life together. It may contribute to a narrative plot, but it is not the message. Scripture is not about defining the "arrangement" *ad infinitum*; it's about living the relationship *ad aeternum*. The covenant was recorded to be a talking point for Jesus, John, Zechariah,

Peter, and Stephen only once each, and for Paul only ten times within his letters. Understandably, Hebrews uniquely addresses its primarily Jewish audience within the context of God's covenant relationship with Israel significantly more than the other letters. However, again, the Testaments' emphasis was not on the legal frameworks themselves; rather, it was on the believer's moral responsibilities empowered by the personal indwelling by the Spirit within the believers of the trusting kingdom:

> Should I offer my firstborn for my sins, my body's fruit for my soul's sin? Mere mortal, he has shown you what is good. So what does the Lord require of you? To act justly, love mercy, and walk humbly with your God. (Mic 6:7–8)

Israel was experiencing its own climactic moment in Jesus' Incarnation; whether they knew it or not, they would see their own kingdom's covenant victory within the grander universal kingdom of God and its victories of every nation.

CONFUSING, MINIMALIST MESSIANIC EXPECTATIONS

Extra-biblical expectations of a messiah were not clear before the Incarnation. Herbert Bateman mentions several examples of profound silence about a messiah between Malachi and Matthew:

> Missing is a concept of a suffering Messiah. Missing is a Messiah whose kingdom and rule extends over the seen and unseen of all creation. Missing is a resurrected Messiah who returns to consummate an already inaugurated kingdom. Missing is a Messiah miraculously born of a virgin in Bethlehem. Missing is a Messiah who is a divine Davidic regal priest.[2]

N. T. Wright describes a diversity in intertestamental messianic hopes but summarizes their unity in at least one kingdom expectation:

> If these disparate movements had anything in common, it was the expectation, forming the context for whatever messianic figure might emerge, that Israel's long history would at last reach its divinely ordained goal. The long night of exile, the "present evil age," would give way to the dawn of renewal and restoration, the new exodus, the return from exile.[3]

---

2. Bateman, "Anticipations," 329.
3. Wright, *Jesus*, 482.

Jews were looking primarily for a "realized" eschatological kingdom. But beyond this, there were few specific and pervasive expectations.

Judaism's expectation of the kingdom of God was that he would physically restore her kingdom and that the rebellious nations would be defeated—a valid expectation given the Old Testament promises. No one could anticipate the time of the Messiah's arrival, but neither were his life circumstances and death anticipated, to say the least: "A Messiah who was executed by the occupying forces was not, after all, the true Messiah."[4] Secondly, the kingdom view of Judaism of an immediately realized kingdom under a geopolitical messiah was mistaken. The Jews were not, and still are not, satisfied with the timing of a realized kingdom that would require at least a two millennia delay once the Messiah had arrived.[5]

Furthermore, their expectations apparently did not include other high-priority messianic responsibilities which were predicted in the Old Testament. Rather than an intense interest in any new mode of sacrificial sin deliverance, the Jews anticipated an immediate political deliverance with great hopes for the restoration of a Davidic kingdom right when the Messiah arrived. However, all should be excused for not having a full and accurate job description for the Messiah with which to show conformity by Jesus. That was what the Incarnation was for. Nonetheless, regardless of others' estimations then and since, the Jewish leadership and populace found the kingdom delay and attenuating circumstances as grounds for rejecting Jesus and his kingdom. Jesus could not be Judaism's Messiah, and Jesus' kingdom could not be Judaism's kingdom. Furthermore, it was not anticipated that the Messiah would bring a new soteriological method, nor would sharing space with an overwhelming number of saved and uncircumcised gentile believers have been within Judaism's worldview. Their messianic kingdom views were wrong in significant ways and incomplete in several others.

---

4. Wright, *Jesus*, 485.

5. Larry R. Helyer gives an example of the results of the disparity between the New Testament and at least one second temple source: "The NT shatters the narrow nationalism of Psalms of Solomon. This very significant difference no doubt played a leading role in the parting of ways between Judaism and Christianity." Helyer, *Jewish Literature*, 391.

CENTRAL HISTORIOGRAPHICAL ERROR

A historiographical presumption and its epistemology affects much of an eschatological emphasis on New Testament theologies of the kingdom of God. A certain determinism of history and its cultural-theological milieu is assumed to have formed Jesus' concept of the kingdom of God. Though a history of religions approach may uncover apparent continuities and developments in religious thought, when the incarnate arrives, one is to listen to him. No presumption of consistency of the revelations by Jesus with the contemporary views needs to apply. This does not mean that there will be no responses to, and even agreements with, prevailing presuppositions, since he would have engaged many of both. But regarding Jesus as the prophet of God, his presuppositions are what matter. One of the most important reasons for his words and works were to correct the prevalent misconceptions about history, Israel, and all creation. All to say, Judaism's prevailing and in many ways inaccurate presumption about the Messiah's purpose was not necessarily the storyline for Jesus.[6] Judaism's realized eschatological expectations could not have been Jesus' revelation. Jesus did not see himself as an inaugurator of a new eschatological kingdom within the context of Israel's salvation history. Jesus insisted by word and deed that he was the coregent King of God's universal kingdom now. Judaism did not set the table for Jesus' message; it set itself as a target, as a foil to his proclamation and demonstration of his mission. His mission was not centrally Israel. Jesus was not a product of his time—he was a product of God's time.

An example of this approach might be N. T. Wright's position, which straps one's exegesis and theology to Judaism's erroneous assumption of the realized kingdom's immediacy. On one hand, one perhaps might agree with Wright:

> But at least we can be sure of this: anyone who was heard talking about the reign of Israel's god would be assumed to be referring to the fulfillment of Israel's long-held hope.[7]

This is apparently true, given the recorded responses to Jesus' pronouncements, but the profound impact of Judaism's additional mistakes about the Messiah discourages the assumption that Jesus was complicit

---

6. Yet this is the common assumption, e.g., "The starting point for Jesus' message was in the Jewish hope for the future Kingdom of God." Pannenberg, *Kingdom of God*, 54.

7. Wright, *Jesus*, 151.

in perpetuating this hope when referring to God's gospel. So, Wright's next conclusion goes too far:

> We may remind ourselves that if Jesus' announcement of the kingdom is to make historical sense, it must make sense *both* as something that would be clearly understood within its Jewish context *and* as the presupposition for the significantly different resonances of "kingdom" in the early church.... It must be set within Judaism, but as a challenge; it must be the presupposition for the church, but not the blueprint.[8]

Wright's presumptions of what "must" be accepted are not necessary, and his approach to history is marginalized when the Word himself appeared to correct the erroneous interpretations of the contemporary culture's definition of the "kingdom of God." A "historical sense" to whomever should always be a consideration but not a determination that overrides a different route that God himself in Jesus took toward the Testaments' more consistent universal kingdom theology. It is inconceivable that Judaism was oblivious to the Old Testament's dual sense of the kingdom of God, national and universal, yet their preference to view it provincially rather than universally is not surprising, just incorrect, so the Messiah arrived to correct it, as well as other messianic misconceptions. As Jonah did, to subordinate God's universal plans for all of creation to his favored nation compromises the breadth and depth of the Testaments' ultimate focus on the nations.

The gentiles would not have been as interested in a kingdom of God defined minimally as Israel's victory.[9] Rather, what caught the attention of the gentile political establishment was the preaching of a kingdom of a god whose main protagonist was said to be greater than the divine Caesar. This points to the Roman's government grasp of a universal kingdom concept and to the reaction of any culture which finds Christian truth too inconvenient in its deconstruction of ultimate power. Furthermore, Luke's summaries of Paul's message to the gentiles show no reluctance by him to prefer proclaiming the universal kingdom of God among the gentiles since the phrase was not constricted by a parochial Jewish thought of the day. Even the Jewish establishment resisted Paul's universal conception of God's kingdom (Acts 28:30–31). Moreover, his letters to gentile

---

8. Wright, *Jesus*, 226.
9. Wright, *Jesus*, 227.

regions are not shy about the kingdom of God (1 Cor 4:20; 6:9–10; 15:24, 50; Gal 5:21; Eph 5:5; Col 1:13; 4:11; 1 Thess 2:12; 2 Thess 1:5).

Wright is an example of those preferring a synthetic kingdom where an immediate Jewish realized kingdom (thesis) and a delayed, future realized eschatological kingdom (antithesis) find their synthesis in the popular "already-not yet" catchphrase. However, Jesus had no interest in endorsing Judaism's prevailing opinions on God's plan for the realization of a perfect creation nor on what the Messiah's total commission entailed. This amounts to a quasi-canonization of an inaccurate historical interpretation of the Messiah and his kingdom. Jesus knew that he would die, that he would disappoint even his own disciples, and that he would defer a perfect domain to the distant future. Israel's obvious role as an ethno-geopolitical center of the Gospels can be overemphasized and become a significant distraction, forming a minimized estimation of Jesus' ministry. The Jews were not expecting a deferred kingdom from their Messiah, nor did the true Messiah who came to rule his current universal kingdom. Judaism's expectation of a realized kingdom came crashing down since it did not materialize under this failed, dead messiah.

The instrumentality of Israel, including her setting for the Incarnation, should not divert one from the authority of the Word himself who identifies and demonstrates the kingdom of God as his and his Father's universal kingdom as the Old Testament predicted. Jesus did not come to "nominate himself for Israel's president."[10] Such a modest political goal to be only nominated, especially by oneself as the leader over a realm so small, is not proportionate to the messianic global predictions of the Old Testament, nor to his divine ontology, since he had been the universal King of all creation already and has been ever since.

RHETORICAL CONTEXTUALIZING

Because of Judaism's incomplete and incorrect views of the Messiah, the message and works of Jesus were bound to be surprisingly counter to its expectations. Schnelle gives a short list of what was missing now in Israel.

---

10. A weak assessment of Jesus and his Incarnation is Scot McKnight's diminutive estimation of his authority: "A more careful examination of the Gospels show a Jesus who unequivocally and without embarrassment nominated himself for Israel's president." McKnight, *King Jesus Gospel*, 121. Such a nominal goal in itself would be an embarrassment for God.

The first striking feature of Jesus's language about the rule/kingdom of God is what is absent: national needs are not addressed, and the ritual separation of Gentiles and Jews no longer plays a role. Table fellowship in Galilean villages, not sacrificial ritual in the temple signals the inbreaking of God's new reality.[11]

A more thorough teleological and biblical continuity is provided by the eternal trajectory of God's universal kingdom rather than pinpointing an inaugural eschatological kingdom. This kingdom is not a parallel or marginal kingdom to a new kingdom; rather, it is the foundational kingdom from which all kingdoms are governed.

One would have hoped that confusion around the Messiah and the kingdom of God would have been settled by Jesus' convincing pronouncements and demonstration of his messianic authority. Nevertheless, Jesus continually met with constricted and deep-seated assumptions of messianic qualifications and narrow estimations of his own messianic kingdom's limitless reign and realm. For instance, the present state of Jesus' universal kingdom was pointed out to the Pharisees when they were considering the wrong question about when the kingdom of God would come (Luke 17:20–21). It was not a potentiality, not soon, nor within the next millennia or two; it was already pervasively present as God's universal kingdom. The messianic kingdom "consubstantiates" creation, not in any mystical sense but in its ubiquity. It is not restricted or localized "over there" or "over here." If one was looking for an army, senate, palace, enthroned king, etc., one was looking in the wrong direction.[12]

Then again, Jesus speaks of a future situation of his universal kingdom. In Luke 19:11–13, 16–17, Jesus discerned his audience's assumption about an immediate coming of a national kingdom of God. Everyone presumed that if he was the Messiah, Israel's kingdom would be restored immediately. His response to their concern acknowledged a timeline of his kingdom, including his leaving and returning, which in itself revealed that he would leave without restoring the national kingdom.[13] But rather than emphasizing the timeline, his response addressed matters of their morality, stewardship, accountability, and obedience until he returned, and even addressed their eventual ruling role after his return. He addressed their sanctification, not their kingdom.

11. Schnelle, *Theology of the New Testament*, 108.
12. See chapter 8 for more detail on Luke 17:20–21.
13. Others were confused another time about the Messiah's departure without meeting Judaism's expectations (John 12:32–36).

> They assumed that the kingdom of God would appear immediately. So he said, "A nobleman went into a far country to receive a kingdom for himself and then return. He called ten of his servants and gave them ten minas and said, 'Engage in business until I come.'" The first came before him, saying, "Lord, your mina has made ten minas more." And he said to him, "Well done, good servant! Because you have been faithful in a little matter, you shall have authority over ten cities."

Jesus' disappointing response to their interest in an immediate national kingdom came in a story, perhaps softening the blow.

The parable of the intransigent tenants warns the Jews further that the centricity of their national kingdom realm was absorbed into the wider and productive realm of the trusting kingdom:

> The kingdom of God will be taken away from you and given to a people who will produce its fruit. (Matt 21:43; also Mark 12:9, Luke 20:16)

The trusting kingdom would no longer be centralized in Israel, though it would remain as an ethno-geopolitical center. God chose by his universal authority, and due to Israel's perpetual recalcitrance, to schedule the transfer of their centricity dynamically and justifiably to the exploding gentile component of his global trusting kingdom.

When asked about Israel's kingdom, Jesus deflected these questions and continued by referring to his broader, more universal commission and kingdom. Jesus answered his disciples' question about when their Israelite kingdom was due. After first mentioning Jerusalem, he does not address the timing of the sub-kingdom of the kingdom of God; instead, he immediately directs their attention to the concentric circles of his universal, global realm: Jerusalem, Judah, and Samaria (Israel), then the globe.

> He appeared to them over a period of forty days and spoke about the kingdom of God.... Then they gathered around and asked, "Lord, now are you going to restore the kingdom to Israel?" He said to them: "You are not to know the times or dates set by the Father by his own authority. But you will receive power when the Holy Spirit comes on you; then you will be my witnesses in Jerusalem, and in all Judea and Samaria, and to the ends of the earth." (Acts 1:3, 6–8)

Understandably, a primary concern of the apostles was Israel's kingdom, their entrenched cultural hope for Israel's victory and reestablishment.

He responded in words reminiscent of Matthew's Great Commission and its universal view of the kingdom. He told them to tend to business, not to look inward and backward but to look outward and forward to God's kingdom surge into the entire world.[14] Commentators are quick to say that Jesus did not reject their question. However, though he acknowledges the question, he basically dismisses it as only a secondary concern to the historically more pressing matter of the global kingdom which should eventually subsume their nationalistic priorities. The change of subject is abrupt, almost, if not a bit disciplinary.

Furthermore, Jesus preferred to self-designate as the generic Son of Man more so than the Son of David. Various reasons could be given for this, yet one of its profound implications is his identity with humanity as a whole rather than concentrating on the Davidic covenant. In fact, in a flair of logic, he baits the Pharisees into revealing their narrow focus on the continuation of the political dynasty of David and the regaining of Jewish independence. Using Ps 110 he redirects their fixation to the Messiah's (his) divinity with the silent deduction that the Messiah (he) was God. Jesus asked the Pharisees, "Whose son is the Messiah?" They replied, "David's son." Jesus responds with the question they could not answer or did not want to answer. "Why would David say the Messiah is the son of David when he calls the Messiah 'Lord'?"[15] In other words, while in many venues Jesus emphasizes his humanity as one of humanity's sons, here he emphasizes he is the vanquishing Lord of humanity; his enemies have become his footstool (Ps 110:1). After all, he is the human/God.

There was plenty that the disciples would experience during this surge that would contextualize their national kingdom within a global scale. As Geerhardus Vos observed, "The Kingdom-hope of the Jews was also politically-nationalistically colored, whereas in the teaching of Jesus its tendency was in the direction of universalism."[16] So what follows in Acts is both a troubling yet elating account of the growth of the trusting kingdom. The book of Acts begins with the parochial interest of the disciples but ends with a contentious exchange between Paul and Jewish

---

14. Dunn regards the disciples' question concerning Israel's kingdom in this passage to be "diverted, but not disowned" by Jesus. Dunn, *Beginning from Jerusalem*, 82. Similarly Haenchen, *Acts*, 141–42. However, the reason for Jesus' diversion here was due to Israel's kingdom having less importance.

15. Matt 22:41–45; Mark 12:35–37; Luke 20:41–44.

16. Vos, *Biblical Theology*, 400.

leaders when he invited them to discuss the kingdom of God during his imprisonment (Acts 28:23–28). The conversation ended with Paul's rebuke of the leaders: "I want you to know that God's salvation has been sent to the Gentiles, and they will listen" (v. 28; cf. Matt 21:43).

It matters whether the kingdom of God refers to God and his universal kingdom or some version of a national kingdom because Jesus is preparing for his trusting kingdom's global commission. Israel will always have a unique covenant relationship with God as his chosen people, but there has always been an overriding covenant relationship all along—the salvation of creation and its nations. The commendable and fruitful efforts to unify the Testaments by building on a covenant theology should be contextualized within the grander scheme of the nature of creation and the eternal design's shepherding and sanctification objective for all nations. While the severity of the human condition has included every nation under the influence of the satanic kingdom, Jesus did not dwell on a story of a particular kingdom with occasional eruptions into creation's history. He did not embark on a ministry of a mere three years by emphasizing a single national view of the kingdom of God when he himself accepted, pronounced, demonstrated, and commanded worldwide obedience even then. Israel's covenant was not considered to be a central topic for Jesus because his urgent commission was his coregency over God's cosmic kingdom.

Without arguing that Jesus was proclaiming his universal kingdom, David Wenham believes a national kingdom was not what Jesus had in mind either.

> Jesus' vision of the kingdom was different from the narrow anti-Roman nationalism of many of his contemporaries. It makes sense that an understanding of his own kingship, if he had such a concept, might also have been different from theirs . . . Jesus himself accepted the designation [messianic king of Israel] but used the concept cautiously, even sometimes secretively, probably because of the sort of nationalism popularly associated with it . . . and also because his understanding of his own role, as well as of the kingdom, was much bigger than that of his contemporaries.[17]

One might object that to not carry the momentum of Israel's Old Testament kingdom role over into the New Testament would be to miss an

---

17. Wenham, *Paul*, 107–9.

opportunity for the Testaments' continuity. The more significant continuity, however, is found in the Old Testament foundational concept of God's universal kingdom as it works through his eternal design from creation through eternity. The core continuity that fills the Testaments' pages more than anything else is the believers' intimate coregency with him in their sanctified shepherding of his creation.

12

Dialectical Kingdom

AFTER ALL THAT HAS been said so far about the kingdom of God, it has avoided the prevailing identity of the kingdom as the "eschatological kingdom." This slight has not gone unnoticed, presumably, while another meaning of God's kingdom in the Testaments, the universal kingdom, has been the preferred and persistent understanding here. Among the reasons for this preference have been the following.

- Comprehensive history is everything that all creation has ever done, from the formless emptiness of earth through eternity. Considerable reductions of the Testaments' central interest to a narrative amounts to emphasizing a parenthesis over the eternal run of history. Biblical theology's interests should emphasize the implications of the eternality of creation and its history and its coextensive created meaning. I have suggested a goal is not merely to theologize about the eternal kingdom of God but to personally shoulder the responsibilities inherent within it as he has made them abundantly clear.

- When God's historical kingdom is inadequately considered by focusing on the parenthetical activity of God solving the sin problem, a heavy focus on the "end times" restricts the importance of the eternal purposes of God even more. It seems a bit odd to reduce Christ's universal and eternal interests in his mere three years of ministry to a future segment of time that ends an immeasurably small fraction of time taken by the parenthetical age. The biblical theology of the natures of creation and its history demand a much wider view than that of an end times focus, regardless of whatever "already" implications it may have.

- God's sovereignty over all creation and its history consists of the entire cosmos including the seven to eight billion people on this planet. If one steps back a ways from the moral rubbish that litters the earth and the souls that occupy it, one sees the common grace of God even in a cursed world: the beauty of God's vast creation, a mother's smile seen by her child, the constructive shepherding by the majority of the world's population, the relative calm hearts of even the unjustified, the bearable weather enjoyed by most, the international peace that is only interrupted by scattered but horrific wars. These are all due to God's universal sovereignty since he does not allow total entropic decay of cultures nor unfettered damage directly from the satanic kingdom. This is not blind cheeriness; it is a reason for greater praise and thankfulness for God's shepherding mercy even while measuring out his justice. Judging God as excessive in his curse and discounting his merciful providence to the world dishonors him and is blind foolishness.

- The Testaments pervasively convey God's coordination of his multiplex of kingdoms as an inestimable effort that will continue endlessly because the heavenly, natural, terrestrial, trusting, and New Earth kingdoms themselves are eternal.

- The Testaments generously reveal God's glory by consistently proving the preeminence of his universal kingdom in his and his Messiah's words and works, as well as those of his biblical heroes.

This chapter lays out why an eschatological kingdom is inadequate in itself when contrasted with the all-inclusive universal kingdom of God. The next chapter will describe several unnecessary paradoxes arising from not opting for Jesus and his followers' understanding of the kingdom of God to be his universal kingdom.

DIALECTICAL KINGDOM DEFINED

Goldsworthy and Caird start at opposite ends of one aspect of Jesus' approach to the kingdom of God: the former says Jesus did not define it;

the latter says he frequently did. Goldsworthy claims Jesus did not need to define it because the people already knew from the Old Testament what it was:

> The fact that Jesus announces the kingdom without explaining what he means by it suggests that he spoke of an already existing idea in the minds of the Jews. It is most likely that the Old Testament will help us understand what the idea was.[1]

On the other hand, Caird claims that Jesus needed to define it extensively to correct current thinking on the subject.

> If the Synoptic Gospels are right to insist that Jesus spent much of his time explaining what *he* meant by the Kingdom, would it not follow that he did not mean what everyone else meant by it?[2]

Though they have opposite views of the *amount* of clear teaching that Jesus provided to define the kingdom of God, both draw justifiable conclusions since the Old Testament provides the key to its definition (Goldsworthy), but it may not have been the definition they expected (Caird). At this point, I would agree with both: Jesus corrected Judaism's choice of an Old Testament national meaning of the kingdom of God and confirmed the Old Testament universal meaning instead. The universal kingdom was a relevant and applicable Old Testament definition of the kingdom of God that was clearly on the table already: "clearly" in that it was apparently hidden in plain sight. This is not to say that either Goldsworthy or Caird would endorse the universal kingdom meaning, just that their separate premises are sound.

Jesus does comment on the kingdom of God in terms of who its king is, when it is, where it is, what it is like, who it belongs to, and who can enter it. Though a precise formal definition in the New Testament, e.g., "The kingdom of God is defined as . . .," what we do have is its frequent description by Jesus' words and, just as frequently, his works. Matthew is especially shy of such a definition formula yet chooses many of Jesus' parables to describe "the kingdom of God/heaven" metaphorically: "The kingdom of God/heaven is like . . ."

I have suggested that the Old Testament's construct of God's universal kingdom is the most consistent meaning of the kingdom of God, given its continuity between Old Testament theology and Jesus' explicit

---

1. Goldsworthy, *According to Plan*, 73.
2. Caird, *New Testament Theology*, 367.

reception of the universal kingdom as his own and as the basis of his ministry. One loses nothing by understanding it as such since any theological benefits of respecting the significance of the kingdom of God when referring to national Israel or salvation history are included within his all-encompassing universal kingdom.

John J. Collins summarizes the diachronic emphases of Judaism's kingdom of God, both the underlying universal meaning and the meaning that was prevalent in Judaism in Jesus' time:

> We have seen that the motif of the kingdom of God was a complex one in Judaism in the period 200 B.C.E.—100 C.E. The basic underlying idea of all conceptions of the kingdom was that God is king of the universe, past, present, and future. In some contexts the kingdom could be understood in a moral or spiritual way, especially in the Hellenistic Diaspora. In the first centuries B.C.E. and C.E., it was expected that the "kingship" of God would be manifested in an eschatological kingdom.[3]

In other words, the meaning of an eschatological kingdom for Judaism had developed a life of its own. David Wenham represents those who assume that Judaism's definition of the kingdom of God impacted Jesus. Jesus' view of the kingdom just had to be Judaism's eschatological view:

> The expression suggests more specifically the coming of the day of divine liberation and of the new society for which Jesus and his contemporaries were longing and waiting. The kingdom of God that Jesus proclaimed is, to use a technical term, the "eschatological kingdom"—the kingdom to come in the last days. It is the coming of the divine rule and of the new world order, for which the Jews were looking.[4]

Jesus' message of the kingdom of God had to be that of his contemporaries, did it not?

Darrell Bock's premise on the subject is equally fallacious. He surprisingly asserts that there was only one Old Testament kingdom construct available from which Israelites could have drawn an understanding of the kingdom of God. In attempting to highlight a centricity of Israel in kingdom theology, he neglects its most general and inclusive Old Testament meaning—the universal kingdom.

---

3. Collins, "Kingdom of God," 95. See also Viviano, "Kingdom of God," 97–107; Goppelt, *Theology of the New Testament*, 1:48–51; Beale, *New Testament Biblical Theology*, 117–28.

4. Wenham, *Paul*, 35.

DIALECTICAL KINGDOM

> At stake is whether an inaugural kingdom is present in Jesus' first coming or whether "kingdom" functions as it did in the Old Testament and intertestamental Judaism as an eschatological term referring exclusively to the consummation of God's rule on earth through Israel.[5]

Without denying that Israel and the world's eschatology is an element of Old Testament theology and Judaism, "kingdom" in the Old Testament definitely did not mean exclusively an eschatological kingdom. Rather, God's universal kingdom is the term's foundational and all-encompassing meaning in both Testaments.

It was pointed out earlier that eschatology can be teleologically deficient since in the temporal sense of teleology, eschatology accentuates the last days of the parenthetical age and maybe a modest amount of the new age. Yet, biblical teleology begins in the epoch of creation and its pre-Fall perfection and continues through the parenthetical age, through the parousia, and through eternity. In addition to its relation to the progression of time, biblical teleology also speaks to purpose more profoundly than eschatology since biblical teleology comes from God's consistent operating principle and objective throughout all epochs, eternally. So, an eschatological view is a finite estimation of history compared to an infinitely wider context with more profound implications, since neither history nor its shepherding design have any last days. "Eschatology" applies literally only to the parenthetical age—its limitations are explicit in its etymology.

An inventive meaning for the kingdom of God is that he now has a new kingship inaugurated by his Messiah's Incarnation, a kingship which will only eventually become complete. This view coins an "already-not yet" nature of God's eschatological kingdom. Redemption and reconciliation, for example, are available "already," but a perfect "not-yet" kingdom will come in the last days. Nevertheless, this understanding of the kingdom of God prioritizes the *future* kingdom, thus the designation "eschatological" kingdom. Yet this view values *present* fulfillments toward the culmination of the world's future perfection. Yet, the center of gravity in the prevailing definition of the kingdom of God is in a future "not-yet" kingdom, not, as I have proposed, a past and current universal kingdom that is never "yet" and recognizes the testamental continuity of God's universal administration of his creation.

---

5. Bock, *Luke–Acts*, 206.

This rendition of the "eschatological kingdom" is not Judaism's eschatological kingdom since the latter was to be instantly a "realized kingdom" for Israel upon the Messiah's appearance. So, three views of the kingdom of God might be abbreviated generally as the following:

- Judaism's kingdom: The kingdom of God will be realized at the Messiah's first and only coming.
- Eschatological kingdom: The kingdom of God was realized already at the Messiah's first coming, yet to be fully realized in the last days.
- Universal kingdom: The universal kingdom of God has always been realized, and it is continued by his Messiah through the last days.

A designation other than "eschatological" is introduced here since "eschatological" is not particularly distinctive in Christian theology's unanimous recognition of an eschatological kingdom by some definition. Not intending to coin a new term, but for this study I will refer to the "(inaugurated) eschatological kingdom" as the "dialectical kingdom." "Dialectical" refers to the polarities that are emphasized by many holding to this view and that will be discussed over the next several pages: for instance, realm/reign, present/future, sovereignty/autonomy, national/universal, appearance/reality, being/becoming, abstract/active-dynamic, deism/theism. Of course all who hold to "the eschatological kingdom" do so in various renditions, so the following critique does not presume that all comments apply to all variations. It should be noted that the designation of the eschatological kingdom as a dialectical *kingdom* is not a derivative from neo-orthodoxy's dialectical *theology*. Nonetheless, the methodology and premises are similar in that both constructs suffer forced concessions to rationality while building theological structures from the straw of tensions, paradoxes, and contradictions. In the case of neo-orthodoxy, a commitment to the Testaments relies on fictionalizing them. In the case of the inaugurated eschatological kingdom, a commitment to the Testaments' historicity includes a distortion of God and his Messiah's sovereignty.

The New Testament's meaning of the kingdom of God depends on which Old Testament meaning it leans on: the universal kingdom or Israel's national kingdom and its derived eschatological implications for the world. But rather than a new dialectical kingdom where the focus of God and Jesus is on the future realized kingdom, the Testaments' focus, instead, is on the present imperfect spiritual, natural, terrestrial, and trusting kingdoms and their interaction among themselves yet under God and his Messiah's perfectly administered universal kingdom. This preferred emphasis is the Old Testament's reason for the Incarnation as Jesus pronounced and modeled it in its harmonic messianic fullness, which will be presented in more detail in chapter 15.

ALREADY-NOT YET

The universal and dialectical kingdoms are not completely contradictory. For instance, Israel has had a hope for their future kingdom. However, their hope has not yet been realized. Gentile believers have a hope for their future as well. Neither has their hope been realized yet. But, a question raised from a theology of history is if everything eventually changes in some way, in what way is an already-not yet narrative unique? The condition of being already-not yet belongs to the nature of all creation's history from subatomic to galactic activity, and it has always been intrinsic to the operation of God's universal kingdom because history and creation are teleological. When one takes the kingdom of God as a chain of cause and effect events that occur whether by the agency of God, humanity, spirits, and nature, then, like everything else in creation, the universal kingdom of God has an indelible already-not yet structure. By accentuating in their eschatology what is common to all reality, the dialectical proponents are not claiming anything distinct from the larger universal kingdom of God. Anything "already" will always be "not yet," so an already-not yet application is not far from a tautology given the inevitability that the "not yet" already will always have an "already." It is the nature of any created existence to "become"; any present entity will be a future entity of some length and description. Relationships, intensity, direction, color, sound, size, or even clarity or manifestation might change, but anything existing will change to its "not yet," even if its "yet" is its eventual extinction, when it becomes "no longer." From the perspective of the universal kingdom, an already-not yet catchphrase, by its "tension," dramatizes the mundane, that is, the eternal cause-and-effect process within all creation. So, one should still use already-not yet terminology pertaining to the routine operation of creation and its history under the authority of the universal kingdom of God, which was inaugurated at creation. Already-not yet is a password to the unnecessary labyrinth of dialectical explanations of the synthesis of an unrealized Judaic realized eschatology and the realized kingdom of New Earth.[6]

Recognizing that salvation history rightfully plays a prominent role in biblical theology, the greatest gain is not from concentrating on only a temporary history of salvation rather than on the universal kingdom and its wider and continual development of the eternal design that propels the temporary salvation history. There is no point where the dialectical kingdom challenges the more comprehensive universal kingdom other than when replacing it with a constricted sense of God's kingdom. Rather than emphasizing an abbreviated kingdom of God that applies to a new inaugurated kingdom in the Savior, the universal kingdom of God was inaugurated at creation and for eternity and proves the glorious nature of God in a most dramatic, merciful, and self-giving, dare I say, humble way. A dialectical kingdom is an unfortunate compromise between Judaism's realized eschatology and Christianity's eschatological realized kingdom.

REIGN AND REALM

Another semantic error has been made frequently when an Old Testament Hebrew equivalent is sought for the New Testament's lone word for kingdom, βασιλεία, meaning either reign or realm, depending on its context in the New Testament as well as in the Septuagint and the wider corpus of ancient Greek.[7] For example, Anthony Thiselton represents those who understand βασιλεία to primarily refer to God's reign in "kingdom of God."

> As is widely appreciated today (in contrast to late-nineteenth century works) kingdom refers in the Gospels to the active, dynamic *reigning* of God as sovereign, even if this reign is in part veiled until its consummation at the *parousia* and last judgment.[8]

---

6. One might say that the Old Testament predicted such an already-not yet scenario, which the New Testament then clarified. This would require of the Old Testament an adequately literal separation between a first and second coming of the Messiah. The universal understanding of the kingdom of God makes such speculation unnecessary.

7. BDB 574–75; BDAG 134–35; Muraoka, *Lexicon to the Septuagint*, 114; Montanari, *Dictionary of Ancient Greek*, 379.

8. Thiselton, *Corinthians*, 377. The distinctive verbiage of many proponents of a dialectical kingdom comparable to Thiselton's "active, dynamic *reigning* of God" will be discussed in the next section. See Allison's list of examples of those holding to this view. *Constructing Jesus*, 168–69.

DIALECTICAL KINGDOM

And Sigurd Grindheim:

> As for the translation of the term βασιλεία, the term may refer both to the idea of a kingdom as a territory and to a kingdom as a dominion, more aptly rendered in modern English as "kingly rule" ... most scholars correctly agree that the dynamic concept of a kingly rule is the primary, if not the only, meaning in the Jesus tradition.[9]

On the other hand, Caird summarizes the diversity in meanings for kingdom in the New Testament:

> It is extremely fortunate that the Greek *basileia* is an ambiguous term which comprehends the three possible senses: sovereignty, reign, and realm. And these three are logically so inseparable that it is no surprise to find the New Testament writers moving freely from one sense to another, and even exploiting the ambiguity.[10]

Allison, apparently, would tend to agree while accurately challenging assertions that βασιλεία means only "reign" or similar definitions:

> Despite the authoritative nature of BDAG and the common opinion that it represents, "kingship" or "royal rule of God" is probably not the exclusive or perhaps even chief meaning of ἡ βασιλεία τοῦ θεοῦ in the Jesus tradition.[11]

Jesus' and Paul's understanding of the kingdom of God are not as distinguishable, as Sigurd Grindheim sees it:

> Whereas the Jesus of the Gospels, at least primarily, envisions the kingdom as a royal power, Paul appears to focus on the kingdom as a territory. He speaks of those who will or, more accurately, will not inherit the kingdom of God (1 Cor 6,9.10; 15,50; Gal 5,21).[12]

---

9. Grindheim, "Kingdom of God," 73. Also, Beasley-Murray presumes a near synonymity between reign and kingdom: "It will be noted that we are using the terms *kingdom* and *sovereignty* interchangeably. That should require no justification today." Beasley-Murray, *Kingdom of God*, 74. If "reign" was the primary meaning of kingdom, one might expect that somewhere ἐξουσία or the like would be connected literally within the context of the kingdom of God phrasing.

10. Caird, *New Testament Theology*, 131. Allison definitively refutes the theorem that βασιλεία and *malkût* mean "active reign" and its like definitions in *Constructing Jesus*, 164–204. He further shows how "kingdom," when used apart from "the kingdom of God" means "a territory ruled by a king, kingdom." *Constructing Jesus*, 178.

11. Allison, *Constructing Jesus*, 169.

12. Grindheim, "Kingdom of God," 75.

However, multiple references in the Synoptics show the realm aspect of the kingdom of God as well, for example: Matt 5:20; 7:21; 18:3; 19:23–24; 23:13; Mark 9:47; Mark 10:15, 23–25 // Luke 18:17, 24–25.

The same is said of words meaning "kingdom" in the Old Testament, where it is said that the use of "kingdom" also primarily means "to reign." However, in search of an equivalent for *basileia*, the lexical subtleties of the Hebrew terms are neglected, and a simplistic conclusion becomes a foundational premise for many in their kingdom theology. This constricted definition of "kingdom" is inconsistent with its breadth of meaning in both Testaments and intervening Second Temple literature.[13] Though one of the Hebrew lexemes, *melûkâ*, fundamentally does mean to reign, the other three in themselves can mean either realm or reign: *malkût*, *mamlakâ*, and *mamlakût*. Furthermore, exegesis of many texts is challenged when either realm or reign fit the context due to the metonymic relationship of the reign and realm concept (more on this below). For instance, *mamlakâ* means reign a number of times but means realm over seventy times. Consequently, the most frequently alleged tandem of βασιλεία and *malkût* specifically is an artificial pairing that ignores the larger Hebrew lexical and semantic field. Hebrew *malkût* leans toward reign, but it is not the lexeme that can be said to mean "reign" primarily in the Old Testament—that claim belongs to *melûkâ*. Furthermore, it is only a guess which one of these four most relevant Hebrew words was in Jesus' mind as a parallel to βασιλεία.[14] *Malkût* is only one Hebrew synonym for βασιλεία and should not be arbitrarily selected as the sole comparand. One should also consider the equally ambiguous *mašal* and its nominal derivatives as parallels to *basileia* that Jesus may have had in mind.[15]

13. This error dates back at least as far as Gustaf Dalman, whom many quote in this regard. He confidently asserts that "no doubt can be entertained that both in the Old Testament and in Jewish literature [*malkût*], when applied to God, means always the 'kingly rule,' never the 'kingdom,' as if it were meant the territory governed by him." Dalman, *Words of Jesus*, 94.

14. What Ben Witherington assumes about an Aramaic etymology could be applied to other Hebrew terms for "kingdom." "Does it refer to a realm or a reign, a state or a divine activity? . . . The Aramaic term malkuta, allows several nuances as determined by the context in which the term is used." Witherington, *Mark*, 78. Witherington suggests using "dominion" over "kingdom" since the former can mean both reign and realm in English. *Indelible Image*, 80. But this only substitutes an English ambiguity with what is already a Hebrew and Aramaic ambiguity, something probably wasted on nearly all who read only Bible translations. The definitions by lexicons of some Hebrew roots meaning "kingdom" already explicitly include the English "dominion," which has this ambiguity already built into what one would hope to be more precise.

15. Another caution is not to assume in the Hebrew poetic literature that parallel

DIALECTICAL KINGDOM

That "kingdom means primarily reign" in both Testaments simply is not verified by the lexicons or this usage in the Testaments; it is only an assertion supported by consensus. Even Ladd admits *malkût* can be used as realm or reign in the Old Testament:[16]

> The fact that there is nothing incongruous in these two facets of the concept but that they are two inseparable parts of a single complex idea can be illustrated by the profane use of the word. The author of Esther can use malkuth to designate both the reign to which Esther has come as queen (Esth 4:14) and the realm over which her husband was king (3:6, 8).[17]

Yet, Ladd abruptly asserts that *malkût* means "God's rule," choosing arbitrarily to narrow his definition of "kingdom," contrary to his conceded examples where the lexical field of *malkût* includes "realm."[18] Again, other Hebrew words for "kingdom" can also mean either realm or reign.[19] One need not isolate an interest on only one option for Jesus' intentions.

The reason for the lexical ambivalence of "kingdom" is easy to understand in both the Hebrew and Greek since English has the same fluctuations in its comparable word, "dominion," which can mean reign or realm. Though kingdom can mean either "reign" or "realm" in both Testaments depending on the context, they have more than a simple homonymous relationship where the same word has two different definitions in a dictionary, definition "1" and definition "2." They also have an inseparable metonymic relationship that any complete meaning of "reign" and "realm" are empty without. "Reign" and "realm" are separate lexemes, but they do not exist independently—lexically separable yet semantically inseparable. They are mutually metonymic, related logically rather than merely metaphorically. Where "crown" is a metonym for

---

structures in the same stich or verse using different derivatives are synonymous—for instance, "dominion, authority, kingdom"—instead, they may be parallel words with intentionally different meanings, both reign and realm.

16. Ladd, *Presence*, 47: "We must also recognize that *malkuth* be used to designate the realm over which a king reigns. See e.g., II Chr. 29:19; Esth 3:6; Dan. 9:1; 11:9; Jer. 10:7. This fact will be important in the analysis of the New Testament concept."

17. Ladd, *Presence*, 130. We would add the Aramaic passages of Dan 4:17; 5:21: "The Most High is ruler over the kingdom [*malkuth*] of humanity."

18. Ladd, *Presence*, 132.

19. Eduard Schweizer attempts to equate realm and reign in an interesting compromise: "The kingdom is more like an area or a sphere of authority into which one can enter, so 'realm' would be a better translation." Schweizer, *Mark*, 45–46. Also Gundry, *Mark*, 64.

"king," it is metaphorical. However, logically does not mean just tautologically, or by definition, e.g., "all unmarried men are bachelors." Rather, "reign" and "realm" are functionally metonymic. They form and share a single concept, kingdom—a realm of one's reign. A ruler at any level without a domain is not a ruler; a realm without a ruler is not a domain. Reigning presumes a realm as its object. It does not always need a literal object, but without at least an implicit realm, reigning is meaningless. Conversely, a realm presumes a ruling entity as its subject. It does not always need a literal subject, but without an implicit ruling entity, realm is meaningless. In other words, the emphasis on a meaning of "reign" at the expense of "realm" is, again, only an assertion supported by consensus, not a linguistic or logical fact. A theological incentive rather than lexical may be in play here, as suggested later.[20]

Furthermore, "kingdom" does not imply a perfectly compliant realm; rebellion always exists to some degree in any regime during the parenthetical age, though no realm can exist as a total anarchy. In other words, "reign" and "realm" are codependent; each implies the other in Hebrew and Greek as it would in any culture; one does not simply have jurisdiction without having a jurisdiction; no one has dominion without having a dominion. One cannot reign over nowhere or nothing. Any notion of the kingdom of God is meaningless without reigning and a realm to reign—they are codependent, thus coterminous.

Schreiner embraces a more holistic meaning of the kingdom of God:

> God's kingdom certainly consists of his rule over angels and human beings, but the emphasis on rule must not blind us to the truth that there is also a realm. History does not take place in an ethereal sphere. . . . So, the kingdom of God has a threefold dimension, focusing on God as King, on human beings as the subjects of the King, and the universe as the place where his kingship is worked out.[21]

Authority and space/time exist simultaneously in both God's providence and his creation kingdom, something a simple concordance search for the frequency of κόσμος (world, earth) would show. His universal realm is just as clearly defined as the kingdom of God as his universal

---

20. Ladd, *Presence*, 130–38. Also Ladd, *Pattern*, 53. More of the theological implications of this lexical preference follows in chapter 14.

21. Schreiner, *Beauty*, xv. Voelz doubles down in his translation in Mark 1:15: "The reign and rule of God," not "the kingdom of God." *Mark 1:1—8:26*, 147.

reign is in both Testaments. Others see the same relationship of "realm" and "reign."[22] David Flusser: "The kingdom of heaven is not simply a matter of God's kingship, but also the domain of his rule, an expanding realm embracing ever more and more people, a realm into which one may enter and find one's inheritance, a realm where there are both great and small."[23] J. I. H. McDonald navigates deftly between realm and reign: "[The kingdom of God] is misrepresented if it is given merely a geographical connotation, and devitalized if it is transposed into abstract categories, such as reign, rule, sovereignty or lordship—not to speak of even more remote theological terminology."[24]

Furthermore, when the meaning of "kingdom" in the Testaments was broached earlier when discussing the eight kingdoms, it was clear that the kingdoms which define creation and its history are all realms, not simply reigns; the heavenly, satanic, natural, terrestrial, believing, and new creation realms and their reigns are not abstractions; they are formidable realms that make up God's universal realm. To say that "kingdom" is not so much a realm as a reign depreciates the role of believers in shepherding their realm. The believer does not simply reign; the believer reigns a significant realm. It would be nonsensical if one was promised to inherit, own, and rule the earth eternally with God but having a realm was incidental. Making God's kingdom an abstraction (power, authority) or something in which God and his Messiah alone engage strips humanity and the believer of their tangible, obedient participation and responsibility to contribute shepherding care for the rest of creation and to lead others to do the same. A realm is hardly "static." All eight of the kingdoms identified are very dynamic with the same metonymy as God's reign and realm. The primary commission and the eternal design require exertion of authority over the realms God has commissioned the trusting kingdom and its citizens to shepherd aggressively but with balance and love. The kingdoms are alive and organic realms, not still landscapes.

So the oft-repeated maxim that "kingdom" primarily means "God's reign" or "God's sovereign activity" cannot be sustained since this view is not supported by either Testament linguistically, exegetically, or theologically. "Reign" does indeed apply to some texts, but it does not apply to many others where the syntax and phrasing do not require it and do not clearly indicate it, or where it would not make sense. The same could

22. E.g., Williams, *Mark*, 30.
23. Flusser, *Jesus*, 110–11.
24. Chilton and McDonald, *Ethics of the Kingdom*, 48.

be said of "realm." A couple examples illustrate where the synecdochical use of "kingdom" pertains to reign or realm: that is, where the kingdom refers to its parts rather than it as a whole.

Realm:

> The Son of Man will send his angels to collect from his kingdom every cause of sin and every lawbreaker, and cast them into the fiery furnace. There will be weeping and gnashing of teeth there. Then the righteous will shine like the sun in their Father's kingdom. (Matt 13:41–43)

Reign:

> He will be great and be called the Son of the Most High. And the Lord God will give to him the throne of his father David, and he will reign over the house of Jacob forever, and his kingdom will have no end. (Luke 1:32–33)

The ultimate significance of this metonymic relation of realm and reign is that it makes both meanings concurrently universal. God and his Messiah cannot own the world if they do not rule it universally, or they could not reign over it universally if they do not own the universal realm. The disembodiment of realm from reign denigrates the significance of God as Creator and owner of creation and might be used to excuse God and his Messiah for universally reigning but not over everything spatially, thus not metonymic, but contingent. The logic, as we will see in some understandings, is that he is not reigning completely if his realm is not completely cooperating. However, in this case it could not be said that Christ upholds the universe (Heb 1:3) or that in him all things hold together (Col 1:17). And temporally speaking, it also invites the perspective that God acts only intermittently in history so that he is not constantly burdened by a stubborn creation-realm that would need continuous action and care. One should not want to marginalize God's realm due to its permanence and continuity. If reign and realm are coextensive and codependent, God's reign over a permanent and continuous realm is implied. This alone questions whether God periodically breaks into history with an "*active reign.*"

GOD'S "ACTIVE" REIGN

I revert nearly a century to Geerhardus Vos and his definition of the kingdom of God that is still repeated in current conceptions of the dialectical kingdom. He begins by overstating that there are "two distinct conceptions" of the kingdom of God in the Old Testament. He then makes an arbitrary distinction by distancing God's *universal* kingdom from his *redemptive* kingdom, not considering an obvious relationship between the two where the redemptive kingdom is a natural function within the universal kingdom.

> In the O.T. the thing later called the Kingdom of God relates as to substance to two distinct conceptions. He designates the rule of God established through creation and extending through providence over the universe. This is not specifically a redemptive Kingdom idea, cf. Psa. 103:19. Besides this, however, there is a specifically-redemptive Kingdom, usually called "the theocracy." The first explicit reference to the redemptive Kingdom appears at the time of the exodus, Ex. 19:6, where Jehovah promises the people, that, if obeying his law, they shall be made to Him "a Kingdom of priests."[25]

Vos discounts the relevant relationship of the universal kingdom only by definition, by negation—it is not redemptive. This is not necessary since God's universal reign designs, initiates, and completes redemption. This dissection, ending in the marginalization of God's universal kingdom, is common among many who see a need for a dialectical kingdom. The importance within the relationship between the universal and redemptive kingdoms is inverted, and the derived redemptive kingdom is artificially prioritized over what is actually its presiding universal kingdom. It has become a foundational premise and methodology for much of the innovative inaugural, eschatological definitions of the kingdom of God. Many still adhere to this particular argument, but I will focus on Ladd and Goldingay as further examples. The Old Testament construction of God's universal kingdom that Eichrodt and Knierim describe should not be dismantled so artificially. God's special redemptive relationship with Israel and ultimately with the globe does not marginalize God's universal kingdom; it is dependent upon it.

Eichrodt:

---

25. Vos, *Biblical Theology*, 398.

The God who chose Israel to be his people, and marked them out by his covenant law, remains at the same time the Creator of the universe, maintaining it by his everlasting decrees, and exercising over the heathen the authority of a king over his subjects.[26]

Knierim:

Yahweh is the liberating creator of Israel precisely because he is the liberating creator of the world.[27]

Vos considers Israel as the "redemptive kingdom" since it is a kingdom of priests, a present kingdom. He also recognizes that the Old Testament speaks of a future kingdom. Vos then juxtaposes these present and future kingdoms and considers the latter variously as an "absolutely new creation," "practically a new kingdom," or "kingdom of God *do novo*" of which God would "make himself the Saviour of and Ruler of Israel."[28] In other words, the inaugurated eschatological kingdom. But it would be unnecessary for God to pronounce himself as Israel's Savior and ruler since he had always been that in his Old Testament universal realm over all nations. It was his decision as the one who reigns to include salvation in his reign.

Moreover, Vos takes three errant lexical steps. First, he claims that the several words for "kingdom" in Hebrew are prevailingly abstract and mean "kingship," an assertion found earlier as lexically invalid since it frequently means realm as well in its various Hebrew lexemes. As mentioned above, other analyses prefer the supposedly less abstract meaning of the "reign of God," minimizing the importance of his realm. Second, he claims that kingship means "the performance of great acts of salvation for a people by which a relationship of leadership is established."[29] However, this is an incomplete, not even its fundamental, meaning. Saving one's people is only one function of a king, a function for God the King that was unnecessary before the Fall and mercifully will not be necessary in New Earth. Vos arbitrarily assigns only one aspect of what a king might do while reigning. Vos makes his points simply by restrictive definitions

---

26. Eichrodt, *Theology*, 1:431.

27. Knierim, *Old Testament Theology*, 210. Though not speaking directly about the verbiage "kingdom of God," he makes the point that redemption is contingent, not independent from God's universal kingdom.

28. Vos, *Biblical Theology*, 399.

29. Vos, *Biblical Theology*, 399.

of terms to the point that his conclusions only appear valid: first in the case of kingdom and then in the case of kingship. Third, he spiritualizes the role of a king by changing the military function into a soteriological metaphor, morphing kingship into the priestly rather than a royal role. He then projects his non sequiturs to Jesus as well: "We may *a priori* be disposed to assume that to Him likewise the abstract idea of 'kingship' would furnish the starting point."[30] Yes, starting with God's kingship is fine, but it also fine to understand that the function of redemption flows from his universal kingship; so he is not forced to inaugurate a new and distinct kingdom to reign. The redemption requirements would be assigned primarily to the Second Person, yet, still, as a continuation of the combined saving efforts of the other Persons.

Again, by discounting the pervasive universal kingdom of God of the Old Testament as non-redemptive, Vos begs the question logically. He eliminates the alternative explanation by declaration, leaving only the national kingdom by which God would only then become its Savior and Ruler. However, it is by the very nature and attributes of God that he saves in his administration of his universal realm. His redemptive plan began in Gen 3:8–9 when he began looking for the Couple to discipline them and save them from their sin. Vacating one's theology of the foundational role of the universal kingdom within God's salvation and sustaining plan is an unfortunate teaching. Yet fortunately, it is not a teaching that most believers either are aware of or cherish in their professing, prayer, and practical lives.

Others are also dismissive of the relevance of God's universal kingdom. For instance, Goldingay believes it "important that everything is under God's ultimate control . . . nothing happens without God's permission . . . God is sovereign in the world as a whole, and nothing happens without his willing it or allowing it." Yet, regardless of these comprehensive descriptions of God's universal rule, for Goldingay his sovereignty can still be too "all-inclusive," actually impractical, it "loses purchase."[31] Similarly, Ladd makes the following questionable distinction comparable to Vos and Goldingay's declarations that marginalize God's universal kingdom.

> God's rule *de jure* exists universally over the heavens and earth; but *de facto*, in this age only when men submit themselves to the

---

30. Vos, *Biblical Theology*, 401.
31. Goldingay, *Biblical Theology*, 215–16.

divine rule. The initiative in bringing God's Kingdom to earth rests with men. However, God's Kingdom will appear eschatologically; and then God will establish his sovereignty *de facto* in all the earth. Before this eschatological event, God's *malkuth* may be more accurately described as an abstract rather than as a dynamic concept. It is always "there," waiting for men to accept it and submit to it. However, it does not "come" until the end of the age.[32]

However, rulers do not cease to reign their realm simply because their denizens disobey its laws or even rebel, especially when the king *allows* disobedience. In this case, the reign is not abstract but remains active and dynamic in all matters of the kingdom, whether it pertains to the rebellion or not. To reduce God's meaningful activity in and with his creation to only redemptive action is yet another element of a parenthetical paralysis.

In a balanced description of the universal kingdom, God does not simply hold the *position* as King, he *acts* as the King.

> Let the nations be glad and sing for joy, for you judge the peoples with equity and guide the nations of the earth. (Ps 67:4)

> He who disciplines the nations . . . He who teaches men knowledge. (Ps 94:10)

If God is in complete control now, then his *active* reign is perfect now since he can only act perfectly. However, God's "active reign" has a much more restrictive denotation within a significant faction of dialectical kingdom theology. This restriction is a result of this faction's emphasis on the parenthetical age and salvation history. The kingdom of God has a pervasive and consistent meaning in the Old, New, and Final Testaments. It concerns God's attribute of sovereignty activated by his reigning, including his instructions for creation's mutual shepherding by his ingrained image. This is not a New Testament development within God's ontology when he becomes even more sovereign or he then begins to reign because he decided to finally start a new kingdom and start saving

---

32. Ladd, *Presence*, 132; also 144. *De jure* implies almost a reluctant concession and also assumes a contrast to *de facto*; however, something can be both. Ladd's characterizing words as abstractions becomes muddled. He affirms that both βασιλεία and its alleged Hebrew equivalent *malkût* are "abstractions" primarily describing the *reign* of God and realm only secondarily. He also prioritizes God's reign over realm, considering *realm* to be an abstraction. And he considers God's realm of reigning to be that of *salvation*, which is an abstraction as well. Ladd, *Presence*, 130, 132, 196.

people. The whole Old Testament is about God as Savior, and it is arbitrary to draw the line between his soteriological and non-soteriological deliverances—they are mostly inextricable. It has been God's loving aim of the eternal design since the creation and will be everlastingly. God is doing more throughout creation than saving souls. He is holding the whole damned world together. Besides, it was a talking point for Jesus and Paul that God blesses the wicked, knowing that all are not and will not be saved. Why would a God, whose active reign is relegated to sin-salvation history alone, send rain to the wicked as well as the righteous and be personally and perpetually engaged with his creation? As Paul says, God reveals "his kindness is in giving you rain from the skies and anticipated crops in their seasons; he provides you with abundant food and fills your hearts with joy" (Acts 14:16–17).

Vos defined two separate and distinct kingdoms: God's universal kingdom and his redemptive kingdom. It is still common to elevate the latter by making it the conduit of salvation history and placing the former in the background. *Heilsgeschichte* is evidently a parallel universe where God reigns to different extents. This requires a presupposed dichotomy to make room for a messianic inaugurated kingdom of which God can now become king. So, Ladd limits the "kingdom of God" to only actions that redeem:

> The Kingdom of God is his redemptive reign of God dynamically active to establish his rule among men, and that this kingdom which will appear as an apocalyptic act at the end of the age, has already come into history in the person and mission of Jesus to overcome evil, to deliver men from its power and to bring them into the blessings of God's reign.[33]

Like Vos and Ladd, Goldingay specifies the denotation of a king's reign. Whereas Vos defines kingship as "the performance of great acts of salvation," Goldingay claims similarly, "God's reign denotes a king's successful assertion of authority and power over forces that oppose it."[34] But, again, one aspect of a king's reign cannot solely define what it means to reign, even less so when sin salvation is not even the role of a king anyway. And again, when God rules the cosmos pre-Eden and post-parousia his reign must no longer be dynamic since his salvation is not needed.

---

33. Ladd, *Presence*, 218, also 188.
34. Goldingay, *Biblical Theology*, 215.

Certainly this verbiage needs reconsideration since its reductionist approach leads to a dishonoring view of God that dims his glory.

Similarly, Schreiner overqualifies the simple biblical lexical meanings of God's kingdom when describing why the kingdom of God is a central biblical theme: "The 'kingdom of God,' if the term is defined with sufficient flexibility, fits well as a central theme of the entire Bible."[35] One learns that "sufficient flexibility" for Schreiner might entail submitting to a theologically imposed structure comparable to Vos, Ladd, and Goldingay, since elsewhere Schreiner segues away from this meaning of kingdom, virtually changing the subject:

> The kingdom of God is a central theme in Jesus' ministry, and the meaning of the concept must be discerned from the Old Testament because Jesus nowhere defines it. When Jesus referred to God's kingdom, he had in mind God's saving power, the fulfillment of his saving promises.[36]

Nothing in the terminology "kingdom of God" denotes salvation, though one might profess it so and place it in Jesus' mind.[37] One wonders what would form a "definition" for the kingdom of God since the Gospels are not treatises with footnotes and glossaries; yet there are several similes: "The kingdom of God is like . . ." Instead, the Gospel's *narrative* of Jesus' words and works defines the kingdom, a narrative that quite frankly has little to say about the effects of the Passion. If one believes Jesus did not define the kingdom, one might be tempted to create a definition for him. Or, one might resort to presuming what Jesus was thinking when defining the kingdom of God as "God's saving power, the fulfillment of his saving promises." It would be better to choose one of the two meanings in the Old Testament, national or universal, rather than creating a new one for Jesus to rule. However, in the end, as said before, stressing either one of the two Old Testament meanings of the kingdom of God

---

35. Schreiner, *Beauty*, xii–xiii.

36. Schreiner, *New Testament Theology*, 26.

37. Witherington's care in handling this discussion is helpful: "Caution is called for in any investigation of Jesus' use of the *basileia* language, and we are not well served by either severe attempts to reduce all the *basileia*=realm texts to *basileia*=dynamic activity, or by attempts to de-eschatologize Jesus' *basileia* teaching that had a definite future and final element to it." Witherington, *Jesus, Paul*, 63. I would agree with most of this statement; eschatology cannot be excised from God's universal kingdom. But, there is no finality to God's *basileia*. Like others using the term "dynamic," Witherington is fond of a distinctiveness in God's reign when it comes to salvation; then it is "dynamic."

implies the other since his redemption acts are sourced in the universal kingdom, and the universal kingdom mercifully provides the redeemer.

The universal kingdom of God which was commissioned to the Messiah was clarified within the context of the Gospels, not according to or dependent on an emphasis by Judaism as to what the Messiah must do immediately upon arrival. Regardless of whether a biblical theology's realm of interest is Israel, as in Judaism, or in a regionalized inaugurated realm in a synthesized dialectical kingdom, these constricted realms treat the rest of God's universal kingdom and its history as marginally relevant.

13

Dialectical Consequences

THE DIALECTICAL KINGDOM'S DESIGNATION of God's eschatological kingdom as a separate saving program is the primary kingdom concern in many theologies. But the natures of God, creation, and history just do not support this route.

- God's sovereignty as constructed from his other attributes cannot be subordinated to his emotional and moral attributes, which in part motivate his salvation plans for creation.
- God's universal kingdom and omniscience of all creation's actions contextualize salvation history within the rest of his several kingdoms' eternity; their equal place in God's eternal design is not challenged by the redemptive immediacies of this parenthetical age. A redemptive eschatological kingdom cannot contain the entire scope of the kingdom of God, nor can it express his eternal teleology for creation.
- The totality of human history as the summation of every effect of creation's events demonstrates its brokenness. However, the eternal design retains creation's physical and social balances by God's generous common graces to his creation in spite of the Curse.
- The Testaments do not reveal a dialectical kingdom as an adequate prism through which to see God and his sovereign interaction with his creation.

DIALECTICAL CONSEQUENCES

In fact, the dialectical or inaugurated eschatological kingdom theology creates unintended and unnecessary consequences. When the dialectical kingdom is the preferred paradigm, it inevitably varies in its premises and themes depending on its proponent. The following examples of the troublesome implications of this paradigm result in less of a God than he in whom the believing kingdom trusts.

Within the various kingdom theologies, words like sovereignty, authority, dominion, reign, realm, rule, king, kingdom, perfect, complete, already-not yet, active, and dynamic are examples of words that are used sometimes synonymously with one or more of the others, sometimes are used as logically connected to others, or are each qualified in a number of ways that only further complicates, even obscures, the conversation about God and his sovereignty and kingdom. I suggest for consideration the following paradigm that connects at least the ideas of kingdom, sovereignty, realm, reign, perfect, complete, universal, active, already-not yet.

- "Kingdom" means reign and/or realm, depending on the context.
- God acts from his attribute of sovereignty through his kingdom reign, which, like his attribute, is universal, absolute, and perfect.
- God's realm is the universal and perpetually unfinished object of God's active reign, and it has always been already-not yet.
- But God's sovereign reign has always been and always will be universal, absolute, and perfect.
- God's universal, absolute, and perfectly sovereign kingdom *reign* cannot be confused with his unfinished, already-not yet universal kingdom *realm*—they are metonymic yet not synonymous.

Frequently one reads something like "though the Old Testament speaks of God's universal kingdom . . . ," which is then followed by qualifications that diminish or marginalize his comprehensive sovereignty. Most cannot deny the Old Testament concept of God's universal kingdom, but many go on to qualify it in compromising ways. For instance, in the current discussion, the dialectical kingdom injects a parallel reality or a hiatus that interrupts God's universal rule with a new and significantly different "saving" kingdom of his that was inaugurated by the Incarnation but will not be successful until some stage of the parousia. It discounts God's current universal rule and casts a God who continuously struggles with his sub-realms.¹ Scobie provides an example of God's deferred sovereignty where he is not "truly" ruling until the Incarnation; only then God begins to rule:

> Since God's purposes have not been fully realized in history and creation, the Old Testament *promises* the ushering in of a new age and a new order in which God will truly reign and creation itself will be renewed. . . . The NT proclaims the *fulfillment* of this promise: with the Christ event the new order has dawned, God's rule is inaugurated, and already there is a new creation.²

DEISM

Attempts to differentiate God's universal kingdom from his "active" or "dynamic" redemptive kingdom were discussed previously. A latent wide-ranging deism lies within the positions of Vos, Ladd, Goldingay, and others[3] in this respect. It is concerning that even though the natures of creation and its history prove themselves so comprehensive, integrative, complex, and eternal, it is suggested that the universal kingdom of God is secondary to its fractional salvation history. How would God's redemptive program be any more active or dynamic reign than it is in his universal reign? Is God's reign merely titular regarding all non-redemptive events within salvation history? Does one become a theist only when speaking of redemption and reconciliation, and a deist in all other matters? This is a high theological price to pay if one elevates salvation history inordinately as the metanarrative of the Testaments. It implies that God is not personally engaged with all creation at all times—that he has not been *the* integral part of all history and forever will be.

God's redemptive action is dramatized by differentiating it as "active" and "dynamic," as if God acts inactively and without dynamism in

---

1. F. Scott Spencer refers to a "the tug-of-war between God and the devil over human destiny." Spencer, *Luke*, 136.

2. Scobie, *Ways of Our God*, 95.

3. See the previous chapter where "active" and "dynamic" qualifiers are reserved for God's redemptive acts rather than all his acts, for instance in Thiselton, Grindheim, and Witherington. Others of this opinion: Marshall believes Jesus' kingdom teaching was about "the action of God in intervening in human history to establish his rule. It refers to the action of God rather than the realm that he establishes." Marshall, *Luke: Historian*, 129. Morris emphasizes God's reigning work: "The Greek term basileia (like the Hebrew malkuth or the Aramaic malku) means not so much a realm as a reign; it is not an area or group so much as God in action." Morris, *New Testament Theology*, 106.

everything else that he does. Rather than substantive qualifiers, these adjectives are no more than punctuation for a superiority of the redemptive kingdom. These embellishing words invite further questions, since, when used, their meaning is incomplete and requires greater precision and rationale. If God's active, dynamic reign denotes his redemptive reign, does it do so exclusively? When is God's reign not active? With this ambiguous application apart from redemption, did God not reign dynamically or actively before the Fall, and will he no longer reign so in new creation when salvation is no longer needed? Will sovereignty even then not have "purchase"? Was God's reign inactive during the intertestamental times? Is he inactive in response to the believer's personal prayer life unrelated to salvation? Is he active, even dynamically, in some places yet not in other places simultaneously? Active-dynamic is an unhelpful choice of accentuation since it diminishes the full force of the meaning of God's sovereignty within the universality of his kingdom.

Personal, social, national, international, natural, and spiritual realms interact only apparently in chaotic, mysterious, and uncontrollable ways throughout history. Only apparently, because though creation is integrated in countless permutations, they are all thoroughly righteously monitored and wisely engaged by God. So, interest in his current shepherding interactions with all of his creation is basic to his corrective measures of deliverance during the parenthetical age. God's current universal reign in this age is equally "active" as it always has been and was continued to be in the Incarnation; it did not start with the Messiah.

Furthermore, a very significant testamental discontinuity is formed by this alleged eruption into history where God's active salvific kingdom erupted at the Incarnation. God was as actively, dynamically saving his believers from sin in the Old Testament. What would be the difference in intensity of God's dynamism then? Or was his dynamism delayed until the dialectical kingdom?

Relegating the universal kingdom to lesser significance than a redemptive kingdom neglects God's active and dynamic daily intervention in the lives of believers and unbelievers by his shepherding blessings, disciplining, and endless deliverances from adversity. When the believer prays for a mother's healing from cancer, for one's rescue from murderous persecutors, and for mercy when facing the carnage of a natural disaster, are they absurdly "waiting for Godot" and his never-coming, active, dynamic presence? Or, do they not hope and pray as if the true God rules overwhelmingly by what he decides to do, not to do, or allows to happen? Most believers are not expecting God to have become active and dynamic in their lives or to "break into history" only when they were regenerated by the Holy Spirit. They trust that he was always active in their personal history, moment by moment, in their time, in their space, in their spirit, in their despair, in their joy, in their midst of two or three. This version of the dialectical kingdom is too minimalist, regardless of whether it is already-not yet. This is not the God whom the laity love and depend on, fortunately.

WORSE, ANARCHY

At least a deistic God can be trusted to have constructed a machine that was well-oiled. That requires a universal machine that has been so intricately programmed that it maintains any current equilibrium within the inanimate and animate cosmos. Conceivable yet not biblical. However, most grapple with a much worse cosmos existing where God is not "actually" in control of creation. For instance, T. Desmond Alexander is quite clear by his phrasings: "The sovereignty of God will be restored and extended over the whole earth"; "re-establish God's sovereignty on the earth"; "God's authority will eventually be extended over the earth."[4] In other words, God is not currently in control of all things. Buist Fanning suggests that God is the ruler, just "not yet": "The point is not simply God's eternal rule as the great King of heaven . . . but that he is about to establish that rule in actuality on earth (cf. Matt 6:10)."[5] Until then, either there is another ruler of all things or there is no ruler of all things; in which case, metonymically speaking, actually there is no realm either: in other words, it is anarchy and administrative chaos that reign.

At this point I would repeat my understanding of God's sovereignty that does not imply a mechanical determinism but supports the significance of the agency of angels and humanity. God knows all creation's potential actions while he administrates his universal kingdom, and when he does not determine them directly, he chooses to allow them and their implications, or to modify them with different implications, or to disallow them completely, usually imperceptibly, and unintelligibly. One can rationally hold to the absolute sovereignty of God and human agency, just not human autonomy.

---

4. Alexander, *Eden to the New Jerusalem*, 82, 110.
5. Fanning, *Revelation*, 339–40; also 357.

Others appear conflicted in their logic as well in whether God is actually sovereign. M. Eugene Boring at one point separates God as King from his lost kingdom; he is a king without a realm.

> God is at present king over the whole of creation, but God's kingdom has been usurped by hostile powers. The coming kingdom of God will thus mean God's mighty reestablishment in fact of a kingship that is presently real but not actualized.[6]

Yet elsewhere, Boring prefers not to speak of God's kingdom as "usurped by hostile powers" against him but as "powers which he has hitherto permitted to operate." In other words, God's kingship has always been "real" and "actualized" in that his permission is required.[7] David Wenham is comfortable with God's partial sovereignty:

> Although there is one sense in which God is eternally and always reigning as Creator, in another sense God's present reign may be seen as partial and compromised. So the Old Testament can look forward to the time when God will reign completely and over everything.[8]

Also, Schreiner:

> In one sense, God is always the King of kings and the Lord of lords reigning over everything that happens. But in another sense, God's rule has been flouted since the fall of humankind, and the Scriptures tell the story of the kingdom regained.[9]

Here is the inevitable discontinuity of theology and a redemptive narrative. God is the eternal universal King, but salvation history tells of a time when he was not and his kingdom needs to be regained. This raises the obvious question: since a realm is always and necessarily reigned by some entity, and if a kingdom is regained by God, then what entity or entities reigned in the meantime? Again, this would be another ruler of all or no ruler of all. A vast realm but no one is reigning it.

---

6. Boring, *Mark*, 52–53.
7. Boring, "Kingdom of God in Mark," 132.
8. Wenham, *Paul*, 39.
9. Schreiner, *Beauty*, xiii.

AT LEAST HE IS TRYING

Another conception of God that is worse than a modified deism where God sets himself pristinely above it all except when pursuing his special project of salvation of the world is a God who has failed to do even that. Goldingay presents a God whose efforts in the past have not been effective enough when he explains that God has "tried" unsuccessfully at gaining enough "willing human acknowledgement," requiring God to try again through Israel:

> God doesn't force people to acknowledge his rule, perhaps because forced acknowledgement is not real acknowledgement. Having tried twice to gain human acknowledgement so as to effect his sovereign purpose in the world through humanity as a whole (see Gen 1–11), God tried a different tactic in settling on one group that might become his bridgehead into the world.[10]

God's multi-millennial struggle with his opposing satanic and terrestrial kingdoms has been exposed. Apparently he has repeatedly overestimated the fallen human heart. God's unsuccessful attempts to get humanity to acknowledge him are not considered his responsibility since most might not want a God so insensitive as to forcibly deliver them from the satanic kingdom.

However, when does God's sovereignty become acknowledged and his expectations obeyed? Under what circumstances would God no longer have to keep trying to get humanity to acknowledge and obey his sovereign reign? It seems that there are few options for a person's obedient acknowledgment as well as the cumulative acknowledgment by all nations and their persons: (1) that one's surrounding conditions for an autonomous salvific choice are changed so that it is harder for one to resist "the call" to acknowledgment; or (2) a new form or intensity of regenerating synergy between the Holy Spirit and a person is developed that is more successful in bringing one to justification; or (3) that God just makes it happen. It will surely take an apocalyptic event to end the deficient acknowledgment of the world, if that is what God is awaiting. However it would have to be even more apocalyptic than the events of the Incarnation, crucifixion, and resurrection since even they were not enough to convince those near them in space and time, nor billions of

---

10. Goldingay, *Biblical Theology*, 216.

people since. How many more tries will it take? Perhaps a millennium will work? Not really; that devolves into a tumultuous, global Armageddon.

Ladd like Goldingay mythologizes salvation history by characterizing God as waiting for something to happen, and when it does not happen he makes it happen in an even more "dynamic" way: "God is no longer waiting for men to submit to his reign but has taken the initiative and has invaded history in a new and unexpected way."[11] What information had God given to all humanity to persuade them to submit to him before God had to finally resort to a dialectical kingdom (Rom 10:14–15)? And how is that working *this* time? Ladd phrases it that God avoided waiting any longer, so he inaugurated his Son's kingdom. Since God's objective is global acknowledgment of him, by this reasoning he is still waiting, and he would need to continue waiting for at least another thousand years during a millennium when universal acknowledgment is still unattained and Armageddon is required.[12] If Christ returned now, it will have been three thousand years of waiting since a remedial kingdom was presumably inaugurated. Admittedly, a thousand years is like one day; then again, inversely, one day is like a thousand years. If God is awaiting a time when there will be total acknowledgment of his universal kingdom by human autonomy, that is, without his universal sovereignty making it happen, an eschaton is only a fantasy. Something drastic and forceful is necessary to happen, so it will. Not another "try" but an event whose true, overpowering fullness of time will have arrived.

God is fully knowledgeable of every implication of all that he does or does not do; otherwise, his actions would be random. His actions might be purposeful but with uncertain results if all potentialities of his and creation's actions were not anticipated by him; his decisions might then be destructive, consequently, even evil. God does not "try" anything; this assumes he does not know the exact time or space of it happening. Instead, his actions are infallibly purposeful, are undistracted, and are propelling creation teleologically by his eternal design. God's actions are not directed toward a temporal "end of history" or to a point where humanity decides to be perfect again and he need not keep trying. Instead, his dynamic actions are directed toward history's purposeful "end"—to shepherd itself under the Great Shepherd. God's omniscience,

---

11. Ladd, *Presence*, 144.

12. The parable of the landowner and wicked vinedressers is not about the rebellious world refusing to submit to him, thus Christ's new eschatological kingdom was needed; it is about Israel's rebellion, specifically (Matt 21:33–43).

omnipotence, and other attributes contribute to his perfect sovereignty that assures his eternal purposes are met despite vehement opposition from creation:

> In him we have acquired an inheritance, since we have been predestined according to the purpose of him who works everything consistently with his will's plan. (Eph 1:11)

> The Lord's plan stands firmly forever . . . to all generations. (Ps 33:11)

> Your works are wonderful, faithful, true, and consistent with your ancient plans. (Isa 25:1)

> I announced from ancient days what has not happened yet. My purpose will be accomplished because I do whatever I want. (Isa 46:9–10)

> I did not shrink from declaring to you the whole purpose of God. (Acts 20:27)

GOD IS NOT QUITE GOD YET

Yet another contradiction within the dialectical kingdom is that God *is* King and is *becoming* King, which is widely esteemed as a profound paradox.

> The kingdom is not something that just appears at the end of time; rather, the whole sweep of redemptive history is driven by the conception of God as both king and becoming king.[13]

However, whereas a kingdom can exist and develop into what it is not yet, the only thing an existing king can become is . . . not a king. This contradiction is avoided by understanding the kingdom of God as the universal kingdom, rather than a king who had the power to create a sub-realm as the redemptive kingdom of which he is only becoming its king.

For Ladd, "God is now the King, but he must also *become* King." This "paradoxical" already-not yet is presented as the only solution to "how the kingdom of God can be both future and present."[14] But there is a better solution that does not force one to be irrational. God's universal kingdom is an already-not yet kingdom with a past, present, and

---

13. Bird, *Evangelical Theology*, 235.
14. Ladd, *Theology of the New Testament*, 61.

future and can be described as such without resorting to contradictions and tensions. Otherwise, God is merely a constrained oligarch with only the conditional sovereignty allowed by the lords and citizens of his sub-realms. Marshall implies that God's perfect rule in the heavenly realm has yet to be fully realized in the global realm: "The period of waiting is over. The heavenly rule of God is becoming a reality here in this world."[15] Bruce Waltke equates the terminology "kingdom of God" and "kingdom of heaven" as interchangeable and believes "the New Testament terms refer to Israel's God becoming king on earth."[16] This sounds as if God is even now, still waiting while he is becoming.

Most who profess this paradox of a king who is becoming a king do not go as far as Wolfhart Pannenberg's logical conclusion from it; thus they are unexcused for stopping short. He accentuates the significance of God's sovereign reign by rightfully relating it to his very being since it is an attribute, though he wrongly isolates it as God's only attribute. For Pannenberg, since God's sovereignty defines him, and since God is "becoming," God does not fully exist. Even his being falls under an open theology.

> What was new was Jesus' understanding that God's claim on the world is to be viewed exclusively in terms of his *coming* rule. Thus it is necessary to say that, in a restricted but important sense, God does not yet exist. Since his rule and being are inseparable, God's being is still in the process of coming to be. Considering this, God should not be mistaken for an objectified being presently existing in its fullness.[17]

The challenge with this oxymoron, God is King while becoming King, is that the textual evidence offered for this conclusion is slight and questionable. For example, the poetic texts of Obad 21 and Zech 14:9 are sometimes cited where God is said to be a "becoming king," but the normal understanding, "will be king," applies better. Otherwise the many passages assigning nations and creation as part of God's universal kingdom would be wrong. The verbal form that is found in these Hebrew texts, *malak*, rarely means "become king"; it means simply to "reign as king." Besides, that God "will be king" does not mean that he has not been king all along; it implies that he will continue to be king. For example,

---

15. Marshall, *Theology*, 61.
16. Waltke, *Old Testament Theology*, 16.
17. Pannenberg, *Kingdom of God*, 56.

if one *is* a member of an organization, one possibly *will be* a member in the future as well. It does not present a change in God's royal position; it changes the temporal reference point when he is king and will be king.

More elaborately, passages in Revelation about the demise of Satan have also been construed to substantiate that God and his Messiah are in the process of becoming kings. I start in 12:10:

> Now the salvation, and the power, and the kingdom of our God and the authority of His Christ have come, for the accuser of our brothers and sisters has been thrown down.

Here the emphasis is laid on the opening word, "now" (Ἄρτι), which is said to indicate that something new is happening, something that has not happened before. The point suggested is that the kingdom of God has now arrived in Revelation in the authority of Christ and is finally the "yet" of the already-not yet kingdom inaugurated at the Incarnation or after the ascension. Yes, "the salvation and power of God" did come in this particular scenario about the demise of Satan (12:1–12). God's salvation and power resulted in casting down Satan. But this is not the first time his salvation and power will have appeared in history for this specific purpose. This is yet another time it is happening. By God's power and salvation, judgment came once before from within the heavenly kingdom when he threw Satan and his minions down from the heavens (Isa 14:12–19; Luke 10:18). Likewise, the kingdom of God, his universal reign and power, has impacted his created realm since its creation, and his salvations have come perpetually since the Fall. The division of God's powerful and saving actions by his universal kingdom are separated syntactically from the "authority of Christ" since Jesus' human component began only at the Incarnation. Once this foundational biblical truth is remembered, putting Satan in his place was a recurrent work of God in the parenthetical age. The strong man had been bound, his kingdom ransacked, and he had been judged already but not with finality. His demise began in Gen 3:15, accelerated at the Incarnation, and will end in hell. So this is not a new feat of God's salvation and power and of his universal kingdom.

Consequently, Satan's terrestrial kingdom will no longer be his sub-domain; the horrid middleman has been eliminated in Revelation, leaving only what was always there—God's universal kingdom. Satan's ploy was to trade what he did not own in order to become "*like* the Most High" by subjugating the Second Person in the wilderness.[18] That was

---

18. Isa 14:14; Satan's temptation that fooled the Couple was that they would be "like

a humiliating failure. Now, in Revelation even Satan's delegated power on earth is finally deactivated. In this sense, it is understood that the terrestrial kingdom now becomes *solely* the kingdom of the Lord and of his Christ and they will continue to reign forever, no longer permitting Satan's destructive distractions (11:15).

It was the Messiah's eternal rule with God that was new, as the conjunction of agents: God, the Second Person and a man. It was not a new parallel kingdom to that of the universal kingdom that was formed for the purpose of redemption. Though one might claim God's God/man has gained a kingdom by "becoming" a king because of these episodes in Revelation, it could hardly be said that the Trinity was becoming sovereign. One might either invent a parallel kingdom or alter the conditions of the current and only one. If there is a "new realm," its newness is in the sharing of the universal kingdom with a human, not in its limited and spiritualized definition by the dialectical kingdom. Jesus' dual nature as the divine man is a guaranteed improvement, even an eternal success for humanity's kingdom and its Edenic primary commission to shepherd creation.

Now, when it comes to 11:17, it becomes a question of presuppositions. The "becoming" camp presupposes that the aorist, ἐβασίλευσας, is to be translated consistent with their interpretation of 11:15, as God's kingdom beginning, as do many Bible translations. This type of aorist is deemed an ingressive aorist: "You have taken Your great power and have *begun to* reign."[19] However, taking the aorist in its basic meaning, it would be translated "You have taken Your great power and reigned." The latter translation fits both Testaments' idea of a God who has always reigned universally.[20] On the other hand, even if one took it as something other than the simple aorist, it may revert to the understanding of 11:15 as God and his Messiah began to reign *solely*. In both cases an interpretive phrasing is imposed: "begun to" or "solely."

Some find confirmation of a becoming God by reaching back to Rev 1:4, 8, and 4:18 and their designation of God as "who is, who was, who is to come." It is stressed that the construct is truncated in 11:17 to designate God as only "who is, who was," leaving out "and who is to come."[21] This

---

God," the Most High.

19. Fanning, *Revelation*, 339.

20. The split in translations is mainly between older translations, pre-twentieth century, and more modern translations. This appears to be more theological than linguistic.

21. Verse 4:18 changes the order, placing the past tense phrasing first: "who was and

is said to indicate a development in Revelation that makes it unnecessary for him to come in the eternal future since he had already just "become" in the Revelation narrative.²² The first three texts, Rev 1:4, 8, and 4:18, pair these tripartite designations of God's existence with that of the triple designation of God's nature, "holy, holy, holy" (4:18), as well as God the "I Am" as the Tetragrammaton, YHWH, and as the "Alpha and Omega" (1:8). These early verses are typical testamental expressions designating God's ontological duration at least, but they are not a foreshadow of his gaining sovereignty or reign as something he did not always have. He is the Almighty (Exod 6:2–3). He does not become the Almighty. So, Rev 11:17 uses the Almighty designation with the same weight as the earlier texts whether it contains the phrase "who is to come" or not. These three early passages are not setting up for a "becoming king" in 11:15–17 any more than they convey a becoming king even among themselves by affirming his eternal stable, reliable existence, not a developing one. These verses reconfirm that when it is expressed in the Testaments that God will be king, it is not implied that he has not been king all along. After all, Rev 1:5 is clear that Christ, as God, is currently the universal King: "[Jesus Christ] is the faithful witness to these things, the first to rise from the dead, and the ruler of all the kings of the world." It does not defer that designation until the eschaton.

THEODICAL SIMILARITIES

An inclination to doubt the current complete sovereignty of God or the universality of his perfect reign might arise because of the trusting kingdom's minority status in the world. This doubt is similar to that of theism's detractors. The classic problem of evil challenges one for a decision: on which horn of a dilemma does one wish to be logically impaled—since there is evil in the world, God is either not all-powerful or not all-loving. The similar challenge is presented to some who may believe that God is only becoming king: since there is evil in the world, God's universal kingdom is either not all-sovereign or he is not all-righteous.

---

who is and who is to come."

22. For example, J. Ramsey Michaels: "God is no longer 'to come' because God has come in power." However, God always acts by his power: might, intense emotions of love or anger, infinite wisdom; in other words, in his full, holy, and glorious being. He does not modulate himself between more or less powerful when his comprehensive nature is considered. Michaels, *Revelation*, 145.

The decision might be that he is not all-sovereign though he remains all-righteous because God could not be totally reigning and righteous now, since the world is dismissive and disobedient to a diabolical extent. However, a response would be that God can be both all-sovereign and all-righteous in an extremely evil world, especially since God brought an ultimate good from the ultimate evil—the crucifixion of his Son. In other words, it is not only when the whole world acknowledges that God and his Messiah have become the Kings of kings but that while there were yet sinners, Christ died for them. Justification came when there was not total acknowledgment; rather, God's sovereign universal reign exploited humanity's gentile and Jewish "kings" and their disobedience that executed his ironic priest.

Christ's reign will have defeated all his enemies only by the end of this parenthetical age, which will be culminated according to a new "fullness of times." But that does not mean that he is not reigning his universal realm perfectly in the meantime; otherwise, it implies that there is currently some deficiency inherent to his reign, which should raise the question whether he is able to complete the task. After all, it is fallen human nature, in fact, it is even a renewed believer's nature in frequent weak moments, to question God's perfect nature: to either accuse God for unrighteously allowing evil or to discount his sovereignty, his abilities, even his reliability to perfectly deal with evil. One might prefer a struggling God over an absolutely sovereign God, since it might excuse him from the evil in this world. Thus it is an attempt at a theodical solution at the expense of one of the poles of the dilemma. If God is struggling, then he is trying his best. If he is not struggling, he does not care. The question is whether a theodicy is attempted by a dialectical kingdom theology.

What would distance a dialectical kingdom from this problem of evil without resorting to an inexplicable "tension"? Some consideration to the following questions might help to distance a "becoming" God from the problem of evil. Can God be reigning currently and completely if the world is not completely and currently perfect? If God and Christ are righteous, omnipotent, and universally sovereign, why does he allow evil? If there is a reason that God and Christ allow evil for unrevealed wise and righteous reasons, thus exonerating their sovereign nature, why would one await them to "become kings"? Do they become kings in proportion to humanity's increasing acknowledgment? In other words, to the extent that missions and evangelism are incrementally successful, does

God's sovereignty or his reign incrementally help him along in gradually becoming king? If God is in the process of becoming king, is this a form of open theology? Would an answer to some of these questions be that God's universal sovereignty is not a divine immutable attribute but an attribute earned by the success of his attempts to save humanity? Must one continue insisting that God's sovereign, universal kingdom is only "abstract"?

There is a true sense where God's rule is defied in that his instructions are not obeyed. However, this has no bearing on his ontology where converging attributes compose his sovereign nature. Nor does it reduce the area of his universal realm. Is God's sovereign reign defied? Yes, most plainly, but it is not reduced. Does his realm of the fallen spirits and humanity resist? Yes, but it does not shrink in size. His sovereignty is not merely an *application* of his attributes shown by his actions; his sovereignty is a necessary and perfect intrinsic element of his nature, so he cannot *become* more or less sovereign. His universal realm requires his universal reign. God is not sovereign because he acts sovereignly; he acts sovereignly because he cannot do otherwise. In other words, God's reign is defied, but it does not modulate from age to age or from person to person depending on human cooperation. He cannot become any more or any less than the universal sovereign of creation because that is his nature and he cannot be or do otherwise.

I now self-plagiarize by substituting "God's sovereignty" for where I had written earlier about "God's glory" in chapter 2: God's sovereignty is an eternal attribute that cannot be enhanced. It can only be increased in creation's perception. Otherwise, God's sovereignty would be mutable and finite; his sovereignty would depend on creation rather than completely on his nature as it certainly was during eternity before creation. To apply this personally for the believer, God does not become any more the Lord of a Christian the more the believer obeys. He was the Lord of all creation and is not becoming Lord; he is the Lord of the believer and is not becoming the believer's Lord. One might reject or deny God's sovereignty, but no one thereby diminishes it. In other words, no one makes God one's King or Lord; he has always been God and Lord of all creation. That is the message Israel was to convey to the nations, that he *is* the only God, not that he is trying to become their God as well.

PHENOMENOLOGY

God and his Messiah reign over everything, but the nations have not acknowledged the fact, and until then his reign is not yet complete. A clear distinction is missing here, between what is real and what is only an appearance. Though appearances are a real experience for the perceiver, appearances do not always reflect reality accurately. Hebrews 2:6–9 provides an example of this regarding humanity's primary commission:

> Someone has testified somewhere, saying, "What is man that you think of him. Or a son of man that you even consider him? You have made him temporarily lower than angels and crowned him with glory and honor. You have put everything in subjection under his feet." . . . But now we do not yet see all things subjected to him. But we do see him who was made for a little while lower than the angels, Jesus.

In other words, it does not appear that humanity is in charge, but one does see Jesus, humanity's proxy, God's Incarnation; one sees the human to whom all of the creation realm is currently subject. So, there was nothing that was "not yet" in the human Jesus' reign of the universal kingdom.

C. E. B. Cranfield cautions against concluding there was a significant lack of acknowledgment of God's comprehensive sovereignty within ancient Israel's orthodoxy. Though Israel's concept of God was that he was King of Israel and the whole world, phenomenologically, his kingship "is referred to in terms of expectation and hope, as something yet to be realized." So, a person "was after all looking forward to the time when God would make manifest and unambiguous that kingdom which he knew was all the time a reality."[23] Cranfield calls for greater care than what permeates many discussions on what I have termed the dialectical kingdom, and it should be applied to the Testaments' universal kingdom:

> We must be chary of explaining the contrast between the kingdom already come with Jesus and the kingdom still to come in terms of a contrast between partial and complete. It is a contrast of veiled and manifest.[24]

---

23. Cranfield, *St. Mark*, 63–64.

24. Cranfield, *St. Mark*, 66. The unnecessary but frequent emphasis on the tension (actually contradiction) between "establishing" God's future kingdom and making what is already true "more manifest" is exemplified by the following reasoning of Theodore Plantinga: "In one sense, making a statement on the problem of evil requires choosing between theodicy and eschatology. I have no theodicy to offer, no justification of God's decisions in the face of evil in the world. Instead I believe we must look ahead

Morna Hooker describes this phenomenological epistemology perfectly:

> The idea of God's kingship is basic in the Old Testament.... But side by side with this declaration went the realization that men and nations did not acknowledge Israel's God as king; though this did not diminish God's omnipotence, their disobedience meant that God was not seen to reign.[25]

The issue is humanity's limited perception and obedience, not God's sovereignty, including his omnipotence.[26]

HUMAN OBEDIENCE

Furthermore, when the extent of the terrestrial kingdom's acknowledgment is included in any qualification of God's sovereignty, what must be meant is obedience to those expectations, not mere acknowledgment of the truth, but following the source and implications of the truth. The real problem lies not in God's sovereignty over his universal kingdom but in humanity's humility within his universal kingdom. It is not an incomplete sovereign reign of God that is the problem; rather, it is the incomplete obedience from the Couple onward. By discounting God's universal kingdom realm, one might more easily speak of God becoming king of his realm while only an abstract king universally. However, one would not want to separate God's realm from his reign in order to maintain that his reign is only a contingent reality yet his realm is a constant reality.

Lack of acknowledgment of God's reign can be for lack of knowledge, though Paul qualifies this reason substantially:[27]

> That which is known about God is evident among them; for God made it evident to them. For since the creation of the world His

---

to the coming triumph over evil, to the establishment of the Kingdom of God, which is already among us but is not yet fully manifest and recognized." Plantinga, *Learning to Live*, 115.

25. Hooker, *St. Mark*, 55. Also Mark J. Boda: "In Zechariah 14, Yahweh once again reveals himself as a victorious warrior over the nations of the earth, which reveals afresh to all that he is truly *king*." Boda, *Book of Zechariah*, 766.

26. However, those like Pannenberg affirm the contingency of God's sovereignty on human obedience: "Theologians of the past correctly asserted that where men comply with the will of God, there is the Kingdom of God. Taking this a step further, they asserted that to extend the sphere of obedience to God's will means the extension and establishment of his Kingdom." Pannenberg, *Kingdom of God*, 51–52.

27. Paul's reasoning itself is phenomenologically challenging.

> invisible attributes, that is, His eternal power and divine nature, have been clearly perceived, being understood by what has been made, so that they are without excuse. For even though they knew God, they did not honor Him as God or give him thanks. (Rom 1:19-21)

So, not appreciating or honoring God is not a deficiency in his sovereignty but in humanity's misinterpretation of what they observe in general revelation concerning his nature and grace. This negligence by humanity leads to errant worldviews, worship, and conduct. It is not that God is becoming more of what he already is; it is that humanity is not becoming more reverent and obedient. The degree to which God and Christ are kings does not depend on the degree to which they are obeyed. His sovereignty is not developing; it is not evolving, which is a form of open theology. Christ is not incrementally gaining his position as the Messiah depending on the status of the satanic or terrestrial kingdoms' compliance. Fortunately, he is not awaiting voluntary acquiescence from humanity as a whole; that will never happen. Besides, for now, he tolerates and uses their intransigence for his perfect ends.

Walther Eichrodt's description of God's sovereignty in the midst of the disobedient terrestrial kingdom makes it clear that there is no need to compromise or forfeit God's immutable nature:

> Indeed, it is the supreme demonstration of his strength that he can incorporate these hostile powers into his own scheme for history, so that in the very insolence of their resistance to God they are constrained to become the instruments of his decrees. . . . The God of the universe, whose decree has gone forth over the whole earth (Isa. 14.26), assuredly combines the destinies of all the various nations in one great unity, and guides the torturous paths of history in accordance with a mysterious and wonderful plan, in order to bring them to the goal which he has ordained.[28]

This is the foundational premise for Paul's expectation that believers pray for all international and national authorities to ensure the peace and tranquility that help foster God's ultimate objective: sanctified and dignified living (1 Tim 2:1-2). God has always been the King of the terrestrial

---

28. Eichrodt, *Theology*, 1:384. "God's reign is sometimes effected by the means of the sovereignties of the superpowers, but that is a rather paradoxical expression of Yahweh's reign, and Yahweh also intervenes in the rule of the superpower to assert his own reign." Goldingay, *Biblical Theology*, 215.

realm to whom believers pray in confidence that his perfect will affects current politics at every level. The trusting kingdom prays without even considering a limited sovereignty of God. They trust that his dynamic activity includes all his planning and responses to creation and its history's events regardless of the intensity of human disobedience. They do not pray as if God is struggling, though they might confess feeling that way many times.

This is the clear assumption of the "Lord's Prayer" where the believer does not only wish that God and his Son's reign will someday arrive in fullness, completion, or consummation in the eschaton; Christ's assumption in modeling this prayer is that God reigns now over the entire realm of creation. Consequently, the Lord's Prayer should be heard and recited in the present tense (Matt 6:9–13; Luke 11:2–4). It does not open with a request that finally at the eschaton the Father's prerogatives will be done on earth as they are in heaven but that the Father's desire will be done today, as it has been done every day and as it has always been done in heaven. This is the only foundation on which one would consider reciting the rest of the Lord's Prayer and requesting God's continuation to provide food (Matt 6:11), forgiveness of sin (12), guidance toward righteousness (13), and protection from evil (13).

Yet, preferring a dialectical theology, many read the prayer as a contradiction: Jesus opens with the hope that someday the will of God could be depended on since it is done perfectly in heaven. Then Jesus encourages the believer to make their daily urgent requests, realizing the will of the Father may not be able to be done as it is in heaven until the last days. This puzzling strategy of Jesus is to start with God's current incomplete sovereignty but to instruct his followers to ask anyway for the most essential basics of life. The cohesiveness of the prayer is found in the universal kingdom's sovereignty, that it will meet the immediate needs of undeserving sinners. If Jesus is modeling prayer, it stands on the certainty that the Father controls the heavenly, satanic, and natural kingdoms rather than praying in uncertainty over exactly how sovereign he may be at the moment.[29]

---

29. For instance, Schreiner in one paragraph asserts a future meaning to the Lord's Prayer request "your kingdom come." In his next paragraph he says the phrase means both present and future. It is not allowed by this circular reasoning to claim the opening phrase of the prayer pertains mainly to the future, since one can just as well interpret the opening phrase as mainly a plea for the continuation of God's present and universal kingdom's grace. The rest of the prayer substantially does this in its concern for the here and now, not the by and by. Schreiner, *New Testament Theology*, 22. In addition

WARPED TIME

A final questionable implication of the dialectical kingdom is represented by Campbell's approach to eschatology. He begins with an apocalyptic understanding of Jesus' death and resurrection and how it began a new cosmic order by their invasion of the satanic kingdom, the resurrection's victory over death, and the creation of a two-realm and two-age eschatological schema. He derives this from what he believes is the inaugural eschatological presupposition permeating Paul's theology. I submit that he appeals to a poetic and dramatic description of the impact of the cross and resurrection in their invasion of the realm of sin and death and the victory that ushers in the new realm of grace and righteousness. The present realm of sin and death now must compete with this inaugurated eschatological realm.

This two-realm construct, however, neglects the kingdom structure of both Testaments where the universal and messianic kingdom governs not only Campbell's two realms but five powerfully interacting realms: the heavenly, satanic, natural, terrestrial, and trusting kingdoms. The realm of grace and righteousness was inaugurated at creation, not at the Incarnation or Passion, and it has encompassed the realm of sin and death throughout the parenthetical age. It was not new. Grace and righteousness have existed wherever and whenever God has interacted with his creation. And planet Earth will enjoy the glory of grace and righteousness within the perfect new creation. The realm within which sin and death flourish spans only the parenthetical age, wherever and whenever Satan and his kingdom interact with God's creation. So, of course these realms exist simultaneously but fortunately not together forever. Again, the kingdom of God is universal and should not be reduced to mean primarily a future kingdom with an impact on the present.

So, what was inaugurated at the Incarnation? First, *when* was the inaugurated realm inaugurated? At the point of the Incarnation in Mary's womb? At Jesus' baptism? At the time of his first miracles of healings, exorcisms, bending nature, and resurrections? These all were before the

---

to this contextual reasoning, a syntactical reason presents itself. The two tandem and tenseless vocatives are ambiguous; "your kingdom come" paralleled with "your will be done" do not demand the meaning to be a present or future kingdom or future will. Logically, however, as parallel expressions they imply either (1) the kingdom of God has not fully come yet and/so the Father's will is not yet fully done on earth, or, (2) since his sovereign will is always fully done on earth, his kingdom has come as well, thus the believer's faith that he will supply the believer's needs.

Passion, predated its supposed invasion and victory, and make up most of each Gospels' narrative, which was the bulk of his ministry. Or was it inaugurated at his exaltation (Phil 2)? Or was the new realm inaugurated in Gen 3:8 when judgment and salvation first appeared? Is there a pre-inaugural inaugurated eschatology, since the new realm allegedly does not occur until the Passion for Campbell? The old age was/is pre-Passion, yet so was the realm of grace and righteousness.

Second, the Passion accomplishes for Jesus what was already true for the Trinity, including the Second Person. It is true that in the Incarnation God engaged history in a new and critical way, yet not by initiating a new kingdom but by personally entering his universal kingdom in the most intimate way. What is inaugurated at the Incarnation is that finally a human is leading the Edenic charge to bring shepherding grace and righteousness to creation and doing so in synergy with the Trinity, which was already doing it before the Incarnation. Jesus bound the strongman before he plundered it as God had, at will, ever since the Fall but *before* the Passion. The Passion may have been apocalyptic, but it was not eschatological apart from the fact that *from now on* humanity would accomplish the primary commission in the Person of Jesus. The Second Person was not experiencing any change in his cosmic authority, but now he shared it with humanity in humanity's flesh. So yes, there is an inaugurated phase under the universal kingdom but eschatological only in its closer step in time toward the eschaton. In this regard, it was no more eschatological than the invention of leather clothing in Eden.

The innovation of a new soteriological realm that only then began to deal with the satanic kingdom and its damage to the present realm is unnecessary. But along with Campbell's two-realm construct is an ahistorical time construct. An attempt to describe the already-not yet more precisely invites an imaginative time warp. Historiography casts the past, present, and future as fixed terms by which creation and its history are calibrated in a real-world understanding of time. However, some proponents of an inaugurated eschatology are comfortable in contorting historical analysis with contradictions which inject an extra-dimensional manipulation of time comparable to science fiction. For example, Campbell:

> Taken together, Christ's death and resurrection effect and mark the end of the old age and the inauguration of the new. Though the old age remains extant after the death and resurrection of

DIALECTICAL CONSEQUENCES

Christ, its days are numbered since its power and grip over humanity have been overthrown.[30]

This approach to the Passion's impact on the past is meant to explain two ages: the old age which is "over" and the new which has now "begun." But "end" does not mean "end" because the old age remains. It must remain because it must coexist side by side with the new age. The meaning of "past" is now broadened to mean present.

Furthermore, the new age, which is the future age, is said to exist now. So, an ahistorical construct merges both the past and future, broadening it to mean the present:

> In an important sense, this [new] realm properly belongs to the future. But since Paul's eschatology has been inaugurated, the realm has already broken into the present. Thus the two realms exist side by side, one naturally belonging to this present age, and the other belonging to the age to come, but both existing at once. . . . This present age is one of sin and death, while the age to come is one of judgement and salvation. But again, Paul's inaugurated eschatology means that the age to come has already broken into the present, thus creating the famed "overlap of the ages." Which is consistent with the eschatology of the whole New Testament. The future has broken into the present, creating two competing realms of authority and orienting believers to believe as belonging to the age to come rather than this present age.[31]

Admittedly, the realm within which grace and righteousness dwell is a future realm, and only in that limited sense does it "belong to the future," since grace and righteousness have always been in the past and present as well. One might just as well say that Christ, holy angels, flora, and fauna belong to the future, but they have also belonged to the past and present too. Grace and righteousness are not "breaking in from the future"; they are continuing on from the past into the present, and they span the time from creation throughout eternity. This type of "paradoxical" language is unwarranted when God's universal kingdom is recognized as what Jesus meant when speaking about the kingdom, yet it is characteristic of some renditions of the dialectical kingdom.

Campbell is not alone in this position on this paradoxical, monistic, historical time warp, since Udo Schnelle attributes an even more extreme metaphysics of time directly to Jesus:

30. Campbell, *Hope of Glory*, 59.
31. Campbell, *Hope of Glory*, 65.

In Jesus' understanding of time, the decisive boundary is between the past and the present, while the present and the future stand in unbroken continuity, *because the future as the dawning kingdom of God has already embraced the present.* The kingdom of God has no past and has its own time: the future already present.[32]

Dunn is even more time-negligent:

> For the resurrection of the dead is itself an apocalyptic category.... To claim that this has already happened in Christ's resurrection, even "the resurrection of the dead" (Rom. 1.4—not just his resurrection from the dead), is again to claim that the normal course of history has been completely broken; a wholly new and qualitatively different dimension of reality has come into play which wholly leaves behind the old.[33]

Campbell, Schnelle, and Dunn apparently believe the cause-and-effect progressive structure of history can somehow be reversed, where a future effect returns to cause the present, which had already caused that future effect. Put simply, an effect becomes its own cause. How does that work in the real world?

Dunn's summary of an eschatological kingdom theology emphasizes its discontinuity with the Old Testament, a disruption of the nature of history as God created it.

> In an *apocalyptic* perspective, the emphasis is on discontinuity between the old and the new, the disruption caused by the inbreaking of the eschatological, the new creation.[34]

Irrational leaps like this are part of the intellectually challenging nature of the dialectical kingdom. One can believe that God enters space and time and their cause-effect process brings biblical miracles into the natural kingdom. However, this wholly new dimension of reality that reconfigures space and time is imperceivable, indeed inconceivable except in paradoxical theological verbiage. Where is this time warp observed so "wholly," to use Dunn's term, throughout all creation and the history of the last two millennia? The biblical understanding of the kingdom of God is its universality, and it operates according to the "normal" teleological nature of creation and its history as we have described it in our first chapter. If this historical mutation of non-linear history is applied

---

32. Schnelle, *Theology of the New Testament*, 99.
33. Dunn, "Paul's Gospel," 375.
34. Dunn, "Paul's Gospel," 367.

wholly, it could be said that all reality exists in the future as the future now has invaded the present, and huge portions, if not all of the eternal future, are already past as the future-infused present has already faded into past history. This temporal monism is not the dimension, epoch, or world where the natural, terrestrial, and trusting kingdoms live. This view of creation and its history is a derivative of the dialectical kingdom's synthesis of the realized kingdom of Judaism and C. H. Dodd with the promise of a realized eschatology of Rev 21—the already-not yet. History and theological writing have gone ahistorical.

The dialectical kingdom's eschatological kingdom of the present is simply the result of God's universal kingdom's evolution on God's timeline toward New Earth. It is not a retroversive apocalyptic invasion from the future. Apparently the present "new" kingdom/age/order/creation/man applies only to the trusting kingdom since the rest of creation and its history is obviously not experiencing it. There is no evidence of a future kingdom impacting the present creation in a post-millennial–like progression toward the eschaton. Creation is just as fallen as it was during the Testaments. God is still awaiting global acknowledgment. One might ask exactly where this "already" is already and how the future is fairing right now in this moment. In this sense, *Heilsgeschichte* can only be conceived by subjecting one's eschatology to a compromising synthesis of the biblical and certain eschaton with Judaism's failed realized kingdom. A salvation history is best considered a chronology of God and humanity's role in the redevelopment of a fallen world but within creation's comprehensive history. If it is considered a "history" that transcends this history or is in some other way a distinct history violating creation's original nature, then I suggest one is only creating a fantasy world that spawns yet other contradictions.

SUMMARY

Some portray a struggling God by marginalizing God's universal kingdom, constricting biblical theology's focus to salvation history and imagining a brand new kingdom within that biblical theology. By emphasizing salvation as its center, the dialectical kingdom misses the broader view of creation's history. It misses the eternal design and its implications for all of creation's compliance or defiance. It affirms the need for creation's salvation but does not answer adequately why a need for salvation relates to humanity's created purpose. However, interpreting the kingdom of God as the universal messianic kingdom does not end in the tensions and contradictions above and is more consistent with Jesus' self-awareness, message, and miracles.

The dialectical kingdom is an unnecessary complication in biblical theology since allegedly God has created a new kingdom with the same historical progression as the universal kingdom. The struggle among the trusting kingdom and the other kingdoms has always tormented it while relying on the universal King to sustain it by innumerable salvific eruptions until New Earth. There is no need midstream to invent a new kingdom where God demoted himself from the universal King and is becoming a new King who becomes the universal King again when humanity acknowledges that he always had been the universal King in the first place.

God's perfect but never completed universal reign and realm is preferred to a position holding various debilitating qualifications to his sovereignty. The trusting kingdom should find its joy in participating constructively in the shepherding eternal design and the purpose it gives to the constructive, productive life that the Testaments describe. The church has a healthy number of trusting kingdom believers within whom the Spirit works, where their hope and persistent, trusting prayers and praise to God presume his complete sovereign reign over all creation and its history, not only one eschatological zone and certain specific events within it.

Fortunately, the trusting kingdom's pastors and laity do not believe in a dialectical kingdom. Their songs of praise, their prayers to the King for his mercy and blessing, and their trust in God's total sovereignty traverse all denominations whose God is unrestricted in his present authority over his universal kingdom. The theological and semantic errors addressed in this chapter result in less of a God than he whom the believing kingdom trusts, a serious unintended consequence. It is detached from the daily theology of the devout pastorate and laity. It may resonate within a theological echo chamber, but it is not how believers worship, fellowship, grow, and thrive in their faith.

14

Muted Messiah

MANY ATTEST THAT JESUS' kingdom message was also a substantial part of Paul's message (chapter 9). Still, a significant difference in the theologies of both Jesus and Paul is regularly assumed in quests beyond literal "kingdom" verbiage, sometimes giving only nods toward Luke's four summaries of Paul's message on the kingdom of God. Yet the analyses of Acts and the letters, generally speaking, render an inaudible or at least a muted Messiah, leaving Jesus' verbal message unattended to. This has deep implications for understanding the kingdom of God in particular and biblical theology in general. Jesus refers to his current universal kingdom rather than a problematic dialectical kingdom, and Luke does not change meanings for the kingdom of God between the two books. Furthermore, Luke's and Paul's references to the interactions between God's sub-kingdoms support their consistency in the dynamism and supremacy of the universal kingdom. Now, we look at another manner in which Jesus' own words about his kingdom message is marginalized by commentaries and theologies when engaging Acts and the apostles' letters.

JESUS' PRIESTLY TEACHING AND INTERPRETATION

The Gospels reveal Jesus the Messiah as the promised royal priest who daily fulfilled the priestly role of teaching God's law; this was reviewed earlier in chapter 7 and will be addressed again in chapter 17. If Jesus' important commissioned function as the law's teacher and interpreter is neglected, this significant purpose of the Incarnation is missed. Jesus was not simply a great teacher. He was a great teacher because he confirmed God's moral law, adding his own commandments and interpretation of both sources as instruction for sanctification. Jesus also contextualized the ceremonial law within the wider and superior scope of the believer's routine righteous behavior. A large part of Jesus' teaching interpreted the depths of the law, as shown in his Sermon on the Mount. In turn, Jesus corrected the scribes' and Pharisees' recurrent misinterpretations and applications of the law when blending them with their mere traditions (Mark 7:13). To subordinate this role to any other messianic expectation mutes Jesus' encouragements, misses his rhetorical genius, screens his shepherding heart, and conveys to his believers a shallow view of the apostles' esteem for the Messiah. A fixation on the concluding soteriological portion of each Gospel can lead to a position that the body of the Gospels is only an introduction. The interpretation and exhorting portions of Jesus' priestly role can be lost among other priestly roles he filled, such as his self-sacrificing role as the ironic priest and his role to rule his universal realm (Ps 110:4; Zech 6:12–13). Nor should the messianic prophetic role of Jesus be surgically separated from his priestly function of teaching the law. Jesus, simultaneously as teaching priest and exhorting prophet, reconfirmed and convicted people by the law when assessing their moral conduct. When not teaching the law, he broached other subjects, and his role was more prophetic: for example when he addressed the kingdom of God, his relationship with his Father, future events, and politics.

Individuals, the crowds, his disciples, the Pharisees, scribes, and Jesus himself frequently referenced him as "teacher." The apostles also refer to his teaching (Eph 6:4; 2 John 9). Jesus passed on his priestly teaching to his disciples so they would teach his royal sanctifying commandments to the world. Luke's and Paul's personal conversations between themselves and others on their journeys surely would have centered on what Jesus taught, including the circulating written or oral non-canonical compilations about Jesus' life.[1] Luke explains in his Gospel (1:1–4) that his

---

1. "There was (evidently) a fair amount of Jesus tradition which must have been known by the earliest Christian churches." Dunn, *Colossians and Philemon*, 236. This also pertains to what Paul considered the content of the "traditions" (1 Cor 11:2; 15:3; Eph 4:20–21; Col 2:6–7; 2 Thess 2:15). For a summary of Paul's familiarity with the early church's cache of Jesus teaching, see Ridderbos, *Paul and Jesus*, 46–53. Witherington is summative and helpful in reference to the agrapha: "It is more blessed to

account is only the latest written narrative. Previous recordings had been handed down by eyewitnesses and were already used for teaching. Christological creeds and hymns were at least in oral circulation by then, if not written. Furthermore, the apostles, including Paul, were quite aware of each other's beliefs and practices by the time of Luke-Acts' circulation. The Jerusalem Council had taken place years earlier, and it is inconceivable that while in Jerusalem, Paul had no interest in the other apostles' recollections of Jesus' teaching.

The apostles include references to Jesus' teaching. A few passages reflect Paul's familiarity with, and confirmation of, Jesus' pronouncements, both agrapha sayings (Acts 20:35; 1 Thess 4:15) and from the Gospels: Matt 5:4, 10–11 => Rom 12:14–15; Mark 7:15–23 // Matt 15:11–20 => Rom 14:14; Matt 10:10 // Luke 10:7 => 1 Cor 9:14; 1 Tim 5:18; Mark 14:22–25 // Luke 22:19 => 1 Cor 11:23–25). Revelation that Paul and Peter received from the "Lord" include the following.

1 Cor 14:37	the things which I write to you are the Lord's commandment
2 Cor 12:1	I will go on to visions and revelations of the Lord
1 Thess 4:2	you know what commandments we gave you by the Lord Jesus
1 Thess 4:15	this we say to you by the word of the Lord
2 Pet 3:2	the commandment of the Lord and Savior spoken by your apostles

Yet, generally, Paul avoided quoting Jesus in his letters as authentication of his own credentials as an apostle. His "documentation" as Christ and the Spirit's mouthpiece included his claim to have a trustworthy relationship with the Lord. Paul's veracity was supported by his delegated apostolic authority from his Lord and further confirmed by his humble submission to the ministry of Jesus' works and words. Peter also is aware of, if not behind, Mark's details of the Baptist's pronouncements as well (Acts 10:36–37; Mark 1:4). This lack of literal quotation, however, is not to say that the apostles did not reference his words often.

---

give than to receive. He notes, "What this saying shows is that there were likely many sayings, even free-floating sayings of Jesus, that were never collected in a Q-like document or a Gospel." Witherington, *Acts*, 626. Moo: "Yet the important point is that, however developed, Paul's teaching stands in continuity with the teaching of Jesus. Paul probably assumes a fair degree of acquaintance among his listeners with the story and teaching of Jesus." *Paul and His Letters*, 27. Also Goppelt, *Theology of the New Testament*, 2:42–46; Dungan, *Sayings of Jesus*, xvii–xxviii.

ARTIFICIAL PRESUPPOSITION

One encounters a fundamental presupposition among those developing an apostolic theology. It is the prevalent, axiomatic, hermeneutical, and theological position against significant apostolic references to Jesus' teaching, preaching, gospel, testimony in their own writings. Unfortunately, finding unity within the New Testament's message has not been helped by this alleged theorem that the New Testament turned from the Gospels' message *from* Jesus to the apostolic message *about* Jesus.[2] Of course, with Jesus' ascension, his real-time words ceased. However, one could not speak *about* Jesus without speaking *about* the words *from* him as teacher and prophet, in which case the phrasing is practically tautological, though its application in many biblical theologies as well as commentaries on the letters is meant to be dichotomous: the message of Jesus and the apostles is significantly different.

Furthermore, even the words that Jesus spoke were *about* himself. Luke begins his second book with "in the first book, O Theophilus, I dealt with all that Jesus began to do and teach"; his first book was *about* Jesus, about his works and teaching in detail. In other words, if the theorem is intended to make a profound distinction, it misses the mark since no distinction is inherent within it. But there is a large difference in how it is *applied* hermeneutically, where the apostolic message that is said to be *about* Jesus rather than *from* him is restricted to his soteriological role, if what exactly it is about Jesus that is meant in a specific text is explained. The focus is not on Jesus' pronouncements but selectively on his Passion—his "work" of his cross and resurrection, not his words. The focus becomes his holy passivity during his execution and resurrection at the exclusion of his holy activity of words and wonders during the years before. In this way, at best, inadvertently, his teaching and prophecy are

---

2. Bultmann's theorem is often quoted but much more pervasively applied: "He who formerly had been the *bearer* of the message was drawn into it and became its essential content. *The proclaimer became the proclaimed.*" Bultmann, *Theology*, 1:33. Examples of those following this theorem would include Jerry L. Sumney: "The ambiguous expression 'the word of Christ' may point to the proclamation about Christ, the teaching of Jesus, or the voice of the risen Christ in the worshipping community... vs. 16 characterizes the church's proclamation as a message primarily about Christ." Sumney, *Colossians*, 223. Benjamin Fiore: "This does not mean the sayings of the Lord, of which the letters give little evidence, but rather refers to the preaching about the Lord." Fiore, *Pastoral Epistles*, 118. Douglas J. Moo on Rom 1:1: "The noun [εὐαγγέλιον] in the New Testament denotes the 'good news' of the saving intervention by God in Christ, referring usually to the message about Christ." Moo, *Epistle to the Romans*, 43. Also Longenecker, *Romans*, 58; Byrne, *Romans*, 325; Kittel, "λέγω, λόγος, κτλ," 4:116.

marginalized. Jesus had his time while incarnate; now it is the apostles' time to speak. This hermeneutical macro-principle or interpretative methodology sings loud while the Messiah's mouth is covered.

I contend below that Jesus' words which he himself proclaimed during his Incarnation became an important reference point in the apostles' writings. Where commentators understand the apostles' pronouncements to be *about* Jesus, they actually refer to Jesus' own pronouncements. To follow the from/about theorem so devoutly canonizes it as a hermeneutical principle that mutes the Messiah with one stroke and indicates only what the apostles' "gospel" is not—it is not the message *from* Jesus.

A surprising opposite perspective to this from/about theorem might be inferred from John 14:26 and 16:12–14:

> The Helper, the Holy Spirit, whom the Father will send in my name, will teach you all things and remind you of everything I have said to you. I have many things yet to say to you, but you cannot bear them now. When the Spirit of truth comes, he will guide you into all the truth, since he will not speak on his own authority, but whatever he hears he will speak, and he will declare to you the things that are to come. He will glorify me by taking what is mine and declaring it to you.

Understandably, the apostles would not remember everything that Jesus had said, but the Spirit brought Jesus' teaching to their minds. This would amount to a gracious inspiration through, or addition to, the oral and written traditions by the gospelers and the many others who were accurately amassing the words and teachings of Christ. While the Spirit taught and reminded the disciples about Jesus' pronouncements, he did more than remind the apostles of Jesus' truths—he simultaneously dispelled inaccurate representations of Jesus' words and works from which false teachings would have inevitably developed. In John we have Jesus' concern that all that he had revealed in his teaching be remembered so it would be promulgated to the world. It would be re-declared to them in light of the forgetfulness of their finite brains. His great commission to his disciples to teach the nations would rely heavily on this promise of the Spirit's safeguarding of Jesus' words.

Some affirm a strong continuity with the message of Jesus that should be expected. Actually, they are too strong in neglecting the Spirit's originality in some revelation to the apostles, apart from Jesus' teachings. Three commentators are examples of those supporting the continuity of

Jesus' teaching into the apostolic age; yet within the same sentence, they silence the Spirit to a great extent.

> The Paraclete, then, simply continues Jesus' revelation, not by providing new teachings, but only by taking what Jesus himself "taught" to a deeper level.[3]

> The Spirit's ministry in this respect was not to bring qualitatively new revelation, but to fill out the revelation brought already by Jesus himself.[4]

> The Spirit brings no new revelation; his task is to point to that which Jesus brought and to enable his disciples to understand it.[5]

This position, as helpful as it is to accentuate the continuity of Jesus' kingdom teaching, proves too much since the Spirit's teaching revealed more than simply an enhancement or in some way a deeper meaning to what Jesus had already said. It neglects the substantive new teaching of the Spirit, e.g., spiritual gifts, church polity, justification, sanctification, the parousia, etc. The error in this interpretation of John 14 and 16 is in its restriction of the Spirit to teach, remind, and expound what Jesus had already said in his Incarnation, when in fact these passages were not intended to imply that there would be no further revelation from the Spirit, including different subjects entirely.

The unfortunate presupposition of the from/about distinction and a centricity of the Passion either contribute to, or are in part due to, a pervasive mistranslation of one common syntactical construction, particularly in Paul. Jesus is silenced in his priestly roles as the commandment teacher, as the royal command giver and enforcer, as the greatest prophet, and as the proclaimer of his Father and his universal kingdom. Understandably, it might sound exaggerated that a modest grammatical imprecision might impact such basic theological matters. But the following premise is not complex or obscure: *When the Epistles apply a specific genitive phrase to Christ, the phrase's meaning is reversed from its precedent meaning elsewhere in the New Testament.*

---

3. Schnackenburg, *St. John*, 3:83. It would be hard to distinguish at what level the Spirit's teaching was only "deeper" and not "new."

4. Carson, *John*, 505.

5. Beasley-Murray, *John*, 261.

PRONOUNCEMENT GENITIVE PRECEDENT

Five pronouncement nouns initiate many Greek genitive phrasings that very broadly designate what God, Jesus, and his followers considered the most significant pronouncements: διδαχή (teaching), κήρυγμα (preaching), εὐαγγέλιον (gospel), μαρτυρία/μαρτύριον[6] (testimony), and λόγος and ῥῆμα (word).[7] These pronouncement nouns are followed by a proper noun or pronoun in the genitive which indicates either the pronouncement's source (subjective genitive) or content (objective genitive).[8] For example, is Christ the source or the object of the following pronouncement genitive?

2 Cor 10:14: ἄχρι γὰρ καὶ ὑμῶν ἐφθάσαμεν ἐν τῷ εὐαγγελίῳ τοῦ Χριστοῦ

Subjective Genitive: For we even came all the way to you with the gospel *from* Christ.

Objective Genitive: For we even came all the way to you with the gospel *about* Christ.

One further interpretation of the pronouncement genitive, a "plenary genitive," is preferred when a commentator believes the biblical author intended both the subjective and objective meanings simultaneously in the same genitive phrase. So this would mean in the text above that Paul was purposefully conveying that the gospel brought to the Corinthians was both from Jesus Christ himself and it was also about Jesus Christ.

Plenary Genitive: For we even came all the way to you with the gospel *from* Christ and *about* Christ.

Since the tautological implications of all pronouncements about Jesus would require all pronouncements from him, an apt response to these three options for these pronouncement genitives would be that they all should be considered plenary. But this is by no means the practice of the

---

6. μαρτυρία (John) Rev 1:2, 9; 12:17; 19:10; 20:4; μαρτύριον (Paul) 1 Cor 1:6; 2 Tim 1:8.

7. λόγος and ῥῆμα are considered synonymous in this study.

8. Only three of over two hundred commentaries that discuss the options designate the genitive differently—and only concerning the subjective designation. So any grammatical complexities of the genitive case in Greek beyond this binomial option are not a concern for commentators' decisions on the pronouncement genitives: "poss. gen. or subj. gen.," Williams, *Mark*, 30; "genitive of possession," Lenski, *Mark*, 64–65; "ablative of source," Stein, *Mark*, 71.

commentaries where, when addressed specifically, the choice is nearly always made between the subjective and objective genitive. We will eventually suggest a reason for this choice is not grammatical or contextual but theological.

Though plenary judgments are recorded in this study, no published translation of the New Testament nor any commentators' own translations reflect literally such a double meaning for their readers, like the example above in 2 Cor 10:14.[9] Furthermore, if an instance is understood as plenary, one would expect someone to explain the implications of that.[10] The plenary genitive is conceivable, but whether this thinking ever makes its way into the written text is imperceptible; it is not verifiable or falsifiable. The plenary has no boundaries, and in the case of a supposed "ambiguity" of these genitive pronouncements, it can become an ironic epistemological presumption that two unproven options can prove something when they are conflated. Fanning recommends caution with plenary genitives: "In most contexts, it is better to choose one sense or the other. Language does not usually allow such a broad range of flexibility."[11] The caution is well-advised, since to resort to double entendres would be a hermeneutical wild card playable in virtually any chapter of the Testaments.

However, a choice for a plenary meaning for the pronouncement genitives might be more rational, though commentators do not reveal this when designating it as plenary. Greg Forbes is an exception when he articulates a rationale for the plenary genitive. He explains this in reference to 1 Pet 1:24–25: "The grass withers, and the flower fades, but the word of the Lord endures forever. This is the word that was proclaimed as the gospel to you." Forbes affirms that the church continued to proclaim

---

9. Dunn reveals his ambivalence when claiming a plenary meaning for the genitive in Rom 1:9 while holding solidly to an objective genitive in 1:3: "To speak of 'the gospel of his Son' so soon after speaking of 'the gospel of God' is striking (similarly 15:16 and 15:19); and while the genitive construction should perhaps be taken in the sense of 'the gospel concerning his Son' (objective genitive—so 1:3), the fact that both phrases are of precisely the same form and are inevitably ambiguous should not be ignored." Dunn, *Romans 1–8*, 29.

10. James Hope Moulton is correct, theoretically: "There is no reason why a gen. in the author's mind may not have been both subjective and objective." Moulton, *Grammar*, 3:210. However, in this case, perhaps a reason could be articulated. Wallace postulates Protestants, in reaction against the multi-valanced interpretation of the Middle Ages, have been traditionally less prone than Catholics to identify plenary meanings. Wallace, *Greek Grammar*, 120.

11. Fanning, *Revelation*, 362.

the words of Jesus, and he believes this is shown by the identification of the pronouncement genitive as plenary: "Given that 'the word was preached to you' (v. 25) is obviously the gospel, both ideas are present (plenary gen.) as the church continues to proclaim about Jesus what he himself proclaimed."[12]

The rare but explicit conclusion by commentators that they are "unsure" whether the genitive is subjective or objective is still meaningful in that after addressing the issue explicitly, the commentators see the possibility of either type, which is still different from a "plenary" conclusion that the genitive in a specific text is both subjective and objective.

The following observation is a baseline for understanding the pronouncement genitives. *All New Testament pronouncement genitives involving the pre-ascension Jesus, the apostles, any orthodox or heterodox teachers, and all other biblical characters are clearly subjective.*[13] For instance, Jesus' use of the pronouncement genitive is always subjective. He warns the disciples about "the teaching of the Pharisees and Sadducees," i.e., the teaching *from* them, not *about* them (Matt 16:12). In the same way, Jesus also warns of "the teaching of Balaam" and "the teaching of the Nicolaitans" (Rev 2:14–15). But he affirms "the preaching of Jonah" (Luke 11:32), the "testimony of John" (John 1:19; 5:36), and the "testimony of two men" (John 8:17)—never *about* them, always *from* them. John, in his Gospel, also intends the genitive to be subjective when referring to pronouncements, such as the "word of Isaiah" (John 12:38) and "the testimony of theirs [martyrs]" (Rev 11:7; 12:11). Peter does the same when he endorses the pronouncements "of the holy prophets" (2 Pet 3:2). Though these genitives are syntactically conceivable either way, they are interpreted exclusively by commentators and translated in all versions of the New Testament as the subjective—*from* these people as *sources*—never as the objective. Luke summarized the response to Peter and the apostles' pronouncements using subjective genitives as *from* Peter and the apostles, not *about* the apostles personally. So those who received "the word of his [from Peter]" (Acts 2:41) subsequently followed "the teaching *from* the apostles" (Acts 2:42). This subjective pattern is continued without exception in several other New Testament passages (John 21:24; Acts 22:18; Rom 2:16; 16:25; 1 Cor 2:4; 2 Cor 4:31; 1 Thess 1:5; 2 Thess 2:14; 2 Tim 2:8). Furthermore, all pronouncement genitives

---

12. Forbes, *1 Peter*, 52.

13. "God" is the lone exception, but these genitives are still predominantly consistent with the subjective precedent.

are presumed subjective when Jesus describes his own pronouncements as the "word(s) of mine" (John 5:24; 12:48). They are always presumed to be subjective as well when others refer to Jesus' pronouncements; he is pervasively presumed to be the source rather than the object, at least thirty times.[14]

The precedent is set then: the genitive is subjective for all pronouncements involving Jesus in the Gospels as well as any mortals throughout the New Testament (over fifty such texts). However, as the following tally shows, this undisputed precedent for the subjective quickly loses its appeal among commentaries which address the pronouncement genitives in Acts, the Epistles, and Revelation when involving "Christ" or "the Lord" ("Jesus" does not occur in these apostolic genitive constructs outside of the Gospels). This adds another forty-seven texts, so around one hundred pronouncement genitive phrases are found in the New Testament.

THE EVIDENCE

One purpose for the following analysis is to discover how *commentators* understand John's and Paul's use of pronouncement genitives (only three texts are not from John or Paul). The ultimate purpose, however, is to observe how commentators' interpretive choices are related to their willingness to use Jesus' pronouncements as reference points for discipling the church or whether they are satisfied not to regularly bring Jesus' own pronouncements directly to the church's attention in their letters. Do they direct their audience to the words that Jesus himself spoke (subjective): his testimony, his preaching, his teaching, his gospel, and his word? Or do they direct their audiences, saved and unsaved, to their own words *about* Jesus (objective)? The from/about dichotomy in large part rests on how these pronouncement genitives are understood: whether Jesus Christ was the source of what they pronounced or the object of what they pronounced. For example, in 2 Cor 10:14, which gospel did Paul bring

---

14. E.g., Matt 7:28; Mark 11:18; Luke 10:39; John 15:7; 18:19; also Rev 3:8. Other examples of Jesus' pronouncement genitives: Matt 24:35 // Mark 13:31 // Luke 21:33; 24:44; Mark 1:22; 4:2; 8:38; Luke 4:32; 6:47; 9:26; 24:7–8; John 3:32–33; 5:24, 38, 47; 7:16–17; 8:14; 12:47–48; 14:15, 21, 23–24; 14:23–24; 15:10, 12; 18:32; 1 John 2:4–5. Jesus says he testifies "about" himself, "Even if I am testifying about Myself . . ." (John 8:14). Yet this is not a pronouncement genitive since we find the explicit preposition for "about," περί, instead: "Κἂν ἐγὼ μαρτυρῶ περὶ ἐμαυτοῦ . . ."

to the Corinthians? The good news *from* Christ or Paul's gospel *about* Christ?[15] It makes a very significant difference in one's theology whether Paul is proclaiming Jesus' gospel or his own gospel about Jesus.

The evidence I cite for the use of this genitive construction includes over three hundred conclusions by over one hundred fifty commentators in their over two hundred commentaries on nearly fifty texts. Obviously, many more commentaries were consulted, yet they did not address this genitive construct at all. Nonetheless, the two hundred commentaries that did comment comprise an adequate sample.[16]

One additional introductory consideration before the evidence is gathered. One might expect that the immediate textual contexts of these genitives would explain a commentary's choice of an objective, subjective, or plenary conclusion. However, the syntax of the pronouncement genitives is so tight and the content is so general that the texts' wider rhetorical context is seldom helpful. Furthermore, these genitives offer no specific content of Jesus' "testimony," "gospel," "word," "preaching," or "teaching."[17] Rather, they are codified phrases filled with unexpressed but presumably expansive meaning for the early church community. These pronouncement phrases became coined repositories carrying their own authority. Consequently, commentaries rarely engage the exegetical contexts to support their conclusions on the genitive, so no consensus develops on how the context affected a preference for the subjective or objective in any given text.[18]

---

15. Translations that prefer the objective interpretation but only rarely amplify the phrase by inserting "about," for instance:

"In this way our testimony about Christ was confirmed and established in you." AMP

"God thus confirming our testimony about Christ among you." NIV

"This confirms that what I told you about Christ is true." NLT

But usually translations leave the text without an explicit tilt toward the subjective or objective genitive.

16. Pronouncement genitive texts that are not counted in this summary include Acts 12:24, in which no one is addressed, and "commands" of God/Christ, which are obviously subjective, or agrapha from Jesus.

17. Exceptions are found only where the subjective genitive is obvious in that they are literal citation of Jesus' words.

18. While explaining when the genitive case is ambiguous between the subjective and objective, Wallace says the decision must rest on "context, authorial usage, and broader exegetical issues." Wallace, *Greek Grammar*, 113, 117. This is correct, so it would be helpful if this interpretive rationale was considered and expressed in the commentaries on these passages.

Genitive "of God"

Consistent with Old Testament precedent, the New Testament pronouncement "the word of God" was always considered the subjective genitive by the commentators covered in this study. However, the perspective changes significantly with "testimony of God" and "gospel of God," where commentators' interpretations per text are mixed but where the preference was fairly consistent with the New Testament's precedent for pronouncement phrases: forty-one subjective, nine objective, and eleven both.

Testimony of God (μαρτυρία/μαρτύριον)

1 Corinthians 2:1 "I did not come with lofty words of wisdom when I proclaimed to you *the testimony of God*." Subj: 2. Obj: 4.[19]

1 John 5:9 "Since we accept *human testimony*, *the testimony of God* is greater since it is the *testimony of God* that he has testified about [περί] his Son." Subj: 9.[20]

Gospel of God (εὐαγγέλιον)

Mark 1:14–15 "Jesus came to Galilee proclaiming *the gospel of God*: 'The time is fulfilled and the Kingdom of God is at hand.'" Subj: 5. Obj: 3. Plenary: 4.[21]

Romans 1:1 "Paul ... set apart for *the gospel of God* which he promised in the holy writings beforehand through his prophets about [περί] his Son." Subj: 10. Obj: 1: Plenary: 2.[22]

---

19. Subj: Lightfoot, *Epistles of Paul*, 171; Brookins and Longenecker, *1 Corinthians 1–9*, 43. Obj: Fee, *First Corinthians*, 33; Garland, *1 Corinthians*, 83; Ciampa and Rosner, *First Corinthians*, 113–14; Barrett, *First Corinthians*, 62.

20. Subj: Jobes, *1, 2, and 3 John*, 223; Smalley, *1, 2, 3 John*, 283; Schuchard, *1–3 John*, 514; Akin, *1, 2, 3 John*, 200; Brown, *Epistles of John*, 600; Kistemaker, *James and 1–3 John*, 356; Kruse, *Letters of John*, 180; Yarborough, *1–3 John*, 285; Haas, *Letters of John*, 121.

21. Subj: Cranfield, *St. Mark*, 62; Maloney, *Gospel of Mark*, 49; Mann, *Mark*, 205; Guelich, *Mark 1—8:26*, 43; Edwards, *Mark*, 45. Obj: Decker, *Mark 1–8*, 17; Gundry, *Mark*, 69; Bratcher and Nida, *Mark*, 3. Plenary: Boring, *Mark*, 49; Bock, *Mark*, 119; France, *Mark*, 91; Donahue and Harrington, *Mark*, 70.

22. Subj: Murray, *Romans*, 1:3; Morris, *Epistle to the Romans*, 40; Dunn, *Romans 1–8*, 10; Moo, *Romans*, 43; Witherington, *Romans*, 31; Cranfield, *Romans*, 2:533;

Romans 15:16 "He gave me the priestly ministry of proclaiming *the gospel of God*." Subj: 3.[23]

2 Corinthians 11:7 "Was it a sin for me to lower myself in order to elevate you by proclaiming *the gospel of God* to you for free?" Subj: 2. Plenary: 1.[24]

1 Thessalonians 2:2 "We had courage from our God to declare *the gospel of God* to you." Subj: 3. Plenary: 2.[25]

1 Thessalonians 2:8 "We were so pleased to share *the gospel of God* with you." Subj: 2. Plenary: 1.[26]

1 Thessalonians 2:9 "We worked day and night not to be a burden to anyone while we proclaimed *the gospel of God* to you." Subj: 1. Plenary: 1.[27]

1 Peter 4:17 "What will the outcome be for those who do not obey *the gospel of God*?" Subj: 6. Obj: 1.[28]

Luke's Pronouncement Genitives in Acts

Christ is considered to be "the Lord" in our pronouncement texts since no text that involves "the Lord" requires God to be the intended divine.[29] Also, many of our pronouncement genitives involving "the Lord" are found in Acts where the fuller designation "the Lord Jesus" is used almost

---

Hodge, *Romans*, 17; Jewett, *Romans*, 102; Fitzmyer, *Romans*, 232; Moulton, *Grammar*, 3:211. Obj: Longenecker, *Romans*, 58. Plenary: Keck, *Romans*, 41; Headlam and Sanday, *Romans*, 5.

23. Subj: Morris, *Romans*, 511; Moo, *Epistle to the Romans*, 890; Moulton, *Grammar*, 3:211.

24. Subj: Barrett, *Second Corinthians*, 282; Plummer, *Second Corinthians*, 303. Plenary: Harris, *Second Corinthians*, 756.

25. Subj Weima, *1-2 Thessalonians*, 133; Richard, *First and Second Thessalonians*, 78; Wanamaker, *Thessalonians*, 92–93. Plenary: Shogren, *1 and 2 Thessalonians* 92; Boring, *I and II Thessalonians*, 81.

26. Subj: Richard, *First and Second Thessalonians*, 101; Hiebert, *Thessalonian Epistles*, 96. Plenary: Keck, *Romans*, 41.

27. Subj: Morris, *First and Second Thessalonians*, 74. Plenary: Keck, *Romans*, 41.

28. Subj: Forbes, *1 Peter*, 52; Jobes, *1 Peter*, 294; Davids, *First Peter*, 171; Achtemeier, *1 Peter*, 141; Schreiner, *1, 2 Peter, Jude*, 228; Grudem, *1 Peter*, 183. Obj: Elliot, *1 Peter*, 801–2.

29. Bruce, *1 and 2 Thessalonians*, 17; Fee: "Paul always and consistently uses 'the Lord' (*kurios*) to refer to Christ." *First and Second Thessalonians*, 173.

twenty times. Third, the designation "Lord Jesus" is used around one hundred times in the New Testament. Compared to the Epistles, commentators rarely address pronouncement genitives in Acts. Compared to the Epistles, very few commentators reflect on which genitive is meant in the relevant Acts texts. Luke's narration in Acts, in its seven instances of the phrase "word of the Lord," is considered in the commentaries as objective nine times and twice as both subjective and objective, contrary to the New Testament precedent (8:25; 13:44, 49; 15:35, 36; 16:32; 19:10). The phrase "teaching of the Lord" is also preferred as the objective three times; one commentator was unsure (Acts 13:12).

Word of the Lord (λόγος or ῥῆμα)

Acts 8:25 "So after [Peter and John] testified and proclaimed *the word of the Lord*, they returned to Jerusalem." Obj: 1.[30]

Acts 13:44 "Nearly the entire city gathered to hear *the word of the Lord*." Obj: 1.[31]

Acts 13:49 "*The word of the Lord* spread throughout the whole region." Obj: 1.[32]

Acts 15:35 "Paul and Barnabas remained in Antioch teaching and proclaiming . . . *the word of the Lord*." Obj: 1. Plenary: 1.[33]

Acts 15:36 "Let us return to visit the believers in every city where we proclaimed *the word of the Lord*." Obj: 1. Plenary: 1.[34]

Acts 16:32 "They spoke *the word of the Lord* to him." Obj: 1.[35]

Acts 19:10 "All who lived in Asia heard *the word of the Lord*." Obj: 2.[36]

---

30. Obj: Fitzmyer, *Acts*, 407.
31. Obj: Schnabel, *Acts*, 586.
32. Obj: Schnabel, *Acts*, 590.
33. Obj: Pervo, *Acts*, 385. Plenary: Schnabel, *Acts*, 661–62.
34. Obj: Pervo, *Acts*, 385. Plenary: Schnabel, *Acts*, 661–62.
35. Obj: Pervo, *Acts*, 398.
36. Obj: Pervo, *Acts*, 462; Schnabel, *Acts*, 794.

Teaching of the Lord (διδαχή)

Acts 13:12 "The proconsul was amazed at *the teaching of the Lord.*" Obj: 3. Unsure: 1.³⁷

John's Genitives with Jesus/Christ

Given that the inherent ambiguity of the pronouncement genitives complicates deciding which is meant, subjective or objective, and given that the context is rarely determinative, thus unarticulated as a key factor, it is not surprising, though unnecessary, that John's commentators are evenly split on his use of the pronouncement genitives regarding "testimony of Jesus" and "teaching of Christ" in 2 John 9 and Revelation respectively: subjective twenty-three times, objective twenty-four, plenary six, and unsure three. However, we saw above that all nine commentators take "testimony of *God*" as the subjective in 1 John 5:9. John intentionally avoids the term "gospel" in his writings, using it only once, and that in Revelation (14:6, "eternal gospel").

Teaching of Christ (διδαχή)

2 John 9 "Everyone who goes beyond *the teaching of Christ*, and does not remain in it, does not have God." Subj: 5. Obj: 10. Plenary: 1. Unsure: 3.³⁸

Testimony of Jesus (μαρτυρία)

Revelation 1:2 "[John], who testified to the word of God and to the *testimony of Jesus Christ* and all that he saw . . ." Subj: 7. Obj: 3.³⁹

---

37. Obj: Peterson, *Acts*, 382; Barrett, *Acts*, 1:619; Schnabel, *Acts*, 560. Unsure: Fitzmyer, *Acts*, 504.

38. Subj: Schnackenburg, *Johannine Epistles*, 286; Westcott, *Epistles of St. John*, 230; Brook, *Johannine Epistles*, 177; Brown, *Epistles of John*, 675; Kistemaker, *James, 1–3 John*, 382. Obj: Rensberger, *1, 2, 3 John*, 154; Marshall, *Epistles of John*, 72; Johnson, *1, 2, 3 John*, 157–58; Lieu, *I, II, and III John*, 258; Painter, *1, 2, 3 John*, 354; Smalley, *1, 2, 3 John*, 332; Strecker, *Johannine Letters*, 242; Jobes, *1, 2, and 3 John*, 270; Akin, *1, 2, 3 John*, 232; Smith, *First, Second, Third John*, 145. Plenary: Schuchard, *1–3 John*, 607. Unsure: Roberts, *Letters of John*, 164–65; Houlden, *Johannine Epistles*, 146; Thompson, *1–3 John*, 155.

39. Subj: Kistemaker, *Revelation*, 78; Aune, *Revelation*, 1:6; Ladd, *Revelation*, 23,

Revelation 1:9 "John . . . was on Patmos for the word of God and *the testimony of Jesus.*" Subj: 1. Obj: 1.[40]

Revelation 12:17 "The dragon was furious with the woman and went off to make war . . . on those who keep the commandments of God and hold to *the testimony of Jesus.*" Subj: 3. Obj 4: Plenary: 2.[41]

Revelation 19:10 "I am a servant with you and your brothers and sisters who hold the *testimony of Jesus* firmly. Worship God, for *the testimony of Jesus* is the spirit of prophecy." Subj: 6. Obj: 3. Plenary: 1.[42]

Revelation 20:4 "I saw the souls of those beheaded for *the testimony of Jesus* and the word of God." Subj: 1. Obj: 2.[43]

Paul's Genitives with Christ/Lord

A formidable precedent is formed by over fifty pronouncement genitives that involve the pre-ascension Jesus, the apostles, heterodox teachers, and other biblical figures, when they are always construed as the subjective genitive. These are always the source of their pronouncement. One would expect that, like John's commentators, commentaries on Paul's letters would at least be split as well for the same reasons of genitive ambiguity and apparent contextual indifference. However, when Paul writes, this precedent has very little sway on his commentators.

The pronouncement genitives' precedent in the New Testament as the subjective is nearly completely reversed when it comes to Paul's commentators who favor the objective 119 times, the subjective only 16 times, and the plenary 14 times. However, even more noteworthy

---

175; Osborne, *Revelation*, 57; Mounce, *Revelation*, 42; Bratcher and Hatton, *Revelation*, 8; Harrington, *Revelation*, 187. Obj: Fee, *Revelation*, 177; Hughes, *Revelation*, 17; Beale, *Revelation*, 184.

40. Subj: Strathmann, "μάρτυς, μαρτυρέω, κτλ," 4:500. Obj: Osborne, *Revelation*, 82.

41. Subj: Harrington, *Revelation*, 187; Strathmann, "μάρτυς, μαρτυρέω, κτλ," 4:500; Mounce, *Revelation*, 242. Obj: Fee, *Revelation*, 177; Aune, *Revelation*, 2:657; Hughes, *Revelation*, 143; Osborne, *Revelation*, 485. Plenary: Beale, *Revelation*, 679; Brighton, *Revelation*, 324.

42. Subj: Harrington, *Revelation*, 187; Caird, *Revelation*, 238; Beckwith, *Apocalypse of John*, 729; Blount, *Revelation*, 34; Strathmann, "μάρτυς, μαρτυρέω, κτλ," 4:500. Obj: Bratcher and Hatton, *Revelation*, 160. Obj: Kistemaker, *Revelation*, 518; Aune, *Revelation*, 3:1038; Fee, *Revelation*, 177. Plenary: Brighton, *Revelation*, 502.

43. Subj: Strathmann, "μάρτυς, μαρτυρέω, κτλ," 4:500. Obj: Fee, *Revelation*, 177; Ladd, *Revelation*, 175.

is that in Paul's pronouncement genitive expressions that use "gospel, εὐαγγέλιον," "testimony, μαρτύριον," and "preaching, κήρυγμα," the genitive conclusions result in 83 for the objective, zero for the subjective, only 6 for the plenary, and 7 were unsure. In other words, contrary to New Testament precedent, and contrary to John's interpreters, *no commentator deciding between the subjective or objective genitive allows the Messiah to be the source of Paul's gospel, testimony, or preaching*. Dissenting voices only infer the subjective in a plenary designation or are unsure.

Word of Christ/Lord (λόγος or ῥῆμα)

Romans 10:17 "Faith comes from hearing, and hearing by *the word of Christ*." Subj: 3. Obj: 7. Plenary: 4. Unsure: 1.[44]

Colossians 3:16 "Let the word of Christ richly dwell in you." Subj: 4. Obj: 14. Plenary: 3.[45]

1 Thessalonians 1:8 "*The word of the Lord* has sounded forth from you." Subj: 4. Obj: 3. Plenary 1.[46]

2 Thessalonians 3:1 "Pray for us, so that the *word of the Lord* may spread rapidly." Obj: 4.[47]

---

44. Subj: Keck, *Romans*, 260; Murray, *Romans*, 2:61; Harvey, *Romans*, 261. Obj: Fitzmyer, *Romans*, 598; Byrne, *Romans*, 325; Moo, *Epistle to the Romans*, 666; Cranfield, *Romans*, 2:533, 2:537; Jewett, *Romans*, 642; Kruse, *Romans*, 418; Schreiner, *Romans*, 566–67; Wuest, *Romans*, 181. Plenary: Dunn, *Romans 1–8*, 620, 623; Hendriksen, *Romans*, 351; Morris, *Romans*, 392. Unsure: Matera, *Romans*, 251.

45. Subj: Wilson, *Colossians and Philemon*, 266; Bruce, *Colossians, Philemon, Ephesians*, 157; Lightfoot, *Colossians and Philemon*, 224; Moule, *Colossians and Philemon*, 125. Obj: Moo, *Colossians and Philemon*, 286; Pokorný, *Colossians*, 173; Hay, *Colossians*, 134; O'Brien, *Colossians, Philemon*, 206; Seitz, *Colossians*, 164; Martin, *Colossians*, 125; McKnight, *Colossians*, 329; Pao, *Colossians and Philemon*, 247; Sumney, *Colossians*, 223; Melick, *Philippians, Colossians*, 303; Deterding, *Colossians*, 146; Wall, *Colossians, Philemon*, 149–50; Wright, *Colossians and Philemon*, 148; Bratcher and Nida, *Colossians and Philemon*, 89; Campbell, *Colossians and Philemon*, 59. Plenary: Dunn, *Colossians and Philemon*, 236, 316; MacDonald, *Colossians and Ephesians*, 142; Thompson, *Colossians and Philemon*, 85–86.

46. Subj: Bruce, *1 and 2 Thessalonians*, 17; Hiebert, *Thessalonian Epistles*, 64; Richard, *First and Second Thessalonians*, 71–72; Wanamaker, *Thessalonians*, 83. Obj: Fee, *First and Second Thessalonians*, 44; Shogren, *1 and 2 Thessalonians*, 68; Weima, *1–2 Thessalonians*, 104. Plenary: Beale, *1–2 Thessalonians*, 58.

47. Obj: Furnish, *1, 2 Thessalonians*, 171; Morris, *First and Second Thessalonians*, 245; Weima, *1–2 Thessalonians*, 585–86; Ellingworth and Nida, *Thessalonians*, 192.

1 Timothy 6:3-4 "Whoever teaches a different doctrine and does not agree with *the sound words of our Lord Jesus Christ* and teaching that conforms to godliness, is arrogant." Subj: 5. Obj: 5. Plenary: 1. Unsure: 1.[48]

Testimony of Christ/Lord (μαρτύριον)

1 Corinthians 1:5-6 "In every way you have been enriched in him . . . even as *the testimony of Christ* was confirmed among you." Obj: 11.[49]

2 Timothy 1:8 "Do not be ashamed then of *the testimony of our Lord* nor of me his prisoner." Obj: 8.[50]

Preaching of Jesus Christ (κήρυγμα)

Romans 16:25-26 "Now to him who is able to strengthen you according to my gospel and the *preaching of Jesus Christ* . . . to the only wise God be glory forevermore through Jesus Christ." Obj: 18. Unsure: 1.[51]

---

48. <u>Subj</u>: Knight, *Pastoral Epistles*, 195, 250; Marshall, *Pastoral Epistles*, 639; Quinn and Wacker, *Timothy*, 488, 491-92; Hendriksen, *1 and 2 Timothy*, 195; Ward, *1 and 2 Timothy, Titus*, 95. <u>Obj</u>: Wall and Steele, *1 and 2 Timothy, Titus*, 140-41; Fiore, *Pastoral Epistles*, 118; Fee, *1 and 2 Timothy, Titus*, 141; Towner, *Letters to Timothy and Titus*, 394; Mounce, *Pastoral Epistles*, 337. <u>Plenary</u>: Kelly, *Pastoral Epistles*, 134. <u>Unsure</u>: Johnson, *First and Second Timothy*, 292.

49. <u>Obj</u>: Fee, *First Corinthians*, 33; Conzelmann, *1 Corinthians*, 27; Barrett, *First Corinthians*, 35; Garland, *1 Corinthians*, 34; Brookins and Longenecker, *1 Corinthians 1-9*, 9; Robertson and Plummer, *First Corinthians*, 6; Lightfoot, *Epistles of Paul*, 148; Ciampa and Rosner, *First Corinthians*, 64; Thiselton, *First Corinthians*, 94; Lockwood, *1 Corinthians*, 32; Ellingworth and Hatton, *First Corinthians*, 13.

50. <u>Obj</u>: Collins, *1 and 2 Timothy and Titus*, 198; Knight, *Pastoral Epistles*, 372; Marshall, *Pastoral Epistles*, 703; Wall and Steele, *1 and 2 Timothy, Titus*, 226; Guthrie, *Pastoral Epistles*, 140; Fiore, *Pastoral Epistles*, 137; Quinn and Wacker, *Timothy*, 594; Bratcher, *Timothy and Titus*, 70-71.

51. <u>Obj</u>: Byrne, *Romans*, 463; Fitzmyer, *Romans*, 754; Witherington, *Romans*, 401; Jewett, *Romans*, 1006; Moo, *Epistle to the Romans*, 938; Murray, *Romans*, 2:241; Black, *Romans*, 216; Keck, *Romans*, 382; Cranfield, *Romans*, 2:810; Kruse, *Romans*, 588; Headlam and Sanday, *Romans*, 433; Middendorf, *Romans 1-8*, 1602; Schreiner, *Romans*, 811; Matera, *Romans*, 347; Stuhlmacher, *Romans*, 257; Morris, *Romans*, 546; Newman and Nida, *Romans*, 299. <u>Unsure</u>: Hodge, *Romans*, 452.

Gospel of Christ/Lord/Son (εὐαγγέλιον)

Romans 1:9–10 "God, whom I serve with my spirit in *the gospel of his Son*, is my witness that I always mention you in my prayers without ceasing." Obj: 12. Unsure: 1.[52]

Romans 15:19 "I have fully proclaimed *the gospel of Christ* from Jerusalem to all the way around to Illyricum." Obj: 5. Unsure:1.[53]

1 Corinthians 9:12 "We endure anything rather than obstruct in any way *the gospel of Christ*." Obj: 5.[54]

2 Corinthians 2:12–13 "When I came to Troas for *the gospel of Christ* . . . my spirit did not rest since I did not find my brother Titus there." Obj: 5. Unsure: 1.[55]

2 Corinthians 9:13 "They will glorify God because of your obedience to your confession of *the gospel of Christ*." Obj: 2. Plenary: 1.[56]

2 Corinthians 10:14 "We even came all the way to you with the *gospel of Christ*." Obj: 2.[57]

Galatians 1:7 "Some are troubling you and want to distort *the gospel of Christ*." Obj: 5. Plenary 2.[58]

---

52. Obj: Murray, *Romans*, 1:20; Keck, *Romans*, 47; Kruse, *Romans*, 60–61; Morris, *Romans*, 58; Byrne, *Romans*, 55; Fitzmyer, *Romans*, 245; Hodge, *Romans*, 25; Matera, *Romans*, 38; Moo, *Epistle to the Romans*, 58; Cranfield, *Romans*, 1:76; Harvey, *Romans*, 20; Wuest, *Romans*, 20. Unsure: Dunn, *Romans 1–8*, 29.

53. Obj: Fitzmyer, *Romans*, 714; Moo, *Epistle to the Romans*, 895; Cranfield, *Romans*, 2:762; Harvey, *Romans*, 360; Newman and Nida, *Romans*, 281. Unsure: Jewett, *Romans*, 914.

54. Obj: Barrett, *First Corinthians*, 207; Brookins and Longenecker, *1 Corinthians 1–9*, 213; Fee, *First Corinthians*, 454; Thiselton, *First Corinthians*, 691; Ellingworth and Hatton, *First Corinthians*, 177.

55. Obj: Belleville, *2 Corinthians*, 78; Seifrid, *2 Corinthians*, 80; Plummer, *Second Corinthians*, 64; Collins, *Second Corinthians*, 62; Omanson and Ellington, *Second Corinthians*, 46. Unsure: Harris, *Second Corinthians*, 237.

56. Obj: Belleville, *2 Corinthians*, 244; Barrett, *Second Corinthians*, 445. Plenary: Harris, *Second Corinthians*, 654.

57. Obj: Barrett, *Second Corinthians*, 445; Omanson and Ellington, *Second Corinthians*, 187.

58. Obj: de Boer, *Galatians*, 41; Soards and Pursiful, *Galatians*, 22; Matera, *Galatians*, 46; Fung, *Galatians*, 45–46; Arichea and Nida, *Galatians*, 13. Plenary: Longenecker, *Galatians*, 16; Dunn, *Galatians*, 43.

Philippians 1:27 "Only let your conduct be worthy of *the gospel of Christ.*" Obj: 2. Plenary: 1. Unsure: 1.[59]

1 Thessalonians 3:2 "We sent our brother Timothy, God's fellow worker in *the gospel of Christ.*" Obj: 4.[60]

2 Thessalonians 1:7–8 "The Lord Jesus will be revealed from heaven with his mighty angels in flaming fire, inflicting retribution to those who do not know God nor obey *the gospel of our Lord Jesus.*" Obj: 5. Plenary: 1.[61]

Other Authors Using Pronouncement Genitives

The three remaining New Testament texts are interpreted by their commentators as the objective genitive or are split:

Mark 1:1 "The beginning of *the gospel of Jesus Christ.*" Obj: 3. Plenary: 3.[62]

Hebrews 6:1 "Let us leave the basic *word of Christ* and go on to maturity." Subj: 2. Obj: 6.[63]

1 Peter 1:25 "The *word of the* Lord endures forever." Subj: 1. Obj: 2. Plenary: 1.[64]

To see this complicated analysis more simply, the following chart removes the "plenary" and "unsure" conclusions by commentators and focuses on the word count pertaining to John's and Paul's pronouncements.

---

59. <u>Obj</u>: Fee, *Philippians*, 162; Loh and Nida, *Philippians*, 38. <u>Plenary</u>: O'Brien, *Philippians*, 148. <u>Unsure</u>: Reumann, *Philippians*, 264.

60. <u>Obj</u>: Green, *1 and 2 Thessalonians*, 160; Wanamaker, *Thessalonians*, 128; Richard, *First and Second Thessalonians*, 141; Ellingworth and Nida, *Thessalonians*, 53.

61. <u>Obj</u>: Hiebert, *Thessalonian Epistles*, 290; Green, *1 and 2 Thessalonians*, 291; Fee, *First and Second Thessalonians*, 258; Shogren, *1 and 2 Thessalonians*, 251; Weima, *1–2 Thessalonians*, 473. <u>Plenary</u>: Beale, *1–2 Thessalonians*, 187.

62. <u>Obj</u>: Boring, *Mark*, 31; Decker, *Mark 1–8*, 2; Guelich, *Mark 1—8:26*, 9. <u>Plenary</u>: Moule, *New Testament Greek*, 36; Collins, *Mark*, 15–16; France, *Mark*, 53.

63. <u>Subj</u>: Bruce, *Hebrews*, 137; Attridge, *Hebrews*, 162. <u>Obj</u>: Hughes, *Hebrews*, 195; Lane, *Hebrews*, 131; Ellingworth, *Hebrews*, 311–12; Mitchell, *Hebrews*, 118; O'Brien, *Hebrews*, 211; Cockerill, *Hebrews*, 261.

64. Quoted from Isa 40:8 where the source is "God" but applied to Christ. <u>Subj</u>: Michaels, *1 Peter*, 79. <u>Obj</u>: Schreiner, *1, 2 Peter, Jude*, 96–97; Achtemeier, *1 Peter*, 141. <u>Plenary</u>: Forbes, *1 Peter*, 52.

COMMENTARY CONCLUSIONS: SUBJECTIVE VS. OBJECTIVE

	gospel		testimony		preaching		word		teaching[65]	
	Subj	Obj	Subj	Obj	Subj	Obj	Subj	Obj	Subj	Obj
Paul	0	47	0	20	0	16	21	35	5	2
John	—	—	18	13	—	—	—	—	6	10

John's uses of the two pronouncement terms' genitive phrases, testimony and teaching, are understood by commentators in a relatively split decision on which genitive is intended, subjective or objective. In other words, there is no consensus, indicating an expected uncertainty given the frequent ambiguity of the genitive in Greek. Nonetheless, this is still inconsistent with the New Testament's precedent for pronouncement genitives to always be subjective when referring to persons, including Jesus in the Gospels. The question remains why after the Gospels the precedent is broken at all. It appears that the reason is to be found in hermeneutical and theological presuppositions that essentially mute the Messiah's revelation found in the Gospels. This hypothesis becomes more clearly substantiated when Paul's pronouncement genitives are considered.

Looking at Paul's commentators when he uses "the word of Christ" or "the word of the Lord" construct, they flout precedence 60 percent of the time. In other words, they see Paul only writing about Christ, not referring to what Christ said. However, when Paul's pronouncements use εὐαγγέλιον, κήρυγμα, and μαρτύριον, his commentators go to the extreme where 100 percent of the time Paul is understood to be writing only about Christ, never allowing Paul to refer to Christ's own words as Paul's gospel, proclamation, and testimony. This is an inexplicable unanimity. This is a strong anti-subjective, anti-precedent sentiment, forming a very united theological subculture—a theological subculture presumably bound only by the from/about influence that has captured all segments of Christendom. Furthermore, no commentator addresses why these three specific

---

65. Paul's one instance of νουθεσία, a near synonym of διδαχή, is considered to be a subjective genitive more often than the objective. There seems to be some leeway given by commentators for Jesus' teaching/instruction to be referred to him by Paul as they do for the "word of Christ/Lord" construct. <u>Subj</u>: Larkin, *Ephesians*, 148; Best, *Ephesians*, 569–70; Thielman, *Ephesians*, 402; Arnold, *Ephesians*, 418; Hoehner, *Ephesians*, 798. <u>Obj</u>: Lincoln, *Ephesians*, 408; O'Brien, *Ephesians*, 447.

terms are so unique from "word" and "teaching." Clearly, an interpretive principle beyond syntax and context is at work, especially in Paul's case.

John and Paul are held by commentators as abnormal in these genitive constructions, and exceptionally so when interpreting Paul, and without any rationale for doing so. One might presume it is a subliminal thought, but more likely, it is the overpowering gravitational pull of the from/about theorem. For this reason, it is referred to here as the "theological genitive" where hermeneutico-theological reasons control the interpretation of the pronouncement genitive exceptionally as the objective genitive. Of course, a "theological genitive" is not found in the grammars since its biblical importance cannot be reduced to a syntactical matter. It is suggested here that these excesses rely on a couple suppositions that build this circular case: (1) the from/about transition and (2) an assumed centricity of the Passion and justification in Paul's message. In other words, generally speaking, even when commentators conclude their "gospel" is about Christ, they limit it to be *about his cross and resurrection.* This does not adequately explain the Messiah's mission and especially *his* message that he commissioned the apostles to evangelize.

INCONSISTENCIES

It would help interpret these seminal New Testament texts if there were explanations for the following logical inconsistencies in interpretation. The burden of proof is on those who interpret the pronouncement genitives as objective genitives, including explanations of how one comes to this conclusion apart from the pervasive application of the theological genitive's presuppositions.

Paul Commentaries

One sees within 1 and 2 Thessalonians the common divergence in interpreting the genitive as subjective or objective from one pronouncement term to another. When viewing "*word* of the Lord," with its allied phrase "*gospel of Christ,*" one sees commentaries shift the preference from the subjective in the former to the objective in the latter. Hiebert, Richard, Wanamaker, and Green regard the genitive in the agrapha in 1 Thess 4:15 as subjective—"by *the word from the Lord.*"[66]

---

66. The means of receiving this particular revelation is debated; however, an

> By the Lord's words we say that we who are still living when the Lord returns will not go before those who have already fallen asleep.

But they vacillate when concluding "gospel of Christ" to be objective in 1 Thess 3:2 and 2 Thess 1:8. There is just something about "gospel, preaching, testimony." No explanation is given for the divergence. If "the word from the Lord" is Christ's own word and considered subjective in a text, why not allow these phrases to refer as well to his own "gospel, preaching, testimony"?[67] The terms are not synonymous, but the unanimous logic that draws the line at "testimony, gospel, preaching" has never been defended. Witherington affirms that 1 Thess 4:15 contains the subjective genitive, "the word from the Lord," but decides in Rom 16:25 on the objective, "preaching about Jesus Christ." Marshall agrees that 1 Thess 4:15 and 1 Tim 6:3–4 should be understood as the subjective in "word of . . .", yet when it comes to 2 Tim 1:8, the genitive is objective: "the testimony about Christ." Knight and Quinn/Wacker accept the subjective in 1 Tim 6:3–4, but in 2 Tim 1:8 it is the objective "testimony about Christ." Morris uses all three of the pronouncement genitive options when approaching those involving Christ, subjective, objective, and plenary: subjective in 1 Thess 1:8 and 4:15 ("word from the Lord"); objective in 2 Thess 3:1 ("word about the Lord"), Rom 1:9 ("gospel about his Son"), and 16:25 ("preaching about Jesus Christ"); plenary in Rom 10:17 ("word from and about Christ").[68] When considering the genitive in 4:15, "word of the Lord," Hiebert, Richard, and Wanamaker apply its subjective meaning to the same phrase in 1 Thess 1:8, whereas Shogren and Weima shift inconsistently from the objective in 1:8 to the subjective in 4:15.

A more glaring inconsistency juxtaposes the gospel of Paul with the preaching of Jesus Christ: "Now to him who is able to strengthen you according to *my gospel* and the *preaching of Jesus Christ*" (Rom 16:25).

---

assumption by many is that it is quoted from Jesus' Incarnation.

67. Outside of these three protected pronouncement nouns (εὐαγγέλιον, μαρτύριον, κήρυγμα), commentators feel freer to opt for the subjective. For example, Eph 6:4: "Bring them up in the discipline and instruction [νουθεσίᾳ] of the Lord." The subjective, "instruction from the Lord," is preferred by commentators twice as many times as the objective. Split decisions also occur on Paul's phrase "word [λόγος or ῥῆμα] of Christ/Lord," where the commentators' decisions still favor the objective twice as many times as the subjective. Nine elect the plenary.

68. In Acts, Schnabel takes the same phrase in five texts, "word of the Lord," differently with no further comments: objective in 13:44, 49; 19:10; plenary in 15:35, 36. See footnotes above on these Acts texts.

Paul's gospel is of course *his*, consistent with the New Testament precedent for non-divines as subjective genitive, here and elsewhere.[69] He even has his own preaching (1 Cor 2:4). But in the same verse where the parallel genitive phrase is connected with Jesus Christ, sixteen decisions in commentaries unanimously disallow Jesus to be the source of his preaching. Paul's reference to "my gospel" does not imply a distinct gospel from Jesus' gospel, only distinct from his and the church's antagonists. G. Friedrich was the sole advocate for the subjective understanding in this verse, and he is careful to distinguish the incarnate Jesus from the risen Christ as a source for the κήρυγμα:

> Christ himself speaks in the gospel of Paul. Paul is not referring to his gospel added to the preaching of the risen Lord. He is emphasizing the agreement of his preaching with that of the earthly Jesus. Hence τὸ κήρυγμα Ἰησοῦ Χριστοῦ can only mean the message which Jesus Christ proclaimed.[70]

Friedrich is the lone voice that allows the Messiah to have a proclamation (κήρυγμα) of his own that Paul honors while preaching his own gospel, which of course was consistent with that of the Messiah.

John's Revelation Commentaries

Commentators show unexplained inconsistencies in their interpretations of the repetitive phrase "the testimony of Jesus" in Revelation. Kistemaker sees it as the subjective genitive in 1:2, but the same phrase in 19:10 as objective. Ladd sees 20:4 as objective when opting for the subjective in 1:2. Osborne accepts 1:2 as subjective but 1:9 and 12:17 as objective. Beale sees 1:2 as objective and 12:17 as plenary. Fanning offers the best attempt at an explanation for interpreting 1:2 and 1:9 as subjective and 12:17, 19:10 (bis), and 20:4 as objective.[71] Otherwise, commentaries are mostly satisfied to rest in the inconsistency.

Comparable to Paul's parallel phrasing in Rom 16:25, "my gospel and the preaching of Jesus Christ," John aligns the parallel genitive construction "the word of God and the testimony of Jesus" (Rev 1:2, 9; 12:17; 20:4) or "the commandments of God and the testimony of Jesus"

---

69. Including Paul's fellow workers: Rom 2:16; 2 Cor 4:3; 1 Thess 1:5; 2 Thess 2:14; 2 Tim 2:8.

70. Friedrich, "κῆρυξ, κηρύσσω, κτλ," 3:716.

71. Fanning, *Revelation*, 362.

(12:17). It is reasonable that the unanimous subjective interpretation by commentaries for "word/commandments of God" be distributed to the parallel genitive, "testimony of Jesus" as well. But each of these passages has advocates for the objective for "testimony of Jesus" regardless of their preference for the subjective genitive for "word/commandments of God."

Acts Commentaries

Two quotations of Jesus clearly use the subjective pronouncement genitive "word of the Lord" and they should be compared with other texts having the same phrase in the same book. Remembrances of Jesus' statements recorded by Luke in Acts should inform his use of the genitive phrase when explaining the spread of "the word of the Lord" elsewhere in Acts.

> I remembered the Lord's word when he said, "John baptized with water." (Acts 11:16)
>
> Remember the Lord Jesus' words: "It is more of a blessing to give than to receive." (Acts 20:35)

Though "the word(s) of the Lord" in these quotations from Jesus are undoubtedly subjective, those who comment on the same verbiage elsewhere in Acts consider them as objective or only plenary (Acts 8:25; 13:44, 49; 15:35, 36; 16:32; 19:10).

First Peter Commentaries

Isaiah is the source for the oft-quoted Hebrew subjective genitive referring to the eternal word *from* God, not the word *about* God: "The grass withers and the flowers fall, but the *word of our God* endures forever" (Isa 40:8 Septuagint). Rather than "the word of our God" in Isaiah, 1 Pet 1:24–25 substitutes the divine "Lord." However, though Isaiah means it as subjective, Paul Achtemeier and Thomas Schreiner change it to the objective. Consistent with the from/about theorem, the eternal word is not from God/the Lord but about the Lord Jesus.[72] One might ask if the word of God is truly eternal, why the meaning of the very verse that expresses that absolute truth might, like the grass, be changed by commentators.

---

72. Achtemeier, *1 Peter*, 141; Schreiner, *1, 2 Peter, Jude*, 96–97.

On the other hand, J. Ramsey Michaels defends the subjective interpretation on the basis of Jesus' own words on the very subject:

> The construction ῥῆμα κυρίου must be understood both in Isaiah and in 1 Peter as a subjective genitive: the word which the Lord spoke. When κυρίου is taken Christologically, the reference is to the message Jesus proclaimed, so that in Peter's context the statement becomes a parallel to Jesus' own pronouncement that "Heaven and earth will pass away, but my words will not pass away" (Mark 13:31 // Matt 24:35 // Luke 21:33). . . . Just as the λόγος was of importance there only because it was God's λόγος, so the ῥῆμα is of importance here only because it is Jesus' ῥῆμα.[73]

IMPLICATIONS

Advocates for the subjective genitive pertaining to Christ can be found in the commentaries. Then why this extended analysis of the pronouncement genitives? I suggest the analysis reveals a theological allegiance to a simplistic hermeneutical bias against allowing Jesus' gospel to compromise Paul's gospel.

- The surprising, unanimous position among Paul's commentators is that his messaging of his "gospel, preaching, or testimony" cannot refer to the message *from* Jesus. Even though Jesus had his own gospel, testimony, and preaching in the Gospels, he has been muted in the Epistles, at least by these objectifications of him. Jesus does not speak in their message and themes of Jesus' preaching. A consistent jargon, so to speak, a dialect of sorts, forms a culture that insolates Paul's message from an apparently competitive message of God in Jesus. Admittedly, this chapter has been a long journey from a single grammatical form to this overwhelming theological error.

- In the data on the Paul's use of other pronouncement terms, "word, teaching," the subjective genitive is allowed but only by a significant minority of commentators, and even then no theological implications are extrapolated. One would expect that when Jesus is allowed into the conversation and his teaching and words are what Paul is referring to, his messages might be given some recognition in the commentaries that opt for the subjective. Does not happen.

---

73. Michaels, *1 Peter*, 79.

- John's commentators are more lenient on allowing Jesus to speak in John's pronouncement genitives. They are evenly split between the subjective or objective in the cases of the only two pronouncement terms that are used in the genitive construction, teaching and testimony, though they are still working against the New Testament precedent of the subjective genitive when opting for the objective. They also do not explain the same theological implications of mainlining Jesus' messages into apostolic theology.

- Of those commentators explicitly interested in the choice of genitive in their interpretations, those who affirm a plenary meaning may have logical reason for their choice, in that "about Christ" would include what he preached, though apart from Forbes, no one says as much. This may amount to a modest and inaudible protest to the from/about theorem.

- The viability of the subjective genitive is affirmed ironically by those who were "unsure" in those texts where they consider the subjective as at least conceivable.

Again, two presuppositions merge to form a "theological genitive" that inverts the linguistic precedent of the pronouncement genitive: (1) a macro-hermeneutical principle where revelation morphs from accentuating the Gospels' pronounced truths *from* Jesus into the apostles' pronounced truths *about* him; (2) Christ's Passion and atonement is the central concern of the apostles' letters.[74]

When commentators explain more fully what their preference for the objective genitive means theologically, they highlight what it is *about* Christ that is most important to them. There is no part of the Messiah's commission found in these explanations apart from the Passion; it is as if a codified meaning of any objective pronouncement genitives is the soteriological gospel, testimony, preaching. All that can be said *about* Jesus, then, when reading the commentaries, is that he died, was buried, and was raised for our salvation. For many, to contextualize these saving events within a much broader understanding of history and by an eternal rather than a parenthetical design would be off-point from this central metanarrative of salvation history. However, the Testaments' teleological emphasis on the purpose of creation and its history exceeds

---

74. Tradition restricts "the Passion" to the crucifixion, yet Jesus' redemptive episode is incomplete without the resurrection, recommending a summative term for the holy three days; "the Passion" is considered the best option.

the instrumentality of salvation, which only puts one back to square one. The centrality of the Passion and justification can blind the believer from what the apostles' letters are truly after. They encourage daily righteousness that blesses, delivers, and disciplines oneself and others as well as using other God-like attributes that makes one human. The eternal design goes way past square one, outpacing salvation history and the parenthetical age into an eternity where God's sub-realms shepherd one another as he himself shepherds them.

The following are examples of a limited understanding of God's design for eternal history when pronouncement genitives are addressed specifically in Mark 1:1; Rom 1:9; 16:25; 1 Cor 9:12; 2 Cor 2:12; 1 Thess 3:2; 1 Pet 1:25.

Frank Matera on Rom 1:9:

> What Paul preaches can be summed up in [a] single word: *euangelion*. Paul proclaims the gospel; the good news of what God has accomplished in Christ's saving death and resurrection.[75]

Graeme Goldsworthy:

> The gospel is the word about Jesus Christ and what he did for us in order to restore us to a right relationship with God.[76]

Leon Morris on Rom 1:9:

> Here Paul speaks of it as "the gospel of his Son'" (cf. 15:19). It centers on Christ's atoning act.[77]

Robert Jewett on Rom 16:25:

> Most commentators find the objective [genitive] more plausible in this context, that is, the preaching *about* Jesus Christ, and with the formula "Jesus Christ" used as a double name, the implication is that the entire life of Jesus is in view. Paul's emphasis in contrast is on Christ crucified and resurrected.[78]

John Elliot on 1 Pet 1:25:

---

75. Matera, *Romans*, 38.
76. Goldsworthy, *According to Plan*, 73.
77. Morris, *Romans*, 58.
78. Jewett, *Romans*, 1006.

From [Peter's] perspective, the word that endures forever is the word about Jesus Christ, his suffering and glorification.[79]

Eugene M. Boring on Mark 1:1:

The "gospel of Jesus Christ" refers not to a book but to the good news of God's saving act in Jesus Christ, the message proclaimed by the church of Mark's day.[80]

Gordon Fee on 1 Cor 9:12:

Anything that would get in the way of someone hearing the gospel for what it is, the good news of God's redeeming grace, can be easily laid aside.[81]

Raymond F. Collins on 2 Cor 2:12:

Identifying "Christ" as the object of his preaching, Paul implies that the good news of the gospel centers on what God has done in the death and resurrection of his Christ.[82]

Earl Richard on 1 Thess 3:2:

If the term's [εὐαγγέλιον] background, origin, and meaning are debated, it is safe to say its NT, and particularly Pauline, meaning is that of "the preaching, message, or working out of God's salvation."[83]

These conclusions on pronouncement genitive texts marginalize Jesus' own pronouncements due to the belief that the Passion radically altered the trajectory of his revelation and that of both Testaments. This exemplifies the parenthetical paralysis of biblical theology.

OBJECTIVE GENITIVE'S MICRO DOMINANCE

The overwhelming New Testament statistical precedent for pronouncement genitives to be understood as the subjective genitive would be sustained if it were not for this "theological genitive." Without this

---

79. Elliot, *1 Peter*, 391.
80. Boring, *Mark*, 49.
81. Fee, *First Corinthians*, 454.
82. Collins, *Second Corinthians*, 62.
83. Richard, *First and Second Thessalonians*, 141. Also Seifrid, *2 Corinthians*, 365; Silva, *NIDNTTE* 3:163; 3:241.

theological overlay the subjective understanding would prevail since there is no syntactical or contextual supporting evidence for interpreting it as the objective genitive in these cases of discourse in the New Testament.

However, the dominance of the objective genitive in these summative pronouncements is now obvious by the accounting of hundreds of conclusions by scores of commentators. This is the objective genitive's *macro* dominance. Yet a *micro* dominance cannot be underestimated in its impact, not only on the texts where they are found but on any discussion of the apostolic and New Testament messages. Again, these pronouncement genitive phrases are not incidental fragments of theological discourse; they are no less than the seminal summaries of the New Testament mission and how it was disseminated.

Returning now to the tautological nature of the from/about mantra, a micro dominance of the objective genitive over the subjective also lies bare in the commentaries' silence on the implicit subjective genitive implications, even when the objective is preferred. That is to say, one might say it does not matter whether these genitives are subjective or objective since even if it was always interpreted as *about* Christ, then all of Jesus' pronouncements, his kingdom gospel, commandments, prophetic revelations and predictions, parables, predictions on his death, etc., would be included. In other words, in essence, a plenary interpretation. This is true theoretically; however, it is by no means the practice. The few excerpts from those commenting on what is important enough "about" Jesus show the momentum toward the Passion.

Occasionally one may find a short reference to the content of Jesus' message as to what would be entailed in pronouncing something about Jesus. Matera and Guthrie represent this but in respect to Jesus' kingdom message alone.

> In proclaiming a message about Jesus, the church relates Jesus own message about the kingdom since the church's proclamation *about* Jesus includes the preaching *of* Jesus.... To proclaim the gospel is to tell the story of Jesus, a story that includes the gospel of the kingdom that Jesus proclaimed.[84]

It is indeed odd and unfortunate that Matera's simple deduction is not applied by him or other commentators pervasively when they explain the implications of the apostolic pronouncement genitives without reference

---

84. Matera, *New Testament Theology*, 8–9.

to what Jesus himself proclaimed. In fact, Matera sounds quite different here than when quoted above: "Paul proclaims the gospel; the good news of what God has accomplished in Christ's saving death and resurrection." Apparently, the difference is that though Jesus had his kingdom gospel, Paul has his Passion gospel. Guthrie also emphasizes the kingdom message of Jesus that is implied within pronouncements about him: "Preaching about Jesus was preaching about the kingdom, because Jesus himself was proclaimed as king."[85] If one were to add to these statements those made by commentators connecting Paul's proclamation of the kingdom of God with that of Jesus (chapter 9), one cannot say there is no awareness that when one speaks about Jesus, they are including his messages. I write "messages" as a plural since Jesus spoke of much more than just the kingdom of God. One should not approach Jesus' teaching with such reductionism.

A fuller explanation of the implications of Jesus' own good news, testimony, words, teaching, or preaching pronouncements for the Epistles might be even more expected by those concluding that a plenary meaning of the genitive Jesus' own words are included in the meaning of the pronouncement in a more intentional way than simply inferred in the word "about." But no more is provided in this regard than when the objective genitive is preferred solely. James Dunn, on Col 3:16, in respect to his preference for the plenary, takes a lone but balancing position by noting the obvious: "Indeed, it would be surprising if the cross and resurrection provided the only subject of early Christian meditation, when there was (evidently) a fair amount of Jesus tradition which must have been known by the earliest Christian churches."[86] Yet, even more disappointing is when those advocating a subjective interpretation to the genitive construct do no more than those who opt for the objective or plenary in explaining the implications of what Jesus' teachings and preaching would be.

All to say, regardless of any interpreter who concludes whether the genitive is the objective, plenary, or even subjective, no emphasis is laid on the implication of Jesus' verbal ministry on the apostles' written pronouncements. What these texts say or imply that Christ himself pronounced is not provided by any interpreter, except on the rare occasion that he is quoted explicitly. Apparently then, the from/about theorem

---

85. Guthrie, *New Testament Theology*, 431.
86. Dunn, *Colossians and Philemon*, 236.

has been proven and the centricity of Jesus' messages have been replaced by the Passion as the new center. Whereas, in the objective and plenary suggestions, the gospel that Jesus proclaimed is only implicit at best and perhaps was not even meant by the author, the subjective "from Jesus" means explicitly that Jesus pronounced something by his testimony, gospel, preaching, and teaching—his words. What the Messiah said cannot be replaced by what he did, on the cross or otherwise. To be clear, of course the Epistles do speak of the kingdom of God explicitly and implicitly. It is just that when a summary statement of the apostles' pronouncements is given, the implications of Jesus' message are not voiced by those commenting on the import of the apostolic pronouncements. Like Luke's review of Paul's pronouncements that are summarized as the "kingdom of God," a preoccupation with what Jesus *did* in the Passion is accentuated at the expense of what Jesus proclaimed and what he demanded his followers to continue proclaiming—his universal kingdom's sanctifying commandments, in addition to the many other subjects he addressed.

In Eph 2:17, Paul does not employ the genitive, yet alternate interpretations given to its plain text reveal the extent to which one renders Jesus inaudible: "[Jesus] came and brought the good news [εὐαγγελίζω] of peace to you who were far away, and peace to those who were near." Klyne Snodgrass's interpretation presents the same reasoning invented by the theological genitive: "Christ's preaching of 'peace to you who were far away and peace to those who were near' (17) refers to *the preaching done by the apostles* and missionaries to Gentiles and Jews respectively, *not literal preaching by Jesus.*"[87] This appears to be a direct application of the from/about theorem. However, Jesus himself encouraged followers with his good news of peace: "These things I have spoken to you so that in Me you may have peace" (John 16:33; also Luke 7:50; 8:48; 10:5; 24:36), and he prayed for unity among them and with God (John 17:20–23). After all, as Peter reminds us, "You know God's message sent to the people of Israel, proclaiming peace by Jesus Christ—he is Lord of all" (Acts 10:36). The apostles proclaimed peace and developed a full theology of reconciliation, but that did not preclude them from referring to Jesus' own proclamations on the subject.

---

87. Snodgrass, *Ephesians*, 131 (italics are mine). Also Hoehner, *Ephesians*, 385; Caird, *Paul's Letters from Prison*, 60; O'Brien, *Ephesians*, 207; Stoeckhardt, *Ephesians*, 150; Schnackenburg, *Ephesians*, 118; Arnold, *Ephesians*, 166. Others poetically consider the cross event to be a "proclamation," e.g., Lincoln, *Ephesians*, 148–49; Patzia, *Ephesians, Colossians, Philippians*, 197.

The objective genitive is not off the table in cases of the pronouncement genitives if the context was to support that meaning.[88] Yet, if one insisted on the predominance of the objective and believed that the phrasing "about" Jesus included his seminal pronouncements, then the specific content and implications of Jesus' important New Testament pronouncements certainly should be addressed. Otherwise, consistency with the New Testament pronouncement genitives used elsewhere would recommend that when "Christ" or "the Lord" are involved, the subjective be the default. While everyone else is considered the source of their own pronouncements in the genitive in the New Testament, in most cases Christ is only an object whose verbal ministry is useful when filtered and edited by the apostles. John's commentators are influenced less by the theological genitive but appear unable to avoid it half the time. So, the burden of proof lies with those who prefer the objective genitive to justify their preference by the immediate textual context, unless, again, one resorts to special pleading by a hermeneutical and theological overlay.

PRONOUNCEMENT GENITIVES PER PRECEDENT

The following Pauline examples render all pronouncement genitives as subjective. These subjective genitive translations are just as intelligible and defensible as the objective translations; their feasibility contrasts with the eloquent hesitancy to cross the red line into a subjective meaning and rather welcomes the Messiah to speak directly by the apostles' pronouncements. Given the ambiguity of the genitive and any obvious contextual evidence to the contrary that one might muster, there might be a few of the following one might consider ineligible for a subjective interpretation. Yet, there are enough examples from Paul's letters below that remain, thus successfully challenging the "theological genitive." The subjective translation may feel strange in some texts, not because they are

---

88. The objective genitive is paralleled by other New Testament Greek phrasing. E.g., by κατά: οὐχ ὅτι καθ' ὑστέρησιν λέγω, ἐγὼ γὰρ ἔμαθον ἐν οἷς εἰμι αὐτάρκης εἶναι ("Not that I speak *about* need") (Phil 4:11). Phrases begun by περί with the genitive noun approximate objective genitives: κηρύσσων τὴν βασιλείαν τοῦ θεοῦ καὶ διδάσκων τὰ περὶ τοῦ κυρίου Ἰησοῦ Χριστοῦ ("[Paul was] proclaiming the kingdom of God and teaching things about the Lord Jesus Christ") (Acts 28:31). Prepositions ἐν and ὑπὲρ are also options for objectifying the following noun (Rom 9:27; 2 Thess 1:4). Where there is simply a verb and the accusative of a proper name, the meaning is objective: εὐθέως ἐν ταῖς συναγωγαῖς ἐκήρυσσεν τὸν Ἰησοῦν ("Immediately he began to proclaim [about] Jesus in the synagogues") (Acts 9:20; also 8:5, 35; 11:20).

inconceivable, but due to a presuppositional inertia they might require some rethinking.

"Gospel from Christ/Lord/Son" (εὐαγγέλιον)

> God is my witness, whom I serve with my spirit in the preaching of the *gospel from His Son*. (Rom 1:9–10)

> From Jerusalem and all around as far as Illyricum I have fully preached the *gospel from Christ*. (Rom 15:19)

> We endure anything so that we will not hinder the *gospel from Christ*. (1 Cor 9:12)

> I came to Troas for the *gospel from Christ*. (2 Cor 2:12–13)

> They will glorify God for your obedience to your confession of the *gospel from Christ*. (2 Cor 9:13)

> We were the first ones to come even as far as you with the *gospel from Christ*. (2 Cor 10:14)

> Some are disturbing you and want to distort the *gospel from Christ*. (Gal 1:7)

> Conduct yourselves in a manner worthy of the *gospel from Christ*. (Phil 1:27)

> We sent Timothy, our brother and God's fellow worker with the *gospel from Christ*. (1 Thess 3:2)

> Those who do not obey the gospel *from our Lord Jesus* . . . (2 Thess 1:7–8)

"Testimony from Christ/Lord" (μαρτύριον)

> Just as the *testimony from Christ* was confirmed in you. (1 Cor 1:5–6)

> Do not be ashamed of the *testimony from our Lord* or from me, his prisoner. (2 Tim 1:8)

"Proclamation from Jesus" Christ (κήρυγμα)

> Now to Him who is able to establish you according to my gospel and the *preaching from Jesus Christ* . . . (Rom 16:25-26)

These subjective genitive translations recommend themselves as critical summative statements of Christ's own pronouncements. This does not suggest a substitute New Testament theological framework, only a much larger one that encompasses these genitives and their underpinnings. Certainly, the apostles and others had new revelation and new collaborating historical accounts and probably had recovered verifiable and credible agrapha about Christ. There was no absence of material *about* Jesus, so the Epistles were not constrained by the subjective genitive precedent and its frequent reference to Jesus' own pronouncements as explicit parts of the letters' theology; the Epistles would only be better informed by this wider context. The apostles' pronouncements on the soteriological implications of the Passion are not lacking by any means, but the New Testament is the poorer when interpretations of the letters do not consider Jesus' good news, testimony, words, teaching, or preaching. The Passion, justification, and reconciliation would not be discounted if one opted for the subjective genitive more often in the Epistles. After all, Jesus' pronouncements spoke explicitly about his Passion within the last year of his ministry and in more cautious language before that. It was a part of his pronouncement repertoire.[89] Furthermore, he surely would have had something to say about his Passion, Isa 53, and the rest of the messianic passages and their implications when he taught hundreds, probably thousands of people from the Old Testament during the forty days between his public resurrection and ascension. In other words, his apostles did not need new, post-ascension revelation to begin proclaiming forgiveness and reconciliation through the Passion; they were already adequately equipped verbally by Jesus to begin the Great Commission.

Admittedly, if allowed into the apostolic messaging, the sheer weight and diversity of the Messiah's pronouncements might overwhelm the content of the otherwise less disturbed Acts and the Epistles. To open the door to Jesus' pronouncements would flood the apostles' teachings. Yet, linguistically, this impact is justifiable, in fact obligatory.

---

89. E.g., Matt 16:21-23 // Mark 8:31-32 // Luke 9:21-22; Matt 17:22-23 // Mark 9:30-32 // Luke 9:43-45; Matt 20:17-19 // Mark 10:32-35 // Luke 18:31-34; Matt 26:32; Matt 26:61 // Mark 14:58; 17:63; Mark 8:31, 34; 11:27-33; 12:1-12; Luke 13:32-33; John 2:19; 3:14; 12:7-8, 32-34; 13:17, 33; 14:25, 29.

Luke makes sure in Acts that Jesus' kingdom gospel, thought by some today to be another gospel than Paul's, was included in his summaries of Paul's pronouncements during his last fifteen years, at least. Through whichever lens this huge New Testament kingdom construct is viewed, Paul's travel and ministry companion accentuated it as a critical talking point in Paul's discussions, preaching, testifying, debating, and teaching while he was also declaring it explicitly in his letters.[90] The theological genitive emphasizes the Passion and mutes the Messiah's kingdom message. It insists on a monocular view of Paul where both Testaments center on an episode in history rather than its eternal teleological design. History contains the trajectory of creation's perpetual sanctification, which relies on justification at a precise time within creation's history on the cross and within each believer's life. Jesus' ethical teaching as a priest and prophet constitutes much of the Gospels' content. Of course, this emphasis on the sanctified life is also a focus for Paul. The harmony of these two preachers of peace and mentors of morality is something that the subjective genitive clearly expresses. Surely, the early church talked *about* Jesus as Savior but not by subordinating *hearing from him* as the teaching priest, as well as King, judge, and prophet—the Messiah's other equally important commission roles.

The pronouncement genitives should be interpreted and translated primarily as the subjective. They are not forced in that direction; rather, it appears the objective has been forced against precedent by an unsustainable preference that objectifies Christ. The contextual and syntactical neutrality of these genitives do not support a theorem that the New Testament message *from* Jesus in the Gospels morphs into the apostles' message *about* him. That presupposition amounts to circular reasoning if, by these purported objective genitives, the incarnate Jesus' own words are not admitted into the theological equation.

---

90. Acts 19:8; 20:25–28; 28:23, 31; Rom 14:17; 1 Cor 4:20; 6:9–10; 15:24, 50; Eph 5:5; Col 1:13; 4:11; 2 Tim 4:1, 18.

15

Harmonic Messianic Message

EARLIER IN CHAPTER 7, the conflation of the Israelite civil administration leadership roles was suggested as God's pattern for the Messiah's commission. This is not an invitation to the imposition of typology.[1] Instead, it acknowledges the pervasive and innate societal functions found within God's common grace to every civilization where, by various designations, there are executive leaders/kings, religious or ideological leaders/priests, moral sages/prophets, regional or familial sub-leaders, legal adjudicators/judges. The Messiah was not only human in ontology; as a human he also personified functionally all human leadership roles.

Nevertheless, monocular and binocular biblical theologies prevail. Some emphasize the ironic priest in salvation; others emphasize the king and his kingdom, yet both of course would say they acknowledge the other. But, whether it is the Passion or the kingdom, either one or even both together miss the wholeness of the messianic commission. Such reductionist limiting of the Messiah's significance marginalizes his priestly teaching, prophetic assessments, adversity deliverances, intercession, and military might. For this reason the New Testament far less frequently refers to Christ as the King (though he surely is that in the most absolute

---

1. To speak of Christ as prophet, priest, judge, King, and the other messianic roles he plays is not to say that the Old Testament civil leadership roles are in themselves "messianic" just because they occur in Israel. They occur in every culture. If one said that any of these and other components of civil leadership in most cultures point to Christ, I would nearly agree since he fills these roles quintessentially.

sense) than it does more broadly to his *messiahship*, repeated so much more often: the Christ/Messiah, Jesus Messiah, Messiah Jesus, Lord Jesus Messiah, Jesus Messiah our Lord. The designation "Christ" might be seen as merely a last name by a believer or the world, but it was never intended to be so reduced in Scripture.

These messianic roles were not simply combined as separate compartments but have overlapping functions held in common with the other leadership roles. In other words, the Messiah's commission was more than multifaceted. The Messianic roles blended their overlaps to form a harmonious whole, which in a perfect being could not conflict. These roles may have conflicted in Israel's society since the official positions were held by fallen and physically separate individuals, but they were perfectly integrated in the ministry of only one Person. The following chart presumes to dissect this un-dissectible nature of the Messiah's commission.

MESSIANIC KINGDOM COMMISSION			
King	Priest	Prophet	Judge
Kingdom's Shepherd	Cultus Leader	Revelator	Judges by the Law
Warrior Savior	Ironic Priest	Moral Teacher	Delivers/Disciplines
Judges by the Law	Moral Teacher	Miracle Deliverer	Warrior Savior
Intercessor	Judges by the Laws	Intercessor	
	Intercessor		

The roles as prophet and judge were not literally "anointed" positions, but their significance cannot be diminished. The royal and priestly roles are those emphasized most frequently, yet even these roles are usually truncated so the focus is usually singular within each. A complete description of the Messiah's commission challenges the minimalist New Testament message, which neglects the totality of what it means for "Jesus to be the Christ." A fuller description acknowledges the Testaments' fundamental interest to lead the nation and its citizens in realizing their obligations in reflecting the moral and amoral attributes of God that equip them for shepherding his creation—in other words, realizing the importance of their sanctification.

The following commentary on the inferences from these civil roles of the Messiah continues from the introduction of the messianic commission in chapter 7 by distilling those roles and demonstrating the value of recognizing a more thorough harmonization of Christ's functions among themselves. The roles will be shown to be (1) sourced in the Godhead, (2) imaged in Israel's polity, (3) fulfilled in the Messiah, and (4) continued in the church and in believers' lives as "imitators of the Godhead" (Eph 5:1).

ROLES AS THE PRIEST

God: God's moral expectations for humanity were exemplified and explained in the law and wisdom from God. He provided the Israelite priesthood for teaching the morality of the law and provided a substitutionary method to compensate for both their inherent and intentional imperfection. God composed a cultus that formed a more intimate and accountable relationship that was beyond mere belief and required an active, bodily commitment to God's sovereignty. His cultus included worship by pilgrimage, recitation, song, feast, and dance, and these were examples of how the love and trust in the Lord from the believer was expressed physically, minimally by verbal assent, but more substantively by adding the hands and feet and even further by its dramatization in the theater of temple sacrifice. Laws that reflected his own unchangeable morality will always be continued, though the ceremonial portions of the law could change by his discretion and timing (Lev 19:23–25) and awaited their expiration date.

Israel's Priests: The pre-Passion priests were the cultus administrators, but they also served harmonically as the teachers of the law, as intercessors, and as judges. Teaching and explanation of God's law required the priests so it would not be broken in the first place and was just as necessary as the management of the complicated sacrifice system that was intended to bring forgiveness for breaking that law. The priests taught what God was expecting morally from the Israelites as representatives within their communities and to the world around them. This was to globally reflect God's own perfectly righteous nature. The priests were also the official community intercessors before the Lord and served as his judges along with community elders.

Messiah: The One's tandem positions as king and priest was anticipated by two explicit texts (Ps 110:1–4; Zech 6:12–13). Yet both functions suffer reductionist explanations that determine whole, even separate, theologies around their limited fields. The Messiah delivers from the darkness and oppression of sin by his death as the ironic priest who becomes the sacrificed Lamb himself. The Messiah, as the incarnate priest and king, personified the balance of power between the two roles. Apart from Jesus' dramatic temple cleansing, any personal affirmation of the Old Testament cultus is virtually absent. Instead, he continues its Old Testament contextualization within the more significant sanctified routine of a life of shepherding by jettisoning what were only Judaism's traditions as well as subordinating the ceremonial law to any conflicting moral obligations (Ps 51:16–17; Hos 6:6; Mic 6:7–8; Matt 23:23; Mark 7:5–13 // Matt 15:1–9). Nonetheless, by his work at the discretion and timing of God, the ironic priest laid himself on the cross for the believer's justification. He thereby abrogated the sacerdotal system and radically changed the highly formal cultus to a lower, better, populist system of ceremony that would only be aggrandized again by unnecessary and inventive human traditions ever since (Acts 15:10, 28–29; Col 2:16–17; Heb 7:12; 10:14).

Much is often made of the Gospels' literary proportions of the Passion narratives compared to the rest of their contents. For some, this supports the supremacy of the Passion as "the gospel." However, whatever proportion one might ascribe to a Gospel's account of the Passion compared to its non-Passion accounts leaves the remaining majority of each Gospel to deal with the miraculous manifestations of the universal kingdom of God by many adversity deliverances as well as the ethical teachings and legal interpretations from this royal priest and prophet. Ironically, this argument in the end proves too much and inadvertently confirms that the majority of each Gospel deals with the more holistic and harmonized commission of the Messiah that is being surveyed, which includes the Passion. Furthermore, if, in this case, arithmetic were such a beneficial hermeneutical tool, then the writers of the Gospels with the lowest proportion of Passion content must have thought it somewhat less important than the other Gospel writers did. Besides, the Passion is told as the prolonged assassination of the universal King, especially in John. It is within this literary context where one sees that the Passion is explicitly as much about humanity's disrespect for the universal King as it is about that priest's substitutionary atonement.

Guthrie provides an example of this mathematical reasoning when describing Mark's "whole gospel":

> Indeed, from a biographical point of view, Mark's gospel is remarkably lopsided. It is as if the rest of the gospel is preparatory to the climax of the passion. It must be supposed for him the whole gospel is a gospel of salvation, expressed more in historic

act than in teaching. The other synoptic gospels, although devoting less space proportionately to the passion, nevertheless show it unmistakably to be the climax towards which the preceding narrative inevitably moves.[2]

A distinction between Jesus' "historic act" and Jesus' acts of teaching is not possible. Even the Passion narratives contain much teaching to the disciples, religious leaders, Pilate, and others, and the remaining non-soteriological narratives are composed of biographical, historical recounting of his messianic works and words. A Gospel's "climax" is not a rhetorical device intended to emphasize a definition of "the gospel." It was a historical and literary climax since it could not have happened sooner in the narrative of Jesus' life, so of course it happens near the end of his teaching to his disciples and his crowds of followers, which extends more than a month after his Passion. In this sense the post-resurrection narratives are more of a climax than the crucifixion since they bring the end to Jesus' full earthly messianic commission, which included his teaching, prophecy, intercessions, death, and resurrection. Nearly seventy times Jesus' literal teaching role (διδάσκω, διδαχή) is referred to including within the synagogues. Scores more times he is recognized as a teacher (διδάσκαλος).

Jesus did more than decree new laws as a king, but like the Old Testament priests he interpreted the existing law as well as his own commands (Matt 5:20–48). He also publicly interpreted the law by his prophetic judgments on the current morality of the people and their leaders. Though he does not act as an elder in the city gates or temple complex as judges did in the Old Testament, still, as the priest and judge he made ethical and condemning judgments, deferring his legal role along with his Father as the final judge in the eschaton. Since the writing prophets were not official court prophets, the role as intercessor rested formally with the priests, and as noted above, Jesus was, and is, that (John 17).

Believers: They continue as as the "kingdom of priests" in the installation of the populist priesthood of the trusting kingdom, which now plays the role that national Israel was supposed to play (Exod 19:6; Rev 1:6). The trusting kingdom has continued through history as "priests," as intercessors, teachers, judges, and servants of God among the church and the terrestrial kingdoms within which they live and have their influence.

---

2. Guthrie, *New Testament Theology*, 436–37.

ROLES AS THE KING

God: The King is the highest shepherding ruler of creation. His royal guidance of humanity toward loving and orderly conduct is among the many ways he blesses creation. He does so in blessing humanity with his commandments to insure health, justice, peace, prosperity—in other words, total fulfilment not only of the individual but of the community that its citizens are responsible for. God's gracious salvation comes to his believers from every sort of adversity and sin; he is the savior warrior to the very end, in battle (Exod 15:3; Rev 18:11) and in sin salvation (Acts 5:31; Jude 1:25). He disciplines and judges humanity to maintain order in the terrestrial kingdom and to further sanctify the believer by the Spirit for godly conduct. This includes instruction in purity, nutrition, harmonious behavior, and economic stability.

Israel's kings: They were to serve under the law and thus were accountable to the priests' teaching of it and prophetic conviction by it, thus maintaining a balance of civil power. Yet a righteous king's own commands were legitimate as well unless they contradicted God's law or wisdom. The monarch delivered the people from adversity, apostasy, and invasions and delivered the innocent by court judgments. The king also interceded between the national kingdom and God, as did the priests. Though not a royal responsibility, in the case of David, Solomon, and Hezekiah, a king could also be a source of revelation, at least in their poetry or wisdom.

Messiah: The Second Person of the Godhead came to perfectly fulfill that divine law and wisdom. Yet, the Good Shepherd King also taught his own commandments for righteous living without contradicting the law. As king he still delivers from every sort of adversity: healing health traumas, rescuing from natural disasters, crushing the satanic kingdom, including the satanic and terrestrial kingdoms' armies at Armageddon. He intercedes for the trusting kingdom (John 17; Rom 8:34; Heb 7:25; 1 John 2:1). The Messiah corrects and disciplines by the principles of the law and his own laws to sanctify those who trust him and the Spirit. Christ currently rules this world, graciously restricting the extent of humanity's wallowing in moral and political madness. He rules during this parenthetical world as any leader at any level does, with his wise balance of any realm's good and evil.

Believers: Members of the trusting kingdom are expected to rule as the Creator and Messiah do and as Israelite kings were to. They are expected to bless creation as part of their primary commission since by the Spirit they are sanctified wholly to be obedient to the commandments of the Trinity and the Incarnate. Having been delivered from sin and as renewed creatures themselves, believers are expected to aid in delivering others from creation's natural adversity and from the personal and cultural debilitations of sin, in their role as testifiers and intercessors, and by their domestic and international evangelistic and relief efforts. Finally, though it is a task that must be done in obedience to God and with great humility, the believer disciplines others and their believing community and wider unbelieving culture by the authority of the commandments and wisdom from God and his Messiah.

ROLES AS THE PROPHET

God: Prophets speak God's mind by the Spirit to the trusting and terrestrial kingdoms about the past, present, and future. The very existence of such a social figure in Israel speaks to the communicative attribute of God, which was demonstrated by him as the initiator and maintainer of the most significant discourse within the Trinity and with humanity. His revelation speaks to the proximity and depth of his shepherding nature rather than his amusement or disinterest from his remote abode while watching humanity try somehow to figure it all out themselves. His words respond to the dependence of human wisdom and success on his wisdom for coping in his cursed world by avoiding, even defeating, the stealth of the intimidating satanic kingdom and the false prophets sown among the wheat of his trusting kingdom.

Prophets: Old Testament prophets were not only one-way conduits of divine information. Of course they revealed encouraging or ominous moral evaluations and predictions about the future, but more importantly and germane to their audience, they were guardians of the law along with the priests and sages. Whereas the priests taught and interpreted the law literally, the prophets were God's channel for his evaluation of the nation's and individuals' moral compliance with those laws. Whereas the priests were responsible for establishing the law, the prophets were responsible for assessing the people's reception and application of it and by the Spirit convicting them of their moral deficiencies. They were the nation and its citizens' "sanctometers." The status of being separate from a fallen world as God is separate was an objective of prophetic prediction when forthtelling the implications of disobedience.

Unlike the priests and kings, the prophets, particularly Moses, Elijah, and Elisha, were also conduits of God's miracles, delivering individuals from the adversities of illness, disease, hunger, anxiety, death, and natural disaster. Prophets were intercessors for Israel as a national sinner (Isa 64:9; Dan 9:4–6; Amos 7:2–3).

Messiah: Jesus was considered a prophet by others and was extolled as such by his fellow travelers to Emmaus: "Jesus of Nazareth, a man who was a mighty prophet in deed and word before God and all the people" (Luke 24:19). He was mighty in his miracles and mighty in his words of authoritative teaching, just as the greatest of the Old Testament prophets. This was his reputation before the Passion, and it continued into the early church. It is unnecessary to enumerate Jesus' ethical teachings and humanity's moral obligations to God and each other to see their preponderance in his prophetic proclamations.

Believers: Believers were expected to share God's mind as well among each other and the world, especially those gifted as evangelists, shepherd/pastors, and prophets/prophetesses.

ROLES AS THE JUDGE

God: God's righteousness includes a balance of his justice and mercy as derivatives of his unbounded love. He applies this love with his equally abundant wisdom that is most frequently and graciously imperceptible to those who could not anticipate or comprehend it or by those presumptuous enough not to agree with it.

Judges: The Old Testament judge blessed, delivered, and disciplined while simultaneously vindicating the innocent and convicting the guilty. This was done often with the priests present and active as the interpreters of the law and who added to the final judgment of the court. This function rewarded righteous living and penalized the opposite. Some judges also served as military leaders whose victories are extolled.

Messiah: Jesus frequently conveyed his judgments on his various audiences but held to his commission restriction to not judge the world but to first deliver it (John 3:17). Eventually, his and the Father's glorious or threatening event of judgment will finally arrive for the innocent and culpable, respectively.

He announces the sanctified as forgiven souls at the final judgment while the others are announced as those condemned to perish. And as the Messiah with universal authority, he judges the nations even now, determining their territorial and moral boundaries and maintaining the current global equilibrium.

Believers: As has been said already, the trusting kingdom's believers are required to make moral judgments, even formal exclusions, from its congregations to maintain the benefits of the Spirit's sanctification of the whole. However, God's grace is exemplified in his balance of grace and justice, not void of reason or restraint but full of love and remedial intention. Believers are to show the same wisdom and restraint in conversations among themselves.

To summarize these roles, the Messiah's commission as the personified consolidation of all human civil leadership roles coalesces around the eternal design's objective, the sanctified shepherding of creation. The King is the ruler, yes, but within that role is the judgment and enforcement of righteous legal behavior that ensures the stability and prosperity of the sanctified community so that it reflects the attributes of the perfectly sanctified communal Trinity. Yes, the priest mediates forgiveness and the Messiah becomes the sacrifice himself. But the purpose for this priestly, loving act of Jesus was to pave the way to the believer's further sanctification defined by his teaching and interpretation of the law. And he is also the current and eventual judge of that righteous behavior. Jesus' role as a prophet conveyed his Father's assessment of righteous behavior and explicitly upheld the law's teaching on many moral issues, as documented in the next chapter. Finally, in his words as a judge he was the guardian of righteous behavior by affirming moral innocence and denouncing the immoral. At the judgment he will exonerate the forgiven and sanctified souls and condemn the guilty who foolishly thought their moral deficiencies did not rise to a convictable case.

The implications of the multi-valanced messianic commission reveal how it harmonizes the Old Testament civil authorities' commission to reveal, teach, interpret, encourage, assess, and enforce God's commandments while interceding for the Israelites in their moral irresponsibility. This paradigm provides a fundamental continuity in God's kingdom management in the Testaments. The civil leadership structure within Israel, which the Messiah personified and applied, better serves the Testaments' trusting kingdom as the venue for the daily shepherding responsibilities within the chosen communities of Israel and the church.

The Old Testament community was constantly reminded by their civil leaders of the importance of the citizens' moral responsibilities to themselves, their neighbor, and their God. The moral emphases in the Testaments grounded believers in the immediate milieu of daily life, not in the by and by but in the day to day. And they give meaning to the routine life within the challenging complexities of the kingdom intersections and clashes as surveyed in chapter 10.

ACENTRICITY OF THE IRONIC PRIEST

I revert for the moment to comments in chapter 7 on whether the designation "Christ" eventually becomes merely a name in the New Testament or retains its purpose as a title throughout. An untenable conclusion about the significance of the designation would be "in virtually every place where 'Christ' occurs in Paul, another name—'Jesus,' 'the Lord'—could have been substituted without any obvious loss of meaning."[3] Earlier, I suggested that to reduce "Christ" to only a name was unreasonable given that the pronouncement "Jesus was the Christ" was a central thesis for the apostles, particularly noted by Luke during Paul's journeys while writing his letters. It is an unnecessary inconsistency to assume he was using it as a name in his letters at the same time using it as a title in his public discourse. That the designation "Christ" is pervasively a title for Jesus is even more strongly recommended now by the centricity of the New Testament message as the Messiah's holistic commission. When it is said that "Jesus is the Messiah," it implies all of his functions, not a subset of them. Furthermore, where "Christ" is compounded with "Jesus," i.e., "Jesus Christ," "Christ Jesus," and "Lord Jesus Christ," the reference to his messiahship as "Christ" is the larger contextual term for the more specific name of "Jesus" and its saving denotation. His sin-saving role was part of what it meant for Jesus to be the prophesied priest, which was part of what it meant for him to be the Messiah. In other words, that Jesus was the Christ/Messiah envelops his priesthood and one of his priestly roles, that of the ironic priest of self-sacrifice. Gerhard Friedrich catches this meaning of the Messiah's name: "If we were to sum up the content of the Gospel in a single word, it would be Jesus the Christ."[4]

---

3. Moo, *Theology of Paul*, 565–66.
4. Friedrich, "εὐαγγελίζομαι, εὐαγγέλιον, κτλ," 2:731.

To demote Christ's title to merely a name contributes to the common practice of constraining what "the gospel" must mean because of an alleged centricity of the Passion. The New Testament message is the totality of the messianic commission, not any portion of it. Rather than seeing the instrumentality of the Passion as its role in the complete messianic commission, it most often becomes the center around which everything else revolves. Caird represents this typical hermeneutic that is committed to finding a geometric center of the New Testament; in his case, in a decisive and momentary historical event. The "focal point" is not a person or a "theme," for example, but a dated episode:

> The focal point of the New Testament is an event which occurred on an April Friday sometime around AD 30. But no event is significant until it has been placed within a framework of interpretation, and on this there will undoubtedly be differences of opinion.[5]

In other words, various interpretive overlays may contextualize the Passion focal point, or center, yet it is still considered the constant among them.

Many of those searching for the "center" of revelation feel they have found it summarized in 1 Cor 15:3–4.[6]

> I delivered to you as of first importance [at the first] what I also received: that Christ died for our sins in accordance with the Scriptures, that he was buried, that he was raised on the third day in accordance with the Scriptures.

But the supremacy of the Passion in Paul's theology based on the translation and interpretation of this text has been revaluated. The prepositional phrase in verse 3, which is invariably translated as if Paul was defining the most important aspect of "the gospel," is an idiom denoting a sequence in time, not of supreme importance. Ancient and Hellenistic Greek, including Jewish religious texts, attest to the only meaning of the prepositional phrase ἐν πρώτοις to be sequential. In other words, the Greek does not say the death, burial, and resurrection were the most important components of "the gospel." Rather the text says that the death, burial, and

---

5. Caird, *New Testament Theology*, 27.

6. E.g., Ciampa and Rosner, *First Corinthians*, 745; Witherington, *Conflict*, 299; Godet, *First Corinthians*, 2:329; Robertson and Plummer, *First Corinthians*, 332. Some prefer the unprecedented meaning of prominence with little or no linguistic discussion: Blomberg, *1 Corinthians*, 295–96; Johnson, *1 Corinthians*, 284; Morris, *First Corinthians*, 201; Taylor, *1 Corinthians*, 371; Gardner, *1 Corinthians*, 649; Keener, *1–2 Corinthians*, 121; Fee, *First Corinthians*, 80–81.

resurrection were "among" (ἐν) the first or initial (πρώτοις) topics Paul pronounced within his total message to the Corinthians.[7]

From Sunday School to sermons to church publications and mission fields to seminaries and their boards and to authors and publishers of the simplest to the most erudite Christian books, the Passion has been the most common "center" for the church and permeates all its layers. The prevailing practice is to hold the Passion and sin salvation as the center of the theology of Paul, the New Testament, even both Testaments. A few comments will suffice to represent this most prevalent position.

> The content of the gospel is, then, centered on the death and resurrection of Jesus, understood as the means through which people can be delivered from their sins and God's judgment upon them.[8]

> The whole content of [Paul's] preaching can be summarized as the proclamation and explication of the eschatological time of salvation inaugurated with Christ's advent, death, and resurrection. . . . it can be said of Paul's gospel in particular that it has its starting point and center in the death and resurrection of Christ.[9]

> Identifying "Christ" as the object of his proclamation, Paul implies that the good news of the gospel centers on what God has done in the death and resurrection of his Christ.[10]

> The gospel is summarized in Christ's death for sinners and his resurrection (1 Cor. 15:3).[11]

> [Paul's] statement in 1 Corinthians 15:3 is specific, in which he clearly says that he had received, as the essence of the Gospel, "that Christ died for our sins in accordance with the scriptures, that he was buried, that he was raised . . . ."[12]

Paul's theology of the cross and resurrection historically has risen to the top position of biblical theological themes. One would expect to hear more of the Passion of Christ in the apostles' message than that of Jesus in the Gospels. However, the reason is more historical than theological since the Passion had not yet happened, and Jesus was politically

---

7. Fredericks, "Question of First Importance," 163–81.
8. Marshall, *Theology*, 476.
9. Ridderbos, *Paul*, 44, 54.
10. Collins, *Second Corinthians*, 62.
11. Schreiner, *New Testament Theology*, 306–7. Also Gorman, *Cruciformity*, 123.
12. Guthrie, *New Testament Theology*, 463.

calculated in his own mention of its process, only rarely hinting about its salvific effect.[13] Jesus does predict for his followers the progression in his Passion—that he would suffer, die, and rise again—but for whatever reasons, he kept obscure the soteriological results to his death, e.g., Mark 8:29–31; 9:31. Not until the Last Supper were the results of his Passion revealed explicitly to be for forgiveness of sin. But his Passion's impact could hardly have been avoided by Jesus in his many post-Passion appearances before his ascension. Could he have emphasized it earlier? Yes, though it is not recorded that he did. Isaiah 53 had no problem explaining it in just a few verses, while Jesus had nearly six weeks to explain the meaning of his recent suffering and dying before his ascension, as Luke recounts it in Luke 24:46–47. Moreover, Jesus gave an extended explanation of his full commission as predicted in the Old Testament while traveling to Emmaus with a couple of his followers. Their conversation of course began with the latest news of the Passion but necessarily turned into an Old Testament teaching on the comprehensive implications of his Messiah commission since the Old Testament spoke significantly more about him than only his redemption of believers. Emmaus helped mark only the beginning to around a month and a half of such public teaching of Jesus (Acts 13:30–31; 1 Cor 15:4–8).

It was not for his priestly self-sacrifice alone that Jesus' universal kingdom is celebrated in Phil 2:1–11. While stressing the ethical theme of humility for the Philippian believers (3–7) Paul elevates his rhetoric by noting the Messiah's perfect example of a righteous, humble, and obedient life that included the cross ("also," καὶ):

> He humbled himself by becoming obedient to the point of death: death on a cross. God exalted him highly for this *also*, and conferred on him the name which is above every name, so that at the name of Jesus every knee will bow, those who are in heaven, on earth, and under the earth, and that every tongue will confess that Jesus Christ is Lord, to the glory of God the Father.

---

13. D. Wenham's conclusion is correct in its reason for a difference in Paul's and Jesus' message but overstates its prominence: "The differences between Paul and Jesus are explicable to a considerable extent. For Jesus the cross lies ahead, and is in a real sense unknown and, as the Gospels suggest, almost impossible to explain to his followers in advance. For Paul the cross has happened and is a massively important datum to be explained; the prominence of it in his thinking is not at all surprising." Wenham, *Paul*, 155.

After all, the Messiah's righteous, submissive obedience to God is his most frequent characteristic in the Old Testament predictions about him and entailed far more than sin salvation.[14] In every way Jesus was God's servant, including his death on the cross.

HARMONIZED PRIEST/KING MESSAGE TEXTS

One should not allow reductionist hierarchies to frame the discussion of biblical theology by emphasizing God's kingdom as most prominent, Christ's sin salvation as most prominent, or Jesus as the moral teacher as the most prominent. The Incarnation brought a multifaceted servant of God. First Corinthians 1:22–23 presents what was and remains the blunt, jarring juxtaposition of the Messiah and the most horrific execution: "But we proclaim *Messiah crucified* [ἡμεῖς δὲ κηρύσσομεν Χριστὸν ἐσταυρωμένον]." Not Jesus crucified, not the Lord crucified. Not even the Savior crucified. The apostolic proclamation was about the crucified *Messiah* in all his roles, as executed King, executed priest, executed judge, executed prophet, executed warrior, executed intercessor, and executed adversity deliverer. In other words, not an executed person with a new last name, "Messiah," but God's divine servant Son (Matt 21:37–39). The following texts reflect this harmonized commentary on the Messiah's commission.

Matthew and Luke present two sides of the coin in their Gospels' closing accounts of Jesus' Great Commissions. In so doing they harmonize the most general messianic role and the more specific roles within it yet with very different emphases. Matthew's commission is most familiar:

> All authority in heaven and on earth has been given to Me. So go and make disciples of all the nations, baptizing them in the name of the Father and the Son and the Holy Spirit and teaching them to follow all that I commanded you. (Matt 28:18–20)

The Great Commission is primarily a discipling commission but implies as a first step the baptism of repentance for the forgiveness of sins. The Messiah's universal kingdom is first firmly planted in verse 18; his kingship is reaffirmed in his coregency with the names of the Father and Holy Spirit; then his royal command to his disciples is for them to disciple others with Jesus' commandments. Three messianic roles are inferred

---

14. See the comments in chapter 7 on this most frequently mentioned expectation of the Messiah expressed in the Old Testament—his righteous submission.

in Matthew's Great Commission; his two priestly roles as the mediator of forgiveness and the teacher of his royal commandments are blended before he concludes by reaffirming his messianic commission as the universal King by his right to demand obedience from all nations.

On the other hand, Luke quotes another Great Commission from Jesus in 24:46–47, when Jesus puts more emphasis on his ironic priestly role than he does in Matthew's commission, yet only after he refers to himself as "the Messiah":

> It is written that the Messiah [τὸν χριστὸν] would suffer but rise from the dead on the third day, so that repentance for the forgiveness of sins would be proclaimed in his name to all nations.

Finally, now Jesus completes his previous teaching to his disciples about his suffering, death, and resurrection and connects it clearly with repentance for the forgiveness of sins that his cross won. His self-designation as the Messiah carried with it all of the messianic commission roles including his command as the universal King, his teaching, prophecy, intercession, and wisdom in all its breadth to be proclaimed globally, to all nations.

Peter summarized his good news tersely as "peace through Jesus Christ, he is the Lord of all" (Acts 10:36). In other words, the Messiah brought peace by his mediating, self-sacrificing role as priest and in his role as the universal King over all. Peter himself had a Jonaic vision as a food blanket descended from the sky (Acts 10:9–15), and he was forced to move on from his national prejudice to embrace the gentiles as his mission. Rather than a mere parenthetical comment as many translations render it, "(he is the Lord of all)," this phrase is nothing less than the dramatic and essential premise for why the good news is also for the whole world. Jesus is the universal King of all.

Paul takes a subtle but profound jab at Ananias in Acts 23:2–5 in the following account of his trial before the high priest:

> Paul said to Ananias, "God will strike you, you whitewashed wall." . . . But those present said, "Are you insulting God's high priest?" Paul said, "Brothers, I was not aware that he is high priest since it is written: 'You shall not speak evil of a ruler of your people.'"

Because Paul knew he was conversing with the recently deposed high priest, Ananias, he did not acknowledge him as the true high priest and thus a ruler of Israel. One cannot conceive of Paul not recognizing who Ananias was; he preferred in his passive resistance to affirm that the rightful high priest was he who laid himself down and who was the ultimate ruler, the King not only of Israel but of all creation.

Hebrews 12:2, like Phil 2, mentions the honored roles of the ironic priest and king: "[Jesus] endured the cross, disregarding its shame, and has sat at the right hand of God's throne," doing so in his role as co-king with his Father.

The message of the New Testament is that the Messiah had arrived as the King, lawgiver, warring savior, judge, intercessor, priest, teacher, revealer, prophet, and miracle deliverer. Since he played these shepherding roles, it should not be said in a false hierarchy that his death and resurrection were his most crucial accomplishments. Those two episodes, however amazing and beneficial, were a means to the greater end of his full commission to shepherd humanity further along in its role in his eternal design. So, attention now is turned to the New Testament's most profound pronouncements about this Messiah and his comprehensive commission, the one who had arrived to continue creation's eternal design to bless itself according to the image, nature, and attributes of the Trinity.

16

New Testament Pronouncements

PREVIOUS CHAPTERS HAVE FOCUSED on the message of the Messiah's commission. Next, we step back to view the New Testament message through the dozens of passages that use "pronouncement" words to introduce any public summations by Jesus and New Testament writers, whether they refer to him or not. By looking at these pronouncements, a more complete idea is formed that supports a harmonic New Testament message. Over two hundred instances of pronouncement terms are considered here. In support of a harmonic message, an analysis of nearly a hundred texts are samples of the most important New Testament pronouncements on any subject. Needless to say, full comments on each text are not possible here, but the following synopses are adequate to further convey the complex nature of the New Testament message.

Attempting to survey the New Testament's primary messages requires sampling without compromising their richness yet accurately reflecting their content. This chapter focuses on the verbalized priorities of those making the pronouncements. Certainly this is not the complete nor only means to understand the most important New Testament messages, but it makes a substantial contribution. This lexical constellation of pronouncement verbs and nouns launches phrasings that reveal what was thought worthy to speak about publicly to various audiences; it indicates what Christ and the apostles thought to be the most significant and broad revelatory topics. There would be objections to a restrictive sampling of this sort, including which specific terms are or are not included in the lexical constellation. Yet, a sampling with reasonable parameters avoids the impossible task of commenting on every public comment in the New Testament.

It has been the practice throughout the foregoing study to use the terms "pronouncement" and "pronounce" as neutral terms for the New Testament's public annunciations, rather than grace any one of the following words as the first among equals. This dispels a presumption that any single pronouncement term owns the right to govern or represent all the others, e.g., εὐαγγέλιον/εὐαγγελίζω, κήρυγμα/κηρύσσω.[1] The pronouncement verbs and nouns used in this synopsis include ἀναγγέλλω, ἀπαγγέλλω, ἀποκρίνομαι, ἀποφθέγγομαι, γνωρίζω, διακατελέγχομαι, διαλέγομαι, διαμαρτύρομαι, διανοίγω, διδάσκω, διδαχή, διερμηνεύω, εἶπον, ἐκτίθημι, εὐαγγέλιον, εὐαγγελίζω, καταγγελεύς, καταγγέλλω, κήρυγμα, κηρύσσω, κῆρυξ, κράζω, λαλέω, λέγω, λόγος, μαρτυρέω, μαρτυρία, μαρτύριον, μάρτυς, ὁμολογέω, ὁμολογία, ἀποφθέγγομαι, ὁρίζω, παραδίδωμι, παρακαλέω, παρατίθημι, παρρησιάζομαι, πείθω, προευαγγελίζομαι, ῥῆμα, συμβιβάζω, φανερόω.[2] Again, words from this list are used to pronounce any number of various profound truths, not just those that one person or another might consider thematic.

The Greek pronouncement terms that are used most frequently are assigned the following English meanings and are used consistently in this synopsis. These are common translations for the terms whose lexical fields are not significantly broader than their English equivalents: κηρύσσω/κήρυγμα—proclaim/proclamation; εὐαγγελίζω/εὐαγγέλιον—bring good news/good news; διδάσκω/διδαχή—teach/teaching; μαρτυρέω/μαρτυρία—testify/testimony; λόγος and ῥῆμα—word. The rest of the terms will be translated by terms commonly agreed upon. The following examples show how the pronouncement terms reflect the New Testament's most profound statements.

---

1. It is common in the guild to emphasize Paul's use of "gospel" to assist in determining his emphasis. This might be helpful, but it can be overestimated at the expense of other words that are in just as clearly public pronouncements.

2. Pronouncement terms used for common or standard speech like, e.g., εἶπον, λαλέω, and λέγω are rarely included in this sampling because they most often introduce routine dialogue rather than general and summary statements of the New Testament's most profound messages. They introduce or accompany narrower discourse and are very often reactive statements within conversations rather than public announcements of conceptual truth. However, another study of the role of these words might be profitable at a different time.

In Acts 26:22-23, Paul uses pronouncement verbs in his public summary of one of his and Christ's messages about the Passion:

> I stand here testifying [μαρτυρέω] to small and great, saying nothing but what the prophets and Moses said would happen: that the Messiah must suffer and being the first to rise from the dead, he would announce [καταγγέλλω] light to our people and the Gentiles.

As we saw in chapter 9, four other Acts passages use seven additional pronouncement terms that summarize Paul's "kingdom of God" pronouncements, Acts 19:8, 20:25, 28:23, and 28:30-31: παρρησιάζομαι, διαλέγομαι, πείθω, κηρύσσω, ἐκτίθημι, διαμαρτύρομαι, διδάσκω.

Pronouncement verbs and nouns occur hundreds of times in the New Testament and often do not indicate any specific content of the pronouncement. That is, very often what it is exactly that is pronounced cannot be determined since the content is too broad; there is nothing specific to work with. For instance,

> I know that Messiah is coming (he who is called Christ); when that One comes, he will announce [ἀναγγέλλω] everything to us. (John 4:25)

> There is no ground for me boasting if I bring good news [εὐαγγελίζω] because that is necessary of me. Woe to me if I do not bring good news [εὐαγγελίζω]![3] (1 Cor 9:16)

> We announce [καταγγέλλω] Christ, warning and wisely teaching everyone so that we may present everyone as mature in Christ. (Col 1:28)

As helpful as these pronouncement phrases are in contributing to their context, they offer nothing specific about their own content.[4] One can import to the phrase what one believes the good news to be, but this would beg the question and assume a conclusion that has not yet been determined.

Attention to these pronouncement terms where any content to the pronouncement is provided results in the following categories:

---

3. Paul uses the redundant cognate accusative, "I brought the good news [εὐαγγελίζω] of the good news [εὐαγγέλιον]" (1 Cor 15:1; also 2 Cor 11:7; Gal 1:11).

4. Only a few other examples where the content is too general: Luke 24:32; John 1:7-8, 18; 16:25; 18:37; 1 Cor 4:17; Gal 1:23; 2 Tim 2:15; Jas 1:18.

Pronouncements Forming No Pattern

Pronouncements with Ethical Content

Pronouncements Reflecting the Messianic Roles

Pronouncements on the Passion Alone

Pronouncements on the Messiah's Universal Kingdom

Messiah's Divine Lordship

Messiah's Kingdom

Pronouncements Harmonizing the Messianic Roles

First, twelve instances of pronouncement terms refer to content that does not amount to a considerable pattern. A second group consists of sixteen pronouncements concerning diverse ethical content. The importance of these passages, however, does not lie in their contribution to or distraction from a New Testament harmonic message about the Messiah. They constitute 25 percent of the total pronouncement texts with terms that carry specific content, leaving the significant majority of texts reflecting a thematic message connected to Jesus Christ.

PATTERNLESS PRONOUNCEMENTS

A few rich passages express the specific content of their pronouncements, yet they do not address any one subject enough to amount to a pattern or New Testament theme.

ἀναγγέλλω (announce)	God's whole purpose	Acts 20:27
ἀναγγέλλω	God is light	1 John 1:5
διαμαρτύρομαι (testify solemnly)	God's grace[5]	Acts 20:24, also v. 32
διδάσκω (teach)	Walk in Christ Jesus the Lord	Col 2:6–7
διδάσκω	Apostolic traditions	2 Thess 2:15
ἐξαγγέλλω (announce)	God's excellencies	1 Pet 2:9
εὐαγγελίζω (bring good news)	Live by God's Spirit	1 Pet 4:6

5. One might limit a definition of "grace" to that of salvation, thereby placing these texts under that category. The same might be said of "peace" in Eph 6:15. However, grace and peace are pervasive greetings by Paul, with no such soteriological limitation; see Eph 2:14–16. On the breadth of meanings of God's "grace," see Bock, *Luke–Acts*, 271–72.

εὐαγγελίζω	Riches of Christ	Eph 3:8
εὐαγγελίζω, εὐαγγέλιον (good news)	God's judgment	Rev 14:6-7
εὐαγγέλιον (good news)	Peace	Eph 6:15
παρακαλέω (encourage) and ἐπιμαρτυρέω (testifying)	God's grace	1 Pet 5:12
παρρησιάζομαι (speak boldly) and λόγος (word)	Lord's word of his grace	Acts 14:3

ETHICAL PRONOUNCEMENTS

A pattern in many pronouncement passages is formed around sanctification by addressing quite general or more specific ethical responsibilities.

ἀγγελία (announcement)	Love one another	1 John 3:11
διαλέγομαι (discuss)	Righteousness	Acts 24:25
διαμαρτύρομαι (testify solemnly)	Repentance and faith	Acts 20:21
διαμαρτύρομαι, and κηρύσσω (proclaim), and λόγος (word), and διδαχή (teaching)	Reprove, rebuke, exhort	2 Tim 4:1-2
διδάσκω (teach)	Temple sacrilege	Mark 11:17
διδάσκω	Beware of scribes	Mark 12:38
διδάσκω	New moral life	Eph 4:20-23
διδάσκω, and παρακαλέω (encourage)	Respect authority	1 Tim 6:2
διδάσκω, and λόγος (word)	Righteousness	Heb 5:12-13
εὐαγγέλιον (good news), and κήρυγμα (proclamation)	Obedience	Rom 16:25-26
εὐαγγελίζω (bring good news)	Thessalonians' faith and love	1 Thess 3:6

κηρύσσω (proclaim)	Repent	Matt 3:1; 4:17; Mark 1:4 // Luke 3:3; Mark 1:14–15; 6:12
παρακαλέω (exhort)	Shepherd your flock	1 Pet 5:1

MESSIANIC PRONOUNCEMENTS

Some ninety pronouncement texts and their two hundred instances of pronouncement terms are the most germane to the harmonic messianic message. A Passion focus stands alone in fourteen of these texts. Thirty-one texts speak of only the Messiah's universal kingdom focus: nine texts specifically refer to his divine lordship, and twenty-two are explicitly about the universal kingdom of which Christ is King and judge. The fifth category has some forty texts where a harmonic message about the Messiah's role is explicitly and simultaneously pronounced.

Pronouncements on the Passion Alone

Various aspects of the Passion are introduced by pronouncement terminology: the suffering, crucifixion, or resurrection of Jesus. Specific results of the Passion are also the explicit content of some: salvation, justification, eternal life, and reconciliation. The following texts present solely Jesus' Passion and its implications. When the Passion is implied in a text designating the Messiah, it is included later under the texts that refer to the harmonization of the messianic commission.

ἀναγγέλλω (announce), and εὐαγγελίζω (bring good news)	Salvation from Christ's suffering and the following glories	1 Pet 1:10–12
διδάσκω (teach), and καταγγέλλω (announce)	Resurrection, including Jesus' own	Acts 4:1–2
εὐαγγελίζω (bring good news)	Jesus' suffering, sacrificial death	Acts 8:32–35
εὐαγγελίζω (bring good news), εὐαγγέλιον (good news)	Brings salvation	Rom 1:16 (cf. 1 Cor 1:18)

καταγγέλλω (announce)	Lord died and will return	1 Cor 11:26
κηρύσσω (proclaim)	Christ's crucifixion	Gal 5:11
λόγος (word)	Reconciliation from God in Christ	2 Cor 5:19
λόγος (word)	Word of eternal life	Phil 2:16
λόγος (word), and λαλέω (speak), and συνεπιμαρτυρέω (co-testify)	Salvation by retribution for sin	Heb 2:3–4
μαρτυρέω (testify)	Lord Jesus' resurrection	Acts 4:33
μαρτυρία (testimony), and εὐαγγέλιον (good news)	God called, saved us Jesus abolished death and brought eternal life	2 Tim 1:8–11
παραδίδωμι (deliver),	Christ died, was buried, and raised	1 Cor 15:1–15
and κηρύσσω (proclaim),	Christ's resurrection	
and μαρτυρέω (testify)	Christ's resurrection	
προευαγγελίζομαι (promise good news)	Nations' justification	Gal 3:8
ῥῆμα (word)	Sin salvation	Acts 11:13–14
φανερόω (disclose) εὐαγγέλιον (good news) κῆρυξ (proclaimer) διδάσκαλος (teacher)	God's calling, salvation, and eternal life in Christ's death	

Pronouncements on the Universal Kingdom Alone

When Christ is referred to as the Lord or the Son of God, it entails his divine royalty as the Messiah and equates him to God, the Lord King, and coregent of the universal kingdom as prophesied (Pss 2:7–8; 110:1; Mic 5:2).

γνωρίζω (reveal)	Power, majesty of the Lord Jesus	2 Pet 1:16–17
διδάσκω (teach)	David's Lord is God and David's son	Mark 12:35–37

εἶπον (say)	Jesus is the Son of God	Luke 1:32
εὐαγγέλιον (good news),	Christ's glory is the image of God	2 Cor 4:4–5
and κηρύσσω (proclaim)	Jesus Christ is Lord	
εὐαγγέλιον (good news)	Good news from God's Son	Rom 1:9
εὐαγγελίζω (bring good news)	Christ is God's Son	Gal 1:15–16
κηρύσσω (proclaim)	Jesus is mightier than John	Mark 1:7
κηρύσσω (proclaim)	Jesus is the Son of God	Acts 9:20–22
κηρύσσω (proclaim)	Jesus Christ as the Son of God Christ, God's Son	2 Cor 1:19

Pronouncements on the Messiah's Kingship Alone

Any reference to the kingdom of God includes the coregency of Christ as well, thus, "the kingdom of our Lord *and* of his Messiah" (Rev 12:10; 11:15; 22:1–3). This includes texts dealing specifically with the Messiah's final judgment, which is performed with his Father. When Christ's kingship is implied in a text designating the Messiah, it is included later under the texts that harmonize his various roles.

ἀπαγγέλλω (announce)	Justice to the nations	Matt 12:15–18
ἀπαγγέλλω (announce)	Diseased are healed, dead are raised	Luke 7:22
διαγγέλλω (announce widely)	About kingdom of God	Luke 9:60
διδάσκω (teach), and κηρύσσω (proclaim), and εὐαγγέλιον (good news)	Good news about the kingdom	Matt 4:23
διδάσκω (teach), and κηρύσσω (proclaim), and εὐαγγέλιον (good news)	Good news about the kingdom	Matt 9:35
εἶπον (say)	Israel's eternal king	Luke 1:32–33

NEW TESTAMENT PRONOUNCEMENTS

εὐαγγελίζω (bring good news)	About the kingdom of God	Luke 4:43–44
εὐαγγελίζω (bring good news)	Good news about the kingdom	Luke 16:16
εὐαγγέλιον (good news), and κηρύσσω (proclaim), and μαρτύριον (testimony)	About the kingdom	Matt 24:14
εὐαγγέλιον (good news)	God, in Christ Jesus will judge	Rom 2:16
εὐαγγελίζω (bring good news),	Good news for every nation	Rev 14:6–7
εὐαγγέλιον (good news)	God's hour of judgment has arrived	
κράζω (shout out),	Jesus was sent by the Father	John 7:27–28
κηρύσσω (proclaim)	Repent, kingdom of heaven is here	Matt 3:1–2
κηρύσσω (proclaim)	Repent, kingdom of heaven is here	Matt 4:17
κηρύσσω (proclaim)	Kingdom of heaven/God is here	Matt 10:7// Luke 9:2
κηρύσσω (proclaim), and εὐαγγέλιον (good news)	Good news from God Kingdom of God is here	Mark 1:14–15
κηρύσσω (proclaim), and εὐαγγελίζω (bring good news)	Good news about the kingdom of God	Luke 8:1
κηρύσσω (proclaim), and λόγος (word)	Word of Christ Jesus who will judge the world	2 Tim 4:1–2
λόγος (word) and διδάσκω (teach)	About the kingdom	Matt 13:19
παρρησιάζομαι (speak openly), διαλέγομαι (discuss), πείθω (persuade)	About the kingdom of God	Acts 19:8

HARMONIC PRONOUNCEMENTS

Again, many pronouncement texts in the New Testament are general statements that do not indicate what exactly is focused on. For instance:

"Woe to me if I do not bring good news [εὐαγγελίζω]" (1 Cor 9:16). This pronouncement does not say what good news was brought. But of the ninety or so that have discernible content, half of them are explicit in their harmonization of Jesus' roles in his designation as the Messiah. The harmonic message is not shown only by the passages that contain two or more roles, but when they are found alone they still imply the diversity within the commission. In other words, the harmonic message is supported when any one role or combination of roles is mentioned. Because the various roles are unified in the Incarnation, passages are considered to imply the full, multifaceted messianic commission when "Messiah" is explicit.

Inevitably, the precision of some conclusions on the following texts would be challenged, but the sheer volume of passages and terms involved would nonetheless support the conclusion that the New Testament presents a harmonized message within the complete messianic commission.

Messiah Alone, Thus Multifaceted Role

Luke 2:10–11: The angel announced good news (εὐαγγελίζω) to the shepherds that the expected Christ/Messiah had come. This Messiah would include being a savior who is no less than "the Lord," the divine Messiah. The messianic "savior" would include his Passion,[6] particularly since the angel had already announced the sin-saving Messiah earlier to Joseph (Matt 1:20–21).

Acts 5:42: Peter and other apostles διδάσκω (taught) and brought the good news (εὐαγγελίζω) that "Jesus was the Messiah." This shortest of New Testament pronouncements is a summary pronouncement that is within the context of the apostles' longer pronouncements in sermons and speeches that include many messianic roles.

Acts 9:22: Paul's conversion led him to his ministry of proving (συμβιβάζω) that "Jesus was the Messiah," meaning all that the messianic commission entailed.

Acts 17:2–3: Paul attempted to convince the Jews that Jesus was the Messiah who served as the ironic priest by various modes of communication: discussing (διαλέγομαι), explaining (διανοίγω), proving (παρατίθημι), and announcing (καταγγέλλω) that Jesus was the Messiah.

---

6. In the Testaments God is the Savior from sin and adversity (Isa 53:4–12; 61:1).

Acts 18:5: See above at 5:42; 9:22; 17:2-3. In this case, Paul is consumed with "the word" (λόγος) and testified solemnly (διαμαρτύρομαι) that Jesus was the Messiah.

Acts 18:28: Again, see above at 5:42; 9:22; 17:2-3; 18:5, where the near creedal refrain that "Jesus was the Messiah" is defended (διακατελέγχομαι).

Acts 28:23-28: Luke ends Acts by including his own Gospel's frequent announcement of the "kingdom" (over thirty times) and Paul's references to it in Acts (Acts 14:22; 19:8; 20:25; 28:31). In these verses, Paul is said to have explained (ἐκτίθημι) and testified profoundly (διαμαρτύρομαι) about God's salvation to prove (πείθω) to others the importance of Jesus from the Old Testament, a topic synonymous with the phrasing "Jesus was the Messiah."

Acts 28:30-31: In this shorter concluding summary, Paul proclaims (κηρύσσω) and teaches (διδάσκω) the harmonic message concerning Jesus: his kingdom and everything concerning the commission of the Lord Jesus Christ.

Messiah and Ironic Priest

1 Corinthians 1:21-23; 2:1-2: The apostles proclaimed (1:21, 23; κήρυγμα) the crucifixion of the Messiah and salvation. Paul announced (2:1; καταγγέλλω) God's testimony (μαρτύριον) to this effect. However, Paul's message is not simply the Passion; he is making an argument in these incisive two words about a "crucified Messiah." In chapter 15, Paul's main topics become the Messiah's resurrection and his kingdom (4:20; 6:9, 10; 15:1-58).

Messiah, Ironic Priest, Adversity Savior, and Nations' Deliverer

Acts 3:12-26: This is one of the most complete New Testament statements of the Messiah's comprehensive commission of universal blessing and his sin salvation to the Jews and the rest of the terrestrial kingdom. Peter responds profoundly [ἀποκρίνομαι] to a crowd amazed by an adversity salvation of a lame man by the authority of Jesus Christ. Peter's theology of history extends from creation until and throughout the age of New Earth and includes the Davidic covenant (24), the suffering servant (13, 26), the servant Messiah's commissioning (20), the Messiah's commission fulfillments (26), the Messiah's return (19), to the blessing of all families in the terrestrial kingdom by their deliverer (25), which is fully restored into a New Earth (21). Peter is blunt to tell the crowd undoubtedly consisting of those who only weeks before yelled "crucify him!" that they had killed God's Messiah, the Holy and Righteous One (Isa 50:7), the prince of life (15), but God had raised him.

Acts 4:8–12: Peter says (εἶπον) the lame man was healed by the power of Jesus Christ over the natural kingdom and blames the leaders for Jesus' death. Peter continues his historic, world-altering claim that Jesus Christ is the lone authority in the world who can deliver the nations.

Acts 8:5–7, 12: Philip proclaimed (κηρύσσω) "the Messiah" to the Samaritans, who responded joyfully with trust and baptism when they heard the good news that Philip brought (εὐαγγελίζω) about him and "the kingdom of God." They believed in the Messiah's reign over the universal realm of God and Christ's authority (name) over the natural kingdom by his adversity salvation of healings and exorcisms.

King and Ironic Priest

Matthew 1:20–21: The angel says (λέγω) to Joseph that Mary's son of the royal line of David should be named "Jesus" because he will be the sin-savior of his people. This presents two roles of the harmonic message—King and self-sacrificing priest.

Matthew 28:18–20: The universal King (18) fulfills his two priestly roles as the mediator of the baptism of forgiveness and the teacher of his royal commandments.

Mark 8:29–31 // Luke 9:20–22: Peter identifies Jesus as God's Messiah and Jesus affirms his commission. He self-identifies as the human Son of Man from Daniel's messianic passage (Dan 7:13–14),[7] and as the ironic and teaching Messiah he begins to teach (διδάσκω) about his death and resurrection.

Luke 18:31–34: The word came (ῥῆμα) from the universal King, the Son of Man (Dan 7:14), who explained to his disciples his Passion that was prophesied in the Old Testament prophets, including how the gentiles of the terrestrial kingdom were complicit in it.

---

7. The designation "Son of Man" occurs nearly ninety times in the New Testament and is taken to refer to Jesus Christ's regal reign and realm that the majestic ceremonial commission of the Messiah introduces in Dan 7.

Luke 24:6-7, 10-11: The women's reported words (ῥῆμα) from the two angels about the empty tomb were foolish to the disciples, despite Jesus' teaching them over months on the subject. As in Luke 18:31-34, the ruling Son of Man would be delivered to sinful men and executed as the ironic priest but would rise.

Acts 2:22-40: Peter was speaking boldly (ἀποφθέγγομαι) in this sermon about the messianic commission roles, including the executed ironic priest. In 22-36, Peter tells the Jerusalemites that though they executed Jesus, God raised him according to his definite plan. But Jesus was raised to rule as the coregent at God's right hand, and they would conquer Jesus' enemies (Ps 110:1). In 37-40, Peter continued, "Repent and be baptized in the name of Jesus Christ for the forgiveness of your sins, and you will receive the gift of the Holy Spirit," and he testified solemnly (διαμαρτύρομαι) about many other matters and encouraged (παρακαλέω) them to save themselves from their perverse world.

Acts 5:28-32: The Jewish leaders are addressed as those who crucified Jesus; thereby, the charged apostles became the prosecutors of this charge against the council. Two roles of the Messiah are identified by the apostles' pronouncements (διδάσκω, διδαχή, μάρτυς). The "Leader and Savior" who had been exalted by God in the Old Testament was crucified and raised for the forgiveness of sin.

Acts 20:20-21, 24-27, 32: Paul announced (ἀναγγέλλω) and taught (διδάσκω) many things to the Ephesian elders, solemnly testifying (διαμαρτύρομαι) to the gentiles as well about repentance and faith (cf. Mark 1:15) and to the good news (εὐαγγέλιον) of "grace," implying the priestly Passion/justification (24). The word (λόγος) of God's grace also sanctifies those who will receive the inheritance of New Earth (32). Paul continuously proclaimed (κηρύσσω) God's universal kingdom (25) by announcing (ἀναγγέλλω) God's whole counsel (27). He encouraged the Ephesian elders to be the better shepherds who were promised in the Old Testament (28-29; Jer 3:15).

Ephesians 1:7-14: The two most frequent roles referred to in the pronouncement constructs are seen again here, where salvation by gracious forgiveness that comes from the priest's substitutionary execution, and the supreme reign of Christ the King in God's eternal design of cosmic administration are found in this rich theological composite. The word (λόγος) of truth is the good news (εὐαγγέλιον) of salvation. God revealed (γνωρίζω) his royal purpose for Christ, to place all of the universal kingdom in his hands as in vv. 9-11.

Colossians 1:15–23: The good news (εὐαγγέλιον) that is proclaimed (κηρύσσω) throughout the universal kingdom does not refer only to the sentence in which these pronouncement terms occur, dealing with Christ's reconciliatory priestly death (21–23). It includes the previous sentences, which convey more than any New Testament passage the kingship and priestly reconciliation of Christ over his creation and church (15–20).

Messiah, King, Ironic Priest, and Nations' Deliverer

Romans 1:1–5: The thrust of these first words of Romans is that "Jesus Christ our Lord" is the Son of God (3–4), Paul's master, and the master of the terrestrial kingdom's nations (5). Paul's good news, like Christ's, was "the good news from God" (Mark 1:14–15), which God promised in the Prophets. Christ Jesus is a son of David who continues and serves as the final King of the eternal Davidic dynasty. Jesus was declared (ὁρίζω) to be the Son of God by his resurrection. This is a harmonic text heavy on messianic expectations: divinity, messiahship, lordship, global impact, and the priest's (death and) resurrection.

Romans 10:8–17: Believers declare (ὁμολογέω) what the word (ῥῆμα) of the apostles declared (ὁμολογέω) and proclaimed (κηρύσσω). The apostolic "word of faith" is that whoever trusts and declares that Jesus is "the Lord" and that God raised him from the dead will be saved and made "rich." Verses 14–16 provide the steps along the road to salvation: from God's sending the apostles, to the apostles bringing good news (εὐαγγελίζω), the "word" (ῥῆμα), to Jews and Greeks who, hearing and trusting the good news (εὐαγγέλιον) for their salvation, are described in verses 8–13. Two roles of the Messiah, his universal kingship as "the Lord of Lords" and his priestly self-sacrifice, are implied by the necessity of his resurrection.

Messiah and Judge

Luke 3:15–18: When John the Baptist was asked whether he was the Messiah, he begins to bring them the good news (εὐαγγελίζω) that the true, mightier Messiah would come with the authority to grant a greater, divine baptism of the Spirit. He adds specifically that the Messiah would be a judge who protects the trusting kingdom while judging and destroying those outside it. John encouraged (παρακαλέω) the people with good news in many other ways as well.

King, Ironic Priest, Adversity Savior, Judge, and Nations' Deliverer

Acts 10:34-43: This is one of the most holistic New Testament addresses on the Messiah's diverse commission, and Luke uses seven different pronouncement terms: λόγος, εὐαγγελίζω, μάρτυς, κηρύσσω, διαμαρτύρομαι, μαρτυρέω, ῥῆμα. By them, he harmonizes many messianic roles: nations' deliverer (34; Ps 72:16-17; Isa 9:1-2; 42:6-7; 49:6-7); the judge (42; Pss 2:9, 12; 72:4; Isa 11:4; 42:1); universal King, "Lord of all nations" (if not all creation; 36); ironic priest (36, 43); adversity deliverer (38).

Messiah, King, and Ironic Priest

2 Timothy 2:8-10: Paul's good news (εὐαγγέλιον), the unimprisoned word (λόγος) of God, blends the messianic roles of Christ Jesus: he is the risen ironic priest and risen Davidic King.

Hebrews 3:1-2, 6: Hebrews combines the two roles of God's commission, forming the harmonic confessions (ὁμολογία) of extolling Jesus as the self-sacrificer and the Son of God whom God has put over his "house" to rule.

Messiah and Ironic Priest

Mark 9:31: It is repeated from Mark 8:31 that Jesus taught (διδάσκω) that he was the Son of Man, implying his broad messianic roles. As the Son of Man, he would be crucified as the ironic priest, but raised, though the effect of his Passion is not disclosed.

Luke 24:25-27: Jesus explains (διερηνεύω) his Passion but within a much broader context of "things about him from all the Scriptures," i.e., the messianic expectations. Two roles are succinctly melded: his most general role as the glorious, divine Messiah and his self-sacrifice.

John 6:68-69: Jesus' words (ῥῆμα; 6:26-59) of eternal life that comes from salvation were believed by his disciples and led Peter to affirm that Jesus was the Holy One from God (Isa 49:7). Peter condensed the harmonic message roles of the divine and royal Messiah with his priestly/prophetic teaching on sin salvation.

Acts 13:29-34, 38-39: Paul spoke (εἶπον) of the messianic role of the Son of God whose kingdom rules (Ps 2) as an extension of the Davidic covenant. Paul announced (καταγγέλλω) forgiveness and justification by Christ for everyone who trusts.

Hebrews 4:14–15: As in 3:1–2 and 10:12–18, the harmonized roles are the objects of the confession (ὁμολογία) of the royal Messiah-Priest. The Son of God, the divine coregent who came from God's heavenly kingdom, is the blameless high priest who gifted himself as the eternal sacrifice.

1 John 4:14: John testifies (μαρτυρέω), as he summarized in his Gospel, that he has seen the evidence that Jesus is the sent Messiah and the savior of his and the Father's world. See also 5:9–11.

Messiah, Ironic Priest, and Nations' Deliverer

Luke 24:46–47: Luke's Great Commission complements Matthew's. Comments on the Messiah's Passion are followed by an urgency to proclaim (κηρύσσω) globally "repentance for the forgiveness of sins" (Luke 3:3; Mark 1:4). The proclamation rests on the authority "in the name" of the Messiah, and it will be given to all the terrestrial kingdom. Three roles are clear: the royal Messiah, his specific role in sin salvation, and the nations' deliverer.

John 1:15, 19–27, 34–36: John the Baptist testified (μαρτυρέω) to Jesus as the one fulfilling the messianic expectations: his preexistence (15, 30; Mic 5:2), Son of God (34; Ps 2:7–8), the self-sacrifice for sins (29; Isa 53:6–12), even the sins of the terrestrial kingdom (29; Isa 42:1, 6–7; 49:6–7). The Baptist thereby marks three roles of the Messiah: as the divine coregent ruler as the Son King, as the deliverer of the nations, and as the ironic priest. And by confessing (ὁμολογέω) he was not the Messiah (19–20), he inferred that Jesus was.

John 6:29–59: These verses include Jesus' teaching on his body as spiritually nutritious bread and drink (6:26–59). He refers to his messianic commission as unfailing submission to his Father's will to bless and deliver the whole world (6:33, 40, 51). He foreshadows his death and the communion meal by describing the ingesting of his body and blood. Jesus taught (διδάσκω) several truths about himself (44, 59): he is the Son of Man from the heavenly kingdom (27, 32–33, 51, 53, 58), the Son of God (40), the sent one who delivers the world (29, 33, 44, 57), and the one who will raise any believer to eternal life (40, 44, 54) due to his self-sacrifice.

Acts 26:20–23, 26: Paul announced (ἀπαγγέλλω) and spoke boldly (παρρησιάζομαι) about repentance and obedience to the God of the universal kingdom, to Jews and gentiles as the nations' deliverer. The Messiah prophesied, announcing (καταγγέλλω) light to all the world, and he was the ironic priest: "the Messiah must suffer . . . and rise from the dead."

King, Ironic Priest, and Nations' Deliverer

1 Timothy 2:5–7: It is a timely testimony (μαρτύριον) that the ruling Son of Man is the priestly mediator between God and humanity in his teaching of all nations through Paul and in his self-sacrifice.

Ironic Priest and Judge

Acts 17:18–19, 30–31: Philosophers were intrigued by Paul bringing good news (εὐαγγελίζω) about Jesus and the topic of the Passion's resurrection. His announcing (καταγγελεύς) foreign deities (God and the Messiah presumably) were new teachings (διδαχή). Paul relays God's announcing (ἀπαγγέλλω) that everybody should repent, since a messianic role is to judge all people in the universal kingdom.

SUMMARY

By this analysis of the New Testament pronouncements, it is not a surprise that they deal primarily with the Messiah. The New Testament message is that the Messiah had arrived to fulfill his complex commission to reign; to deliver from sin and adversity; to teach, judge, intercede, prophesy; to be the military deliverer of his trusting kingdom and the deliverer of all nations. The complete list of his messianic responsibilities is never explicit in any text, but it is implied whenever his title, Χριστός, is mentioned, whether alone as a single designation or in its several different compound designations. Theologies often reveal simplified, isolated subsets of the Messiah's comprehensive commission's assignments and marginalize the remaining roles, if they are even seriously considered. However, in so doing, God's full design for eternal creation is constricted from the breadth of God and his Messiah's universal shepherding impact on his creation.

17

Sanctified Shepherding

WHEN ONE STEPS BACK from the Testaments to view their most common subject matter, one sees their overwhelmingly ethical landscape. Metanarratives, in all their elaborate architecture, can obscure God's message of his intentions and enforcement of a sanctified shepherding creation while expecting the most from humanity, his image-bearing pinnacle of creation. Furthermore, the Messiah's most frequent portrayal in the Old Testament is his humble, righteous obedience while serving as the coregent of God's universal kingdom, precisely the chief end of creation, including humanity—righteous shepherding under the Shepherd. Creation, including humanity, is equipped for this chief end, since it did not become totally depraved at the Fall, since the image of God which was formed within creation is still here, though needless to say, it has degenerated considerably. The natural kingdom still operates generally as created in nature, even to the extent that it still demonstrates the nature of God (Rom 1:19–20) and fulfills its role in the eternal design. God's nature is still seen in humanity, but it is miraculously enhanced wherever the Holy Spirit has regenerated and continues to sanctify the trusting soul. And this sanctification includes the amoral attributes that enhance the human condition since its God-like nature empowers creative, exhilarating, brilliant, productive, and complex endeavors, even in this pathetic parenthetical age.[1]

---

1. McConville captures this element of human potential: "Work and art have in

As we approach the chronological end of this book, I now wrap creation's purposive end of the eternal design back to its origin, back to the shepherding God and his shepherding creation. This study has stressed that God's universal kingdom's eternal design advances from its initial perfect age into this compromising parenthetical age but is perfected again for New Earth. The Messiah's commission had many roles to fill in order to continue moving the parenthetical age toward the eternal Final Testament by providing continued guidance for humanity to assist him in the eternal design by the commandments and encouragements from the first and second Testaments.

God's nature was also an early focus in this study. It is the pattern for creation's derived nature and its history as it is imaged especially by humanity as his primary shepherding stewards. God created the animate natural kingdom to produce offspring after its "kind" (Gen 1:21, 24), just as he produced offspring after his kind. God's nature is purposive and eternal, and it includes several other attributes that comprise his infinitely glorious nature that makes him unique, holy, and thus separate from his finite creation. Humanity, by its godly nature, contributes to the eternal design, and it is most successful when the believers of the trusting kingdom are holistically sanctified by the Holy Spirit in righteousness as well as in the other attributes of God's glorious nature. The Spirit's power recreates a segment of humanity during this crippled parenthetical age to better assist in the shepherding design which God has modeled for all creation. The holiness and glory of God and humanity are the basis of this holistic sanctification, which is this final chapter's central concern.

BIBLICAL INSTRUCTION

The central concern of the Testaments is not the parenthetical age's transactions such as redemption or reconciliation, nor is it the eschaton. Instead, the most consistent testamental concern is the eternal sanctified shepherding of creation and its emulation of God's moral and amoral attributes. Everything else is only a means to that end. The objective is for all of creation to eventually reflect God's nature perfectly again and to

---

common their sense of making real, or discovering, what is implicit or possible within God's creation." After identifying Old Testament terms for wisdom, insight, and knowledge, McConville describes their contribution to creativity: "These together suggest both God-given talent and the disciplines of learning and application, with their outcome in the experience that produces good judgment." McConville, *Being Human*, 179.

engage his eternal design productively. The Spirit inspired the Scriptures and for millennia has personally maintained the trajectory of the eternal design especially by empowering believers to apply the Testaments' principles to oneself and to the rest of creation. The harmonic messianic roles converge on this central matter in the Testaments. The priests were to teach and interpret the covenant law; the prophets were to remind, encourage, and convict by that law; and the judges and kings were to enforce that law. The sages added normative moral and practical aphorisms as guardrails for moral excellence, sometimes paralleling or borrowing from natural law and the human conscience reflected in surrounding cultures, sometimes reinforcing covenantal law but never contradicting it. Together, these sources of ethical expectations, and the historical and prophetic assessment of compliance by the individual or nation, make up at least a plurality of the Old Testament material found in the Torah, history, prophetic, poetic, and wisdom sections. The reason for Israel's chosen status was to advertise to the nations the *shalom* collaboration between humanity and the only God, Israel's God. "If you truly obey my voice and keep my covenant, then you will be my own possession among all the peoples, realizing that all the earth is mine" (Exod 19:5).

This raises a heart-searching question for the believer: what is the primary motivation for righteous and wise conduct—is it primarily to confirm one's eternal life, thus a personal hedonism, itself a sin, or is it because whether there is an eternal life or not, a believer would still be driven to love, trust, and obey God regardless? According to some theologies, this would have been all the Israelites could hope to experience. Believers have always been more concerned with their functional relationship with God right now, which might look forward to the by and by but looks more often and closely to the day by day. And, when they reflect on life properly, they are concerned with their moral and amoral contributions to their current personal successes or failures as well as the concerns of others. One should not think of Paul as extraordinary in his difficult preference to remain and shepherd the believers rather than to be with Christ.

> For me to live is Christ, and to die is gain. If I am to live in the flesh, that means fruitful labor for me . . . . I am convinced and know that I will remain to continue with you all in your progress and joy in the faith. (Phil 1:21–22, 25)

Humanity was not created to obsess on the future; it was created to effectively shepherd the present, yet understandably, with an eye on the future implications of their conduct. This should motivate the renewed believer as it did for Paul. Believers are satisfied to focus on the "already" and to leave any "not yet" for then. Current, comprehensive, sanctified shepherding is God's expectation of his believers in this parenthetical age; the eternal design is more comprehensive than one's justification and eternal life. Both priorities are important but are only the means to continue the routine behavior of acting like God in one's present and eternal life.

Pannenberg is correct in acknowledging that "in Jewish tradition, the hope of God's coming Kingdom was more of an appendix to a piety shaped by the law given by Moses." But as he completes his thought, it is incorrect to contrast Jesus' teaching with that of moral excellence: "With Jesus the eschatological hope itself became the only source of knowledge and guide for living."[2] This is the implication of another future-laden and mistaken identification of Jesus' kingdom message as well as an overpowering distraction by the dialectical kingdom. Rather, both Testaments revealed sanctified obedience to God as his objective for the routine life of the believer, regardless of the nature and timing of creation's eventual utopia. To appear blameless at the judgment is only one impetus for sanctified living. Believers anticipate Christ's return and their resurrection even before then, but the daily and hourly challenge before them appropriately demands their immediate application of their renewed godly attributes to their realm of responsibility.

The following chart shows examples of the continuity of the Testaments on specific expectations for sanctified living:

Standard	Law	Wisdom	Prophets	Christ	Apostles
Adultery	Exod 20:14; Lev 18:20	Prov 22:14; 23:26–28	Jer 23:10; Ezek 33:26	Matt 5:27–28; Mark 7:21	Heb 13:4; Jas 2:11
Prostitution	Lev 19:29; 21:9	Prov 6:26; 23:27	Isa 57:3–4; Hos 4:11	Luke 15:29–30	1 Cor 6:15–16
Homosexuality	Lev 18:22; 20:13				1 Cor 6:9–10; 1 Tim 1:10

---

2. Pannenberg, *Kingdom of God*, 54.

Incest	Lev 18:10; Deut 27:20-23		Ezek 22:10-11		1 Cor 5:1
Gluttony	Deut 21:20	Prov 23:19-21; 28:7		Matt 11:19	Titus 1:12
Drunkenness	Deut 21:20	Prov 20:1; 23:29-35	Isa 5:22; 28:1-3	Luke 12:45-46; 21:34	Rom 13:13; Eph 5:18
Impartial courts	Exod 23:6; Deut 24:17; 27:19	Job 29:12-17; Prov 13:23	Isa 1:23; Lam 3:35-36	Matt 23:23 // Luke 11:42	1 Cor 6:2-5; 1 Tim 5:19
False testimony	Exod 20:16; 23:1-2, 7	Prov 19:5, 9; 21:28	Ezek 22:9	Matt 15:19; Mark 10:19	Acts 5:4-10; 1 Tim 1:10
Care for widows	Exod 22:22-24; Deut 14:29	Job 24:21;	Isa 1:17; Mal 3:5	Mark 12:38-40	Acts 6:1; 1 Tim 5:3
Care for orphans	Deut 16:11, 14; 24:19-21	Job 24:9; Prov 23:10	Jer 22:3; Ezek 22:7		Jas 1:27
Care for handicapped	Lev 19:14; Deut 27:18	Job 29:15		Matt 4:24; 8:5; Luke 13:11	Acts 3:6-8; 14:8-10
Care for the poor	Deut 15:7, 11; 24:14	Job 30:25; Prov 14:21, 31	Isa 3:15; Amos 4:1	Luke 14:13; 18:22	Acts 4:34-35; Jas 2:15-16
Care for servants	Lev 25:39-40; Deut 15:12-14	Prov 31:15; Eccl 7:21-22	Jer 34:8-10		Eph 6:9; Col 4:1;
Withholding wages	Lev 19:13; Deut 24:15	Job 24:10-11	Jer 22:13; Mal 3:5	Matt 20:8-9	1 Tim 6:18; Jas 5:4
Lending	Exod 22:25-26; Deut 23:19	Prov 19:17; 28:8	Ezek 18:8-9; 22:12	Matt 5:42; Luke 6:34-35	
Care for animals	Exod 23:12; Deut 22:6-7	Prov 12:10; 27:23			1 Cor 9:9; 1 Tim 5:18
Respect parents	Lev 19:3; Deut 27:16	Prov 19:26; 28:24		Matt 15:4-6; Mark 7:10	Col 3:20; 2 Tim 3:2
Divorce	Exod 21:10-11; Deut 24:1-4		Jer 3:1; Mal 2:16	Matt 5:31-32; 19:3-8	1 Cor 7:7-8, 15, 39-40
Idolatry	Lev 26:1; Deut 27:15	Job 31:26-28	Hos 8:4-6; Zeph 1:4		1 John 5:21; 1 Pet 4:3

Sorcery	Deut 18:10		Jer 27:9; Mal 3:5		Gal 5:20; Rev 21:8
Lying	Lev 19:11	Prov 4:24; 12:22; 19:22	Isa 59:12–13; Jer 9:5		Col 3:9; 1 Tim 1:10
Coveting	Exod 20:17; Deut 5:21	Job 31:1, 9, 11	Mic 2:2	Mark 7:21–22; Luke 12:13–15	Acts 20:33; 1 Cor 5:10–11
Murder	Lev 24:17; Num 35:30	Job 24:14; Prov 29:10	Jer 22:17; Hos 4:2	Mark 7:21; Luke 18:19–20	1 Tim 1:9–10; 1 Pet 4:15
Slave dealing	Exod 21:16; Deut 24:7				1 Tim 1:10
Stealing	Exod 20:15; Deut 5:19	Job 20:19; 24:2–3	Mic 2:2; Mal 3:8–9	Luke 3:14	Eph 4:28; Titus 2:10
Limit "royal" privilege	Deut 17:14–20	Prov 16:12; 29:4	Jer 22:14–15; Isa 10:1	Matt 23:25–35	1 Pet 5:1–3; 2 Pet 2:2–3

HOLY SPIRIT'S COREGENCY

The New Testament message of the Messiah and his multiple assignments included his priesthood which, according to the law, made him responsible for teaching and interpreting it. And as a king who was under the law and fulfilled it, he was a lawgiver himself who added his own commandments, which he taught and interpreted simultaneously. And as a prophet he confronted Jews and gentiles with the standards and implications of God's and his own commandments. And as the judge he will finally sentence the individual on the basis of those instructive commandments. As the Messiah, he set the table for the infinitely mighty Holy Spirit to continue his role as the Person responsible for the transforming process of the old man reconstructed into the new. In this process the Spirit uses what he inspired: the commandments, wisdom literature, prophets, exemplary biographies, historical narratives, the Gospels, Acts, and the letters. The Spirit's revelatory interests include every subject matter in the Testaments; none should be diminished, but they should be seen as contributing to humanity's thinking like God, loving like God, and shepherding like God, drawing on the power of God to act like him in every way and in the most edifying and productive ways.

Though rarely articulated in the Testaments, the truth is no less potent—God is the Spirit, the Spirit is God (2 Cor 3:17–18; Acts 5:3–4). The Holy Spirit is an equally powerful Person of the Trinity who communicates and activates from within its perfect harmony. So, humanity's disobedience defies not only the authority of the Father and Son but the Spirit as well. Israel frequently resisted the Holy Spirit (Acts 7:51–53), and her constant rebellion personally grieved him (Isa 63:10), and the church does the same, even now (Eph 4:30). As a massive force in God's administration, the Spirit's role has been integral in epochal biblical creations and re-creations, e.g., Gen 1, the procreation of Jesus, the believers' re-creation, and the New Earth's re-creation (Isa 32:14–15). His Old Testament impact was hardly quiet while moving over the surging seas and while inspiring Old Testament revelation, including that of the vigorous prophets. He was the might behind the miracles of Jesus and his apostles, the inspiration behind Jesus' radical pronouncements, the fire behind Pentecost, and the thrust behind the surging church toward a world empire that has molded many nations and their cultures.

The Spirit's power and authority are matched by his love and commitment to the Trinity's eternal design. When the New Testament comments on all three Persons of the Trinity working together in the same text, often it describes the Trinity's shepherding. For example:

> [To those] who are chosen according to the foreknowledge of God the Father, by the sanctifying work of the Spirit, to obey Jesus Christ and be sprinkled with His blood. (1 Pet 1:1–2)

> He who establishes us with you in Christ and anointed us is God, who also sealed us and placed the Spirit in our hearts. (2 Cor 1:21–22)

> May the grace of the Lord Jesus Christ, the love of God, and the fellowship of the Holy Spirit, be with you all. (2 Cor 13:14)

> God has sent the Spirit of His Son into our hearts, crying, "Abba—Father." (Gal 4:6)

> There is one body and one Spirit . . . one Lord, one faith, one baptism, one God and Father of all who is over all and through all and in all. (Eph 4:4–6)

> How much harsher punishment do you think he will deserve who has trampled underfoot the Son of God and has regarded the covenant's blood that sanctified him as unclean, and has insulted the Spirit of grace? (Heb 10:29)

Marginalizing the Spirit, even if in a commendable pursuit of honoring Christ, should be avoided. One should not emphasize the instrumentality of the Passion in order to elevate the Messiah's significance at the expense of God and his Spirit's final goal—the powerful regeneration and sanctification of humanity.[3] After all, salvation by the sanctifying work of the Spirit predated the cross and any eschatological kingdom. Otherwise, the fallen nature of Old Testament humans was ontologically and spiritually superior to the fallen nature of post-Pentecost humans to the extent that an Israelite was capable of pleasing God without the Spirit's regeneration and sanctifying power. Admittedly, this perspective on the Spirit's job description challenges a schedule of salvation history where his work might be postponed to an inaugurated eschatological kingdom. Nonetheless, regardless of one's position on the Holy Spirit's work in the times of the Old Testament, intertestamental, and pre-Passion New Testament, and whether a believer received salvation by a self-generated faith plus obedience or by a Spirit-infused faith that led to obedience, bottom line, the Testaments' expectation was moral shepherding in compliance with God's law and wisdom.

RE-IMAGING AND TRANSFORMATION

Humanity's fall from its initial reflection of God's glory requires its re-glorification by the Spirit's regeneration and renewal.[4]

---

3. Sinclair Ferguson expresses what can be a danger in overemphasizing progressive revelation in biblical theology: "Any biblical theology of the Spirit's work must recognize the progressive and cumulative character of historical revelation. But systematic or logical considerations invite the conclusion that the Spirit's activity in the OT epoch involved personal renewal of a moral and spiritual nature." Ferguson, *Holy Spirit*, 25. This study has assumed an adequate depiction of God as at least a Trinity in the Old Testament. Without rehearsing centuries of debate, C. John Collins is quoted here with an adequate conclusion: "If the Christian doctrine of the Trinity is true, then the referent was present in Genesis 1. This is not the same as claiming that the author or a pious Israelite reader must have been able to see it, only that the narration allows it." Collins, *Genesis 1–4*, 61. I would apply this same logic to the specific regenerating role of the Holy Spirit in the Old Testament, thus rejecting the circuitous reasoning that the Old Testament does not speak of a Trinity because each text considered is not enough in itself to contribute to a cumulative pattern, i.e., a text does not imply the Trinity because it has not been allowed in any other possible instances.

4. For a helpful exegetical review of the image of God, primarily in the New Testament, see Kilner, *Dignity and Destiny*, 60–82.

> We all, seeing the glory of the Lord with unveiled faces, are being transformed into the same image from one degree of glory to another. (2 Cor 3:18)
>
> I am again in the pain of childbirth until Christ is formed in you. (Gal 4:19)
>
> Put on your new nature, which is being renewed to a true knowledge like the image of the One who created it. (Col 3:10)
>
> Imitate God since we are his children. (Eph 5:1)
>
> We know that when he appears we will be like him. (1 John 3:2)

The promise of one's predestination to conformity to the Son's image is a promise to the believer that one will eventually conform to the nature of the Trinity (Rom 8:28).[5] The believer's glory is the objective of one's rebirth and renewal as a new creation, which results in progressing toward the image of God by progressing toward the more tangible image of his incarnate Son. God's ultimate objective is not only to declare sinners as innocent but to renew them for glorified and productive eternal action, including now. This is why sanctification is not mentioned specifically in the *ordo salutis* of Rom 8:29. All stages of salvation fall within the sanctification process. God's foreknowledge and predestination lead to a person's call, which is accepted by a somehow-generated faith to which God responds with justification. This legally sets the believer apart by forensic acquittal and adoption so that faith continues the believer's regeneration in moral and amoral sanctification that culminates in one's ultimate salvation at glorification.

> Those whom he foreknew he predestined to be conformed to the image of his Son.... Those whom he predestined he called, and those he also justified, and those he also glorified. (Rom 8:29–30)

Sanctification is the totality of salvation, and it is the process that Paul was commissioned by Jesus to evangelize. Paul combined components of sanctification, regeneration, renewal, and justification while testifying to Agrippa and when writing to Titus, and the apostles write, sometimes

---

5. Humanity is so like God that people are called "gods" in the Old and New Testament, though the exaggerated metaphor should not be too proudly grasped (Ps 82:6–7; John 10:35; cf. Acts 17:28–29). Thus the sons and daughters of God: Matt 5:9; Rom 8:14, 19; 9:26; Gal 3:26; 4:6; Eph 2:10; 4:20–24; Heb 12:7. But, any concept of becoming gods or part of God even in spite of "union" with Christ is foreign to biblical teaching.

confusingly, about one or more of these components within this temporal and logical series of the Persons' saving roles.

> To *open their eyes* [regeneration] so that they may turn from darkness to light, and from the power of Satan to God, that they may receive *forgiveness of sins* [justification] and an inheritance among those who have been *sanctified* by faith in me. (Acts 26:18)

Paul combines these different separating effects of sanctification in Titus as well.

> [God our savior] saved us not on the basis of works which we did in righteousness, but by his mercy, by the washing of *regeneration and renewing* by the Holy Spirit, whom he poured out upon us richly through Jesus Christ our Savior, so as *justified* by his grace we would be made heirs with the hope of eternal life [glorification]. (Titus 3:5–7)

Holiness is not a synonym for righteousness, though righteousness is included along with all of God's other glorious attributes. So sanctification, separateness, and holiness emphasize something's uniqueness when everything else is merely common and ordinary.[6] The relationship that God wants for his people is where he draws them to be separate *from* this evil age and closer *into* his separate sphere—a sphere that is separate from sin, from one's old man, from darkness and foolishness, and consequently, further into his sphere of glorious attributes.

It has been a basic premise in this study that God's nature determines his actions, that is, God is not righteous because he acts righteously; rather, he acts only righteously because he is righteous by nature. Similarly, the believer is not righteous because one acts righteously, rather one acts righteously because one is righteous by a nature recreated by the Spirit: "We know that no one sins repeatedly when born of God" (1 John 5:18).

---

6. An additional definition of sanctification is the separation of common from uncommon—a separation based primarily on the ceremonial consecration of an otherwise common thing, whether a human, cloth, oil, bowl, etc. More theologically, however, God is uncommonly holy by his nature as the infinite, complete, and perfect God, thus separate from all else which is finite and "common." Therefore, what should have been eternally common was the "goodness" of creation as the finite (thus still separate) representation of God's nature in all reality. However, the Fall separated creation from its intended common goodness, and it became impure, ungodly, and the new "common." In New Earth, all of creation that was cursed and unclean, thus only common, will become uncommonly clean again, radiating God's glory as morally perfect and amorally "good" in all of its finite original pre-Fall meaning.

This new nature reflects the fruits of the Spirit, including love, respect, wisdom, and honesty. God has not only blessed humanity with a static image but has blessed humanity with the means to personally activate God's image by an internal freshness of one's spirit and mind.[7]

> Do not conform to this world, but be transformed by the renewing of your mind. (Rom 12:2)

> Though our body is wasting away, our inner self is renewed day by day. (2 Cor 4:16)

> Anyone in Christ is a new creation since the old things pass away but new things have come. (2 Cor 5:17)

GREATEST WAR

The Lord's exchange with Cain confirms what was already revealed in the Couple—morality is a spiritual battle against sin's desire instigated directly by Satan or by the new and treacherous sinful nature of humanity.

> If you do what is right, you are acceptable. But if you do not do what is right, sin crouches at the door, desiring to control you. So, you must rule over sin. (Gen 4:7)

There is no reference to Satan making Cain do anything. Presumably it was the power of original sin, the "old man" that presented its threat to Cain and Abel. The Lord defines salvation for Cain, namely *trusting* obedience—doing right by one's righteous nature. The alternative to trusting obedience is to surrender to sin's stalking and pouncing assault. Rather than succeeding in the primary commission's instruction to subdue, one loses the battle by moral slackness.

Others in the Testaments were aware of this subdue-or-be-subdued struggle. Realizing the predatory nature of sin, David pleads for the Lord's help against it, and when David fails he sees his own Cain-like scenario.

> Restrain your servant from deliberate sins; do not let them rule over me. (Ps 19:13)

> My iniquities have overtaken me. (Ps 40:12)

---

7. McConville reviews the very subjective human ontology that is not only expressed by "parts" of a person, e.g., heart, soul, mind, spirit, breath, but by the totality, the synergy of these, the "human constitution" that presumes a social context and venue for the outer life of these internal components. McConville, *Being Human*, 47–59.

Ezekiel repeats the ultimatum:

> Turn away from all your sins or they will destroy you. (Ezek 18:30)

Paul reaffirms the zero-sum axiom, reminding the believer who must be the master:

> Do not let sin reign in your body and obey its evil desires.... Sin is not your master anymore. (Rom 6:12, 14)[8]

> Do not be conquered by evil; conquer evil with good. (Rom 12:21)

His encouragement is a call to the lethal violence required for victory in the believer's war with sin:

> So, put to death what is earthly in you. (Col 3:5; cf. Rom 8:13)

For Paul, sanctification is a war of liberation for which the transformed believer has been adequately equipped by God through the strengthening power of the Holy Spirit (Rom 6:12–23). Sanctification is not an occasional border skirmish that will eventually lose steam. Sin is more persistent and pernicious than that. The renewed believer must hold on to the territory of light within rather than allow the darkness to raid and stake its own sinister territory.

Mature believers are not only equipped for the battle, as Paul describes in Eph 6:10–17, but they are practiced, "having trained to distinguish between good and evil" (Heb 5:14). It will be relentlessly debated whether one can resist and reject the regenerative process before justification, but what is not in question is that believers can and must resist sin in one's post-justification sanctification. But God is patient in awaiting the maturation of those hearts surrendered to him. It is a process demanding tenacity with countless responsibilities along the journey:

> Diligently add virtue to your faith, and by virtue add knowledge, and by knowledge add self-control, and by self-control add perseverance, and by perseverance add godliness, and by

---

8. The coregency of God and a person's subjugation of sin and the satanic kingdom is a theme from Cain to Paul and beyond (Gen 4; Rom 6:12). It goes too far to anchor Paul's understanding of "the kingdom God" on the idea of reigning and victory over sin specifically, per Grindheim, "Kingdom of God." Yes, the primary commission requires subjection of sin and Satan, but human reigning requires far more than that, i.e., shepherding one's fallen nature is only a part of all creation.

> godliness add brotherly affection, and by brotherly affection add love. (2 Pet 1:5–7)

In other words, the believer must bear fruit as well as bear arms (John 15:1–5).

Jesus was not distracted from this emphasis on obedience, and his insistence marginalized even hallowed maternal relations in what some might consider harsh responses:

> "The womb that carried you and the breasts that nursed you were blessed!" But he responded, "On the contrary, those who hear the word of God and follow it are to be blessed." (Luke 11:27–28)

> "Your mother and brothers are standing outside, wanting to see you." But he responded and said to them, "My mother and brothers are these who hear God's word and obey." (Luke 8:20–21; also Matt 10:37)

Furthermore, Jesus is quite direct about anyone's self-adulation for their obedience:

> When you do all the things which were commanded you, then say, "We are unworthy slaves; we have done *only* that which we ought to have done." (Luke 17:10)

Sanctification is a command in both Testaments, not optional extra credit. Bluntly stated, "Be separate as God is separate." This does not mean to be only morally unique but unique in all of the godly attributes which form one to be human.

John is particularly concerned with obedience and one's faith. Believers will "keep the commandments of God and the testimony from Jesus" (Rev 12:17). One might be inclined to rush to somehow moderate Jesus and John's unvarnished comments on obedience: "The one who says, 'I have come to know him,' and does not keep his commandments, is a liar'" (1 John 2:4). But John also encourages believers since those who keep the commandments from Jesus are no less than his friends (John 14:15, 21; 15:14).

SYNERGY OF SANCTIFICATION

The Spirit cooperates with the Messiah within the Trinity's coregency over creation. The Spirit also, like the Messiah, enters a coregency with the justified but in one's subsequent sanctification. Like the Father and Son, all of God's attributes apply to the Spirit. As the indwelling Spirit, he has regenerated, renewed, sanctified, and empowered hundreds of millions of believers in the Testaments and around the world. This is accomplished as they reign together over the flesh, contend with the satanic kingdom's destructive intents, and serve as shepherds to their local and global trusting kingdom and to the surrounding terrestrial kingdoms.

So we return now to the synergy of the eternal design as the impetus for the synergy of sanctification: God shepherds his shepherding creation. In his messianic role as King, Jesus confirmed the Old Testament sanctifying moral standards that he supplemented. Furthermore, as the coregent King, he deferred to the Spirit by requesting that his Father send him to convict the world of sin (John 16:8), to multiply the trusting kingdom into a global kingdom, and to continue as the force behind the trusting kingdom and its members' sanctified shepherding (John 6:7–11). The Spirit's commission is within the context of the commissioned Messiah, in whom all things are summed (Eph 1:10). Justification is God's unilateral verdict due to one's Spirit-infused faith and Christ's perfect life and death. However this does not override nor is it synonymous with the equally important affirmation that one's sanctification is due to God and one's synergy founded on this new Spirit-infused nature: "You were washed, you were sanctified, you were justified in the name of the Lord Jesus Christ and by the Spirit of our God" (1 Cor 6:11). Believers are "in Christ" since they are under his merits and lordship within his realm of the trusting kingdom. However, believers are also under the Spirit's lordship when submitting to him by obedience to God's standards.

The believer's moral sanctification forms a new coworker with God, just as the eternal design is a statement of the synergy of God and humanity. The downloaded, God-imaging nature is ready for activation by the believer: "Activate your salvation with fear and trembling, for God works in you to will and to work for his good purposes" (Phil 2:12–13). God the Spirit has worked into the believer's new nature the desire and power to will and to work for God's good purposes. Yet, where exactly do the Testaments provide all of this guidance on what God's grace has provided within the new self? An answer to this might be, "Well, the Spirit has written them on the believer's heart; the Law is no longer needed." In this case the apostles would only have needed to encourage the trusting kingdom to "follow their heart." The forceful exhortations and granular ethical instructions would have been unnecessary.

However, this was not God's estimation of even the believer's renewed heart. So, the majority of the Testaments' contents provides the ethical guidance in their commandments, wise observations, pithy proverbs, exemplary biographies and stories, prophetic and apostolic encouragement and rebukes, parables, poetic prayers, speeches, letters, and visions. And yes, ethical guidance is available from natural revelation and the human conscience where significant portions of the law are already written even in the unbeliever's heart (Rom 2:14–15). All of these revelations describe God's moral expectations derived from his character and judged through his responses. The most substantive and pervasive content of the Testaments is the requirements for sanctification, the recorded human performance, the responses from God, and the further implications of positive or negative performance.

The Spirit empowers the believer by this renewal, which prepares the believer who is now capable for good works synergistically with the Spirit. Trying to be righteous by appearing righteous is the Pharisaic fallacy, but being righteous because of a Spirit-created new nature is commendable (Gal 3:3). This is not the legally imputed righteousness declared by God but the subsequent righteousness that flows from a transformed nature that is now capable of genuine love for, and trust in, God.

This synergy of God or the Spirit with the believer is inseparable in several passages. For example:

> The Shepherd equips the believer: Heb 13:20–21; 2 Pet 1:3; Eph 3:20.
>
> God strengthens the believer: Eph 3:16; 2 Tim 1:7; 2 Thess 2:16–17.
>
> God has installed the desire to do good: 2 Cor 8:16; Phil 2:12–13.
>
> The Spirit guides to righteousness: Gal 5:16.
>
> The Spirit frees the believer: 2 Cor 3:17.
>
> The Spirit allows one to kill bodily sin: Rom 8:13.

REPENTANCE, TRUST, OBEDIENCE

The synergy initiated by the Holy Spirit requires the believer's intentional activation of what the Spirit has already prepared. One enters the kingdom without works, yet one continues in the kingdom with works that are done diligently by faith and obedience. After the Fall, humanity was not fired from the job of shepherding intensively and productively. Moral passivity concedes to the surrounding apathetic moral "spirit," misses the shepherding moment, and becomes complicit in the demise of one's own or another person's life or leads to further cultural dissolution in one's society. The believer's efforts, even exertion, should be from the most informed, purposive, and integrated act of one's will—like God's efforts. Yet, unfortunately, satisfied with mediocrity while standing in the foyer of the kingdom, many believers suffer an "arrival syndrome": once inside the trusting kingdom's door, they begin looking for the most comfortable lounges.

When Jesus pronounced his gospel of his universal kingdom he demanded a particular response: repent and trust in God and his universal reign (Mark 1:15). It was his call to sanctification just as it was God's call throughout the Old Testament.[9] It was his royal command to repent, to "turn" away from sin, to set oneself apart from sin and from the culture around. Separating one's conduct from the remaining "old man" and progressing toward the image of Christ/God is the sanctification implied in Jesus' "gospel of God." To paraphrase, "Separate yourself from sin and trust, *because* the kingdom of God is at hand" shows that the ethical dimension is demanded by the king; kingdom morality is explicit in the kingdom's enhanced presence in the God/man. The Old Testament paradigm to trust God and repent is continued in Jesus' proclamation of the kingdom of God. Jesus' kingdom gospel was not "be saved" but "be sanctified." All of Jesus' subsequent ethical teaching and modeling as well as the apostles' letters are footnotes to Mark 1:14–15, the message of both Testaments. Not only unbelievers were in Jesus' crowds; repent and trust applied equally for those who were already believers since repentance and trust are not an episode leading only to "get into" the trusting kingdom by justification but a process throughout one's spiritual transformation. So Jesus' kingdom gospel was discipleship as well as evangelism.

> God's kindness should lead you to repentance. But your stubborn and unrepentant heart is gathering God's wrath for the day of wrath . . . . . Those who obey the Law will be justified. (Rom 2:4–5, 13)

Yet, again, sanctification is not only moral; it is becoming more mature in every way, in every created attribute, in purposefulness,

---

9. In repentance and rest you will be saved, and in quietness and trust you will be strong. But you were unwilling. (Isa 30:15)
Those who repent will be revived by righteousness. (Isa 1:27)
A Redeemer will come to Zion, and to those who turn from transgression. (Isa 59:20)

willingness, creativity, knowledge, emotion. Paul encourages the believer's moral and amoral experiences: "The kingdom of God is not eating and drinking, but righteousness, peace, and joy, inspired by the Holy Spirit" (Rom 14:17).[10] Though moral sanctification is the most explicit objective in Scripture, there will be astounding restoration of our human potential for amoral transformation as well. Both transformations are required for sanctification and shepherding since they are inseparable. In many amoral ways we will be relieved from the encumbrances of the Eden Curse since the Fall restricted humanity and nature from realizing their full potential. Amoral uniqueness was necessary, and it was instilled in humanity at creation to separate it from the dominion that it was given as chief shepherds under God to help lead creation's history in the eternal design. But the Couple's disobedience resulted in clouded minds, imbalanced emotions, stilted creativity, less energy, finite life, spiritual vulnerability; in other words, there is more to renew than our moral nature.

One's moral and amoral decisions can appear nearly indistinguishable, but a wise decision may not always be a decision based on morality but one of skill, often a choice between goods, not necessarily between good and evil. For example, should a gift be fifty dollars or sixty dollars? This may not be a moral decision; it may be a wisdom decision. In fact a person who conceives every decision as a moral decision will inflict unnecessary anxiety or false guilt on oneself or others. Most decisions are not moral. They are results of one's unique nature and personality, inclinations, giftings, or unique circumstances, responsibilities, and priorities. This is the pleasure of free decisions that will be enjoyed eternally, when there will be no sinful nature or a confused mind to compromise any wise decision.

Certain spiritual *gifts* are examples of amoral reflections of God's nature which he shares with selected believers. Examples of these gifts are given, but the lists are not complete (1 Pet 4:10; Rom 12:6–8; 1 Cor 12:8–10, 28–30). We consider them amoral in that all believers are not morally responsible to exhibit each of them. On the other hand, the spiritual *fruits*, for example in Gal 5:22–23, are profound moral responsibilities expected from all believers. The spiritual gifts, however, are not

---

10. Craig Bartholomew catches the spirit of the comprehensive sanctification that is powered by the transforming Holy Spirit: "As the close link between the Spirit, creation, and recreation suggest, the work of the Spirit in redemption is not to produce religious cranks, but to open up our humanity and to enable us to become what God always and by creation intended us to be: his fully human image-bearers." Bartholomew, "Wisdom Literature," 33.

moral in themselves since all believers do not receive each one, yet they have a moral dimension in that they are to be used generously for the edification or shepherding of the trusting kingdom (1 Cor 12:7; 14:12; Eph 4:11–12). Yet, Paul mentions a few gifts that some have to a great extent in Rom 12:6–8; nevertheless, they should be shown by all believers and thus are close to spiritual fruit. For example, service, encouragement, giving, and mercy are of course to be shown by all, but those especially and spiritually equipped in these regards are held to a higher standard of frequency, quality, and intensity.

All spiritual gifts reveal God's own infinite attributes, and as the diversity in gender reveals the likeness of God (Gen 1:27), so the diversity in gifting reflects his nature. And since these gifts reflect God's nature and edify the trusting kingdom, they were not withheld by the Spirit until the New Testament but were given to various Old Testament believers as well: prophecy, healing, miracles, artistry, courage, physical strength, evangelism, administration, hospitality, discernment, knowledge, and wisdom. Though maybe the ancient believers were unable to identify the Spirit's role in these Old Testament giftings, Walther Eichrodt explains the profound implications of God's equipping a person for the comprehensive responsibilities for being fully human. Though it reads without identifying what the "spirit" (small s) is, Eichrodt describes the breadth of what it means to be human within a holistic biblical theology:

> Hand in hand with this experience of the Spirit's guidance in the present goes *the effort to bring greater and greater areas of life within the scope of its dominion.* Thus political activity, and the whole field of art, whether it be inspired poetry or the many varieties of craftmanship, are subsumed under the operation of the spirit, and any skill in these directions is thankfully venerated as given by it. Here are the very definite beginnings of a systematic understanding of the *whole* of life as proceeding from the power of the spirit, the aim of which is to actualize the will of God in all forms of human existence. To achieve the major goal of becoming a holy people every power and every gift must experience the renewing influence of the spirit.[11]

---

11. Eichrodt, *Theology*, 2:63.

Conclusion

WE BEGAN BY LOOKING at what is common to all of God's creation, and it was proposed that what is common is the perceivable *design* that is patterned after the attributes of God's nature. It is an *eternal* design for all of creation and its eternal history: for all spirits, for all of nature, for self, family, society, and all nations. This eternal pattern envelops all narrower histories that reflect the limited interest of any historian, whether economic history, Asian history, natural history, or salvation history. More specifically, the eternal design is the foundation and context by which the most popular theological matters should be formed: for example, creation and its history, the kingdom of God, the Messiah, eschatology, morality, the new creation, justification, sanctification, and "the gospel." Components like these are contextualized within this design that is reflected throughout the Testaments. Biblical theology focuses on the corrective parenthetical age rather than on the ultimate and eternal objective of that correction. The preference to apply the eternal design to creation from its beginning through eternity and to apply it to the Testaments' significant interests, including the most pervasive, sanctified shepherding, has led to this volume, *Rethinking Biblical Theology*.

THE ETERNAL DESIGN

God has provided the comprehensive, universal design, where the teleological nature of creation and its history has always embraced all creation, time/space, astronomy, and humanity. That universal story is told in terms of God and his Messiah's universal kingdom, which actively shepherds his creation. He blesses his creation in the most significant way by imparting his attributes to all creation including to the spirit and natural kingdoms as these assist his shepherding creation and inevitably reflect his nature. But he was extremely generous with his attributes while creating humanity in his image by giving it similar attributes that render it gloriously separate from the rest of creation.

The Trinity's loving and coordinating nature is seen among itself, and it shares that nature with creation so pervasively that its eternal design is seen in natural revelation as well as in human and natural history—*God shepherds his shepherding creation*. The eternal teleological meaning for creation, then, is to shepherd itself as God shepherds it. God's eternal relationship with his creation is his perpetual blessing of it, even during this parenthetical age when to bless creation requires its deliverance and discipline until it is perfect again in New Earth. Likewise, creation is equipped with God's image to eternally bless itself among its various kingdoms, including this parenthetical age's requirement for deliverance and discipline.

Humanity's relentless search for the purpose to life, to an extent, finds it already in enjoying relatively peaceful lives in families, neighborhoods, and communities. Admittedly, this equilibrium is interrupted by fallen human predators, who, more than most others, hunger for the greatest portions of power and property. Yet, terrestrial kingdoms shepherd their residents with various measures of care rather than creating a literal and perpetual hell on earth for all. However, our race finds it difficult to wrench itself from the hold of the satanic kingdom and all its enticements to prey on other sheep rather than to shepherd them. Nonetheless, more stable cultures have found ways to connect the dots around them and form a communal ethos of mutual support/shepherding. Until New Earth, God's complete attention to his creation brings blessing, deliverance, and discipline directly and indirectly through his sub-kingdoms' shepherding roles.

THE KINGDOM OF GOD

God's universal kingdom and its eternal design have been the central concerns in this study, because all of creation and its history (realm) are subject to these means of his sovereignty (reign). The natures of creation and history are inseparable as codependent thus coexistent. Their natures are comprehensive in that every created entity produces its history regardless of how minute the event may be. So, every single event is historical and integrated in God's boundless awareness and scrutiny. Furthermore, creation and history are eternal, so eschatology is only a relative concept applicable only to this parenthetical age. And due to the cause-effect nature of creation and the history it produces, there is an inherent teleology that passes from creation through the parenthetical age and into everlasting New Earth. Throughout the Testaments, a kingdom structure within God's universal kingdom is composed by the interaction of the coregent messianic kingdom as well as the sub-kingdoms: the heavenly, satanic, natural, terrestrial, trusting, as well as the eventual New Earth kingdom of the Final Testament.

THE MESSIAH'S UNIVERSAL KINGDOM

God shares his universal kingdom with humanity in the reigning incarnate Jesus who is sustaining all of creation and its kingdoms' interactions, both positive and negative. Creation's diverse kingdoms interact now under a modified Trinitarian coregency in God's universal kingdom where the Second Person's rule is merged with a human to guarantee that the shepherding primary commission of Gen 1 is accomplished by a human as the Couple were intended to do. The Messiah announces the arrival of the same universal kingdom yet under a new management arrangement. This did not inaugurate a new eschatological kingdom; it simply continues the universal kingdom toward the completion of the parenthetical age. This new arrangement did not require a parallel kingdom with which God and his Messiah currently struggle. This messianic commission harmoniously incarnated the typical leadership roles of most of humanity's societies: ruling, teaching, adjudicating, healing, interceding, warring, and offering sacrifices for sin. The messianic kingdom is not a one- or two-dimensional hierarchical structure where the Messiah is a royal saving priest; it is a horizontal structure as well as a community and social order that actualizes the eternal design.

Mark 1:14–15 is equally a revelation and a reassurance. As a revelation, we are told that a new phase in history has come. As a reassurance, we are told that still, it is God's universal kingdom, not a revelation of God's delay in his eventual, always successful, sovereign presence in the world. It is a reassurance that the Trinity of the Old Testament and its shepherding of its creation continue in its eternal trajectory through a more visible

Second Person and a better understood Third Person. It is an encouraging pronouncement that his eternal universal kingdom continues now in an intimate, personal incarnation which ends the burdensome ceremonial accoutrements of forgiveness and uncovers the Spirit's role of renewing one's life to be holy and separate as God is holy and separate.

Acts represents Paul's articulated theology, centering on Jesus' message of the kingdom of God and the responsibilities it entailed for humanity (19:8; 20:25; 28:23; 28:30–31). Acts also reveals that the apostolic message was immersed in the context of the intersecting kingdoms under the universal kingdom of God and his Messiah. The apostles' letters encourage believers to navigate their lives under the Spirit's influence, even lordship among the satanic, terrestrial, natural, and trusting kingdoms. These encouragements continue the Testaments' objective for the believer to shepherd oneself, one's trusting community, and the surrounding world.

THE MUTED MESSIAH

However, it appears that those responsible for translating the apostles' writings to a lesser or greater extent mute the Messiah's kingdom gospel and other teachings, preferring a truncated message *about* him and, even then, most often only about his Passion. When Christ's priestly and prophetic words allegedly started to wilt under the overpowering message of his Passion is hard to date. Rather than this unnecessary transition, it has been contended that his teaching and commandments, as well as his general prophetic utterances, were extended not only in the publication of the Gospels but during the apostles' journeys and within their letters. This would be the expectation of the apostles in their faithful commitment to both the Matthean and Lukan "great commissions."

THE SPIRIT'S SANCTIFICATION

To the extent that one discounts the universal kingdom of God, one misses a powerful commission emanating from the Trinity's coregency, particularly, the active work of the Holy Spirit and his sanctifying work. The sovereign Spirit's unique commission was to personally renew the image of God and sanctify the believer morally and amorally. He equips the believer to live a more moral life as well as to live it more wisely and productively by the application of the amoral attributes of God which one is to mirror as well. The divine attributes combine to make God the most effective sovereign shepherd. Likewise, the renewed attributes combine to make the believer a most effective sovereign shepherd. This is a result of sanctification, to attain a glory that does not match yet reflects the glory of the Trinity. The image that God shared perfectly with created humanity, and with his Messiah, is the Testaments' most prevalent message. But this message weight is not restricted to renewal because even if there had been no Fall, so without the need for renewal, the image of God is still required to effectively accomplish the primary commission and its impact on the eternal design forever. One can become an expert in theological and hermeneutical exercises, but it can become an obsession with them at the expense of God's designed interest—the daily practicality of acting like him.

Starting with the biblical meaning of holy, "to be separate," sanctification is not just part of the *ordo salutis*, it *is* the *ordo salutis*. It is both the ultimate objective as well as the only means of achieving that objective. Under the Spirit's power, the believer is separated by the "call," regenerated by the Spirit from rebellion to trust, separated by the legal declaration of perfection in Christ, separated from the unregenerate by adoption by the Father, and perpetually regenerated by the Spirit for progressive separation from this world's degenerate and infectious spirit.

THEOLOGICAL INERTIA

Anyone attempting to describe a predominant biblical theology should expect only to fail. There is no greater diversity in the world of ideas than that found in the world of Christianity, which reveals and revels in its innumerable variations on any theme. Nevertheless, I have chosen in this study to look at the metanarratives of salvation history and the inaugural eschatological kingdom and their narrow perspectives on God's creation and its history. There appears to be a frequent marginalization of God's universal kingdom in deference to a "more urgent" matter that is given center stage—the story of salvation.

No lack of ink has been spent on burrowing deeply into Israel's history and its series of covenant episodes leading to the saving death of the Messiah. However, this has led some to an unnecessary synthesis of fallible Judaism with the infallible Word, resulting in a theory that God

CONCLUSION

initiated a kingdom that is still under construction since he is struggling to someday completely rule it. Israel is the context of this extension from the Old Testament into Judaism's expectations of a realized eschatology which morphs into the New Testament's center as the already-not yet reign of the Messiah. This dialectical kingdom has unintended logical consequences that may in the end compromise the sovereignty of God to which supposedly all subscribe. Judaism's realized eschatology becomes a burden as a theological presupposition of the inaugurated eschatological kingdom. The dialectical kingdom carries the heavy water of yet another misunderstanding of Judaism's Messiah while minimizing God's current absolute and universal sovereignty that is clearly revealed in the Testaments.

Fortunately the laity and church leaders trust in God's universal kingdom daily and know little of, or think seldom of, an inaugural eschatological kingdom. They can see clearly what for some is hidden in plain sight. They depend daily on God's universal kingdom as expressed in Jesus' exemplary prayer. Their hope is not that God's kingdom may eventually come or that his will may be done on earth but that his kingdom authority will bring them food now, forgiveness now, and daily deliverance from temptation and other evils now. In spite of patience for God's answer to this prayer, their trust is not that God will keep trying to meet their needs but that he is currently meeting their needs as his wisdom, love, and mercy guide him.

The eternal design requires vigorous activity from the trusting kingdom now rather than resting in a current status or waiting for some future bliss. God has planned an endless interactive *journey* for humanity and the rest of his creation with him, now and forever. There is never finality or an eternal resolution to God's eternal design and creation's shepherding role within it. Instead, history abounds with an infinite number of exciting roads to unimaginable destinations. Christ came to continue the eternal design, not just to end the parenthetical age. So, the pivotal moment in all history, the eschaton moment, will be when Christ returns a perfected world to the Trinity again. The eternal design's course is toward a grander human history of creative, industrious, and fruitful activity in the eternal new Eden.

The goal of this study has not been to raise lofty philosophical or theological ideas. Quite the opposite: the goal has been to direct biblical theology's attention to the practical and routine activity of the believer. For all of the church's emphasis on the cross and justification by whatever definition it engenders within Christianity's diverse tribes, God's central concern is not that. Rather, it is what has always been his central objective for humanity—being and acting like him. Not believing like him and not flattering him on Sunday while reaching around to pick his back pocket of all his benefits, but to be and act like him—to be unique as he is unique—to be sanctified.

Finally, most history will always be amoral; its comprehensiveness far transcends the parameters of human morality. There is so much more of reality with which to build a comprehensive worldview. Biblical theology will remain in its adolescence as long as its focus is on salvation rather than God's universal kingdom and the extent of its design and its eternal implications. The humanism and hedonism that many Christian leaders should denounce pervades their own theology and "gospel": "How can I get people saved to live forever?" Instead, spiritual maturity asks, "How can I encourage people to be like God and shepherd with him?" Perhaps this is "the gospel"?

Bibliography of Cited Works

Achtemeier, Paul J. *1 Peter*. Philadelphia: Fortress, 1996.
Akin, Daniel L. *1, 2, 3 John*. Nashville: Broadman and Holman, 2001.
Alexander, T. Desmond. *Face to Face with God*. Downers Grove, IL: IVP Academic, 2022.
———. *From Eden to the New Jerusalem: An Introduction to Biblical Theology*. Grand Rapids: Kregel, 2008.
Allison, Dale C. *Constructing Jesus: Memory, Imagination, and History*. Grand Rapids: Baker Academic, 2010.
Atkinson, Kenneth. *An Intertextual Study of Psalms of Solomon: Pseudepigrapha*. Lewiston, NY: Edwin Mellen, 2001.
Attridge, Harold W. *The Epistle to the Hebrews*. Philadelphia: Fortress, 1989.
Arichea, Daniel C., Jr., and Eugene A. Nida. *A Translator's Handbook on Paul's Letter to the Galatians*. Stuttgart: UBS, 1976.
Arnold, Clinton E. *Ephesians*. Grand Rapids: Zondervan, 2010.
Aune, David E. *Revelation*. Vol. 1, *Revelation 1–5*. Dallas: Word, 1997.
———. *Revelation*. Vol. 2, *Revelation 6–16*. Nashville: Thomas Nelson, 1998.
———. *Revelation*. Vol. 3, *Revelation 17–22*. Nashville: Thomas Nelson, 1998.
Barrett, C. K. *The Acts of the Apostles*. 2 vols. Edinburgh: T&T Clark, 1994.
———. *Commentary on the First Epistle to the Corinthians*. New York: Harper & Row, 1968.
———. *Commentary on the Second Epistle to the Corinthians*. New York: Harper & Row, 1973.
Barth, Christoph. *God with Us: A Theological Introduction to the Old Testament*. Grand Rapids: Eerdmans, 1991.
Barth, Markus. *Ephesians 1–3*. Garden City, NY: Doubleday, 1974.
Bartholomew, Craig. "The Wisdom Literature." In *A Biblical Theology of the Holy Spirit*, edited by Trevor J. Burke and Keith Warrington, 24–33. Eugene, OR: Cascade, 2014.
Bateman, Herbert W., IV. "Anticipations of the One Called Son." In *Jesus the Messiah: Tracing the Promises, Expectations, and Coming of Israel's King*, edited by Herbert W. Bateman IV et al., 303–29. Grand Rapids: Kregel, 2012.
Bauer, Walter, et al. *Greek-English Lexicon of the New Testament and Other Early Christian Literature*. 2nd ed. Chicago: University of Chicago Press, 1979.

BIBLIOGRAPHY OF CITED WORKS

Beale, G. K. *1–2 Thessalonians*. Downers Grove, IL: InterVarsity, 2003.
———. *The Book of Revelation*. Grand Rapids: Eerdmans, 1999.
———. *A New Testament Biblical Theology*. Grand Rapids: Baker Academic, 2011.
Beasley-Murray, G. R. *Jesus and the Kingdom of God*. Grand Rapids: Eerdmans, 1986.
———. *John*. Waco, TX: Word, 1999.
Beckwith, Isbon Thaddeus. *The Apocalypse of John*. Grand Rapids: Baker, 1967.
Belleville, Linda L. *2 Corinthians*. Downers Grove, IL: InterVarsity, 1996.
Berkhof, Louis. *Systematic Theology*. Grand Rapids: Eerdmans, 1949.
Best, Ernest. *A Critical and Exegetical Commentary on the Epistle to the Ephesians*. Edinburgh: T&T Clark, 1998.
Bird, Michael F. *Evangelical Theology: A Biblical and Systematic Introduction*. Grand Rapids: Zondervan, 2013.
Black, Matthew. *Romans*. Grand Rapids: Eerdmans, 1973.
Bloch, Marc. *The Historian's Craft*. New York: Knopf, 1953.
Blomberg, Craig. *1 Corinthians*. Grand Rapids: Zondervan, 1995.
———. "Messiah in the New Testament." In *Israel's Messiah in the Bible and the Dead Sea Scrolls*, edited by Richard S. Hess and M. Daniel Carroll R., 111–41. Grand Rapids: Baker, 2003.
Blount, Brian K. *Revelation*. Louisville: Westminster John Knox, 2009.
Bock, Darrell. *Dispensationalism, Israel and the Church: The Search for Definition*. Grand Rapids: Zondervan, 1992.
———. *Mark*. Cambridge: Cambridge University Press, 2015.
———. "Messianic Trajectories in Jeremiah, Ezekiel, and Daniel." In *Jesus the Messiah: Tracing the Promises, Expectations, and Coming of Israel's King*, edited by Herbert W. Bateman IV et al., 169–89. Grand Rapids: Kregel, 2012.
———. *A Theology of Luke–Acts*. Grand Rapids: Zondervan, 2012.
Boda, Mark J. *Zechariah*. Grand Rapids: Eerdmans, 2016.
Boring, M. Eugene. *I and II Thessalonians*. Louisville: Westminster John Knox, 2015.
———. "The Kingdom of God in Mark." In *The Kingdom of God in 20th-Century Interpretation*, edited by Wendell Willis, 131–45. Peabody, MA: Hendrickson, 1987.
———. *Mark: A Commentary*. Louisville: Westminster John Knox, 2006.
Brannon, M. Jeff. *The Heavenlies in Ephesians*. London: T&T Clark, 2011.
Bratcher, R. G. *A Translator's Handbook to Paul's Letters to Timothy and to Titus*. London: UBS, 1983.
Bratcher, R. G., and Eugene A. Nida. *A Translator's Handbook on the Gospel of Mark*. Leiden: Brill, 1961.
———. *A Translator's Handbook on Paul's Letters to the Colossians and to Philemon*. London: UBS, 1977.
Bratcher, R. G., and H. A. Hatton. *A Handbook on the Revelation to John*. London: UBS, 1993.
Bright, John. *The Kingdom of God*. New York: Abingdon, 1953.
Brighton, Louis. *Revelation*. St. Louis: Concordia, 2000.
Brook, A. E. *A Critical and Exegetical Commentary on the Johannine Epistles*. New York: Scribner's Sons, 1912.
Brookins, Timothy A., and Richard N. Longenecker. *1 Corinthians 1–9*. Waco, TX: Baylor University Press, 2016.
Brown, Francis, S. R. Driver, and Charles A. Briggs. *A Hebrew and English Lexicon*. Peabody, MA: Hendrickson, 2012.

BIBLIOGRAPHY OF CITED WORKS

Brown, Raymond E. *The Epistles of John*. New York: Doubleday, 1982.
Bruce, F. F. *1 and 2 Thessalonians*. Grand Rapids: Eerdmans, 1982.
———. *The Book of Acts*. Grand Rapids: Eerdmans, 1988.
———. *The Epistle to the Hebrews*. Grand Rapids: Eerdmans, 1990.
———. *The Epistles to the Colossians, to Philemon, and to the Ephesians*. Grand Rapids: Eerdmans, 1984.
Brueggemann, Walter. *Theology of the Old Testament: Testimony, Dispute, Advocacy*. Minneapolis: Fortress, 2005.
Bultmann, Rudolf. *Theology of the New Testament*. 2 vols. New York: Scribner's, 1965.
Butterfield, Herbert. *Writings on Christianity and History*. New York: Oxford University Press, 1979.
Byrne, Brendon. *Romans*. Collegeville, MN: Liturgical, 1996.
Caird, G. B. *The Language and Imagery of the Bible*. Philadelphia: Westminster, 1980.
———. *New Testament Theology*. Oxford: Clarendon, 1994.
———. *Paul's Letters from Prison: Ephesians, Philippians, Colossians, Philemon*. Oxford: Oxford University Press, 1976.
———. *The Revelation of St. John the Divine*. New York: Harper & Row, 1966.
Campbell, Constantine. *Colossians and Philemon*. Waco, TX: Baylor University Press, 2013.
———. *Paul and the Hope of Glory*. Grand Rapids: Zondervan Academic, 2020.
Carson, D. A. *The Gospel According to John*. Leicester: InterVarsity, 1991.
Casserly, J. V. L. *Toward a Theology of History*. London: Mowbray, 1965.
Charles, R. H. *The Apocrypha and Pseudepigrapha of the Old Testament*. 2 vols. Oxford: Clarendon, 1913.
Chilton, Bruce. *The Kingdom of God in the Teaching of Jesus*. Philadelphia: Fortress, 1984.
———. *Pure Kingdom: Jesus' Vision of God*. Grand Rapids: Eerdmans, 1996.
Chilton, Bruce, and J. I. H. McDonald. *Jesus and the Ethics of the Kingdom*. Grand Rapids: Eerdmans, 1987.
Ciampa, Roy E., and Brian S. Rosner. *The First Epistle to the Corinthians*. Grand Rapids: Eerdmans, 2010.
Clements, R. E. *Prophecy and Covenant*. London: SCM, 1965.
Cockerill, Gareth Lee. *The Epistle to the Hebrews*. Grand Rapids: Eerdmans, 2012.
Collins, Adela Yarbro. *Mark*. Minneapolis: Fortress, 2007.
Collins, C. John. *Genesis 1–4: A Linguistic, Literary, and Theological Commentary*. Phillipsburg, NJ: P&R, 2006.
Collins, John J. "The Kingdom of God in the Apocrypha and Pseudepigrapha." In *The Kingdom of God in 20th-Century Interpretation*, edited by Wendell Willis, 81–95. Peabody, MA: Hendrickson, 1987.
Collins, Raymond F. *1 and 2 Timothy and Titus*. Louisville: Westminster John Knox, 2002.
———. *Second Corinthians*. Grand Rapids: Baker Academic, 2013.
Conzelmann, Hans. *1 Corinthians*. Philadelphia: Fortress, 1975.
Cranfield, C. E. B. *A Critical and Exegetical Commentary on the Epistles to the Romans*. 2 vols. Edinburgh: T&T Clark, 1979.
———. *The Gospel According to St. Mark*. London: Cambridge University Press, 1959.
Dalman, Gustaf. *The Words of Jesus*. Edinburgh: T&T Clark, 1909.
Davids, Peter. *The First Epistle of Peter*. Grand Rapids: Eerdmans, 1990.
De Boer, Martinus C. *Galatians*. Louisville: Westminster John Knox, 2011.

Decker, Rodney G. *Mark 1–8: A Handbook on the Greek Text*. Waco, TX: Baylor University Press, 2014.
Deterding, Paul E. *Colossians*. St. Louis: Concordia, 2003.
Donahue, John R., and Daniel J. Harrington. *The Gospel of Mark*. Collegeville, MN: Liturgical, 2002.
Dungan David L. *The Sayings of Jesus in the Churches of Paul*. Philadelphia: Fortress, 1971.
Dunn, James D. G. *Beginning from Jerusalem: Christianity in the Making*. Grand Rapids: Eerdmans, 2009.
———. *The Epistle to the Galatians*. Peabody, MA: Hendrickson, 1993.
———. *The Epistles to the Colossians and to Philemon*. Grand Rapids: Eerdmans, 1996.
———. "How New Was Paul's Gospel? The Problem of Continuity and Discontinuity." In *Gospel in Paul: Studies on Corinthians, Galatians, and Romans for Richard N. Longenecker*, edited by L. Ann Jervis and Peter Richardson, 367–88. London: Bloomsbury, 1994.
———. *Romans 1–8*. Dallas: Word, 1988.
Edwards, James R. *The Gospel According to Mark*. Grand Rapids: Eerdmans, 2002.
Eichrodt, Walther. *Theology of the Old Testament*. 2 vols. Philadelphia: Westminster, 1967.
Elliot, John H. *1 Peter*. New Haven, CT: Yale University Press, 2001.
Ellingworth, Paul. *The Epistle to the Hebrews*. Grand Rapids: Eerdmans, 1993.
Ellingworth, Paul, and Eugene A. Nida. *A Translator's Handbook on Paul's Letters to the Thessalonians*. New York: UBS, 1975.
Ellingworth, Paul, and H. A. Hatton. *A Handbook on Paul's First Letter to the Corinthians*. London: UBS, 1985.
Fanning, Buist. *Revelation*. Grand Rapids: Zondervan, 2020.
Fee, Gordon. *1 and 2 Timothy, Titus*. Peabody, MA: Hendrickson, 1988.
———. *The First Epistle to the Corinthians*. Grand Rapids: Eerdmans, 2014.
———. *The First and Second Letters to the Thessalonians*. Grand Rapids: Eerdmans, 2009.
———. *Pauline Christology: An Exegetical-Theological Study*. Peabody, MA: Hendrickson, 2007.
———. *Paul's Letter to the Philippians*. Grand Rapids: Eerdmans, 1995.
———. *Revelation*. Eugene, OR: Cascade, 2010.
Ferguson, Sinclair. *The Holy Spirit*. Downers Grove, IL: InterVarsity, 1996.
Fiore, Benjamin. *The Pastoral Epistles*. Collegeville, MN: Liturgical, 2007.
Fitzmyer, Joseph A. *The Acts of the Apostles*. New York: Doubleday, 1998.
———. *The One Who Is to Come*. Grand Rapids: Eerdmans, 2007.
———. *Pauline Theology: A Brief Sketch*. Englewood Cliffs, NJ: Prentice-Hall, 1967.
———. *Romans*. New York: Doubleday, 1993.
Flusser, David. *Jesus*. Jerusalem: Magnus, 1997.
Forbes, Greg W. *1 Peter*. Nashville: B&H, 2014.
France, R. T. *The Gospel of Mark: A Commentary on the Greek Text*. Grand Rapids: Eerdmans, 2002.
Fredericks, Daniel C. "A Question of First Importance." *Bulletin for Biblical Research* 32.2 (2022) 163–81.
———. *Shepherds: The Believer's Outline of Theology*. Eugene, OR: Wipf & Stock, 2017.
Friedrich, Gerhard. "εὐαγγελίζομαι, εὐαγγέλιον, κτλ." In *TDNT* 2:707–37.

———. "κῆρυξ, κηρύσσω, κτλ." In *TDNT* 3:683–718.
Fung, R. Y. K. *The Epistle to the Galatians*. Grand Rapids: Eerdmans, 1988.
Furnish, Victor Paul. *1 Thessalonians, 2 Thessalonians*. Nashville: Abingdon, 2007.
Gardner, Paul. *1 Corinthians*. Grand Rapids: Zondervan, 2018.
Garland, David E. *1 Corinthians*. Edinburgh: T&T Clark, 2003.
Godet, Frederic. *Commentary on St. Paul's First Epistle to the Corinthians*. 2 vols. Edinburgh: T&T Clark, 1886.
Goldingay, John. *Biblical Theology: The God of the Christian Scriptures*. Downers Grove, IL: IVP Academic, 2016.
———. *Do We Need the New Testament? Letting the Old Testament Speak for Itself*. Downers Grove, IL: IVP Academic, 2015.
———. *Old Testament Theology*. 3 vols. Downers Grove, IL: IVP Academic, 2009.
Goldsworthy, Graeme. *According to Plan: The Unfolding Revelation of God in the Bible*. Downers Grove, IL: InterVarsity Press, 1991.
Goppelt, Leonhard. *Theology of the New Testament*. 2 vols. Grand Rapids: Eerdmans, 1981–82.
Gorman, Michael J. *Cruciformity: Paul's Narrative Spirituality of the Cross*. Grand Rapids: Eerdmans, 2021.
Green, Gene L. *1 and 2 Thessalonians*. Grand Rapids: Eerdmans, 2002.
Grindheim, Sigurd. "The Kingdom of God in Romans." *Biblica* 98 (2017) 72–90.
Grudem, Wayne. *1 Peter*. Leicester: IVP, 1988.
———. *Systematic Theology: An Introduction to Biblical Doctrine*. Grand Rapids: Zondervan, 1994.
Guelich, Robert A. *Mark 1—8:26*. Dallas: Word, 1989.
Gundry, Robert H. *Mark: A Commentary on His Apology for the Cross*. Grand Rapids: Eerdmans, 1993.
Guthrie, Donald. *New Testament Theology*. Leicester: InterVarsity, 1981.
———. *The Pastoral Epistles*. Downers Grove, IL: IVP Academic, 1990.
Haas, C. M., et al. *A Translator's Handbook on the Letters of John*. London: SCM, 1972.
Haenchen, Ernst. *The Acts of the Apostles*. Oxford: Basil Blackburn, 1971.
Harrington, Wilfrid J. *Revelation*. Collegeville, MN: Liturgical, 1993.
Harris, Murray J. *The Second Epistle to the Corinthians*. Grand Rapids: Eerdmans, 2005.
Harvey, John D. *A Commentary on Romans*. Grand Rapids: Kregel, 2020.
Hay, David M. *Colossians*. Nashville: Abingdon, 2000.
Headlam, Arthur, and W. Sanday. *A Critical and Exegetical Commentary on the Epistle to the Romans*. Edinburgh: T&T Clark, 1902.
Helyer, Larry R. *Exploring Jewish Literature of the Second Temple Period*. Downers Grove, IL: InterVarsity, 2002.
Hendriksen, William. *1 and 2 Timothy*. Grand Rapids: Baker, 1957.
———. *Exposition of Paul's Epistle to the Romans*. Grand Rapids: Baker, 1980.
Hiebert, D. Edmond. *The Thessalonian Epistles: A Call to Readiness*. Chicago: Moody, 1882.
Hodge, Charles. *Commentary on the Epistle to the Romans*. Grand Rapids: Eerdmans, 1955.
Hoehner, Harold W. *Ephesians*. Edinburgh: T&T Clark, 2002.
Hooker, Morna. *St. Mark*. Peabody, MA: Hendrickson, 1997.
Houlden, J. L. *A Commentary on the Johannine Epistles*. London: A & C Black, 1994.

Hughes, Philip Edgecumbe. *A Commentary on the Epistle to the Hebrews*. Grand Rapids: Eerdmans, 1977.

———. *Revelation*. Grand Rapids: Eerdmans, 1990.

Hult, Adolf. *The Theology of History*. Rock Island, IL: Augustana, 1960.

Jacob, Edmond. *Theology of the Old Testament*. New York: Harper & Brothers, 1958.

Jewett, Robert. *Romans*. Minneapolis: Fortress, 2007.

Jobes Karen H. *1, 2, and 3 John*. Grand Rapids: Zondervan, 2014.

———. *1 Peter*. Grand Rapids: Baker Academic, 2005.

Johnson, Alan F. *1 Corinthians*. Downers Grove, IL: InterVarsity, 2004.

Johnson, Thomas. *1, 2, 3 John*. Peabody, MA: Hendrickson, 1993.

Johnson, Luke Timothy. *Acts of the Apostles*. Collegeville, MN: Liturgical, 1992.

———. *The First and Second Letters to Timothy*. New York: Doubleday, 2001.

Johnston, Gordon H. "Messianic Trajectories in Zechariah." In *Jesus the Messiah: Tracing the Promises, Expectations, and Coming of Israel's King*, edited by Herbert W. Bateman IV et al., 191–209. Grand Rapids: Kregel, 2012.

Keck, Leander. *Romans*. Nashville: Abingdon, 2005.

Keener, Craig. *1–2 Corinthians*. Cambridge: Cambridge University Press, 2005.

———. *Acts: An Exegetical Commentary*. 4 vols. Grand Rapids: Baker Academic, 2012–15.

Kellum, L. Scott. *Acts*. Nashville: B&H, 2020.

Kelly, John N. D. *A Commentary on the Pastoral Epistles*. New York: Harper & Row, 1963.

Kilner, John F. *Dignity and Destiny: Humanity in the Image of God*. Grand Rapids: Eerdmans, 2015.

Kistemaker, Simon. *Exposition of the Acts of the Apostles*. Grand Rapids: Baker Academic, 1990.

———. *James and 1–3 John*. Grand Rapids: Baker Academic, 1986.

———. *Revelation*. Grand Rapids: Baker Academic, 2001.

Kittel, Gerhard. "λέγω, λόγος, κτλ." In *TDNT* 4:69–143.

Kittel, Gerhard, and Gerhard Friedrich, eds. *Theological Dictionary of the New Testament*. Translated by Geoffrey Bromiley. 10 vols. Grand Rapids: Eerdmans, 1964–76.

Knierim, Rolf. *The Task of Old Testament Theology: Method and Cases*. Grand Rapids: Eerdmans, 1995.

Knight, George W. *The Pastoral Epistles*. Grand Rapids: Eerdmans, 1992.

Köstenberger, Andreas. *A Theology of John's Gospel and Letters*. Grand Rapids: Zondervan, 2009.

Kruse, Colin G. *The Letters of John*. Grand Rapids: Eerdmans, 2000.

———. *Paul's Letter to the Romans*. Grand Rapids: Eerdmans, 2012.

Ladd, George E. *A Commentary on the Revelation of John*. Grand Rapids: Eerdmans, 1972.

———. *Pattern of New Testament Truth*. Grand Rapids: Eerdmans, 1968.

———. *The Presence of the Future: The Eschatology of Biblical Realism*. Grand Rapids: Eerdmans, 1974.

———. *A Theology of the New Testament*. Grand Rapids: Eerdmans, 1993.

Lane, William. *Hebrews*. Dallas: Word, 1991.

Larkin, William J. *Acts*. Downers Grove, IL: InterVarsity, 1995.

———. *Ephesians: A Handbook on the Greek Text*. Waco, TX: Baylor University Press, 2009.
Lenski, R. C. H. *The Interpretation of St. Mark's Gospel*. Minneapolis: Augsburg, 1964.
Lieu, Judith M. *I, II, and III John*. Louisville: Westminster John Knox, 2008.
Lightfoot, J. B. *Notes on the Epistles of Paul*. Grand Rapids: Zondervan, 1895.
———. *Saint Paul's Epistles to the Colossians and to Philemon*. Grand Rapids: Zondervan, 1895.
Lincoln, Andrew T. *Ephesians*. Dallas: Word, 1990.
Lockwood, Gregory J. *1 Corinthians*. St. Louis: Concordia, 2000.
Loh, I-Jin, and Eugene A. Nida. *A Translator's Handbook on Paul's Letter to the Philippians*. New York: UBS, 1977.
Longenecker, Richard N. *The Epistle to the Romans*. Grand Rapids: Eerdmans, 2016.
———. *Galatians*. Waco, TX: Word, 1990.
MacDonald, Margaret Y. *Colossians and Ephesians*. Collegeville, MN: Liturgical, 2000.
Maloney, Francis J. *The Gospel of Mark*. Peabody, MA: Hendrickson, 2002.
Mann, C. S. *Mark*. Garden City, NY: Doubleday, 1986.
Maritain, Jacques. *On the Philosophy of History*. Clifton, NJ: A. M. Kelly, 1973.
Marshall, I. Howard. *The Epistles of John*. Grand Rapids: Eerdmans, 1978.
———. *Luke: Historian and Theologian*. Grand Rapids: Zondervan, 1971.
———. *New Testament Theology*. Downers Grove, IL: IVP Academic, 2003.
———. *The Pastoral Epistles*. Edinburgh: T&T Clark, 1999.
Martin, Ralph P. *Colossians: The Church's Lord and the Christian's Liberty*. Grand Rapids: Zondervan, 1972.
Matera, Frank J. *Galatians*. Collegeville, MN: Liturgical, 1992.
———. *New Testament Theology*. Louisville: Westminster John Knox, 2007.
———. *Romans*. Grand Rapids: Baker Academic, 2010.
McCartney, D. G. "*Ecco Homo*: The Coming of the Kingdom as the Restoration of Human Viceregency." *Westminster Theological Journal* 56 (1994) 1–21.
McConville, J. Gordon. *Being Human in God's World: An Old Testament Theology of Humanity*. Grand Rapids: Baker Academic, 2016.
McKnight, Scott. *The King Jesus Gospel: The Original Good News Revisited*. Grand Rapids: Zondervan, 2016.
———. *The Letter to the Colossians*. Grand Rapids: Eerdmans, 2018.
Melick, Richard R., Jr. *Philippians, Colossians, Philemon*. Nashville: B&H, 1991.
Michaels, J. Ramsey. *1 Peter*. Dallas: Word, 1988.
———. *Revelation*. Downers Grove, IL: InterVarsity, 1997.
Middendorf, Michael P. *Romans 1–8*. St. Louis: Concordia, 2013.
Middleton, Richard J. *A New Heaven and a New Earth: Reclaiming Biblical Eschatology*. Grand Rapids: Baker Academic, 2014.
Mitchell, Alan C. *Hebrews*. Collegeville, MN: Liturgical, 2007.
Montanari, Franco. *The Brill Dictionary of Ancient Greek*. Edited by Madeleine Goh et al. Leiden: Brill, 2015.
Moo, Douglas. *The Epistle to the Romans*. Grand Rapids: Eerdmans, 1996.
———. *The Letter to the Romans*. Grand Rapids: Eerdmans, 2018.
———. *The Letters to the Colossians and to Philemon*. Grand Rapids: Eerdmans, 2008.
———. *A Theology of Paul and His Letters: The Gift of the New Realm in Christ*. Grand Rapids: Zondervan Academic, 2021.
Morris, Leon. *The Epistle to the Romans*. Grand Rapids: Eerdmans, 1988.

———. *The First and Second Epistles to the Thessalonians*. Grand Rapids: Eerdmans, 1991.
———. *The First Epistle of Paul to the Corinthians*. Leicester: InterVarsity, 1985.
———. *New Testament Theology*. Grand Rapids: Zondervan, 1986.
Moule, C. F. D. *The Epistles to the Colossians and to Philemon*. Cambridge: Cambridge University Press, 1957.
———. *An Idiom Book of New Testament Greek*. Cambridge: Cambridge University Press, 1959.
Moulton, James Hope. *A Grammar of New Testament Greek*. 5 vols. Edinburgh: T&T Clark, 1963.
Mounce, Robert. *The Book of Revelation*. Grand Rapids: Eerdmans, 1997.
Mounce, William. *Pastoral Epistles*. Nashville: Thomas Nelson, 2000.
Muraoka, T. *A Greek-English Lexicon to the Septuagint*. Louvain: Peeters, 2009.
Murray, John. *The Epistle to the Romans*. 2 vols. Grand Rapids: Eerdmans, 1968.
Newman, B. M., and Eugene A. Nida. *A Translator's Handbook on Paul's Letter to the Romans*. Stuttgart: UBS, 1973.
O'Brien, Peter T. *Colossians, Philemon*. Waco, TX: Word, 1982.
———. *Ephesians*. Grand Rapids: Eerdmans, 1999.
———. *The Epistle to the Philippians*. Grand Rapids: Eerdmans, 1991.
———. *The Letter to the Hebrews*. Grand Rapids: Eerdmans, 2010.
Omanson, R. L., and J. Ellington. *A Handbook on Paul's Second Letter to the Corinthians*. New York: UBS, 1993.
Osborne, Grant. *Revelation*. Grand Rapids: Baker Academic, 2002.
O'Toole, Robert. "The Kingdom of God in Luke–Acts." In *The Kingdom of God in 20th-Century Interpretation*, edited by Wendell Willis, 147–62. Peabody, MA: Hendrickson, 1987.
Painter, John. *1, 2, 3 John*. Collegeville, MN: Liturgical, 2002.
Pannenberg, Wolfhart. *Theology and the Kingdom of God*. Philadelphia: Westminster, 1969.
Pao, David W. *Colossians and Philemon*. Grand Rapids: Zondervan, 2012.
Patrick, Dale. "The Kingdom of God in the Old Testament." In *The Kingdom of God in 20th-Century Interpretation*, edited by Wendell Willis, 67–79. Peabody, MA: Hendrickson, 1987.
Patzia, Arthur. *Ephesians, Colossians, Philippians*. Peabody, MA: Hendrickson, 1990.
Perrin, Nicholas. *Jesus as Priest*. Grand Rapids: Baker Academic, 2018.
Perrin, Norman. *Jesus and the Language of the Kingdom*. Philadelphia: Fortress, 1976.
Pervo, Richard I. *Acts*. Minneapolis: Fortress, 2009.
Peterson, David G. *The Acts of the Apostles*. Grand Rapids: Eerdmans, 2009.
———. *Hebrews*. Downers Grove, IL: IVP Academic, 2020.
Plantinga, Theodore. *Learning to Live with Evil*. Grand Rapids: Eerdmans, 1982.
Plummer, Alfred. *A Critical and Exegetical Commentary on the Second Epistle of Paul to the Corinthians*. Edinburgh: T&T Clark, 1915.
Pokorný, Petr. *Colossians*. Peabody, MA: Hendrickson, 1991.
Polhill, John B. *Acts*. Nashville: Broadman, 1992.
Quinn, Jerome D., and William C. Wacker. *The First and Second Letters to Timothy: A New Translation with Notes and Commentary*. Grand Rapids: Eerdmans, 2000.
Rensberger, David K. *1, 2, 3 John*. Nashville: Abingdon, 1997.
Reumann, John. *Philippians*. New Haven, CT: Yale University Press, 2008.

Richard, Earl. *First and Second Thessalonians*. Collegeville, MN: Liturgical, 1995.
Ridderbos, Herman N. *Paul: An Outline of His Theology*. Grand Rapids: Eerdmans, 1975.
———. *Paul and Jesus: Origin and General Character of Paul's Preaching of Christ*. Grand Rapids: Baker, 1958.
Roberts, J. W. *The Letters of John*. Austin: R. B. Swete, 1968.
Robertson, Archibald, and Alfred A. Plummer. *A Critical and Exegetical Commentary on the First Epistle of Paul to the Corinthians*. Edinburgh: T&T Clark, 1914.
Routledge, Robin. *Old Testament Theology: A Thematic Approach*. Downers Grove, IL: IVP Academic, 2008.
Rutledge, Fleming. *The Crucifixion: Understanding the Death of Jesus Christ*. Grand Rapids: Eerdmans, 2015.
Schnabel, Eckhard J. *Acts*. Grand Rapids: Zondervan, 2012.
Schnackenburg, Rudolf. *The Epistle to the Ephesians*. Edinburgh: T&T Clark, 1991.
———. *God's Rule and Kingdom*. Montreal: Palm, 1963.
———. *The Gospel According to St. John*. 3 vols. New York: Crossroad, 1990.
———. *The Johannine Epistles*. New York: Crossroad, 1992.
Schnelle, Udo. *Theology of the New Testament*. Grand Rapids: Baker Academic, 2007.
Schreiner, Thomas R. *1, 2 Peter, Jude*. Nashville: B&H, 2003.
———. *The King in His Beauty: A Biblical Theology of the Old and New Testaments*. Grand Rapids: Baker Academic, 2013.
———. *New Testament Theology: Magnifying God in Christ*. Downers Grove, IL: Baker Academic, 2008.
———. *Romans*. Grand Rapids: Baker Academic, 1998.
Schuchard, Bruce G. *1–3 John*. St. Louis: Concordia, 2012.
Schweizer, Eduard. *The Good News According to Mark*. Atlanta: John Knox, 1970.
Scobie, Charles. *The Ways of Our God: An Approach to Biblical Theology*. Grand Rapids: Eerdmans, 2003.
Seifrid, Mark A. *2 Corinthians*. Grand Rapids: Eerdmans, 2014.
Seitz, Christopher R. *Colossians*. Grand Rapids: Brazos, 2014.
Shaw, Mark, and Wanjiru M. Gitau. *The Kingdom of God in Africa: A History of African Christianity*. Carlisle: Langham Global Library, 2020.
Shogren, Gary S. *1 and 2 Thessalonians*. Grand Rapids: Zondervan, 2012.
Silva, Moises, ed. *New International Dictionary of New Testament Theology and Exegesis*. 5 vols. 2nd ed. Grand Rapids: Zondervan, 2014.
Smalley, Stephen S. *1, 2, 3 John*. Nashville: Thomas Nelson, 1984.
Smith, D. Moody. *First, Second, and Third John*. Louisville: John Knox, 1991.
Snodgrass, Klyne. *Ephesians*. Grand Rapids: Zondervan, 2009.
Soards, Marion L., and Darrell J. Pursiful. *Galatians*. Macon, GA: Smyth & Helwys, 2015.
Spencer, F. Scott. *Luke*. Grand Rapids: Eerdmans, 2019.
Stein, Robert H. *Mark*. Grand Rapids: Baker Academic, 2008.
Stoeckhardt, Georg. *Commentary on Ephesians*. St. Louis: Concordia, 1987.
Strathmann, Hermann. "μάρτυς, μαρτυρέω, κτλ." In *TDNT* 4:474–514.
Strauss, Mark L. *Mark*. Grand Rapids: Zondervan, 2014.
Strecker, Georg. *The Johannine Letters*. Minneapolis: Fortress, 1996.
Stuhlmacher, Peter. *Paul's Letter to the Romans*. Louisville: Westminster John Knox, 1994.
Sumney, Jerry L. *Colossians*. Louisville: Westminster John Knox, 2008.

Taylor, Mark. *1 Corinthians*. Nashville: B&H, 2014.
Thielman, Frank. *Ephesians*. Grand Rapids: Baker Academic, 2010.
———. *Theology of the New Testament*. Grand Rapids: Zondervan, 2005.
Thiselton, Anthony C. *The First Epistle to the Corinthians*. Grand Rapids: Eerdmans, 2000.
Thompson, Marianne Meye. *1–3 John*. Downers Grove, IL: InterVarsity, 1992.
———. *Colossians and Philemon*. Grand Rapids: Eerdmans, 2005.
Towner, Philip H. *The Letters to Timothy and Titus*. Grand Rapids: Eerdmans, 2006.
Trafton, Joseph L. "What Would David Do? Messianic Expectation and Surprise in Ps. Sol. 17." In *The Psalms of Solomon: Language, History, Theology*, edited by Eberhard Bons and Patrick Pouchelle, 155–74. Atlanta: SBL, 2015.
Viviano, B. T. "The Kingdom of God in the Qumran Literature." In *The Kingdom of God in 20th-Century Interpretation*, edited by Wendell Willis, 87–107. Peabody, MA: Hendrickson, 1987.
Voelz, James W. *Mark 1:1—8:26*. St. Louis: Concordia, 2013.
Von Balthasar, Hans Urs. *A Theology of History*. New York: Sheed and Ward, 1963.
Vos, Geerhardus. *Biblical Theology: Old and New Testaments*. Grand Rapids: Eerdmans, 1948.
Wall, Robert. *Colossians and Philemon*. Downers Grove, IL: InterVarsity, 1993.
Wall, Robert, and Richard B. Steele. *1 and 2 Timothy, Titus*. Grand Rapids: Eerdmans, 2012.
Wallace, Daniel B. *Greek Grammar Beyond the Basics: An Exegetical Syntax of the New Testament*. Grand Rapids: Zondervan, 1996.
Waltke, Bruce. *An Old Testament Theology: A Canonical and Thematic Approach*. Grand Rapids: Zondervan, 2006.
Walton, John. *Old Testament Theology for Christians*. Downers Grove, IL: InterVarsity, 2017.
Wanamaker, Charles A. *The Epistles to the Thessalonians: A Commentary on the Greek Text*. Grand Rapids: Eerdmans, 1990.
Ward, Ronald. *Commentary on 1 and 2 Timothy and Titus*. Waco, TX: Word, 1974.
Weima, Jeffrey A. D. *1–2 Thessalonians*. Grand Rapids: Baker Academic, 2014.
Wenham, David. *Paul: Follower of Jesus or Founder of Christianity?* Grand Rapids: Eerdmans, 1995.
Wenham, Gordon J. *Genesis 1–15*. Nashville: Nelson, 1987.
Westcott, B. F. *The Epistles of St. John*. Grand Rapids: Eerdmans, 1957.
Wheelwright, Phillip. *Metaphor and Reality*. Bloomington: Indiana University Press, 1962.
Williams, David J. *Acts*. Peabody, MA: Hendrickson, 1990.
Williams, Joel F. *Mark*. Nashville: B&H Academic, 2020.
Wilson, Robert. *Colossians and Philemon*. London: T&T Clark, 2005.
Witherington, Ben, III. *The Acts of the Apostles: A Socio-Rhetorical Commentary*. Grand Rapids: Eerdmans, 1998.
———. *Conflict and Community in Corinth*. Grand Rapids: Eerdmans, 1995.
———. *The Gospel of Mark: A Socio-Rhetorical Commentary*. Grand Rapids: Eerdmans, 2001.
———. *The Indelible Image*. Downers Grove, IL: IVP, 2009.
———. *Jesus, Paul, and the End of the World*. Downers Grove, IL: InterVarsity, 1992.
———. *Paul's Letter to the Romans*. Grand Rapids: Eerdmans, 2004.

Wright, Christopher J. H. *Mission of God: Unlocking the Bible's Grand Narrative*. Downers Grove, IL: IVP Academic, 2006.
Wright, N. T. *The Climax of the Covenant*. Minneapolis: Fortress, 1992.
———. *The Epistles of St. Paul to the Colossians and to Philemon*. Grand Rapids: Eerdmans, 1986.
———. *Jesus and the Victory of God*. Minneapolis: Fortress, 1996.
Wright, Robert B. *The Psalms of Solomon: A Critical Edition of the Greek Text*. New York: T&T Clark, 2007.
———. "The Psalms of Solomon: A New Translation and Introduction." In *The Old Testament Pseudepigrapha*, edited by James H. Charlesworth, 2:639–70. Peabody, MA: Hendrickson, 1983.
Wuest, K. S. *Romans in the Greek New Testament*. Grand Rapids: Eerdmans, 1955.
Yarborough, Robert W. *1–3 John*. Grand Rapids: Baker Academic, 2008.
Zimmerli, Walther. *Old Testament Theology in Outline*. Atlanta: John Knox, 1978.

Scripture Index

OLD TESTAMENT

Genesis

	88, 94
1	38, 326, 327n3
1–11	232
1–14	80
1:17–18	79
1:21	321
1:21–22	78
1:22	38
1:24	321
1:26	37n9, 46
1:26–28	35, 78, 148
1:27	337
1:28	37n9, 81, 88, 142, 148, 175
3:4–6	175
3:8	246
3:8–9	221
3:15	78, 175, 236
4	331n8
4:7	330
4:17–22	82
9:9–17	78
9:16	91
11:8–9	81n36
12:1–2	81n36
12:3	130, 191
12:6–7	81n36
14:18–20	112
16:7–13	72n13
18:1–14	72n13
18:18	130, 191
19:1	73n20
19:15–22	73n20
21:17–18	72n13
21–22	185
22:10–18	73n20
22:18	130, 191
24:5–7	73n20
24:40	73n20
26:4	191
28:14	191
32:1–2	73n20
48:15–16	32n4
49:24	32n4
49:25	30

Exodus

3:7–8	81n36
6:2–3	238
8:19	146n36
9:29	68n3
14:19	73n19
14:21–22	124
15:3	292
15:18	71n8
18:4	30
19:5	69n4, 190, 322
19:6	85, 219, 291
20:11	42, 68n2
20:14	114, 122, 323
20:15	115, 122, 325

Exodus (cont.)

20:16	114, 122, 324
20:17	114, 122, 325
21:10–11	114, 122, 324
21:16	325
22:22–24	114, 122, 324
22:25–26	114, 324
22:26–27	122
23:1–2	324
23:6	114, 122, 324
23:7	324
23:8	122
23:9	122
23:12	324
23:20–23	72n13, 73n19
24:40	72n13
32:34	73n19
34:6–7	32

Leviticus

8:10–11	42
10:8–11	104, 113
18:10	122, 324
18:20	323
18:22	323
19:2	42
19:3	324
19:6	42
19:11	122, 325
19:13	114, 122, 324
19:14	114, 324
19:18	114
19:23–25	150, 289
19:29	114, 122, 323
19:35–36	122
20:13	323
21:9	323
24:17	115, 122, 325
25:39–40	122, 324
26:1	122, 324

Numbers

5:29–30	116n37
5:29–31	104
6:22–26	104
12:13–16	124
20:14–16	73n19
27:16–18	32n4
35:30	325

Deuteronomy

2:5	81n36
2:9	81n36
2:12	81n36
2:19–21	81n36
4:6–7	90
4:19	79
4:35	187n2
4:39	187n2
4:39–40	191
5:19	122, 325
5:21	325
7:6	42
10:14	68n3
14:29	324
15:7	114, 122, 324
15:11	114, 324
15:12–14	324
16:11	122, 324
16:14	324
17:8–10	116
17:8–12	104
17:14–20	115, 122, 325
18:10	122
18:15	121
18:18	121
18:19	325
19:15–19	104, 116n37
19:17	116
20:1–4	104
21:1–5	104
21:5	116
21:20	114, 122, 324
22:6–7	324
23:1–5	116n37
23:19	324
24:1–4	324
24:7	325
24:8	104, 113n30
24:14	324
24:15	324
24:17	324
24:19–21	324

27:14–26	104, 113n30
27:15	324
27:16	324
27:18	324
27:19	324
27:20–23	324
31:9–12	104, 113n30
32:8	81n36
33:2	72n10
33:8–10	104, 113n30
33:10	113

Joshua

1:2–4	81n36
3:10	81n36
5:13–15	73n19

1 Samuel

2:6	74
2:9–10	187
28:11–15	74

Judges

6:11–21	72n13
13:2–21	72n13

2 Samuel

6:13–18	104
7:10	81n36
7:12–16	121n43
7:13	168n16
7:14	121n43
8:18	104
15:2–6	104
24:13–15	73n22
24:25	104

1 Kings

17:14	124
17:17–24	124
19:4–8	73n20
22:17	32n4

2 Kings

2:8	124
2:11	74n25
2:14	124
4:4	124
4:34	124
4:43	124
5:1	70
5:10–14	124
6:15–17	73n19
19:15	81n34
19:35	73

1 Chronicles

15:27	104
16:23–26	187n2
16:24	191
16:26	191
21:11–14	73n22
21:28	104
28:5	132
29:11	68, 132

2 Chronicles

6:33	191
17:7–9	113n30
18:16	32n5
19:8	116n37
20:6	81n34, 191
29:19	215n16

Nehemiah

8:1–3	113
9:6	72n11

Esther

3:6	215, 215n16
3:8	215
4:14	215

Job

	74n26
1:6	72n11
2:1	72n11

Job (cont.)

14:12	74n25
19:25–27	74n25
20:19	325
24:2–3	325
24:10–11	324
24:14	325
24:21	324
24:29	324
26:7	78
29:12–17	324
29:15	324
30:25	324
31:1	325
31:9	325
31:11	325
31:26–28	324
34:13	70n6
37–41	38
38	79
38:4–12	68n2
38:6–7	72n11
38:19–38	68n2
38:33	39, 78
38:41	78
41:11	68

Psalms

	88
2	81, 96n1, 178, 317
2:6	111n25
2:7–8	309, 318
2:7–9	123
2:8	136, 152
2:9	124, 317
2:10–12	130
2:12	124, 317
5:2	70
6:2–3	126
8	78
8:3–4	68n2
8:4–6	44
8:5–6	36
8:6	81
8:6–8	148
10:16	70n6, 71n8
16:9–11	74n25

19:1	26, 68n2
19:13	330
19:16	38
22:7	84n40
22:26	74n25
22:28	68, 81n34
22:28–29	132
24:1	68n3, 81
28:9	32n4
33:5	78
33:6	68n2
33:11	234
33:20	30
34:7	73n20
35:6	73n20
40:12	330
41:12	74n25
45:6–7	106
46:5	147
46:10	84n40
47:2	69, 71
47:6–7	71
47:7	69
47:8	69n4
49:7	119
49:15	74n25
50:6	119
50:10–12	68n3
51:16–17	115, 290
52:14	119
53:3–9	119
60:6–8	81n36
61:4–8	74n25
66:3–4	84n40
66:7	81n34
67:1–3	191
67:4	222
68:17	72n10
68:30–32	84n40
72	81, 96n1
72:2–4	110n24, 125
72:4	125, 317
72:8	136, 152
72:12–14	110n24, 128
72:16–17	317
72:17	84n40, 130
73:24–26	74n25
74:12	147

75:9–10	74n25	115:16	81, 148
77:20	32n4	115:17–18	74n25
78:52	32n4	119:76	32n4
78:71–72	32n4	121:1–2	30
79:10	192	121:2	68n2
79:11–13	32n4	124:8	30, 68n2
80:1–3	32n4	126:1–3	192
82:6	75n28	126:2–3	84n40
82:6–7	328n5	134:3	68n2
86:9	81n36, 84n40	135:6	70n6
89:5–7	72n11	135:10–13	81n36
89:11	68	136:5–9	68n2
90:2	68n2	136:7–9	79
91:11	73n20	136:9	38
93:1	68n2	145:1–2	74n25
94:10	222	145:9	78
95:3–5	68n3	145:10–11	68n2
95:6–7	40	145:11–13	132
95:7	32n4	145:21	84n40
96:10–13	80n33	147:4	68n2
96:11–13	92	148:1–2	72n11
97:1	69n4	148:11–13	192
97:8	136n11	148:11–14	84n40
98:7–9	80n33		
99:1	69n4	**Proverbs**	
99:6–9	136n11	3:19–20	68n2
100:3	32n4	4:24	325
102:21–22	84n40	6:26	323
103:17–19	71	8:15	187
103:19	69, 132, 219	8:22–29	68n2
103:20	72n11	10:25	74n25
104	78, 80	12:10	324
104:5	59, 68n2	12:19	74n25
104:19–20	68n2	12:22	325
107:41	32n4	13:23	324
110	81, 96n1, 202	14:21	324
110:1	107:41, 111, 111n27, 180, 202, 309, 315	14:31	324
		14:32	74n25
		15:24	74n25
110:1–2	111, 140n21	16:12	325
110:1–4	103, 289	19:5	324
110:2	85, 111n25, 147	19:9	324
110:4	85, 112, 252	19:17	324
110:5	111	19:22	325
110:5–6	124	19:26	324
114:2	69n4, 132	20:1	324
115:9–11	30	21:1	187
115:15	68n2		

Proverbs (cont.)

21:28	74n25, 324
22:14	323
23:10	324
23:19–21	324
23:26–28	323
23:27	323
23:29–35	324
25:1	103
27:23	324
28:7	324
28:8	324
28:24	324
29:4	325
29:10	325
31:1	103
31:15	324

Ecclesiastes

1:4	59
2:24–25	179
7:21–22	324
8:2–5	83
8:11	83
11:5	68n2
12:9–12	103

Isaiah

	88, 91, 275, 276
1:17	122, 324
1:23	122, 324
1:25–26	84n39
1:27	335n9
2:4	84n40
3:15	122, 324
4:3–4	84n39
5:22	122, 324
5:23	122
6:3	43, 72n11
9	96n1
9:1–2	317
9:6	106, 108, 141
9:7	110, 111n25
9:9–10	110
10:1	325
11	96n1
11:1	111
11:1–3	80n33
11:2	110n21
11:2–3	110n22
11:4	110n21, 110n24, 125, 317
11:5	110n22
11:6	80
11:6–9	80n33, 91
11:8	80
12:4–5	84n40
12:6	147
14:12–14	175
14:12–19	236
14:14	236n18
14:26	243
19:20–25	84n40
24:16	109
24:22–23	69n4
25:1	234
25:6	84n40
25:6–9	69n4
25:8	74n25
26:19	74n25
27:1	69n4
28:1–3	324
30:15	162, 335n9
32:14–15	326
32:15–16	84n39
35:1–2	80n33
35:9	91
37:16	68n2
37:20	187n2, 191
40:8 LXX	275
40:9	32
40:9–11	32n4
40:11	32
40:15	187
40:17	187
40:22–24	187
40:25	109
40:26	68n2
42	81, 96n1
42:1	111, 111n26, 125, 317, 318
42:1–4	84n40, 112
42:3–4	110n23
42:6	111n26, 130

42:6-7	128, 317, 318	55:22	80n33
42:10-12	84n40	56:6-7	84n40
43:6-7	27	56:11	32n5
44:28	81n35	57:3-4	122, 323
45:1-3	81n35	59:12-13	122, 325
45:18	68n2	59:20	335n9
45:22-26	84n40	60:7	84n40
46:9-10	234	60:20	91n45
48:9	27	61:1	110n24, 149, 312n6
48:13	68n2	61:1-2	96, 123n46, 128
49	81, 96n1	61:2	110n24
49:1-6	112	61:5-7	84n40
49:5	111, 111n26	63:10	326
49:5-6	108	63:11	32n4
49:6	130	64:9	294
49:6-7	317, 318	65:17	91
49:7	111, 111n26, 137, 152, 317	65:17-18	92
49:9	32n4	65:17-25	80n33
50	96n1	65:25	91
50:4	123, 129	66:1-2	68
50:4-5	111	66:18-19	84n40
50:4-9	112	66:22	91
50:5	110n22, 112		
50:5-7	110n23	**Jeremiah**	
50:7	314	1:5	81, 192
50:7-8a	111n26	2:8	32n5
50:9	111n26, 125	2:26-28	113
50:11	125	3:1	122, 324
50:52-53	112	3:15	315
51:3	80n33	3:15-16	32n4
51:3-4	91	3:17	84n40
52	81	8:1-2	113
52:13—53:12	84n39	9:5	325
52-53	96n1	10:7	81n34, 215n16
53	119, 285, 299	10:10	81n34
53:4-12	312n6	10:21	32n5
53:6	32n4	11:3	122
53:6-12	318	12:10	32n5
53:7-9	110n23	13:11	27
53:7-12	98	14:9	147
53:8	130	17:14-16	32n4
53:9	110n21	22:3	122, 324
53:10	111	22:13	122, 324
53:11	109, 110, 130	22:14-15	122, 325
53:12	111	22:17	122, 325
55:3-5	84n40	23	96n1
55:12-13	91		

Jeremiah (cont.)

23:1	32n5
23:1–2	110
23:3	110
23:3–4	32n4
23:5	110, 111n25
23:5–6	110, 130
23:6	110n21
23:10	122, 323
25:31	32n5, 83
25:34	32n5, 83
27:9	122, 325
30	96n1
30:8–9	111n25, 130
31:10	32n4
31:31–32	84n39
33	96n1
33:2	68n2
33:15	111n25
33:15–16	110, 110n21
33:17–18	118
33:20	38, 79
34:8–10	122, 324
50:6	32n5
50:17–19	32n4, 32n5
50:44	32n4
51:15–16	68n2

Lamentations

3:35–36	324

Ezekiel

7:10	113
18:7	122
18:8–9	324
18:30	331
20:14	27
21	96n1
21:25–27	111n25
22:7	324
22:9	122, 324
22:10–11	122, 324
22:12	324
22:26	113
23:24	32, 32n4
28:11–19	72, 77
33:26	323
34	96n1
34:2–8	32n5
34:5	32n4
34:11–16	32n4
34:20–21	32n5
34:23	32n4
34:23–24	111n25
34:24	141
34:28	91
34:31	32n4
36:22–23	27
36:25–26	84n39
36:30	80n33
37	96n1
37:23–24	84n39
37:24	193
37:24–25	111n25
37:24–26	32n4
44:15	104
44:23	104, 113n30
44:24	104, 116

Daniel

	88, 132
2:20–21	81n35
2:37–45	81n35
2:44	69n4, 81n34, 136, 136n12, 152
3:28	73n20
4:3	70n6, 71n8, 132, 137
4:13	73n18
4:17	68, 73n18, 81, 215n17
4:23	73n18
4:34	71n8, 137
5:18	81n35
5:21	69n4, 81n34, 81n35, 215n17
6:22	73n20
6:26	137
7	81, 96n1, 314n7
7:10	72, 72n10
7:12–22	81n35
7:13	111
7:13–14	88, 108, 108n20, 123n45, 168n16, 178, 314

7:14	88, 89, 111n25, 137, 152, 314	**Obadiah**	
7:16	73n14	21	235
7:18	88, 148		
7:21–22	88	**Micah**	
7:22	88n4, 148	2:2	122, 325
7:27	84n40, 87, 88, 148	2:12	32n4
8:16	72n12	4:1–5	84n40
9	96n1	4:3	84
9:1	215n16	4:8	32n4
9:4–6	294	5	81, 96n1, 106
9:21	72n12	5:2	107:41, 111n25, 112, 309, 318
9:21–23	73n14		
9:23	141	5:2–4	32n4, 134
10:5–21	73n14	5:3	108
10:12–13	73	5:4	111, 111n26, 112, 137, 152
10:13	72		
10:20–21	73	6:7–8	115, 195, 290
11:9	215n16		
12:1	72n12, 73n19	**Habakkuk**	
12:2	74n25	2:14	84n40
12:13	74n25		
		Zephaniah	
Hosea		1:4	113, 324
2:18	38, 78	2:11	84n40
2:21–22	80n33	3:4	113
2:28	80n33	3:5	147
3	96n1	3:9	84n40
4:1–6	104, 113n30	3:15	147
4:2	325	3:17	147
4:11	323		
6:6	290	**Haggai**	
8:4–6	122, 324	2:11–13	113n30
11:9	147	2:21–23	81n35
12:7	122		
		Zechariah	
Joel		1:9–11	73n14
2:27	147	1:10–11	73n18
		1:19	73n14
Amos		2:5	147
4:1	324	3	96n1
4:13	68n2	3:1–8	77
5:8	68n2	3:7–8	118
7:2–3	294	3:9–10	130
9:6	68n2	6	96n1

Zechariah (cont.)

6:7	73n14, 73n18
6:11	111n25
6:12–13	103, 112–13, 117, 252, 289
6:13	111n25
8:20–22	84n40
9	81, 96n1
9:10	136, 152
9:16	32n4
10:2	32n4
11:4–7	32n4
11:5	32n5
11:8–9	32n5
11:17	32n5
12	96n1
12:1	68n2
13:7	32n4
14:7	91n45
14:9	235
14:11	92
14:16	84n40
25:10–11	147

Malachi

1:11	84n40
2:4–8	104
2:7	113
2:8	113
2:16	324
3	96n1
3:1–4	118
3:3	125
3:5	125, 324, 325
3:8	113n31
3:8–9	325

APOCRYPHA AND PSEUDEPIGRAPHA

Wisdom of Solomon

6:1–3	69
10:10	132

1 Enoch

9:4	69, 133
9:5	69, 133
84:2	69, 133
84:3	69, 133

Assumption of Moses

9:6	69, 133
10:1	69, 133
10:7	69, 133

Psalms of Solomon

	133
2:34	70
5:10–13	70
5:18	132
5:21	70
6:7–8	196n5
17	133, 134
17:3	70
17:4	70, 133
17:5	133
17:51	70, 133
18:1	70
18:3	70
18:5	70

NEW TESTAMENT

Matthew

	88, 301
1:1	120n42
1:2–16	108
1:6	120n42, 145n33
1:16–17	120n42
1:20	120n42
1:20–21	312, 314
1:21	140n21
2:4–6	145n33
2:6	32n6, 110
2:41–45	107:41
3:1	308
3:1–2	311
3:12	125
4:5–6	73n21

4:7	76	11:19	114, 324
4:8–9	172	11:25	70, 112
4:8–10	173	11:27	139, 152
4:10	76	11:28–30	129
4:11	73n21	12:6	104
4:17	146, 308, 311	12:6–8	117m40
4:23	310, 324	12:7	115
4:24	114	12:11	32n6
5:4	253	12:11–12	115
5:5	36, 148	12:15–18	310
5:9	328n5	12:15–21	112
5:10–11	253	12:22–23	120n42
5:16	87	12:28	146
5:17–48	116	12:28–30	173
5:20	214	12:29	77, 172
5:20–48	291	12:30	173
5:23–25	115	12:38–40	119n41
5:27–28	114, 323	12:41	104
5:31–32	114, 324	12:42	104
5:34–35	70	13:19	311
5:35	112	13:31–32	148
5:42	114, 324	13:33	148
5:44–45	84	13:35	145n34
5:46–47	82	13:37–42	73n23
6:9–13	244	13:37–43	173
6:10	72, 230	13:40–43	140
6:11	244	13:41	138n14
6:12	244	13:41–43	218
6:13	244	13:43	91n45, 140n19
6:26–30	78	13:44–46	147
6:33	147	13:49–50	73n23, 173
6:34	129	13:57	123
7:21	214	14:25	124
7:28	260n14	14:28	124
8:5	324	14:32	124
8:26	124	14:33	106
9:27	120n42	15:1–9	290
9:35	146, 310	15:4–6	324
9:36	32n6, 111, 129, 149	15:11–20	253
		15:19	114, 324
10:7	146, 311	15:22	120n42
10:10	253	15:24	32n6, 193
10:28–31	129	16:12	259
10:37	332	16:13–14	123n48
11:3	97	16:15–16	97
11:4–5	96	16:16	96, 98
11:5	128	16:20	97
11:11	147	16:21–23	119n41, 285n89

Scripture Index

Matthew (cont.)

16:22–23	96
16:28	140n19
17:9–12	120n41
17:22–23	119n41, 285n89
17:25–27	83n38
18:3	214
18:10	74n24
18:12–14	32n6
18:23–35	147
18:34–35	125, 140n21
19:3–8	324
19:23–24	214
20:1–16	147
20:8–9	114, 324
20:17–19	120n41, 285n89
20:21	148
20:25–28	173
20:28	26, 119, 120n41
20:30–31	120n42
21:9	120n42
21:15	120n42
21:31	148
21:33–43	233n12
21:36–39	120n41
21:37–39	300
21:43	201, 203
21:46	123n48
22:2–13	148
22:21	83n38, 173
22:41–42	120n42
22:41–45	202n15
23:13	148, 214
23:23	114, 115, 290, 324
23:25–35	115, 325
24:3–36	174
24:14	311
24:30	178
24:35	59n2, 260n14, 276
25:1–13	148
25:31–32	32n6
25:31–40	174
25:32	125
25:34	36, 88n4, 93, 145n34, 148, 183
26:1–4	120n41
26:12	120n41
26:24	120n41
26:25–32	120n41
26:28	119
26:29	140n19
26:31–32	120n41
26:32	285n89
26:51–53	174
26:52–53	72
26:61	120n41, 285n89
26:63–65	107:41
27:11	125n50, 174
27:29	174
27:37	174
27:42	174
27:46	112
27:54	106
28:2	73
28:2–8	175
28:5–7	73n17
28:18	89, 116, 139, 145n31, 152
28:18–19	81n34
28:18–20	35, 175, 300, 314
28:19	192

Mark

	290
1:1	270, 278, 279
1:4	162, 253, 308, 318
1:7	310
1:13	73n21
1:14–15	136, 144, 145, 161, 162, 262, 308, 311, 316, 335, 340
1:15	143n26, 152, 167, 216n21, 315, 335
1:22	260n14
1:23–28	145
1:24	172
1:32–39	172
1:38	102
2	128
2:26–28	115
2:28	117m40
3:1–6	115
3:11	106
3:23–26	173

4:2	260n14	14:25	148
4:26	148	14:27	32n6, 120n41
4:30–32	148	14:47	174
4:41	78	14:58	120n41, 285n89
6:12	308	14:61–62	97, 172
6:15	123n48, 193	15:2	174
6:34	32n6	15:4–6	114
7:5–13	290	15:12	174
7:10	324	15:18	174
7:10–12	115–16	15:26	174
7:13	116, 252	15:32	174
7:15–23	253	16:2–6	175
7:21	115, 323, 325	16:5–7	73n17
7:21–22	114, 325	17:63	285n89
8:27–28	123n48		
8:28	193		
8:29	96, 97		

Luke

8:29–31	115n25, 117, 299, 314		135, 154, 159, 254, 317
8:31	120n41, 285n89, 317	1:1–4	252
		1:3	158, 158n3
8:31–32	285n89	1:6	158
8:34	120n41, 285n89	1:11–14	73n16
8:38	125, 260n14	1:13	73
9:30–32	120n41, 285n89	1:18–20	73
9:31	299, 317	1:19	72n12, 73n16
9:31–32	119n41	1:26	72n12
9:47	214	1:26–36	73n16
10:15	214	1:27	120n42
10:19	324	1:32	120n42, 310
10:23–25	148, 214	1:32–33	145n33, 168n16, 218, 310
10:32–35	120n41, 285n89		
10:42–45	173	1:33	137
10:45	26, 119	1:68	140n20
11:17	307	1:69	120n42
11:18	260n14	1:77	140n21
11:27–33	285n89	2:4	120n42
12:1–12	120n41, 285n89	2:9–12	73n16
12:9	201	2:10–11	312
12:17	83n38, 173	2:11	120n42
12:31	114	2:32	130
12:35–37	107:41, 202n15, 309	2:49	112
		3:3	162, 308, 318
12:38	307	3:14	115, 325
12:38–40	114, 324	3:15	97
13:3–37	174	3:15–18	316
13:31	59n2, 260n14, 276	3:23–38	108
14:22–25	253	4:5–7	172

SCRIPTURE INDEX

Luke (cont.)

4:6–8	173
4:9–10	73n21
4:12–43	155
4:16–30	123n46
4:18–19	128
4:32	260n14
4:34	109, 172
4:41	97
4:43	102, 135, 154, 155, 159
4:43–44	193, 311
5:47	260n14
6:1–2	115
6:5	117m40
6:20	136, 155
6:27	89
6:32–33	82
6:34–35	324
7:14–15	124
7:16	123n48
7:22	96, 310
7:28	136, 147, 155
7:50	282
8:1	136, 155, 159, 311
8:10	159
8:20–21	332
8:28	77
8:48	282
8:54–55	124
9:2	136, 146, 155, 311
9:8	123n48
9:11	136, 146, 155, 159
9:18–19	123n48
9:20	96, 97
9:20–22	314
9:21–22	119n41, 285n89
9:26	260n14
9:43–45	120n41, 285n89
9:60	310
10:1	77
10:5	282
10:7	253
10:9–11	136, 155
10:17–19	175
10:17–20	172
10:18	172, 236
10:39	260n14
11:2–4	244
11:18	74
11:18–20	173
11:20	136, 155
11:21–22	172
11:27	106
11:27–28	332
11:32	259
11:42	324
11:52	148
12:8–9	74n24
12:13–15	325
12:22–31	129
12:31–32	136, 155
12:32	87
12:37	26, 30
12:42–44	88n4
12:45–46	114, 324
12:51–52	173
13:11	324
13:18	148
13:20	148
13:28–29	148
13:29	130
13:32–33	120n41, 285n89
13:33	123
14:13	114, 324
15:4–7	32n6
15:29–30	114, 323
16:16	136, 155, 311
17:10	332
17:20–21	15n8, 136, 145, 146, 155, 200, 200n12
17:21	146
18:17	214
18:19–20	325
18:22	324
18:24–25	214
18:29	136, 155
18:31–34	120n41, 285n89, 314, 315
18:38–39	120n42
19:8	159
19:11	136, 155
19:11–13	200
19:16–17	200

SCRIPTURE INDEX

19:38	162	1:19	259
20:16	201	1:19–20	318
20:25	83n38, 159, 173	1:19–27	318
20:41–44	120n42, 202n15	1:20–25	123
21:7–36	174	1:29	98, 119, 318
21:31	136, 155	1:30	104, 318
21:33	59n2, 260n14, 276	1:34	318
21:34	324	1:34–36	318
22:19	253	1:36	98, 119
22:19–20	119	1:41	96, 98
22:29–39	140n19	1:43–44	124
22:30	136, 155	1:45	98
22:42	112, 184	1:49	98
22:43	73n21	2:19	120n41, 285n89
22:49–51	174	2:19–22	117
22:66–71	108	2:22	120n41
22:69	111n27, 145n32	3:14	120n41, 285n89
23:2	102, 174	3:16	90
23:2–3	162	3:16–17	125
23:3	174	3:17	116, 125, 294
23:37–38	162, 174	3:32–33	260n14
23:42	136, 155	3:35	137, 145n31, 152
23:43	74	4:19	123n48
24:1–6	175	4:23–26	96
24:4–7	73n17	4:25	305
24:6–7	315	4:25–26	97, 98, 121
24:7–8	260n14	4:42	130
24:10–11	315	4:44	123
24:19	123n48, 294	5:13	128
24:23	73n17	5:19	83
24:25–26	120n41	5:22–27	125
24:25–27	317	5:24	260, 260n14
24:32	305n4	5:36	259
24:36	282	5:38	260n14
24:44	260n14	5:47	260n14
24::46–47	155	6:7–11	333
24:46–47	154, 155, 299, 301, 318	6:14	124
		6:26–59	318
24:47	162	6:27	318
28:23	158, 159	6:29	318
28:31	158, 158n3, 159	6:29–59	318
		6:32–33	318
John		6:33	318
	290	6:38	112, 112n28
1:7–8	305n4	6:40	318
1:15	106, 318	6:44	318
1:18	305n4	6:51	318
		6:53	318

SCRIPTURE INDEX

John (cont.)

Reference	Pages
6:54	318
6:57	318
6:58	318
6:59	318
6:68–69	317
6:69	109
7:16–17	260n14
7:25–27	98
7:27–28	311
7:31	98
7:40–41	124
7:41–42	98, 145n33
8:1–8	116n38
8:12	130
8:14	260n14
8:17	259
8:26	123
8:58	106
9:17	123n48
9:30–38	128
9:39	125
10:1–29	32n6
10:11	110
10:24	98
10:27–29	140n21
10:30	106n16
10:35	328n5
10:35–36	75n28
11:27	97
11:47–48	175
12:6–8	120n41
12:7–8	285n89
12:27	102
12:31	74, 77, 172
12:31–32	84
12:31–34	175, 176
12:32	130
12:32–34	120n41, 285n89
12:32–36	200n13
12:34	98, 108
12:38	259
12:46	130
12:47–48	260n14
12:48	260
13:3	139, 152
13:17	285n89
13:33	120n41, 285n89
14	256
14:1–4	129
14:10	123
14:15	260n14, 332
14:16–19	129
14:21	260n14, 332
14:23–24	260n14
14:25	120n41, 285n89
14:26	129, 255
14:28	112, 112n28
14:29	120n41, 285n89
14:30	74
14:30–31	176
14:31	111
15:1–5	332
15:7	260n14
15:10	260n14
15:12	260n14
15:14	332
15:14–15	86
15:19	89
16	256
16:1	78
16:7–11	178
16:8	333
16:8–10	130
16:11	74, 172
16:12–14	255
16:15	139, 152, 164
16:25	305n4
16:33	176, 282
17	291, 292
17:2	139, 145n31, 152
17:4	112, 112n28
17:5	30n3
17:10	139, 152
17:11–15	129
17:20–23	282
17:22	27
17:24	106n16
18:10–11	174
18:19	260n14
18:32	260n14
18:36	72n9, 140n19
18:36–37	174
18:37	102, 121, 172, 305n4

SCRIPTURE INDEX

19:10–15	174	3:24	313
19:11	72n9, 81, 178	3:25	314
19:12	102, 188	3:26	112, 313
19:19	174	4:1–2	308
20:9	26	4:7	176
20:12	73n17	4:8–12	314
20:12–13	26	4:24	68n2
20:17	112	4:26–28	178
20:28	106	4:27	42, 109, 112
20:30	129	4:29–30	176
20:30–31	149	4:30	109, 112
21:13	30	4:33	309
21:15–17	32n6, 166	4:34–35	324
21:24	259	5:3–4	326
21:25	129	5:3–10	176
		5:4–10	324
		5:12–16	176
		5:28–32	315

Acts

	98, 135, 154, 159, 160, 162m13, 162, 163, 172, 177, 181, 193, 194, 202, 251, 264, 275, 286, 313, 325	5:29–31	178
		5:31	145n32, 292
		5:42	97, 100, 155, 312, 313
		6:1	324
		6:8	176
1	64	7:35	73n15
1:3	136, 153, 154, 155, 159, 201	7:38	73n15
		7:51–53	326
1:6–8	178, 201	7:52	109
1:8	154, 155	7:53	73n15
1:11	72	7:55–56	111n27
2:1–12	178	7:56	145n32
2:22–36	315	8:5	283n88
2:22–40	315	8:5–7	314
2:31	97, 155	8:6–7	176
2:33	145n32	8:12	136, 155, 159, 162, 163n14, 314
2:37–40	315		
2:41	259	8:12–13	176
2:42	259	8:25	275
3:6–7	176	8:25–28	264
3:6–8	324	8:32	119
3:12–26	313	8:32–35	308
3:13	112, 313	8:35	283n88
3:14	109	9:20	283n88
3:15	314	9:20–22	310
3:19	314	9:22	97, 100, 155, 312, 313
3:20	97, 155, 313		
3:21	178, 314	9:34	176
3:22	121	9:40–41	176

373

Acts (cont.)

10:9–15	301
10:34	317
10:34–36	81n34
10:34–43	317
10:36	138, 145n31, 282, 301, 317
10:36–37	253
10:38	176
10:42	125n50, 317
10:43	81n34, 317
11:13–14	309
11:16	275
11:20	283n88
12:20–23	81
12:21–23	73, 179
12:24	261n16
13:10	176
13:10–11	176
13:12	264, 265
13:22–23	120n42
13:29–34	317
13:30–31	299
13:38–39	317
13:44	264, 273n68, 275
13:46–48	177
13:47	130
13:49	264, 273n68, 275
14	177
14:3	167, 307
14:8–10	324
14:11–17	179
14:14–15	68n2
14:14:22	313
14:15–17	180
14:16–17	84, 223
14:17	79
14:21–22	156n2, 157
14:22	136, 155, 181
15:10	115, 117, 150, 290
15:14	140
15:16	120n42
15:17	140n20
15:19–21	115
15:28–29	290
15:35	264, 273n68, 275
15:36	264, 273n68, 275
16:18	176
16:32	264, 275
17	177, 183
17:1–3	100
17:2–3	312, 313
17:3	97, 155
17:6–7	125n50
17:7	162
17:16	180
17:18	179
17:18–19	319
17:22–31	179
17:24	70
17:26	69n4, 81n36
17:27–28	15
17:28–29	328n5
17:30–31	319
17:31	125, 125n50, 140n21
18:2–5	100
18:5	97, 100, 155, 313
18:28	97, 100, 155, 313
19:8	136, 155, 156, 156n2, 162, 181, 286n90, 305, 311, 313, 341
19:10	264, 273n68, 275
20	165
20:18–35	167
20:20	167
20:20–21	315
20:21	167, 307
20:24	160, 167, 306, 315
20:24–25	161n9
20:24–27	315
20:25	136, 155, 156, 156n2, 158, 160, 161, 162, 163n14, 166, 181, 305, 313, 315, 341
20:25–28	165, 286n90
20:27	30, 63, 164, 184, 234, 306, 315
20:28	167
20:28–29	32n6, 315
20:32	88n4, 161n9, 166, 167, 306, 315
20:33	325

374

SCRIPTURE INDEX

20:35	253, 275
22:14	109
22:18	259
23:2–5	301
23:4–5	118
24:25	307
26:17	192
26:18	176, 329
26:20–23	318
26:22–23	305
26:23	130
26:26	318
27	177
27:22–24	179
28:23	155, 156, 156n2, 160n8, 162, 163n14, 181, 286n90, 305, 341
28:23–28	203, 313
28:28	203
28:30–31	154, 155, 156, 181, 198, 305, 313, 341
28:31	135, 154, 155, 156n2, 160, 162, 283n88, 286n90, 313
28–31	167
28:32	156
32	167
33	167
34	167
35	167

Romans

1	182, 183
1:1	254n2, 262
1:1–5	316
1:3	258n9
1:3–4	316
1:4	42, 248
1:5	316
1:9	258n9, 273, 278, 310
1:9–10	269, 284
1:16	308
1:18–32	180, 181
1:19–20	45, 179, 320
1:19–21	243
1:20	26
1:21–32	179
1:22–23	79
1:23	181
2:4–5	335
2:7	47
2:13	335
2:14–15	82, 334
2:14–16	181
2:15–16	180
2:16	125, 140n21, 259, 274n69, 311
4:17	68n2
5:17	89
6:12	331, 331n8
6:12–23	331
6:14	331
8:13	331, 334
8:14	328n5
8:16–17	88n4
8:17	148
8:18	91
8:18–20	180, 182
8:18–22	91
8:19	328n5
8:20–22	80
8:25–28	78
8:28	328
8:29	328
8:29–30	328
8:34	117, 145n32, 292
8:37–39	87, 180, 182
9:5	106, 139, 145n31
9:17	177
9:26	328n5
9:27	283n88
10:8–13	316
10:8–17	316
10:14–15	233
10:14–16	316
10:17	267, 273
11:13	81, 192
11:36	27, 68, 68n2
12:2	330
12:6–8	336, 337
12:14–15	253
12:21	331

Romans (cont.)

13:1	83
13:1–2	81n35
13:1–7	180, 182
13:3–7	83
13:6–7	83
13:13	324
14:9	125n50
14:9–11	145n31
14:14	253
14:17	158, 286n90, 336
15:16	258n9, 263
15:19	258n9, 269, 278, 284
15:25	259
16:20	76, 78, 89, 175, 180, 182
16:25	273, 274, 278
16:25–26	268, 285, 307
17:24–25	84

1 Corinthians

	139n17, 157
1:5–6	268, 284
1:6	257n6
1:6–8	180
1:12–13	180
1:18	308
1:20–24	181, 182
1:21	313
1:21–23	313
1:21–27	49
1:22–23	300
1:23	313
2:1	262, 313
2:1–2	313
2:4	259, 274
2:6–8	177, 183
2:6–10	150
2:12–13	177, 183
3:18–20	183
3:21–23	148
3:22–23	88n4
4:8	88
4:9	74n24, 177, 183
4:17	305n4

4:20	139n17, 157, 199, 286n90, 313
5:1	324
5:2–3	88
5:5	77
5:10–11	325
6	213
6:2–3	76
6:2–5	324
6:9	36, 148, 313
6:9–10	88n4, 139n17, 157, 199, 286n90, 323
6:10	313
6:11	333
6:15–16	323
7:7–8	324
7:15	324
7:39–40	324
8:4–6	181
8:6	27, 68n2, 68n3
9	213
9:9	324
9:11	278
9:12	269, 279, 284
9:14	253
9:16	305, 312
10	213
10:19	181
10:26	68n3
11:2	252n1
11:10	74n24
11:23–25	253
11:26	309
12:7	337
12:8	110n21
12:8–10	336
12:28–30	336
14:12	337
14:37	253
15	135
15:1	305n3
15:1–15	309
15:1–58	313
15:3	252n1, 297, 298
15:3–4	297
15:4–8	299
15:23–24	77n31

15:24	157, 199, 286n90	**Galatians**	
15:24–25	3	1:4	56, 75n27
15:24–28	125n50, 139n17, 183	1:7	269, 284
		1:15–16	310
15:27	138, 152	1:16	192
15:28	60	1:23	305n4
15:49–50	158	2:11	305n3
15:50	36, 88n4, 139n17, 148, 199, 213, 286n90	3:3	334
		3:8	309
		3:19	73n15
		3:26	328n5
2 Corinthians		4:6	326, 328n5
1:19	310	4:7	88n4
1:21–22	326	4:19	328
2:12	278, 279	5	213
2:12–13	269	5:11	309
3:12–13	284	5:16	334
3:17	334	5:20	325
3:17–18	326	5:21	36, 88n4, 139n17, 148, 157, 199
3:18	328		
4:3	274n69	5:22–23	336
4:3–4	183	6:10	89
4:4	42, 66, 75n28	21	213
4:4–5	310		
4:16	330	**Ephesians**	
4:31	259		167
5:8	74	1	165
5:10	125	1:7–10	150
5:17	330	1:7–14	315
5:19	309	1:8–10	163, 164, 165
5:21	109	1:8–12	183
6:14–15	87	1:9–10	145, 164, 184
8:16	334	1:9–11	315
9:13	269, 284	1:10	125n50, 164, 333
10:4–6	181, 183	1:10–11	145n34
10:14	257, 258, 260, 261n15, 269, 284	1:11	88n4, 234
		1:13	75n27
11:7	263, 305n3	1:15	168
12:1	253	1:20	111n27, 117, 145n32
12:2–3	74n26		
12:4	74	1:20–21	138, 168n16
12:7	77	1:20–22	125n50, 145n31
13:14	326	1:22	138, 152
19:8–10	104	1:22–23	86, 183
		2:1	184
		2:1–10	183
		2:2	74

Ephesians (cont.)

2:6	86
2:10	328n5
2:12–18	168
2:14–16	86, 306n5
2:17	282
2:19	86, 158
3	165
3:2	145n34
3:8	307
3:8–11	164–65, 180
3:8–16	184
3:9	68n2, 69n4
3:9–11	145n34
3:10	177
3:10–11	102
3:16	334
3:20	334
4:1–16	168
4:4–6	326
4:11	32n6
4:11–12	337
4:19	168
4:20–21	252n1
4:20–23	307
4:20–24	328n5
4:22	168
4:25–29	168
4:26	168
4:27	89
4:28	168, 325
4:29	168
4:30	326
4:31—5:2	168
4:31–32	168
5:1	45, 86, 103, 328
5:3	168
5:4	168
5:5	36, 88n4, 140, 148, 157, 168, 199, 286n90
5:18	168, 324
5:18–20	168
5:21	168
5:22–33	168
5:23	140n21
5:29–33	86
6:1–3	168
6:4	115, 168, 252, 273n67
6:5–8	168
6:9	168, 324
6:10–17	331
6:11–12	87, 184
6:12	56, 77
6:15	306n5, 307
6:18	168
6:23	86

Colossians

	139n17
1:2	86
1:12	88n4
1:13	75n27, 86, 125n50, 139n17, 199, 286n90
1:13–14	158
1:13–20	184
1:15–20	316
1:15–23	316
1:16	81n34, 106, 145n31, 152
1:16–17	164
1:16–20	125n50
1:17	138, 139, 218
1:21–23	316
1:28	305
2:2	150
2:6–7	252n1, 306
2:8	87
2:8–10	181, 184
2:9	106
2:10	81n34, 145n31
2:15	76
2:16–17	290
2:18–23	181, 184
3:1	117, 145n32
3:5	331
3:9	325
3:10	328
3:11	164
3:15	111n27
3:16	138, 267, 281
3:20	324
3:24	88n4

4:1	324
4:11	86, 139n17, 157, 199, 286n90

1 Thessalonians

	272
1:5	259, 274n69
1:8	267, 273
2:2	263
2:8	263
2:9–10	263
2:11–12	158
2:12	139n17, 199
3:2	270, 273, 278, 279, 284
3:6	307
3:11	140n21
4:2	253
4:15	253, 272–73

2 Thessalonians

	272
1:4	283n88
1:5	139n17, 199
1:7	72n11
1:7–8	270, 284
1:7–9	73n23
1:8	273
2:14	259, 274n69
2:15	252n1, 306
2:16–17	140n21, 334
3:1	267, 273

1 Timothy

1:1	140n21
1:3–4	181, 184
1:9–10	325
1:10	323, 324, 325
1:11	42
1:17	71n8
1:20	77
2:1–2	180, 185, 243
2:3	140n21
2:5–7	319
3:6	78
3:15	86
3:16	177
4:7	181, 184
4:10	140n21
5:3	324
5:18	253, 324
5:19	324
5:21	74n24, 177
6:2	307
6:3–4	268, 273
6:13	68n2, 177
6:14	157
6:15	125n50
6:15–16	140
6:18	324

2 Timothy

1:7	334
1:8	257n6, 268, 273, 284
1:8–11	309
1:10	64, 140n21
2:8	259, 274n69
2:8–10	317
2:10–12	88n4
2:11–12	89
2:15	305n4
3:2	324
4:1	125n50, 286n90
4:1–2	157, 307, 311
4:8	157
4:18	74, 286n90

Philippians

1:21–22	322
1:23–24	74
1:25	322
1:27	270, 284
2	246, 302
2:1–11	299
2:3–7	299
2:6	141
2:6–11	125n50
2:7–8	109
2:8–11	112, 138n15, 184
2:9–10	145n31
2:10	138

Philippians (cont.)

2:12–13	184, 333, 334
2:16	309
2:25	86
3:20	86, 140n21, 184
3:20–21	184
3:21	145n31
4:11	283n88

Titus

1:3	140n21
1:4	86, 140n21
1:12	324
2:10	140n21, 325
2:13	89, 140n21, 157
2:14	140
3:1	83
3:4	140n21
3:5–7	329

Hebrews

	88, 101n12, 195
1:1–4	152, 186
1:3	65, 111n27, 131, 138, 145n32, 218
1:7	73n23
1:8	106, 139
1:8–13	152
1:9	109
1:13	111n27, 145n32, 186
1:15	73
2:1–10	152
2:2	73n15
2:3–4	309
2:5	186
2:6–9	241
2:8–10	186
2:10	27, 68n2
2:14	77, 77n31, 102
2:14–15	110
2:17	102
3:1–2	111, 317, 318
3:4	68n2
3:6	86, 317
4:13	20
4:14	109
4:14–15	318
4:18	117
5:12–13	307
5:14	331
6:1	270
7:11	112
7:12	118, 150, 290
7:14	118
7:22–23	117m39
7:25	292
8:1	111n27, 145n32, 152, 186
8:2	68n2
8:4–6	117m39
9:11	68n2
9:24	68n2, 117
10:12	152, 186
10:12–13	111n27, 145n32
10:12–18	318
10:13	152
10:14	150, 290
10:29	326
11:3	68n2
12:2	111n27, 145n32, 152, 186, 302
12:6	126
12:7	328n5
12:22–24	72
12:23	125, 140n21
12:24	117m39
12:28	88n4
13:4	323
13:20	32
13:20–21	334

James

1:17–18	68n2
1:18	305n4
1:27	324
2:5	88n4
2:11	323
2:15–16	324
2:19	77
2:23	86
3:5–8	51
3:7	36

4:4	83	2:9–13	186
4:7	87, 89	2:11	72n11
5:4	324	2:12	78
		3:2	253, 259

1 Peter

		3:5	68n2
	276	3:7	80n32
1:1–2	326	3:7–10	91
1:10–11	150	3:10	80n32
1:10–12	308	3:10–13	80n33
1:20	145n34	3:12	80n32
1:20–21	150		
1:24–25	258, 275	## 1 John	
1:25	259, 270, 278	1:5	306
2:9	306	2:1	292
2:9–10	85, 140n20	2:4	332
2:13–14	83, 186	2:4–5	260n14
2:25	32, 32n6	2:14	87
3:21–22	111n27, 138, 145n31, 145n32, 186	2:16–17	185
		2:17	80n33
		2:18	77
4:3	324	2:20	109
4:6	306	2:22	77
4:10	336	3:2	86, 328
4:11	125n50	3:8	77, 102, 172, 185
4:15	325	3:11	307
4:17	263	4:3	77, 185
4:19	68n2	4:14	90, 318
5:1	308	5:9	262, 265
5:1–3	325	5:9–11	318
5:2–4	32n6	5:18	329
5:4	32	5:19	74
5:8	75	5:21	324
5:9	86, 89		
5:12	167, 307	## 2 John	
		7	77, 185

2 Peter

		9	115, 252, 265
1:3	334	13	86
1:5–7	332		
1:11	168n16	## Jude	
1:16–17	309	1:6	77
2:2–3	325	1:14–15	72n10
2:4	77	1:25	71, 292
2:4–5	186	6–10	186
2:4–15	186		

Revelation

	58, 73n14, 80, 94, 185, 188, 238, 265
1:2	257n6, 265, 274
1:4	237, 238
1:5	81n34, 138, 185, 238
1:5–6	125n50
1:6	85, 148, 185, 291
1:8	237, 238
1:9	266, 274
1:9–10	257n6
1:13	108n20
2:14–15	259
2:26	88, 148
2:26–27	185
3:5	74n24
3:8	260n14
3:11	185
3:12	112, 140
3:21	88n4, 185
4:8	42
4:11	68, 68n2
4:18	237, 237n21, 238
5:9–10	185
5:10	88n4, 90, 148
10:5–6	68n2
11:7	259
11:15	140, 168n16, 237, 310
11:15–17	238
11:17	237, 238
12:1–12	236
12:4	77
12:5	32n6
12:7–9	185
12:9	77n31
12:10	140, 236, 310
12:11	259
12:17	257n6, 266, 274, 275, 332
13:8	145n34
14:6	265
14:6–7	81n34, 192, 307, 311
14:7	68n2, 69
14:14	108n20
14:14–20	73n23
16:1–21	73n23
17:12–14	77n31
17:14	81n34, 125n50, 140, 185
18:11	292
19:10	257n6, 266, 274
19:15–16	185
19:16	125n50, 140
19:20	185
20:1–3	172, 185
20:2	74n24, 77n31
20:4	257n6, 266, 274
20:4–15	185
20:6	148
20:9	185
21	249
21:1	80n33, 90n44, 91n45
21:3	140n20
21:4	91, 92
21:8	325
21:27	92
22:1–3	141, 310
22:3	92, 148
22:3–5	88
22:5	88n4, 91n45, 148, 185

Author Index

Achtemeier, Paul J., 263, 270, 269
Akin, Daniel L., 262, 265
Alexander, T. Desmond, 113, 230
Allison, Dale C., 145, 212–13
Atkinson, Kenneth, 132
Attridge, Harold W., 270
Arichea, Jr., Daniel C., 269
Arnold, Clinton E., 271, 282
Aune, David E., 265–66

Balthasar, Hans Urs von, 2
Barrett, C. K., 163, 262–63, 265, 268–69
Barth, Christoph, 70
Barth, Karl, 162
Barth, Marcus, 165
Bartholomew, Craig, 336
Bateman IV, Herbert W., 195
Beale, G. K., 37, 59, 208, 266–67, 270, 274
Beasley-Murray, G. R., 59, 144, 213, 256
Beckwith, Isbon Thaddeus, 266
Belleville, Linda L., 269
Berkhof, Louis, 42
Best, Ernest, 271
Bird, Michael F., 234
Black, Matthew, 268
Bloch, Marc, 4–5, 10
Blomberg, Craig, 99, 297
Blount, Brian K., 266
Bock, Darrell, 99, 108, 112, 123, 131, 144, 208–9, 262, 306
Boda, Mark J., 242

Boring, Eugene M., 143, 207, 231, 262–63, 270, 279
Brannon, M. Jeff, 74
Bratcher, R. G., 262, 267–68
Bright, John, 114–15
Brighton, Louis, 266
Brook, A. E., 265
Brookins, Timothy A., 262, 268–69
Brown, Raymond E., 262, 265
Bruce, F. F., 263, 267, 270
Brueggemann, Walter, 39, 104
Bultmann, Rudolf, 254
Butterfield, Herbert, 6–7, 147
Byrne, Brendon, 254, 267–69

Caird, G. B., 58, 144, 206–7, 213, 266, 282, 297
Campbell, Constantine, 75, 246–48, 267
Carson, D. A., 256
Casserly, J. V. L., 2
Charles, R. H., 69, 132
Ciampa, Roy E., 262, 268, 297
Chilton, Bruce, 132, 144, 217
Clements, R. E., 59
Cockerill, Gareth Lee, 270
Collins, Adele Yarbro, 270
Collins, C. John, 327
Collins, John J., 208
Collins, Raymond F., 268–70, 279, 298
Conzelmann, Hans, 268
Cranfield, C. E. B., 141, 244, 262, 267–69

Dalman, Gustaf, 214
Davids, Peter, 263
de Boer, Martinus C., 269
Decker, Rodney G., 262, 270
Deterding, Paul E., 267, 269
Dodd, C. H., 247
Donahue, John R., 262
Dungan, David L., 253
Dunn, James D. G., 158, 202, 248, 258, 262, 269, 281

Edwards, James R., 262
Eichrodt, Walther, 219-20, 243, 337
Elliot, John H., 263, 279
Ellington, J., 269
Ellingworth, Paul, 267-70

Fanning, Buist, 230, 270, 258, 274
Fee, Gordon, 99, 139, 262-63, 266-70, 279, 297
Ferguson, Sinclair, 327
Fiore, Benjamin, 254, 268
Fitzmyer, Joseph A., 97, 107, 263-65, 267-69
Flusser, David, 217
Forbes, Greg W., 258-59, 263, 270, 277
France, R. T., 143, 145, 262, 270
Fredericks, Daniel C., 32, 35, 298
Fung, R. Y. K., 269
Furnish, Victor Paul, 267

Gardner, Paul, 297
Garland, David E., 262, 268
Gitau, Wanjiru, M., 94
Godet, Frederic, 297
Goldingay, John, 61-62, 104, 113, 219, 221, 223-24, 228, 232-33, 243
Goldsworthy, Graeme, 124, 144, 206-7, 278
Goppelt, Leonhard, 99, 123, 208, 253
Gorman, Michael J., 298
Gray, Buchanan G., 132
Green, Gene L., 270, 272
Grindheim, Sigurd, 213, 228, 331
Grudem, Wayne, 107, 135, 263,
Guelich, Robert A., 262, 270
Gundry, Robert H., 144, 146, 215

Guthrie, Donald, 268, 280-81, 290-91, 298

Haas, C. M., 262
Haenchen, Ernst, 202
Harrington, Daniel J., 262
Harrington, Wilfrid J., 267
Harris, Murray J., 263, 269
Harvey, John D., 267, 269
Hatton, H. A., 266, 268-69,
Hay, David M., 267
Headlam, Arthur, 263, 268
Hiebert, D. Edmond, 263, 267, 270, 272-73
Helyer, Larry R., 196
Hendriksen, William, 196, 267-68
Hodge, Charles, 263, 268-69
Hoehner, Harold W., 272, 282
Hooker, Morna, 242
Houlden, J. L., 265
Hughes, Philip Edgecumbe, 141, 266, 270
Hult, Adolf, 2

Jacob, Edmond, 7, 30
Jewett, Robert, 263, 267-69, 278
Jobes, Karen H., 262-63, 265
Johnson, Alan F., 297
Johnson, Thomas, 265
Johnson, Timothy Luke, 135-36, 154, 268
Johnston, Gordon H., 92

Keck, Leander, 263, 267-69
Keener, Craig, 160-61, 297
Kellum, L. Scott, 160
Kelly, John N. D., 268
Kilner, John F., 37, 327
Kistemaker, Simon, 160-61, 262, 265-66, 274
Knierim, Rolf, 62, 191, 219-20
Knight, George W., 268
Köstenberger, Andreas, 30, 81
Kruse, Colin G., 262, 267-69

Ladd, George E., 77, 159, 215-16, 219, 221-24, 228, 233-34, 265-66, 274

AUTHOR INDEX

Lane, William, 270
Larkin, William J., 161, 271
Lenski, R. C. H., 257
Lieu, Judith M., 265
Lightfoot, J. B., 262, 267-68
Lincoln, Andrew T., 271, 282,
Lockwood, Gregory J., 268
Loh, I-Jin, 270
Longenecker, Richard N., 254, 262-63, 268-69

Maloney, Francis J., 262
Mann, C. S., 262
Maritain, Jacques, 10
Marshall, I. Howard, 97-98, 161-62, 228, 235, 265, 268, 273, 298
Martin, Ralph P., 267
Matera, Frank J., 99, 267-69, 278, 280-81
McConville, J. Gordon, 37, 320-21, 330
MacDonald, Margaret Y., 267
McDonald, J. I. H., 217
McKnight, Scott, 199, 267
Melick Jr., Richard R., 267
Michaels, J. Ramsey, 238, 270, 276
Middendorf, Michael P., 268
Middleton, Richard J., 80
Mitchell, Alan C., 270
Montanari, Franco, 212
Moo, Douglas, 63-64, 100, 108, 253-54, 262-63, 267-69, 296
Morris, Leon, 98, 140, 159, 228, 262-63, 267-69, 278, 297
Moule, C. F. D., 260, 267
Moulton, James Hope, 258, 263
Mounce, Robert, 266
Mounce, William, 268
Muraoka, T., 212
Murray, John, 262, 267-69

Newman, B. M., 268-69
Nida, Eugene A., 262, 267-70

O'Brien, Peter T., 267, 270-71, 282
Omanson, R. L., 269
Osborne, Grant, 266, 274
O'Toole, Robert, 143

Painter, John, 265
Pannenberg, Wolfhart, 197, 235, 242, 323
Pao, David W., 267
Patrick, Dale, 68, 132, 143, 187
Patzia, Arthur, 282
Perrin, Nicholas, 113,
Perrin, Norman, 142-43
Pervo, Richard I., 160, 162, 264
Peterson, David G., 59, 265
Plantinga, Theodore, 241-42
Plummer, Alfred, 263, 268-69, 297
Polhill, John B., 161
Pokorny', Petr., 267
Pursiful, Darrell J., 269

Quinn, Jerome D., 268, 273

Rensberger, David K., 265
Reumann, John, 270
Richard, Earl, 270, 272-73, 279
Ridderbos, Herman N., 75, 138, 252, 298
Roberts, J. W., 265
Robertson, Archibald, 268, 297
Rosner, Brian S., 262, 268, 297
Routledge, Robin, 43
Rutledge, Fleming, 87

Sanday, W., 263, 268
Schnabel, Eckhard J., 158-61, 264-65
Schnackenburg, Rudolf, 143, 256, 265, 282
Schnelle, Udo, 101, 187, 199-200, 247-48
Schreiner, Thomas R., 163, 171, 216, 224, 231, 244, 263, 267-68, 270, 275, 298
Schweizer, Eduard, 215
Schuchard, Bruce G., 262, 265
Scobie, Charles, 29, 64, 136, 228
Seifrid, Mark A., 269, 279
Seitz, Christopher R., 267
Shaw, Mark, 94
Shogren, Gary S., 263, 267, 270, 273
Smalley, Stephen S., 262, 265
Smith, D. Moody, 265
Snodgrass, Klyne, 282

AUTHOR INDEX

Soards, Marion L., 269
Spencer, F. Scott, 228
Steele, Richard B., 268
Stein, Robert H., 144, 257
Stoeckhardt, Georg, 282
Strauss, Mark L., 161
Strecker, Georg, 265
Stuhlmacher, Peter, 268
Sumney, Jerry L., 254, 267

Taylor, Mark, 297
Thielman, Frank, 92, 271
Thiselton, Anthony C., 212, 228, 268
Thompson, Marianne Meye, 265, 267
Towner, Philip H., 268
Trafton, Joseph L., 134

Viviano, B. T., 208
Voelz, James W., 144, 216
Vos, Geerhardus, 202, 219-21, 223-24, 228

Wacker, William C., 268, 273
Wall, Robert, 267-68
Wallace, Daniel B., 258, 261

Waltke, Bruce, 90, 132, 149-50, 235
Walton, John, 63
Wanamaker, Charles A., 263, 267, 270, 272-73
Ward, Ronald, 268
Weima, Jeffrey A. D., 263, 267, 270, 273
Wenham, David, 159, 161, 202, 208, 231, 299
Wenham, Gordon J., 37
Westcott, B. F., 265
Wheelwright, Phillip, 143
Williams, David J., 161, 257
Williams, Joel F., 217
Wilson, Robert, 267
Witherington III, Ben, 146, 214, 224, 228, 252-53, 262, 268, 273, 297
Wright, C. J. H., 59, 62-63, 107
Wright, N.T., 97, 99-100, 267
Wright, Robert B., 132-34
Wuest, K. S., 267, 269

Yarborough, Robert W., 262

Zimmerli, Walther, 104